Thomas Jefferson's
SCRAPBOOKS

Thomas Jefferson's SCRAPBOOKS

Poems of
Nation, Family,
& Romantic Love

Collected by
AMERICA'S
THIRD PRESIDENT

Edited and Introduced by
JONATHAN GROSS

STEERFORTH PRESS · HANOVER, NEW HAMPSHIRE

For information about permission to reproduce
selections from this book, write to:
Steerforth Press L.C., 25 Lebanon Street
Hanover, New Hampshire 03755

The photographs are courtesy of the University of Virginia Library, and of Scrapbooks of clippings compiled by Thomas Jefferson's family, MSS5948, -a, Special Collections, University of Virginia Library.

Library of Congress cataloging-in-publication data is available from the publisher.

ISBN-10: 1-58642-107-7
ISBN-13: 978-1-58642-107-6

Book design by Peter Holm, Sterling Hill Productions

FIRST EDITION

CONTENTS

Part Two: Poems of Family

Part Three: Poems of Romantic Love

ACKNOWLEDGMENTS

T would like to thank James Horn for inviting me to the Robert H. Smith International Center for Jefferson Studies, where I served as a visiting fellow in December 2002. The library at the center, and its knowledgeable staff, made this project possible. Andrew Jackson O'Shaughnessy, Saunders Director of the International Center, and the researchers and staff at the center have supported my work in numerous ways. Professor Peter Graham, Clifford A. Cutchins III Professor of English at Virginia Tech, first made me aware of the International Center for Jefferson Studies and has been encouraging at every stage of the project; Professor Malcolm Kelsall's groundbreaking *Jefferson and the Iconography of Romanticism* helped me see important connections between British Romanticism and Thomas Jefferson. Bryan Craig, librarian at the Jefferson center, made my stay at Monticello productive, directing my research in helpful ways. My thanks to the seminar participants at the International Center, including Austin Graham, for comments on an essay on Wordsworth and Jefferson. Two University Research Council Awards (2003, 2005) at DePaul helped defray expenses involved in photographing the collection in December of that year; a summer stipend (2003) helped me undertake further research at the Alderman Library, complete the annotations, and write the introduction. Special thanks to the Virginia Foundation for the Humanities for a visiting fellowship (2006), which has enabled me to continue work on this project.

My special thanks to Chip Fleischer, who saw merit in this book, and to Robin Dutcher, Laura Jorstad, and Kristin Sperber for their deft editorial assistance.

Thomas Jefferson would smile down on Alderman Library, University of Virginia, and the librarians at the Rare Book Room who work there. By graciously allowing me to photograph the collection, they helped make this project possible; their late hours, even during holiday seasons, also helped. Special thanks, too, to Carrie Taylor, in the Curatorial Department of Monticello, for making the volume at the visitor center available. I am also grateful to the American Antiquarian Society and the rare book rooms and microfilm centers at University of Chicago, the Newberry Library, and the University of Illinois–Chicago for the use of their collections. Professor Bill Fahrenbach, chair of the Department of English, and my other colleagues at DePaul — Paula McQuade, Michele Morano, June Chung, Ted Anton, Shailja Sharma, and Eileen Seifert — were an ideal audience with whom to share my findings at a Faculty Research Seminar at DePaul.

As always, Michele Rubin, editor at Writer's House, has been a great friend and inspiration, helping me to conceive of this project as a book for the general reader. Jonathan Etes was a key research assistant, finding information on Thomas Fessenden and Philip Freneau; his close reading of the manuscript in March 2005, his patience with an endlessly changing table of contents, and his generosity with his time assisted me in meeting my deadline. Professor Peter Graham read a late draft of the introduction and provided helpful suggestions, almost all of them incorporated. For their help with queries and historical research, I am grateful to Randi Russert, David Jakalski, and Shannon Siggeman (for leading me to Royall Tyler). My thanks, too, to members of my graduate seminar in bibliography and literary research at DePaul (2003), especially Laura Fitzpatrick-Dibs, Randi Russert, and Lyndee Yamshon, whose thoughtful essays on Irish politics and Jefferson's marriage influenced my approach. Andrew Burstein and Jefferson Looney helped with the historical questions, saving me from several errors. My gratitude to them and to Philip Gould, Karl Kroeber, Jay Fliegelman, Douglas Wilson, and Jonathan Arac for reading the manuscript and providing constructive suggestions. Any remaining errors are mine alone.

Finally, a word of thanks to my own domestic circle, Jacqueline Russell and Shiri Nicole, who helped make my work on eighteenth-century families particularly meaningful.

For
PETER GRAHAM

I was bred to the law; that gave me a view of the dark side of humanity. Then I read poetry to qualify it with a gaze upon its bright side; and between the two extremes I have contrived through life to draw the due medium.

THOMAS JEFFERSON,
quoted in John Bernard,
Retrospections of America, 1797–1811

INTRODUCTION

During the month of December 2002, I found myself in Roosevelt cottage at Kenwood, a seventy-eight-acre estate on the slopes of Monticello, land once owned by Thomas Jefferson. At night, I was editing an eighteenth-century novel by the duchess of Devonshire, published three years before Jefferson wrote the Declaration of Independence. By day, I was supposed to be working in the Jefferson library of the Thomas Jefferson Foundation, where I had keys as a scholar-in-residence. On the walls of the stone cottage were photographs of Franklin Roosevelt, who had apparently spent a weekend there on May 2 and 3, 1941; the cottage had been built expressly for him by a senior aide and close friend, Major General Edwin M. Watson of Kenwood. The *Life* photographs portrayed Roosevelt as a good democrat, a man who enjoyed Coca-Cola, just like everyone else, and a refrigerator stocked with Schlitz.

I was at the Jefferson library in Monticello to write a book about Thomas Jefferson's interest in Romantic poetry, but I had little to go on. The library was daunting, filled with volumes on Jefferson and gardening, Jefferson and architecture, everything, it seemed, but Jefferson and poetry. By the third week of my stay, feeling more dejected than usual, I drove down to the bottom of the mountain. At the visitor center, I bought some Jefferson soaps and a Jefferson pencil, getting ready to make the long journey back to the Midwest. At the cash register, exchanging pleasantries, I glanced at a title in black cloth binding, published by Rowman and Littlefield: James and Alan Golden's *Thomas Jefferson and the Rhetoric of Virtue.* Turning to the back of the volume, I noticed an appendix treating a newspaper clippings book of poetry that had been discovered too late to include in the main text. The book had just come out. I jumped in my silver Honda Civic and drove back up the little mountain for which Monticello is named, almost forgetting to pay for my Jeffersonian memorabilia. With Golden's reference in hand, I unearthed two thick binders of newspaper clippings, evidently xeroxed from microfilm. I had photocopying privileges that month, and with all the idealism of a graduate student (with only seven days left of my monthlong fellowship), I began copying portions of the manuscript. As the copier whirred and sent off light in all directions, I wondered if these books might not contain another side to Thomas Jefferson: An admirer of women writers, perhaps? A fan of abolitionist verse? A closet Anglophile?

Anxiety soon followed exhilaration. What if Jefferson had nothing to do with these books? I pictured a small girl of eight or nine, cutting out poems from the newspaper and gluing them on scrap paper.[1] Her mother ambled to her side and helped her paste a poem in her scrapbook. Perhaps the little girl was Ellen Coolidge, Jefferson's most literary granddaughter. Anne C. Bankhead, Cornelia Randolph, and Virginia J. Trist[2] apparently had collections of their own as well. Try as I would, however, I could not picture the author of the Declaration of Independence with scissors and paste, gluing poems about owls and parrots on the back of his own correspondence.

And yet this, it would seem, was precisely what he did. Scholars had previously assumed Jefferson's granddaughters collected the poems, but opinions on this, and other matters, were beginning to change. "Four Scrapbooks previously regarded as the work of Thomas Jefferson's grandchildren were actually compiled by the nation's third President," Lee Smith wrote in the *Washington Post* on September 30, 1999. Robert McDonald, assistant professor of history at the US Military Academy, and James Horn, Saunders Director of the International Center for Jeffersonian Studies at Monticello, vouched for their authenticity. "It conforms to everything we know about the aspects of his character," Horn stated. Dan Jordan, president of the Thomas Jefferson Memorial Foundation, called the scrapbooks "a major find because of the insight they offer into Jefferson's personality and intellectual interests."[3]

"Must have been a slow news day," Jefferson Looney said when I alluded to the article in 1999; "we've known about them for years." *Then why was nothing done?* I felt tempted to ask. But the formidably erudite Looney was encouraging, or meant to be. He suggested an electronic edition, and I began to think about the years it might take to put the complete poems before the public. All the potential mistakes! The embarrassments! Glancing at the staff of ten scholars who were busy editing Jefferson's retirement papers, I reminded myself that Jefferson's forty-volume correspondence had only reached 1800. He wrote sixteen thousand letters in his lifetime;[4] there was still more than twenty years' worth of letters to edit, including those written during his presidency. And this extraordinarily disciplined group of scholars and its counterpart in Princeton had been working on Jefferson's papers since 1957. Jefferson's newspaper clippings could wait.

To get a better sense of the task at hand, I decided to consult the original scrapbooks. There were four: two devoted to prose and two to poetry (see appendix four). One was in the visitor center at Monticello, where I'd first come across the Goldens' book. Tourists visited the center every day and viewed this newspaper scrapbook from behind Plexiglas. The secret was in plain sight. When I tried to take photographs of the volume, however, I was discouraged, which only whetted my desire to get a letter of permission to consult the original. The other volume, in the rare book room at Alderman Library on the campus of University of Virginia, was more readily accessible, but had also been ignored. And this had occurred at Jefferson's own university, where a life-sized statue looks down on the students who assemble in the academic village he designed.

In December 2003, I took a propeller plane on the final leg of my journey, from Chicago to Charlottesville by way of Washington, visiting Alderman Library and the visitor center, where the manuscripts were held. A year later, I drove the fourteen hours to Charlottesville straight, until the Blue Ridge Mountains seemed to burst through my windshield. I took digital photographs of every page of both books, screwing my body up into strange positions to make use of the natural sunlight that helped light up the yellow pages of the newspaper clippings. It gets dark early in December. Leaving my Econo Lodge hotel at 7:30 AM for the library, I emerged at 5:00 PM to what seemed like the utter darkness of rural Virginia. I made my way down the hill from the University of Virginia campus to Cary's Camera and Imaging, where I tried not to look at the bill for the photographs I had taken that day. The store manager gave me tips on light meters and aperture settings. Librarians at the University of Virginia and at the International Center for Jefferson Studies were extraordinarily patient, allowing me to photograph the manuscript myself, thereby enabling me to work on the collection at home in Chicago.

The more I read about Jefferson, especially his letters to his granddaughters, the more convinced I became that Robert McDonald and the *Washington Post* were right: Jefferson had assembled this book, and his granddaughters had books of their own. Theirs no longer survive, but his does.[5] The primary proof is that the poems are annotated in his hand. They appear on the back of his own White House correspondence. I'll never forget the day an oak leaf popped out of one book, pressed, as it was, against a page containing a sentimental poem titled "To Clara." The oak leaf had appeared even in the microfilm shot in 1957. It was still there! Jefferson's spirit seemed to haunt this book, beckoning the researcher, as he had encouraged so many scholars, to study his life, his interests, and hobbyhorses. It was an intensely personal book: a mature genius's leisure-hours retrospective, not the work of a child. Like the manuscript Victor Frankenstein leaves to Robert Walton, or Kurtz leaves for Charlie Marlow — like Byron's memoirs entrusted to Thomas Moore — Jefferson's newspaper clippings book was full of self-justifications and ironic reflections, an autobiography of the heart more revealing than *Anas*, his published reminiscences. Washington, Burr, Hamilton, and other friends and foes of his political career appear like ghosts from the past. Sentimental poetry dominates the collection, as do poems about poppies, grasshoppers, and the seasons.

As I studied Jefferson's scrapbooks, I was surprised to find evidence of his own penciled emendations. After Barbauld's "Hymn to Content," he decided to change the pagination and place that poem in a different section of the collection. When Burger's "Leonora" didn't fit, he folded the poem so it would. Next to a passage from *Mirror for Magistrates*, he wrote, "as good now as when it was written." When a bit of newspaper print was smudged, Jefferson provided the missing word. Not one was missing.

Like Monticello itself, which was always under construction during Jefferson's life, these volumes were subject to the caprice and ever-changing interests of the man who compiled them. He changed the order of the collection, toying with thematic and chronological arrangements, providing at least two sets of numbering systems. His handwriting on the poems themselves, their subject matter, and their relationship to themes in his correspondence, point directly to his organizing intelligence.[6] Even the physical appearance of this volume, bound in dark brown boards, matches what we know of Jefferson's work on the New Testament. For two days in early February 1804,[7] Jefferson assembled a version of the New Testament that included only Jesus' sayings — and did so in four different languages (Greek, French, English, and Latin). This Enlightenment project bears interesting similarities to the newspaper clippings book, which was also assembled while Jefferson was president.[8] The methodology used in both is the same: comparison and contrast, juxtaposition, careful arrangement of received material. In both cases, Jefferson sent the book he assembled to be bound at a bookseller.[9]

Even as he kept his own scrapbook, then, Jefferson sent poems to help his granddaughters to read, memorize, and foster a love of poetry. Perhaps he also kept his own book to compare with theirs. Though I have tried to edit this sprawling interdisciplinary collection in a scholarly manner, I hope I have followed the spirit of Jefferson's project in editing this work for the general reader, even the youthful reader with whom portions of it were first shared, rather than the academic specialist.

One clear value of this collection is that it provides evidence for Jefferson's continuing interest in literature after the construction of his literary commonplace book in 1767. This has not been the predominant view. Some have argued that Jefferson knew little to nothing about poetry, citing his own remarks on the subject. When John Daly Burk asked Jefferson to comment on Joel Barlow's *The Vision of Columbus*, Jefferson confessed that he would be an inadequate judge.

> To my own mortification, [* * *] of all men living, I am the last who should undertake to decide as to the merits of poetry. In earlier life I was fond of it, and easily pleased. But as age and cares advanced, the powers of fancy have declined. Every year seems to have plucked a feather from her wings, till she can no longer waft one to those sublime heights to which it is necessary to accompany the poet. So much has my relish for poetry deserted me that, at present, I cannot read

even Virgil with pleasure. I am consequently [utterly] incapable to decide on the merits of poetry. The very feelings to which it is addressed are among those I have lost. So that the blind man might as well undertake to [faded in manuscript] a painting, or the deaf a musical composition.[10]

Yet this letter has been taken out of context. Jefferson had written a "substantial" essay on English prosody in 1786,[11] in which he debated with the marquis de Chastellux whether English prosody's principal characteristic was quantity, as Samuel Johnson maintained, or accent; after arguing the wrong side of the question, Jefferson came to the conclusion that accent is "the basis of English verse."[12] His technical knowledge included a detailed comparison of accentual and syllabic scansion, and an account of the "charms of music" that any "well-organized ear" can hear. "What proves the excellence of blank verse is that the taste lasts longer than that for rhyme," he wrote in his *Essay on Prosody*. "The fondness for the jingle leaves us with that for the rattles and baubles of childhood."[13]

A better explanation for Jefferson's self-effacing remarks concerning his knowledge of poetry might be the rhetorical occasion. Jefferson prudently refrained from judging a friendly correspondent's verse (enclosed in the letter) or commenting on the merit of Barlow's. After all, Barlow was a propagandist for the Republican cause, too useful to risk alienating. If Jefferson was truly mortified by a growing insusceptibility to the beauty of poetry, he did not remain so for long. This letter may well have been the catalyst for Jefferson to assemble two volumes of newspaper verse. He did so that same year, judging from the dates of the earliest entries;[14] interestingly, Barlow's poem appears in volume one.

Yet Jefferson's 1801 letter to Burk is unconvincing in other respects as well. A year and a half earlier, for example, he was reading Homer, enjoying him "in his own language infinitely beyond Pope's translation of him,"[15] so he had not given up on Greek or Roman poetry entirely. If Jefferson believed that one's taste for verse evolved from rhyme to blank verse, he did not foresee that his role as a grandfather would return him to the very compositions he thought he had outgrown. Jefferson's modesty belies his erudition. In fact, it is hard to think of recent American presidents, with the exception of John F. Kennedy and Abraham Lincoln, who cultivated such a catholic love of literature before, during, and after their term in the Oval Office. As a college student at William and Mary, Jefferson enjoyed James Macpherson's poetry and copied down whole passages from Shakespeare, Milton, and Chaucer. Shortly after his term as governor of Virginia ended, he shared his love of James Macpherson with the marquis de Chastellux in the spring of 1782, having previously written to the poet's brother, Charles, to obtain copies of the Gaelic originals in 1773.[16] As president, he watched the rise of Romantic poetry with more than ordinary interest. The loving attention he paid to the rhymed verse of Thomas Moore, Walter Scott, Robert Southey, Amelia Opie, Anna Barbauld, and Charlotte Dacre — clipping and pasting these poems, despite or because of their "jingle" — is surprisingly fashionable. Almost every writer he admired, though mostly ignored for the past fifty years, has reemerged from obscurity. Jefferson appears to have been as prescient in his literary tastes as he was in his political judgment. An undergraduate who reads only a third of this volume will have a wider education in Romantic poetry (British and American) than most college English majors.

———

What is the value of Jefferson's scrapbooks? We read the poems, in large part, less for their literary quality than for the insight they give us into Jefferson's mind. They form a portrait of his age and offer, by contrast, a portrait of our own. If a verse seems sentimental and cloying, trivial or charming, it illustrates how our attitudes towards nation, family, and poetry itself have changed: The poems read us.

Jefferson lived, emotionally, through the poetry and fiction he shared with his family. Shortly before his wife died, they read and transcribed portions of *Tristram Shandy* together, sharing ideas and thoughts that lay too deep for tears. "Read good books," he instructed Peter Carr on August 10, 1787, "because they will encourage as well as direct your feelings. The writings of Sterne, particularly, form the best course of morality that ever was written."[17] When he was weakened by his own approaching death and could not fully communicate, he directed his daughter to a poem he had composed that would express the emotions he felt for her.

To read Jefferson's letters to his family, then, is to grasp how important poetry was to him as a means of communicating with those he loved. On April 3, 1808 — only months before he would step down as president — Jefferson sent a four-line poem to his granddaughter Cornelia Jefferson Randolph. "I have owed you a letter two months, but have had nothing to write about, till last night I found in a newspaper the four lines which I now inclose you: and as you are learning to write, they will be a good lesson to convince you of the importance of minding your stops in writing." This letter shows that clipping poetry was Jefferson's way of keeping up with the mental life of his grandchildren, as if he were running a correspondence school from the White House. "I allow you a day to find out yourself how to read these lines so as to make them true," he continued. "If you cannot do it in that time you may call in assistance." Martha encouraged her father to play this role in her children's lives, for fear they would turn out "blockheads."[18] For Jefferson, the scrapbooks, like the letters he wrote to his grandson, prepared him for his retirement years, when he would draw up plans for the University of Virginia. They also encouraged him to think about the place of poetry in his own life, when he was a younger man.

> I've seen the sea all in a blaze of fire.
> I've seen a house high as the moon and higher
> I've seen the sun at twelve o'clock at night
> I've seen the man who saw this wonderous sight.[19]

The last line of Jefferson's poem remains with me. "I've seen the man who saw this wonderous sight." Reading Jefferson's scrapbooks gave me the eerie feeling that I had finally "seen the [private] man" described most recently as an American sphinx.

Staying in the Roosevelt cottage, however, also led me to consider Jefferson's public persona, to imagine Jefferson through Franklin D. Roosevelt's eyes. What drew Roosevelt to Monticello while World War II was raging? What did America's forty-third president see in Thomas Jefferson; why did he retreat to the cottage I had first inhabited when I "discovered" these books?[20] For privacy, fellowship, a romantic tryst? Some of these questions cannot be answered, but the consequences of Roosevelt's pilgrimage are clear. For Roosevelt, Jefferson became the "Apostle of Freedom." So important was he that Roosevelt ordered a rotunda built on the Tidal Basin in Washington, DC, dedicating it on April 13, 1943, with Jefferson's words inscribed on the inside of the dome: "I have sworn upon the altar of God eternal hostility against every form of tyranny over the mind of man." For Jefferson, tyranny took the form of clerical opponents in Connecticut who accused him of atheism; he was firmly "sworn" to defend the separation of church and state, hopeful that no intimidating clerics, nor national church, would threaten free thought in the United States. For Franklin Roosevelt, tyranny appeared as the spectre of Hitler and Mussolini. Roosevelt used Jefferson as a symbol to fight European fascism. Like Jefferson in 1808, Roosevelt pursued isolationist policies until military action (in 1812 and 1942) became inevitable. He wrote the famous "Four Freedoms" speech and quoted Jefferson in his "We the People" radio broadcast of 1941. Several days before the Normandy invasion on June 6, 1944, Roosevelt returned to rural Virginia to await the results, this time eschewing the privacy of the Roosevelt cottage to stay with "Pa" Watson in the main house at Kenwood.

The photograph in Roosevelt cottage, where he first stayed in 1941, shows a smiling African American woman, Arlene Wardlaw, serving the president's breakfast to him in Monticello. What was she thinking, I wondered, as the photographer from *Life* took the photo? "It was just a mock-up," a scholar said to me derisively when I alluded to these photographs. But I insisted on the historicity of this moment; not only had Roosevelt stayed where I had spent the last month, but this woman had served him his breakfast: a pair of four-minute eggs, two strips of crisp bacon, toast, marmalade, coffee, a copy of the *Washington Star*, three cigarettes, and a rose freshly plucked from the garden.[21] Perhaps she was happy to be noticed in a national magazine; perhaps she had voted for Roosevelt, or not voted at all. I was reminded of Langston Hughes's "Theme for English B." "Sometimes perhaps you don't want to be a part of me. / Nor do I often want to be a part of you. / But we are, that's true!" What was certain was that the owner of Kenwood, Major General Edwin M. ("Pa") Watson (Roosevelt's senior aide), had the cottage built for Roosevelt three weeks before the president arrived on May 2, 1941.[22] A few years later, Roosevelt designed "Top Cottage" in Dutchess County, New York, which has a simple layout not unlike where he stayed in 1941.

Sitting in a replica of Jefferson's Campeachy chair, which had been constructed by John Hemings, the talented brother of Sally, I wondered if the link between Roosevelt and Jefferson was not now complete, at least in my own mind. Two aristocratic men, one a New Yorker, the other a Virginian, helped foster principles of liberal democracy. They were moral exemplars, fighting the tyranny of George III and of fascism in their own lifetimes. But these men — like Georgiana, duchess of Devonshire, the author of the novel I was editing at Roosevelt cottage — led complex private lives. For a month, I enjoyed the remoteness of Roosevelt cottage, perhaps one of the last private places on earth. Up the hill was the most public building imaginable: Monticello, ostensibly a private home. Dignitaries and tourists came in droves, even in Jefferson's lifetime, and he hung Venetian blinds (louvered shutters) between the pillars to escape their peering gaze.[23] When that failed, he built a Bedford County retreat he named Poplar Forest just to get away.

Certainly, Jefferson's secrets have drawn the attention of America's newest generation of historians.[24] But Jefferson would not have been surprised. "In speaking of the calumnies which his enemies had uttered against his public and private character with such unmitigated and untiring bitterness," Sarah Randolph wrote, "he said that he had not considered them as abusing him; they had never known him. They had created an imaginary being clothed with odious attributes, to whom they had given his name."[25] In an era of sexual McCarthyism, as Alan Dershowitz has perceptively called it, political leaders are too often held to the standards of a Procrustean Puritanism;[26] such standards are applied, without historical perspective, to figures such as Benjamin Franklin and Thomas Jefferson, as Andrew Burstein rightly argues.[27] Journalistic practice is not so different in the twenty-first century than it was at the beginning of the nineteenth, as William Safire's recent dramatized history, *Scandalmonger*, suggests.

Despite attacks, Jefferson lives on, in part, because of his own optimism. If he was perhaps too philosophical about his own limitations, he captured the meaning of hope in a poem he wrote that I stumbled upon in the Library of Congress archives. Interestingly, Jefferson's "To Ellen" embodies the three categories of nation ("heroes fight in hopes of fame"), family ("when true love a visit pays"), and romanticism ("to poetic lays") that mark his newspaper clippings.

> 'Tis hope supports each noble flame,
> 'Tis hope inspires poetic lays,
> Our heroes fight in hopes of fame,
> And poets write in hopes of praise.
>
> She sings sweet songs of future years,
> And dries the tears of present sorrow
> Bids doubt in mortals cease their fears,
> And tells them of a bright tomorrow.
>
> And when true love a visit pays,
> The minstrel hope is always there,
> To soothe young Cupid with her lays,
> And keep the lover from despair.[28]

Perhaps Jefferson's sense of hope, as portrayed in this poem, led William Jefferson Clinton, another southern governor, to make a pilgrimage to Monticello before beginning his duties as president. Both were called demagogues, but both incarnated a sense of optimism and faith in democracy that Clinton memorably described, in his own campaign book, as "putting people first." Clinton's second campaign book, *Between Hope and History*, was no less Jeffersonian.

Jefferson's newspaper clippings did much to nourish his heart, an attribute that is sometimes difficult to measure when assessing the accomplishments of statesmen. But not only the personal note is struck in this newspaper clippings book or in the poems he wrote himself. In the two hundredth anniversary of

Jefferson's second term — when American values are being redefined in the name of illusory versions of the founding fathers' original intent — Jefferson's clippings may well help readers grasp how Jefferson hoped Americans would see their country and its values at its inception. Such a vantage point might make readers more sympathetic with Jefferson despite his perceived moral shortcomings; more admiring of the scope and accomplishments of the man who was, after all, a single parent and a widow. To read the poetry Jefferson admired — some of it abolitionist verse — is to become indoctrinated in the values of the early Republic. It may have been easier for him to profess those values than to practice them, but are we any better on that score?

At a gathering of forty-nine Nobel Prize recipients at the White House on April 29, 1962, John F. Kennedy noted that never before had such talent been assembled in one room, except, perhaps, when Thomas Jefferson dined alone.[29] This collection of some of Jefferson's favorite poems is offered to the common reader in a spirit of admiration and celebration, then; for Jefferson assumed the common reader's wisdom as part of his democratic faith. Jefferson was not only America's third president, but America's first Romantic president. He turned the country away from Federalism, for better or worse. Jefferson's scrapbooks, no less than his inaugural address, shows him returning the country to what he came to think of as the spirit of '76.[30]

PART ONE

Poems of
NATION

Thomas Jefferson's collection of political verse includes at least twenty hymns to July 4, and four "Odes to Liberty." When one considers that Jefferson personally clipped these poems and pasted them in two books — over at least an eight-year period while president of the United States — they might be viewed as a second declaration of independence. If the first declared liberty from Great Britain, the second considered the manner in which that liberty should be celebrated. For Jefferson, the spirit of '76 required renewal, and his administration would provide it. The first volume of Jefferson's clippings reflects the rush of excitement that attended these times, which Jefferson latter dubbed the revolution of 1800, "as real a revolution in the principles of our government as that of 1776 was in its form."[1] Jefferson's scrapbooks, which begin in 1801, charts this important change through the poets, the unacknowledged legislators, who described it.

In the twenty-first century, however, a selection titled "Poems of Nation" might require some explanation. Samuel Johnson called patriotism the last refuge of a scoundrel.[2] More recently, Benedict Anderson and Ernest Gellner have questioned nationalism from a different standpoint, rightfully seeing it as responsible for twentieth-century atrocities. But modern theorists who are antinational may not be the best guides to a nation in formation, or the brand of civic pride Jefferson endorsed. As Henry Adams observed, America in 1800 did not have "even enough nationality to be sure it was a nation," and "Jefferson, in particular, aspired beyond the ambition of nationality, and embraced in his view the whole future of man."[3]

In the poems of nation, America does not appear anxious to force its will on other nations. Instead, Jefferson sought to consolidate gains made by a country that had turned away from English monarchical principles. In his first inaugural address, he summed up this republican creed succinctly: "equal and exact justice to all men, of whatever state or persuasion, religious or political; peace, commerce, and honest friendship, with all nations — entangling alliances with none; the support of the state governments in all their rights, as the most competent administrations for our domestic concerns . . . the honest payment of our debts and sacred preservation of the public faith; encouragement of agriculture, and of commerce as its handmaid. . . ."[4] Though he declared that "we are all Republicans — we are all Federalists," in that same speech after a contentious election, he remained vigilant lest English ideas about nationalism and empire infect the country. The author of the Kentucky Resolutions in 1798 would ensure, even by clipping poems about July 4 celebrations in specific states, that the government honored states' rights. During his administration, he restored freedom of the press after Adams's Alien and Sedition Acts, returned the period of naturalization from fourteen (under the Federalists) to five years, "drastically" reduced the army and navy despite a war on the Barbary pirates, repealed the Judiciary Act of 1801 (thus curtailing Federalist judges), abolished internal taxes, replaced presidential formality with "Jeffersonian simplicity," and retired the debt over a period of sixteen years.[5]

Jefferson declared cultural independence from Great Britain on more than one occasion, and the poems he gathered from American newspapers reveal his preference for poets and rebels against English monarchy. Poems such as "The Grave of Russel," for example, celebrate the handsome Irish hero Thomas Russel, friend of Wolf Tone, who was hung on the gallows and then beheaded for high treason on October 21, 1803, for founding the United Irishmen and supporting their cause as early as October 18, 1791. His epitaph, identical to the poem's title, reads simply "The Grave of Russel." Other poems, such as "The Death of W. Wallace,"[6] indicate Jefferson's support for a hero, William Wallace (1270–1305), who thwarted King Edward's claim to overlordship of Scotland. Wallace's military skill and the gruesome manner of his death — quartered and disemboweled with his limbs mounted on four separate gates — made Wallace a hero and a symbol of resistance to English oppression.

Often, and somewhat surprisingly, Jefferson clipped poems that celebrate military valor, such as "A Dead March,"[7] for he counted General Kosciusko and the marquis de Lafayette as close friends and correspondents.[8] When Jefferson stood for president in 1800, journalists and poets uncharitably reminded audiences of Jefferson's reputation as a poor wartime governor (though he was exonerated in his own state from such a charge). Threatened with invasion by Colonel Tarleton and Lord Cornwallis, Jefferson left Monticello rather than face arrest or oppose, unarmed, a troop of British soldiers. Yet Thomas Green Fessenden and William Cullen Bryant mocked his retreat to Carter's mountain while Alexander Hamilton insinuated, in 1792, that Jefferson and Madison's lack of military experience made them politically suspect, with a "womanish attachment to France and a womanish resentment against Great Britain."[9] Jefferson's years as ambassador to France led many to consider him overly sympathetic to French interests.

By contrast, Hamilton's experience as Washington's aide-de-camp during the Revolutionary War ensured a special relationship to America's first president that Jefferson never enjoyed. Of Hamilton's wartime union, Jefferson wrote, "A man as timid as he is on the water, as timid on horseback, as timid in sickness, would be a phenomenon if the courage of which he has the reputation in military occasions were genuine."[10] Hamilton's reputation was based, among other exploits, on his heroic defense of New York, near Bunker Hill, as an artillery captain and a well-executed bayonet charge during the battle of Yorktown.[11] During the war, Colonel Hamilton repeatedly asked to exchange his desk job for a military command, though he had the reputation for recklessness in battle, as did his close friend John Laurens.[12]

With this background in mind, it is amusing to think of Jefferson clipping a poem titled "To the Memory of Gen. Hamilton," for example, that praises him as "Great Hamilton!" and criticizes Aaron Burr's "dark, malignant hand, / Who *coldly* shot a fellow creature, / A man belov'd by all our land." Jefferson seems to be taking the measure of the public's response to both of his rivals. As secretary of state, Jefferson had vied with Secretary of the Treasury Alexander Hamilton for the ear of George Washington regarding American fiscal policy; with Aaron Burr for no less a prize than the presidency of the United States. When a tie extended the election until March 1801, Hamilton, of all people, helped throw the election in in Jefferson's favor, by planting a fear of Burr's unpredictability. And Jefferson subsequently accused Burr of conspiring to separate certain western states from the Union, forcing his first-term vice president to stand trial for treason. Jefferson's long battle with Hamilton over a national bank, and his suspicion of paper currency and economic machinations, appears in the witty "The Ghost of Continental Money, to the Embryo of the New Emission."[13] Though some of the details of such a poem might be lost on a modern reader who is not also an economist, Jefferson's wide-ranging interest in hard currency and soft hearts (his opposition to Hamilton's ideas) emerges from this poem and shows his ongoing debate with Hamilton, even after the latter's death. Jefferson kept a bust of Hamilton at Monticello, which faced his own, remarking to visitors that the two opposed each other in death, as in life.

Jefferson used his clippings book to take note of the emergence of a new political style. Thus his poem "To America, on the Retirement of Geo. Washington" seems to be included because it offers a republican version of leadership, one that Jefferson deliberately contrasts with "His Majesty's Birth Day," by H. J. Pye. If "To America" celebrates George Washington's contribution in founding America, "His Majesty's Birth Day" offers nothing so inspiring. Washington's greatness lies precisely in the acts of violence he did not execute.

> What tho' no pageant titles deck the SAGE —
> No murderer's millions haunt the Hero's mind;
> Yet shall the leaves of Time, as they unfold,
> Still rank thy GEORGE among the first of men.[14]

For Pye, by contrast, a soldier's willingness to shed blood proves his loyalty: "Rush to the field where George and Freedom lead, / Glory and fame alike the warriors' meed, / Brave in their country's cause, who conquer or who bleed." Soldiers who die for a virtuous man (Washington) limn those who die for an incompetent king. In describing George Washington as "the first of men," the poet may have had Lighthorse Henry Lee's toast to George Washington in mind: "first in war, first in peace, and first in the hearts of his countrymen."[15] Nevertheless, Jefferson's clipping of this valedictory, like the elegy of Hamilton, should not blind the reader to the fact that Jefferson, as Washington's secretary of state, criticized Washington's pro-British policies, and objected to his militaristic handling of the Whiskey Rebellion. In this collection, however, George Washington is far preferable to George III, whose "Freedom" seems inextricably connected to the pursuit of empire. In Pye's poem, the phrase *George and Freedom* rings hollow, since British foreign policy abroad so often meant colonization prompted by commercial imperatives (at least from Jefferson's standpoint).

Some poems indicate Jefferson's early interest in celebrating the Fourth of July as a national holiday. One example is R. T. Paine's song "sung at Boston, on the celebration of the 4th of July." Jefferson clearly played a hand in promoting festivities that honor this day, as Pauline Maier has noted,[16] but he did so in a way that respected states' rights. The fact that he clipped poems commemorating his own role in producing the conditions in which American liberty could thrive gives further evidence that Jefferson worked behind the scenes to advance his own reputation. Jefferson's scrapbooks show that he encouraged July 4 as a national holiday as early as July 4, 1801, for example, while he was president of the United States, and long before the American Jubilee of 1826, which celebrated America's fiftieth birthday.[17] Jefferson was not averse to self-promotion, even as he seemed to shy away from any appearance of such ungentlemanly activity.

Even as he worked to have July 4 honored as a national holiday, he also understood how a free press could divide public opinion. For Jefferson, the United States could be compared, metaphorically, to an oak tree, "For oft a worm destroys an oak, / Whose leaf that worm would bury." R. T. Paine's "Wide o'er the wilderness of waves" develops the oak as a symbol of tradition and ancestry, tall and proud, but susceptible to worms if not protected. Moving, figuratively, from oak trees to dogs, this same poem explains how Jefferson triumphed over Federalists' "yelp and bark" and refers, in passing, to Jefferson's triumph over John Adams in the 1800 election ("And Burr and all his host undone"). Certain elements in Jefferson's party (mainly the editor of the New York newspaper *American Citizen*) anathematized Burr as well as the high federalists.

If not exactly exulting in the defeat of his political rivals, Jefferson is hardly the disinterested figure passed down to us by some biographers.[18] He seems to have enjoyed the cult of mystery that followed him up to the mountain at Monticello, inspiring a poem published in the *National Aegis*, written by "A Squatter."

> Kind reader, if you'll deign to hear,
> I'll tell a tale that's something queer;
> Where Monticello's summits rise,
> In tow'ring columns to the skies,
> There lives a man as fame relates,
> Who makes great clamor in these States;

Some tell he's learned, just and wise,
While others say these tales are lies,
And call him idiot, knave and fool, . . .

Jefferson's mountaintop retreat and his strange inventions led Federalist satirists such as Royall Tyler, Joseph Dennie, and Thomas Green Fessenden to depict him as eccentric. "Of Mr. Jefferson I know nothing," Joseph Dennie wrote, "& in this I am not singular. From his sullen & retired habits, few know more than myself."[19] John Quincy Adams mocked Jefferson's preoccupation with natural history and mastadons discovered by Meriwether Lewis and William Clark. He mocked Joel Barlow's "On the Discoveries of Captain Lewis" as fatuous self-promotion for the Jefferson administration.

Despite his detractors, Jefferson was comfortable with complexity, a trait best captured by the literature he read and enjoyed. He alluded to Cervantes's *Don Quixote* on several occasions,[20] recommending it to his daughters to help them learn Spanish. The whipping that Quixote tries to prevent at the beginning of Cervantes's novel is replayed in interesting ways in "The Irish Drummer," a poem that displays the irony of unintended consequences. In Cervantes's work, the boy whom Quixote "saves" is whipped more brutally after his departure than if Quixote had never intervened. Similarly, in this poem, a man recounts his misdirected efforts to flog a fellow soldier with compassion.[21]

Sheridan used the story of the Irish drummer to humor his audience into acknowledging the injustices of British imperialism in India during the Warren Hastings trial. Byron admired Sheridan's wit enough to refashion it for his own speech on Catholic Emancipation (June 1, 1813). In the poem Jefferson clipped, the hapless Irishman comes in for much harsher scrutiny.

Less than one month before he died, Jefferson continued to be sympathetic toward the underdog (a quality he shared with Sheridan and Byron). "The mass of mankind has not been born with saddles on their backs, nor a favored few, booted and spurred, ready to ride them legitimately, by the grace of God," Jefferson wrote in June 1826. Even this quintessentially American comment, prepared for a July 4 celebration, echoes the words of the Puritan soldier Colonel Richard Rumbold, who delivered a famous speech on the gallows in 1685 before he was hanged for treason: The phrases *saddles on their backs* and *a favored few, booted and spurred, ready to ride them*, appear in both. Jefferson owned English histories that reprinted Rumbold's speech.[22] Even when most nationalistic, "Poems of Nation" reflects the shadow of English culture.

That same influence is also evident in the many hymns that appear. Jefferson, who had a reputation for "nearly always humming some tune, or singing in a low voice to himself,"[23] played violin "no less than *three hours* a day" and brought his instrument with him to the Continental Congress, so his interest in poetry set to music is hardly surprising.[24] The most common songs include "Anacreon in Heaven" by John Stafford Smith, a British composer whose melody Francis Scott Key used for "The Star Spangled Banner": Even national anthems could be borrowed tunes. Jefferson also clipped a number of poems set to "Yankee Doodle Dandy," indicating his interest in the American vernacular. In Royall Tyler's 1785 drama *The Contrast*, a character threatens to take "Yankee Doodle" to seventy-six verses. If Jefferson felt this tune was ridiculous, he did not suggest so here.

Thomas Green Fessenden, by contrast, dubbed "Yankee Doodle Dandy" "a ludicrous musical air, which I believe was first invented by the English, in derision of the Americans, whom they styled 'Yankees.'" Fessenden found much to bemoan and quoted a few lines:

> At length came in the deacon's Sal
> From milking at the barn, sir,
> And faith she is as good a gal
> As ever twisted yarn, sir.

While college graduates like Fessenden cringed at American folk songs, Jefferson saw such songs as the beginning of a national literature.

A number of the homelier poems Jefferson collected, such as "An Ode. Composed for the Baltimore Typographical Society,"[25] celebrate state festivals in Delaware, New Hampshire, or other states, and include choruses sung to a specific melody. When not overtly political (as in Selleck Osborn or William Ray's July 4 orations), they are often lyrical ballads, not unlike those collected in Bishop Thomas Percy's *Reliques of Ancient English Poetry*, and remind readers that two years before Jefferson became president of the United States, Wordsworth and Coleridge paid homage to the democratic implications of rural verse. Hazlitt described the *Lyrical Ballads*, with its compassion for beggars and the destitute, as a second French Revolution in verse. Sympathetic to the French experiment, Jefferson and Wordsworth had much in common, both viewing the language of everyday life as something worth preserving and cherishing (with the republicanism implicit in this act of reverence). Both understood how nature and human affection keep the heart responsive.

Jefferson was also interested in the songs and melodies native to other countries. There are more than five songs by the blind Irish bard Carolan. Songs by Burns appear under Romantic poetry in this collection, for Jefferson took a keen interest in Scottish, Irish, and English music.

The last important grouping that appears in this section concerns poems about the embargo. With the formation of the Third Coalition against Napoleon in 1805, all Europe was at war and the United States became the most significant neutral nation.[26] In June 1807, a British ship fired on an American frigate, the *Chesapeake*. At first, Jefferson tried to use this event as a lever to negotiate with the British. When this failed, he signed the Embargo Act into law on December 21, 1807, closing American ports to foreign trade and placing all American merchant ships under the jurisdiction of the United States; the president cleared any ship sailing to a foreign port. The Louisiana Purchase showed the wisdom of Jefferson's foreign policy, especially his diplomacy with Napoleon: Jefferson had waited until Santa Domingo had become ungovernable for Napoleon before gaining Louisiana and the port of New Orleans by purchasing them. The embargo was less successful; it did little to prevent British impressment of American sailors and less to prevent the Barbary pirates from capturing American vessels off the coast of Algiers. Escalating tension with Great Britain, the decimation of trade in New England, and the War of 1812 were the inevitable, catastrophic results. The embargo was a noble and idealistic, if misguided, experiment; a chance to counter Hamiltonian finance with Republican schemes. One of the few positive consequences of the embargo was that Jefferson managed to avoid war long enough to allow American agriculture and industry to prosper.

Prompted by his Federalist-leaning father, thirteen-year-old William Cullen Bryant complained about the policy, while others defended Jefferson, most notably Henry Mellen and William Ray. Ray was a poet from Albany who had been imprisoned in Algiers; he was a strong supporter of Jefferson. Ray's "Cash" reveals the same suspicion about paper money and national banks that Jefferson articulated throughout his political career.

If Jefferson's term began in a flash of patriotism, it ended, perhaps inevitably, in controversy. Jefferson sought to determine whether the national debt and the wars it fostered — aspects, Jefferson believed, of Hamilton's system — could be avoided through a pacifist embargo. "Never did a prisoner, released from his chains, feel such relief as I shall on shaking off the shackles of power,"[27] he noted the day before Madison's inauguration.

The Music of the following excellent SONG,
was admirably performed by the Band, at the
Ball in this town, on Monday evening last —
but the words could not then be obtained.

JEFFERSON AND LIBERTY.
[Anonymous]

THE gloomy night before us flies:
The reign of terror now is o'er,
Its gags, inquisitors and spies,
Its hordes of harpies are no more.
  Rejoice! Columbia's sons rejoice
  To tyrants never bend the knee,
  But join with heart, and soul, and voice,
  For JEFFERSON and LIBERTY
O'er vast Columbia's varied clime;
Her cities forests, shores and dales,
In rising majesty sublime,
Immortal Liberty prevails.
  Rejoice! Columbia's Sons, &c.

. . .

No lordling here with gorging jaws,
Shall wring from industry its food,
No fiery bigot's holy laws,
Lay waste our fields and streets in blood.
  Rejoice! Columbia's sons, &c.
Here strangers from a thousand shores,
Compell'd by tyranny to roam,
Shall find amidst abundant shores,
A nobler and a happier home.
  Rejoice! Columbia's sons, &c.
Here art shall lift her laurel'd head,
Wealth, industry and peace divine,
And where dark pathless forests spread,
Rich fields and lofty cities shine.
  Rejoice! Columbia's sons, &c.
From Europe's wants and woes remote,
A dreary waste of waves between,
Here plenty cheers the humble cot,

And smiles on every village green.
    Rejoice! Columbia's sons, &c.
Here free as air's expanded space,
To every soul and feet shall be,
That sacred privilege of our race,
The worship of the Deity.
    Rejoice! Columbia's sons, &c.
These gifts, great Liberty, are thine;
Ten thousand more we owe to thee!
Immortal may their mem'ries shine,
Who sought and died for liberty
    Rejoice! Columbia's sons, &c.
What heart but hails a scene so bright,
What soul but inspiration draws,
Who would not guard so dear a right,
Or die in such a glorious cause.
    Rejoice! Columbia's sons, &c.
Let foes to freedom dread the name,
But should they touch the sacred tree,
Twice fifty thousand swords shall flame,
For JEFFERSON and LIBERTY.
    Rejoice! Columbia's sons, &c.
From Georgia up to Lake Champlain,
From seas to Mississippi's shore,
Ye sons of freedom loud proclaim,
THE REIGN OF TERROR IS NO MORE
    Rejoice! Columbia's sons, rejoice!
    To tyrants never bend the knee,
    But join with heart, and soul, and voice,
    For JEFFERSON and LIBERTY.

I:I

This poem is the first to appear in Jefferson's clippings book; it captures the tone and tenor of Jefferson's presidency. Republicans cast their election as a return to the spirit of '76, an overthrow of tyrants who would impose the Alien and Sedition Acts on the American public. After eight years in office, Jefferson began to sympathize with Adams's position, modulating his belief in freedom of the press with indignation at the libels he read on a daily basis in American newspapers. The poem includes an interesting reversal of a phrase, associating the reign of terror with the Federalists rather than with Robespierre and the French Revolution.

THE following SONG, sung on the 4th of MARCH, at an entertainment given by the American Consul at the Hotel, London, has merit which entitles it to high rank among our popular airs.

[Anonymous]

TUNE — "Anacreon in Heaven."

[I]

Well met, fellow freemen!
   let's cheerfully greet,
The return of *this day*, with a
   copious libation.
For freedom this day in her cho-
   sen retreat,
Hailed her favourite JEFFERSON
   Chief of our nation.
 A chief in whose mind
 Republicans find,
Wisdom, probity, honor and
   firmness combined.
Let our wine sparkle high, whilst
   we gratefully give,
The health of our Sachem, and
   long may he live.

[II]

Political frenzy howl'd o'er the
   earth,
Ambition and rapine with blood
   ting'd the ocean.
While JEFFERSON rip'ning sage
   systems for birth,
Found the peaceful legitimate
   path to promotion.

With reason his guide,
    At WASHINGTON's side,
His virtues and talents full-often
        were tried.
Now he's chief in command let
        the universe see,
How happy a nation of freemen
        can be!

        III.
Whilst Europe's proud Chiefs
        wield the sword or the pen,
By force or by fraud to acquire
        new possessions;
Our rulers speak "peace & good
        will towards men," —
And their practice accords with
        their cordial professions:
    But should foreign foes
        Their rancor disclose,
And by discord or arms dare dis-
        turb our repose,
Let our Chief give the word, and he
        safely may trust,
That those haughty disturbers
        shall soon "bite the dust."

        IV.
May JEFFERSON's genius sublime-
        ly control,
The carping of envy, the frenzy
        of faction:
At his bidding let union attune
        each free soul,
And Godlike philanthropy spring
        into action;

Thus blessing and blest,
By his country carest,
Sweet peace shall forever illumi-
nate his breast!
Admiring his virtues, again let
us give,
The health of our Sachem, and
long may he live.

1:2

James Hall wrote "Anacreon in Heaven," a song with the same melody as "The Star Spangled Banner." Several poems in Jefferson's collection are set to this song. Though some of the praise of Jefferson is fatuous ("May JEFFERSON's genius sublimely control, / The carping of envy, the frenzy of faction"), Jefferson himself did not hesitate to include verse from the *Port Folio*, edited by Joseph Dennie, which was harshly critical of his administration. This poem refers to Jefferson as "our Sachem," a term used in Republican Tammany lodges in New York, where political leaders often dressed as Algonquin Indians and took nicknames.

THE PEOPLE'S FRIEND,
Sung at Philadelphia, 4 July, 1801.

[Anonymous]

NO more to subtle arts a prey,
Which fearful of the eye of day;
    A nation's ruin plann'd:
Now entering on th' auspicious morn,
In which a people's hopes are born,
    What joy o'erspreads the land!

While past events portended harm,
And rais'd the spirit of alarm,
    Uncertain of the end:
Ere all was lost, the prospect clear'd,
And a bright star of hope appear'd,
    The People's chosen friend.

Devoted to his country's cause,
The rights of Man and equal Laws,
    His hollow'd pen was given:
And now those Rights and Laws to save
From sinking to an early grave,
    He comes, employ'd by Heav'n.

What joyful prospects rise before!
Peace, Arts and Science hail our shore,
    And through the country spread:
Long may these blessings be preserv'd,
And by a virtuous land deserv'd,
    With JEFFERSON our head!

CHORUS.

REJOICE, ye States, rejoice
    And spread the patriot flame;
Call'd by a nation's voice;
    To save his country's fame;
And dissipate increasing fears,
Our favorite JEFFERSON appears.

Let every heart unite,
    Th' eventful day to hail;
When from the Freemen's Right,
    The people's hopes prevail;
That hence may horrid faction cease,
And honor be maintain'd with PEACE.

                                        1:2

This poem is interesting, in part, because it shows that Jefferson clipped poems from the first year of his presidency (July 4, 1801). The great majority of his political verse is culled from newspapers during his second administration.

The Land of Love and Liberty.
[By Thomas Paine]

TUNE — "Rule Britannia."

HAIL, great republic of the world!
    The rising empire of the west!
Where fam'd Columbus, with mighty mind inspir'd,
    Gave tortur'd Europe scenes of rest.
    Be thou forever, forever great and free,
    The land of love and liberty!

Beneath the spreading mantling vine,
    Beside thy flow'ry groves in spring,
And on thy lofty, thy lofty mountain's brow,
    May all thy sons and fair ones sing,
    Be thou forever &c.

From thee may rudest nations learn
    To prize the cause thou first began,
From thee may future, may future tyrants know,
    That sacred are the rights of man.
    Be thou forever, &c.

From thee may horrid [illeg.] discord fly,
    With all her dark, her gloomy train,
And o'er thy fertile, thy fertile wide domain
    May everlasting friendship reign.
    Be thou forever, &c.

Of thee may lisping infancy
    The pleasing wondrous story tell;
And patriot sages in venerable mood
    Instruct the world to govern well.
    Be thou forever, &c.

Ye guardian angels watch around,
    From harm protect the new-born state;
And all ye friendly nations join,
    And thus salute the Child of Fate —
      Be thou forever great and free;
      The Land of Love and Liberty.

1:3

This poem celebrating the United States as "The Land of Love and Liberty" is sung, oddly enough, to the tune of "Rule Britannia." Paine's *Common Sense* was published in January 1776, months before the Declaration of Independence.

ODE INSCRIBED TO THE 4th of JULY, 1805.

[Anonymous]

HENCE, laureate *Flattery*'s lambient strain,
Profuse, mellifluent, loud, and vain,
    To puff a monarch's sway;
At Freedom's shrine, where *Patriots* bow,
We'll pledge our renovated vow,
    And hail her holyday.

Impulsive more is *Law*'s command,
Than gorgon *Terror*'s lifted hand,
    To move a nation's soul;
Since fond desires propel to bliss
This golden age of happiness,
    We'll grateful hearts control.

Here *Agriculture* clothes her fields,
And much to Nature's children yields,
    O! Nature's ancient pride —
When shepherds sang to streams and groves,
Their cheerly tasks and spotless loves,
    Where gods would fain reside.

Commerce, her cheerful *handmaid*, pours
Earth's richest gifts on Freedom's shores,
    E'en *Luxury*'s board supplies;
Thus let us waft from every zone,
A world's rare virtues to our own,
    And fast to glory rise.

Science unlocks great Nature's springs,
And humbly takes her holy things,
    And pours them on the mind;
She bids us count our blessings dear,
And soothing shows that Freedom here
    An endless reign shall find.

On flowery grades *desert* ascends,
No tyrant *test* its hand extends,
      To lead the mind awry;
Conscience her awful GOD adores,
Nor strange oblation heartless pours,
      In forc'd idolatry.

What rash foe dares the realm molest,
Where swains are soldiers but undrest,
      And every neighbor, friend.
Who, with his hous[e]hold, shares his toil
The livelong day, to dress the soil,
      Can best that soil defend!

The faithless *Power of Barbary*'s clefts,
No more shall, with his dastard thefts,
      Our conscious flag offend;
Where thousands of our *wealth* we gave
To pass in peace the midland wave,
      A thousand *deaths* we'll send.

Let mad *Ambition*'s venal tools
Affect to blanch our civic rules,
      As mere politic self;
We'll tell the *World* by maxims sound,
At length a blest REPUBLIC's found,
      Where MAN CAN RULE HIMSELF!

1:7

The process of celebrating a national holiday started at least twenty-five years before the fiftieth anniversary. The poem distinguishes America from those countries that would "puff a monarch's sway," but Federalists might well have challenged the assumption that a republic was a place "Where MAN CAN RULE HIM-SELF." According to Montesquieu's definitions, America was an aristocratic republic, ruled by an elite group of educated men like Jefferson and Madison. Federalists charged Republicans with conflating *democracy* and *republic*, two words that could not have been more antithetical.

If a country is formed through a community of newspaper readers, as Benedict Anderson has argued, then Jefferson's newspaper clippings show how poets used this medium to become what Shelley, in his *Defense of Poetry*, called "the unacknowledged legislators of the world." That not all Americans would have agreed with the sentiments of this poem can be gleaned from the fact that Joseph Dennie referred to Thomas Paine as a "drunken atheist."[28]

Triumph of principles, in the election of Governor
TOMPKINS. — *Quidism deprecated.*
[Anonymous]

Call'd to the governmental chair
    By half a million's voice;
A character so bright, so fair,
    Is worthy of the choice.

A name, expiring envy owns,
    Has robb'd her of her breath;
And fell detraction vents her groans,
    As in the pangs of death;

And malice casts a dying glance,
    And bites her serpent-tongue —
For all she ever could advance,
    Was — "Tompkins is too young."

And youth is an atrocious crime, —
    — Devoid of sense or wit —
So Walpole, on a certain time
    Declar'd to William Pitt.

When William, saucy youth, replied,
    — Tho' vast your life appears,
Your crimes, your follies and your pride,
    Are equal to your years.

No matter whether *young* or *old* —
    Where born, of *whom* or *when*;
For true republicans all hold
    To *principles* — not *men*.

And now, while war impending low'rs,
    And threatens to descend;
From discord, O ye gracious pow'rs,
    Our citizens defend!

From governors, tho' grey with age,
    Who base apostates prove,
And sacrifice to party rage
    Their patriotic love; —

From senators who strive to bribe
    The councils of the state,
And all the treason-fav'ring tribe,
    However *would-be* great: —

From demagogues of ev'ry name,
    Who all their arts employ,
The people's passions to enflame —
    The people to destroy.

The monarchist, we often find,
    Is loyal to his king;
The hog acts after his own kind,
    The scorpion hath his sting;

Some fed'ralists are men of *worth*,
    Some virtues have, tho' hid;
But of all animals on earth,
    O save us from the *Quid*!

                  1:9

De Witt Clinton and his brother-in-law, Judge Ambrose Spencere, tried to prevent the re-election of the Livingstons' candidate, Governor Morgan Lewis. On February 16, 1807, Clinton and a Repubican caucus nominated Daniel D. Tompkins and John Broome for governor and lieutenant governor. Clintonians called their opponent, Morgan Lewis, "Quid." This poem has been described as "probably the first song written to advocate the principle of party regularity." In American newspapers, *quid* also refers to *tertium quid*, a third-party movement within the Republican party. As Andrew Burstein has noted, anyone who threatened a state political interest was branded "quid" during the first decade of the nineteenth century.[29]

SONG,

Written for the Anniversary of American Independence, and sung at the last celebration, by a society
of the friends of the People in Philadelphia.

[Anonymous]

While the slaves of a tyrant his birth day revere,
    And honor the despot who robs them of bread;
Whilst thousands are starving and sunk in despair,
    And the big tears of misery too often are shed;
Shall a nation so free and so happy as we
    Not partake of much gladness from year unto year:
        To a freeman most truly,
        Each fourth of July,
The birth day of freedom shall ever be dear.

We'll remember the heroes who bled in the field,
    We'll remember the sages who counsel'd at home,
We'll remember the foe whom they forced to yield,
    We'll remember the contest for ages to come;
        The heroes and sages,
        Thro' numerous ages,
Shall live in the delight of the friends of mankind;
        And while on the ground,
        E'er a freeman is found,
Shall the birth day of freedom be present in mind.

See the old haughty foe on your shores now advance,
    Led on by the spirit of selfish ambition;
Let them come when they please, we will give them a dance
    By the route Saratoga and York, to perdition:
        Let them come when they will,
        They will find we are still,
Such men as they found us at old Bunker's hill;
        Ever ready to show,
        To an insolent foe,
That the blessings of freedom and virtue we know.

1:9/8

Determined to reject the pompous model set by the "haughty foe" Great Britain, the poet emphasizes that Americans celebrate July 4 rather than a presidential birthday. Jefferson deliberately contrasted this poem with the next, which celebrates Washington's achievements rather than the date of his birth.

ODE to Columbia's Favourite SON.

[Anonymous]

1.

GREAT WASHINGTON, the Hero's come,
   Each heart exulting hears the sound,
Thousands to their Deliv'rer throng,
   And shout him welcome all around!
      Now in full chorus join the song,
      And shout aloud great WASHINGTON!

2.

There view Columbia's favorite Son,
   Her Father, Saviour, Friend, and Guide!
There see th'immortal Washington!
   His Country's Glory, Boast, and Pride;
      Now in full chorus, &c.

3.

When the impending storm of War,
   Thick clouds and darkness hid our way,
Great WASHINGTON, our Polar Star,
   Arose; and all was light as day.
      Now in full chorus, &c.

4.

'Twas on yon plains thy valour rose,
   And ran like fire from man to man;
'Twas here thou humbled Paria's foes,
   And chac'd whole legions to the main!
      Now in full chorus, &c.

5.

Thro' countless dangers, toils and cares,
   Our Hero led us safely on —
With matchless skill directs the wars,
   'Till Vict'ry cries — The day's his own!
      Now in full chorus, &c.

5. [sic]

His country sav'd, the contest o'er,
   Sweet peace restor'd his toils to crown,
The Warrior to his native shore
   Returns, and this his fertile ground.
      Now in full chorus, &c.

7.

But soon Columbia call'd him forth
Again to save her sinking fame,
To take the helm, and by his worth
To make her an immortal name!
Now in full chorus, &c.

8.

Nor yet alone thro' Paria's shores
Her fame, her mighty trumpet blown;
E'en Europe, Africa, Asia, hears,
And emulate the deed he's done!
Now in full chorus, &c.

1:10/9

Washington was, indeed, a hero abroad. Byron alluded to him in his "Ode to Napoleon Bonaparte" as "the first — the last — the best, / The Cincinnatus of the West." The alteration of the eighth stanza, and the newspaper's note of this, marked the moment when Washington became an icon abroad. In "The Vision of Judgment," Byron recognized as heroes Washington, Horne Tooke, and Franklin but not Jefferson; Blake also minimized his role in "America."

POEMS OF NATION

FOR THE MIRROR.
THE PROGRESS OF FEDERALISM.
[Anonymous]
TUNE — "The leaves so green O."

When Congress I was sent
Delaware to represent,
Tout ensemble, — *debonair,*
How I made their folks to stare;
Told each loggerheaded wigh
I could turn the day to night,
If they'd join in my farcical scene O.
   Lie and swear
   All was fair,
   Mind myself,
   Get the pelf;
Heigh down, ho down, derry, derry down,
If they'd join in my farcical scene O.

When serv'd up in *fed'ral* dishes,
Were the precious *loaves* and *fishes*;
Snatch'd a few for father *Bass* — *
Then a *Justice* — next, an *Ass*:
Some four hundred pounds, or more,
That was gleaned from the poor;
All to keep up the farcical, scene O.
   Fire and thunder!
   War and plunder!
   Stamps and stills
   Pay the bills.
               Heigh down, &c.

When a *judge* my daddy grown,
Higher still he rais'd his tone;
On the bench demurely sit;
Shew'd his *learning* and his *wit*;
Merciless to all their crimes
Not remembering *old times*
When he join'd in each, farcical scene O.

"Silence there"!
Lawyers stare!!!
"Clerk — the docket"
"Curse the blockhead"
     Heigh down, &c.

Times are alter'd now I wot,
Daddy's *fishes* gone to pot;
Democrats begin to find
"After cat is after kind"
And that turn about is meet
When I must resign my seat,
It will finish the farcical scene O:
  Toll the bell,
  Fare you well,
  Without doubt
  I'll be out.
     Heigh down, &c.

New Castle.

*Judge Bassett.

       1:10/9

A censorious judge forgets his youthful transgressions. This portrait of elitism and snobbery depicts Federalists as a psychological as well as social type, born to privilege.

Richard Bassett served in the Revolutionary War; he was elected governor of Delaware, and then served as a member of the old Continental Congress, helped form the Constitution, and served in the Senate. He was one of the judges placed on the federal bench by John Adams, and was removed by Jefferson's Judiciary Act in 1802.

On the discoveries of Captain Lewis.
BY JOEL BARLOW, ESQ.

Let the Nile cloak his head in clouds and defy,
The researches of science and time,
Let the Niger escape the keen traveller's eye,
By plunging or changing his clime —

Columbia! not so shall thy boundless domain,
Defraud their brave sons of their right;
Streams, midlands and shorelands, illude us in vain,
We shall drag their dark regions to light.

Look down sainted sage from the synod of Gods:
See, inspired by thy venturous soul,
Mackenzie roll northward his earth-draining floods,
And surge the broad waves to the pole.

With the same soaring genius thy Lewis ascends,
And seizing the car of the sun,
O'er the sky propping hills and high waters he bends,
And gives the proud earth a new zone.

Potomac, Ohio, Missouri had felt,
Half the globe in her cincture comprest,
His long curving course has completed the belt,
And tam'd the last tide of the west.

Then hear the loud voice of the nation proclaim,
And all ages resound the decree —
"Let our Occident stream bear the young hero's name,
Who taught him his path to the Sea."

These four brother floods, like a garland of flowers,
Shall entwine all our states in a band,
Confirm and confed'rate their wide spreading powers,
And their wealth and their wisdom expand.

From Darien to Davis one garden shall bloom,
Where war's wearied banners are furl'd,
And the far-scenting breezes that waft its perfume,
Shall settle the storms of the world.

Then hear the loud voice of the nation proclaim,
And all ages resound the decree —
"That our Occident stream bear the young hero's name,
Who taught him his path to the Sea."

1:16/15

Comparing Lewis and Clark's expedition to a biblical parting of the Nile, the poet views Jeffersonian exploration a messianic: "We . . . drag their dark regions to light." "Look down fainted sage from the synod of Gods: / See, inspired by thy venturous soul, / Mackenzie roll northward his earth-draining floods, / And surge the broad waves to the pole." The poet juxtaposes Mackenzie's path through Canada with Lewis's through "Potomac, Ohio, [and] Missouri."

Barlow felt that a united country could "settle the storms of the world." The newly discovered river (which Barlow thought should be called the "Lewis" rather than the Columbia) would supplement the Potomac, the Ohio, and the Missouri. Such grandiose language was bound to inspire a satire, and John Quincy Adams provided one in *The Monthly Anthology,* by describing what Lewis did not find:

He never with a Mammoth met
However you may wonder;
Not even with a Mammoth's bone,
Above the ground or under —

And from the day his course began,
Till even it was ended,
He never found an Indian tribe
From Welchmen straight descended.[30]

THE DEVIL AND THE CONSUL.

[Anonymous]

AS the Devil in Paris was taking a walk.
He met Bonaparte, and they had some fine talk;
What, Hero! Says Satan, pray how do you do? —
I'm well, cried the Consul, and glad to see you.

> Derry down, down, &c.

What news do you bring from your empire below!
How is OLIVER CROMWELL? — but very so so:
I fancy he envies your glories so great:
For he vows he ne'er reigned in such splendour and state.

> Derry down, &c.

Tho' he often exerted himself in my cause,
The Britons, from him had some excellent laws:
How much below you all his merit must fall,
Who rules this Republic without laws at all!

> Derry down, &c.

ALEXANDER and CAESAR — fine heroes in story!
Are jealous, I know, of your deeds and great glory;
Tho' they push'd through the globe all that conquests *pell mell*,
And rul'd monarchs on earth, now they're subjects in hell.

> Derry down, &c.

'Bout religion at Rome, you once made a great pother,
Have pull'd down one Pope, and then set up another:
In Egypt I've heard of your wonderful works,
How MAHOMET you worship'd to humbug the Turks.

> Derry down, &c.

The deeds you there acted with poison and ire,
In my realms are recorded in letters of fire;
Not an imp in my service but boasts of your fame,
And horribly grins when he mentions your name.

> Derry down, &c.

You boast much, friend Consul, of Liberty's tree,
And say that the Dutch and the Swiss are quite free:
If such freedom as this to give England you aim,
Try your skill — that the sooner yourself I may claim.

                              Derry down, &c.

When the time shall arrive that's determin'd by fate,
That you quit for Invasion, your Consular seat;
Fear not; if bold Britons should prove your o'erthrow,
You shall have a snug birth in my kingdom below.

                              Derry down, &c.

To my dark dominions, soon as you descend,
The damn'd shall rejoice at the sight of their friend;
And I'll give you as long as with me you reside
The hottest of corners at the Devil's fire side.

                              Derry down, &c.

Parblieu! Cried the Consul, and dropped on his knee;
A much cooler lodging would satisfy me.
Hold! Hold! Satan cries, such a mighty Commander,
Shall roast by the side of his friend Alexander.

                              Derry down, &c.

                                            1:22

The poet pictures Oliver Cromwell, Alexander, and Caesar admiring Bonaparte because he is more despotic (and alive!) than they are; they took advantage of their positions as leaders of the people to impose tyranny on their respective countries. This poem's satiric strategy bears comparison with Southey and Coleridge's "The Devil's Walk," which was not acknowledged by them until 1827. Before that time, Byron's "The Devil's Drive" (1813) and Shelley's "The Devil's Thoughts" (1799) appeared, conscious echoes of Southey and Coleridge's poem, which they thought had been written by Richard Porson.

[Anonymous]

A republican's picture is easy to draw,
He can't bear to *obey*, but will *govern* the law;
His manners unsocial, his temper unkind,
He's a rebel in conduct, a tyrant in mind.

He's envious of those, who have riches or pow'r,
Discontented, malignant, implacable, sour!
Never happy himself, he would wish to destroy
The comfort and blessings, which others enjoy.

Our forefathers of old, by his arts were deceiv'd,
Presbyterians they trusted — *fanatics* believ'd;
But, the throne overturn'd, John Bull found, to his cost
He had fifty oppressors, for one he had lost!

Till at length the whole nation were glad to restore,
That good constitution, which bless'd them before;
They no longer endur'd the republican yoke,
But hallow'd the boughs of the fam'd royal oak!

1:25

A Federalist poet reworks the symbolism of
the oak tree to point out America's bond
with England.

FROM THE AMERICAN CITIZEN.
TO THE MEMORY OF GEN. HAMILTON.

[Anonymous]

I.

Wafted by our nation's sigh,
Thy soul is gone to realms above,
　To meet its Washington on high,
Kindred souls! pure as the dove.

II.

Spirit of the heavenly regions,
Crown'd with never-ending fame,
　List and hear how earthly legions
Consecrate thy deathless name.

III.

From that blest, that holy dwelling,
Where, midst fields of glory bright,
Thou the sacred anthem swelling,
　With white-rob'd ministers of light.

IV.

Behold the patriot's bosom burning,
The virgin's tears descend for thee;
　Columbia's sons *indignant* mourning,
The soldier of humanity.

V.

Vengeance lights each *honest* feature,
'Gainst the dark, malignant hand,
　Who *coldly* shot a fellow creature,
A man belov'd by all our land.

VI.

Our empire's union's great defender,
Lies mouldering in the silent tomb,
　Its foes will *now* strive hard to rend her;
Uncertain is our nation's doom!!

VII.

Great Hamilton! thy country's story
To latest time will clearly prove,
How great thy worth and martial glory,
Embalm'd with all Columbia's love.

PATRIOTICUS.

1:26/25

This poem is remarkable for depicting Hamilton in heaven ("Thy soul is gone to realms above, / To meet its Washington on high, / Kindred souls!"). Jefferson may not have agreed with the depiction of Hamilton's soul as "Pure as the dove." Hamilton's strong partisan interests as a Federalist have been subsumed by this patriotic poet who depicts him as "the soldier of humanity" (stanza four). Patrioticus alludes to the "dark, malignant hand" of Burr, though Burr remains unnamed.

An ODE,

Most respectfully inscribed to his Excellency General WASHINGTON, on being chosen President of the United States.

I.

Where fair Columbia spreads her wide domain
O'er many a lengthen'd hill and sylvan plain,
In mystic vision wrapt, far to the south,
Array'd in all the gloom of rosy youth,
   A cherub form arose,
O'er the blue Heavens her snowy pinions spread,
Celestial tints illum'd her starry head,
Bright as the radiant God of Day,
Soft as the fleecy cloud, or milky-way,
   Her shining vestment flows.
Her hand sustains the trump of fame,
Its blasts aloud her will proclaim;
   As high in air she hung,
O'er where Mount Vernon's odours breathe,
She dropt immortal Glory's wreathe,
   Then, northward floating sung —
The music of the spheres resounding to her tongue;

II.

"Heaven born Freedom, sent to save,
"By actions, glorious as brave,
"With every Godlike virtue fraught,
"Which either peace or war has taught,
   "Behold your hero come!
"Call'd by his country's urgent voice,
"O'er her high councils to preside;
"By every breast's united choice,
"Call'd, the storm-beat helm to guide,
   "He leaves his rural dome.
"On all his steps see smiling Concord wait,
"And harmony pervade each happy State —
"See Public Confidence her arms expand.
"While glad'ning gratulations echo o'er the land.

III.

"With soul at unambitious rest,
"Yet glowing for the public weal;
"Still must Columbia's dear bequest
"O'er philosophic ease prevail.
　　"To hold with shady hand,
"A free, a just restricting rein,
"Wild jarring discord to restrain;
"As government's revolving car,
"Through placid peace, or horrid war,
　　"Obeys his mild command.
"Thine be the bliss, great Son of Fame!
"(As still hath been thy only aim)
"To bid stern Justice poise her equal scale —
"Reviving Commerce spread the swelling sail,
"With golden prospects fraught, from ev'ry gale.

IV.

"Those laurel-trophies won through seas of blood,
"Unequall'd in historic fame;
"Those priceless labours for the public good
"Had well immortaliz'd thy name,
　　"And claim'd a world's applause
"Now all the honors of the field
"All splendid conquest e'er could yield,
"Combine with universal praise,
"On high thy matchless worth to raise,
　　"The guardian of our laws,
"Not rear'd by tumult in a giddy hour,
"The crested idol of despotic power;
"But sacred Freedom's delegated voice,
"Thy grateful country's uncorrupted choice.

V.

"No Alexander's mad career,
"Nor Caesar's dictatorial reign,
"No dazzling dome that scepters wear,
"Thy soul with thirst of power could stain.
　　"A greater honour's thine,
"Approving millions place in you

"That power they would reflective view —
"Diffusing all that's good and great
"Through each department of the State:
  "Thy bright'ning virtues shine,
"With more effulgence round thy head,
"With more essential honors spread,
"Than sparkling toys that gild the tyrant's brow;
"Worn but to court his cringing slaves to bow.

VI.

"As yon bright spheres that circling run,
"With lucid splendour or round the Sun,
  "Diffuse their borrow'd blaze;
"So may that senatoran band,
"Assembled by a virtuous land,
  "As in thy worth they gaze;
"Reflect the light thy virtues yield,
"The sword of justice bid thee wield,
  "And anarchy erase.
"The Federal Union closer bind,
  "Firm public faith restore:
"Drive discord from the canker'd mind,
  "Each mutual blessing pour:
"Then, when the glorious course is run,
"Which Heav'n assigned her WASHINGTON;
"His soul let cherub-choirs convey
"To all the triumphs of eternal day."

                                              S. K

Bladensburg, April 16, 1789.

1:29

If odes are written in praise of someone, this poem more than fulfills its genre, praising Washington as a godlike figure: "Heaven born Freedom, sent to save, / By actions, glorious as brave." The poet suggests that America's first president resists tyranny.

"His integrity was most pure," Jefferson wrote of Washington, "his justice the most inflexible I have ever known, no motives of interest or consanguinity, of friendship or hatred, being able to bias his decision."[31]

TO AMERICA,
On the Retirement of Geo. Washington.
[Anonymous]

"Virtus, repulsae, necescia, sordidae
"Intaminatis fulget honoribus
"Nec semit, aut ponit secures
"Arbitrio popularis *aurae.*   Hor.

SAD as thou strayest through the sullen cloud
That hang, portentious, round thy nut-brown front;
Slow though thy pace is, thro' the lofty pines
That bend their green tufts to the warring winds;
That, on thy shores high beats the surf of war,
Tho' round thy commerce storms and tempests rage,
And the worn pilot quits, the stubborn helm;
Yet shall thy bards still tempt thee to a smile,
Shall loose thy dark hair to the western breeze,
And drive pale fear from thy maternal breast; —
Thy son, unseen, shall still direct the course,
And Empire's ship ride high above the storm.

What tho' no pageant titles deck the SAGE —
No murder'd millions haunt the Hero's mind;
Yet shall the leaves of Time, as they unfold,
Still rank thy GEORGE among the first of Men.

If Greece could raise its worthies to a name,
And sail them onward, with the stream of years,
For the towns, and petty islands sav'd;
In the long list of Roman heroes rolls
Along the pages of immortal song,
For thousands butcher'd — Nations — Kings enslav'd;
If Fame has blazon'd to th'admiring world,
And in her temple plac'd some Modern names,
Who fear'd adventur'ous, her imperial fire,
Impel'd by honors, or impress'd by pride:
Yet when THY SON, AMERICA, appears,
Girding the horizon with setting ray,
The Grecian, Roman, Modern names fast fade
Before the Brilliance of a western sky.

Led by a nymph from Heaven, gay Liberty,
Timoleon ventur'd on a land oppress'd,
And lest fair Corinth and its spires behind,
Its fam'd Colossus, and its towers of brass;
The stranger-chief, still led Sicilian on
To Battle, Conquest, Liberty, and Ease:
Grown old, retir'd, yet still his honor'd name,
And his last Councils, guided still the isle,
Whilst every breath was incense to his age
Timoleon sav'd a small and foreign State; —
OUR CHIEF his Country sav'd, and half a World!

Ye blest companions of his early years,
Who saw the youth fast rip'ning into man.
Lend your glad praises to his spotless morn.
WARRIORS! escap'd from Braddock's slaughter'd train,
With all your race — attend, with voices tun'd
To the high strain of a Deliverer's praise.
Virgins and Youths, if e'er you hope to lay
Your hearts, high beating, to the breast of Love,
Join in the chorus of my grateful verse.
Ye Veteran Bands, brave partners of his toil!

Who drove thro' frost and fire at his command
Thro' all the changes of eventful war,
Sound the loud clarions to your General's praise,
The great conductor of your Lightning arms.
Ye Sires! who train the Law, and ye who Judge,
Rise from your seats, and on the Hero's head
(Retiring fast to radiate other worlds)
Plant with your rev'rend hands the honored wreath,
Rich woven by the Fathers of the Land.
And may the Land, from all its mountains, send
A general echo, to the great applause,
Till the long peal of praise, America,
Rolls o'er thy cloud-topt hills — sounds thro' thy woods —
Floats onward with thy streams — surrounds thy shores —
And sweeping o'er the wide Atlantic waves,
Resounds the plaudit thro' the Eastern World!

European worlds, brown dame, tho sad thou sit'st,
Lonely, amongst the rocks of thy domains,
(Moaning for fancied treasures idly gain'd,
As fury ventur'd and as idly lost)
Torn by mad monarchs, who wou'd grasp a world,
And by Republics aping ancient Rome,
Owns not a balsam for its streaming wounds.
Not from the reign of Theseus,* until now,
Thro' the long record of illustrious names,
Thro' the stone tablets of eternal Fame,
Can Europe raise her forehead to the sky,
Where beams the mirror of celestial Truth,
And point one equal of this Son of Thine!
                              AMERICAN.

*The first established Government that we read of was
under him.

[Norfolk Herald.]

1:30/29

Jefferson juxtaposed Washington's "being chosen" president with his retirement. The quotation from Horace celebrates Washington as a man of virtue, seeing him in light of Greece and Rome and modern names (presumably Napoleon) that "fast fade" before America's "western sky." According to the poet, Washington compares favorably with Timoleon, who overthrew the tyranny of his brother, retired, and then returned to public life to unseat Dionysus II. He also compares favorably with Theseus, legendary lawgiver of Greece. The "stone tablets of eternal Fame" seem to be a reference to Moses.

HIS MAJESTY'S BIRTH DAY.
Ode for his Majesty's Birth-day, 1804.
By H. J. Pye, Esq. P. L.
(To be performed This Day at St. James's)

I.

As the blest guardians of the British Isles,
   Immortal Liberty, triumphant stood,
And view'd her gallant sons with favoring smiles
   Undaunted heroes of the field or flood;
From Inverary's rocky shores,
Where loud the Hyperborean billow roars,
To w[h]ere the surges of the Atlantic wave,
Around Cornubia's western borders rave.
While Erin's valiant warriors glow,
With kindred fire to crush the injurious foe,
From her bright lance the flames of vengeance stream,
And in her eagle eye shines glory's radiant beam.

II.

Why sink those smiles in Sorrow's sigh?
Why Sorrow's tears suffuse that eye?
Alas! While weeping Britain sees,
The baleful fiends of pale disease
Malignant hovering near her throne,
And threat a Monarch all her own.
No more from Anglia's fertile land,
No more from Caledonia's brand,
From Erin's breezy hills no more
The panting legions crowd the shores
The buoyant barks the vaunting host,
That swarm Gallia's hostile coast,
The anxious thought no longer share,
Lost in a nearer, dearer care,
And Britain breathes alone for George's life her prayer.

POEMS OF NATION

III.

Her prayer is heard, th'Almighty Power,
   Potent to punish or to save,
Bids health resume again her happier hour;
   And as across the misty wave
The freshening breezes sweep the clouds away
That hid awhile the golded orb of day,
So from Hygeia's balmy breath
Fly the drear shadows of disease and death.
Again the manly breast beats high,
And flames again the indignant eye,
While from the cottage to the throne,
This generous sentiment alone
Lives in each heart with patriot ardour warm,
Point, every sword, nerves every Briton's arm,
"Rush to the field where George and Freedom lead,
"Glory and fame alike the warriors' meed,
"Brave in their country's cause, who conquer or who bleed."

1:30/29–1:31

This completes a series contrasting two democratic tributes to Washington, with Pye's sychophantic ode, which even the British of George III's day probably found unctuous. Jefferson seems to take pride in the simple eloquence that democracy fosters. George III underwent periodic fits of madness. Stanza three describes his recovery from one of them: "the shadows of disease and death" that turned out to be madness induced by porphyria, a rare blood disease. The last line of the poem strikes a rather despondent note, suggesting that sacrificing one's life for George III's cause, even for his whims, is worthy and patriotic.

Note: Cornubia, a term used during Roman and immediate post-Roman Britain, means "people of the horn" and refers to the Land's End section of the Cornish peninsula.

*The following Song, was written by R. T. Paine,
Jun. Esq. and sung at Boston, on the celebration
of the 4th of July.*

SONG FOR JULY 4th, 1805.

TUNE — "Whilst happy in my native land."

WIDE o'er the wilderness of waves,
    Untrack'd by human peril,
Our fathers roam'd for peaceful graves,
    To deserts dark and sterile:
No parting pang — No long adieu
    Delay'd their gallant daring;
With *them*, their *Gods*, and *Country* too,
    Their pilgrim keels were bearing.
All hearts unite the patriot band,
Be Liberty our natal land.

II.

Their dauntless hearts no meteor led.
    In terror o'er the ocean:
From fortune and from man they fled,
    To Heaven and its devotion.
Fate cannot bend the high born mind
    To bigot usurpation: —
They, who had left a world behind,
    Now gave that world a nation.

III.

The soil to till, to freight the sea,
    By valor's arm protected —
To plant an empire brave and free,
    Their sacred view directed:
But more they feared, than tyrant's yoke,
    Insidious faction's fury:
For oft a worm destroys an oak,
    Whose leaf that worm would bury.

IV.

Thus rear'd, our giant's realm arose,
  And claim'd our sovereign CHARTA: —
Her life-blood warm from heroes rose,
  And all her sons from *Sparta*.
Be Free, *Columbia!* proudest name,
  Fame's Herald wafts in story:
Be Free, thou youngest child of Fame,
  Rule, brightest heir of Glory!

V.

The Public, mid the battle's ire,
  Hath Afric's towers dejected:
And Lybia's sands have flash'd with fire,
  From EATON's sword reflected.
Thy groves, which erst from hill or plain,
  Entrench'd from savage plunder,
To Naiads turn'd, must cleave the main,
  And sport with *Neptune's* thunder.

1:32/31

This song by Robert Treat Paine described the real perils risked by the founders of a new nation: "They, who had left a world behind, / Now gave that world a nation" (stanza two). An "empire" was planned rather than a democracy. Anachronistically, the poet argued that faction (such as that between Federalists and Republicans) was feared more than tyranny. Paine depicted the young America as more like Sparta than Athens. Daniel Eaton (1764–1811) was an American naval hero appointed Navy agent for the Barbary region (May 26, 1804) and led the attack on Derne on April 27, 1805.

A SONG,

FOR THE NEW-HAMPSHIRE ELECTION,

1805.

[Anonymous]

TUNE — "JEFFERSON and LIBERTY."

ALL hail, ye noble, generous souls,
Whose bosoms glow with freedom's fire;
Push round the full convivial bowls,
And strike your harps, ye tuneful quire.
      CHORUS.
    Rejoice, New-Hampshire's sons rejoice,
    This day again declares you free:
    While Heaven and earth approve your choice,
    And LANGDON guards your Liberty.

Again the vast concave resounds
With freeman's Heaven inspired acclaim,
While distant spheres echo the sounds,
"Still dear to us in freedom's name."
    Rejoice, New-Hampshire's sons, &c.

When Albion's proud, insulting host,
To crush Columbia cross'd the sea;
When prowling legions throng'd our coast.
Then LANGDON fought for liberty.
    Rejoice, New-Hampshire's sons, &c.

And when our freedom was secur'd
And liberty triumphant reign'd,
On Langdon was the task confer'd
Of guarding rights so dearly gain'd
    Rejoice, New-Hampshire's sons, &c.

Our firm, immortal fabric rear'd,
(The dread and wonder of the world!)
Soon demagogues their bolts prepar'd
And Langdon felt the first they hurld.
    Rejoice, New-Hampshire's sons, &c.

But spite of all those base designs
Pursu'd by parasites and knaves,
Behold, conspicuous freedom shines
And bids her votaries never be slaves.
    Rejoice, New-Hampshire's sons, &c.

And hark! from Heaven's high-arch'd alcove,
Methinks in soft, mellifluous sound,
Like Orpheus' gentle notes of love,
I hear this sweet response resound,
    "Rejoice, New-Hampshire's sons, rejoice,
    "This day again declares you free;
    "While Heaven and earth approve your choice,
    "And LANGDON guards your liberty.

"Assemble, all ye youthful train,
"Nor age decline the jubilee;
"Henceforth determine to maintain,
"Your Langdon and your liberty.
    "Rejoice New-Hampshire's sons, rejoice,
    "This day again declares you free,
    "While Heaven and earth approve your choice,
    "And LANGDON guards your Liberty."
                    S. C.

Washington, 1805.

            1:32/31

In this poem, the poet refers to America as Columbia and celebrates John Langdon as the defender of liberty. No atheist, Langdon is a Jeffersonian who has the approval of "Heaven and earth." Langdon was governor of New Hampshire (1805; 1809–11) and a staunch supporter of Jefferson during the embargo. As early as 1802, Jefferson relied on Langdon for news of political events in New Hampshire, which he refused to believe was a "satellite of Massachusetts."

"Although we have not yet got a majority into the fold of republicanism in your state," Jefferson wrote to Langdon in June 1802, "yet one long pull more will affect it. We can hardly doubt that one twelve month more will give an executive and legislature in that state whose opinions may harmonize with their sister states. Unless it be true as is sometimes said that N. H. is but a satellite of Massachusetts. In this last state the public sentiment seems to be under some influence additional to that of the clergy and lawyers. I suspect there must be a leaven of state pride at seeing itself deserted by the public opinion, and that their late popular song of *Rule New England* betrays one principle of their present variance from the union. But I am in hopes they will in time discover that the shortest road to rule is to join the majority."

A SONG,
For the Fourth of July, 1806.
[Anonymous]

YANKEE DOODLE is the tune
    Americans delight in:
'Twill do to whistle, sing, or play,
    And *just the thing* for fighting.

        CHORUS.
    Yankee doodle, boys; Huzza!
    Down outside, up the middle —
    Yankee doodle, fa, sol, la,
    Trumpet, drum, and fiddle.

Should Great Britain, Spain, or France,
    Wage war upon our shore, sir,
We'll lead them such a *woundy* dance,
    They'll find their toes are sore, sir.
                Yankee doodle, &c.

Should a haughty foe expect
    To give our boys a caning,
We *guess* they'll find our boys have *larnt*
    A *little bit* of training.
                Yankee doodle, &c.

I'll wager now a mug of slip,
    And bring it on the table,
Put Yankee boys aboard a ship,
    To beat them they are able.
                Yankee doodle, &c.

Then if they go to *argufy*,
    I *rather guess* they'll find, too,
We've got a set of *tonguey blades*,
    T'out-talk 'em, if *they're mind* to.
                Yankee doodle, &c.

America's a *dandy* place;
    The people are all brothers;
And which one's got a *pumpkin pye*,
    He shares it with the others.
                    Yankee doodle, &c.

We work, and sleep, and pray in peace —
    By industry we thrive, sir,
And if a drone won't do his part,
    We'll scout him from the hive, sir.
                    Yankee doodle, &c.

And then on INDEPENDENT DAY
    (And who's a better right to?)
We eat and drink, and sing and play,
    And have a dance at night, too.
                    Yankee doodle, &c.

Our girls are fair, our boys are tough,
    Our old folks wise and healthy;
And when we've every thing we want,
    We *count* that we are wealthy.
                    Yankee doodle, &c.

We're *happy, free,* and *well to do,*
    And cannot want for knowledge;
For almost every mile or two,
    You find a *school* or *college.*
                    Yankee doodle, &c.

The land we till is all our own;
    Whate'er the price, we paid it;
Therefore we'll fight *till all is blue,*
    Should any dare invade it.
                    Yankee doodle, &c.

Since we're so bless'd, let's eat and drink,
    With thankfulness and gladness;
Should we kick o'er our cup of joy,
    It would be *surtin* madness.
                    Yankee doodle, &c.

1:33–1:34

The speaker idealizes America as a place where "the people are all brothers" who can share "a pumpkin pye." Americans are busy bees who do their part or are driven from the "hive," a quality that still exists (describing at once the American work ethic and American conformity). They do not seek foreign wars (a contrast with the previous poem) but will defend their land when attacked. In fact, America's army and navy would not give it negotiating advantages until more than a century later. At the dawn of American literature, it is interesting to see a distinctly Yankee vernacular underscored in newspaper verse, characterized by such words as *surtin*.

POEMS OF NATION

PATRIOTIC SONG.

BY WILLIAM RAY.

TUNE — "Anacreon in Heaven."

MORE free than the Mohawk that glides thro' our plains,
   Republicans! meet round this joyous libation;
From freedom blest millions resound the bold strains —
   From earth-tilling peasants, the lords of our nation —
      Loud echoes to fame,
      The day shall proclaim,
      That gave Independence her blood written name;
And own'd Nature's equal, eternal decree —
Heav'n ne'er form'd us slaves — man was born to live free

While JEFFERSON o'er us sublimely sits head,
   No treason the league-union'd states can dissever;
Of freedom the guardian — of tyrants the dread —
   His name will grow dearer and dearer forever;
      When worlds cannot save —
      Green garlands shall wave,
      And Liberty blossom o'er Jefferson's grave,
To prove Nature's equal, eternal decree —
Heav'n ne'er form'd us slaves — man was born to live free.

From no haug[h]ty lordlings our tenors we hold,
   From natives we bought the rich soil we inherit,
Our great and our mighty — the wise and the bold,
   The badge of their power, is the pledge of their merit;
      If traitors, they yield
      The blood purchas'd field,
      No wreath shall avail them — do dignity shield;
They curse Nature's equal, eternal decree —
Heav'n ne'er form'd us slaves — man was born to live free.

Where late yell'd the savage, and wolves howled for prey,
   Gay villages rise and the arts flourish round us;
And science forth beams like the dawning of day,
   Nor earth holds our commerce, nor ocean can bound us;

Lo! India's vast shore
Our seamen explore!
See Lybia's wild deserts an EATON march o'er!
To prove Nature's equal, eternal decree —
Heav'n ne'er, form'd us slaves — man was born to live free.

Those heav'n born heroes, who fought, bled & died
    To give us our wisdom-built free constitution,
Stars mounting, the ruins of time shall o'erride —
    Their virtues out-blazon the earth's dissolution.
        T[h]rough death's darkest gloom
        Fresh laurels shall bloom,
        And youth spring immortal from Washington's tomb!
To prove Nature's final, eternal decree —
Heav'n ne'er form'd us slaves — man was born to live free.

Then free as yon Mohawk that glides through the plains,
    Republicans meet round this joyous libation:
From freedom-blest millions resound the bold strains,
    From earth-tilling peasants, the lords of our nation,
        Loud echoes to fame,
        The day shall proclaim,
        They gave Independence her blood written name,
And own'd Nature's equal, eternal decree —
Heav'n ne'er made us slaves — man was born to live free.

Amsterdam, N. Y. July 4, 1807.

1:34

William Ray found democratic Americans "more free than the Mohawk that glides thro' our plains." The fascination with American Indians as a cultural point of comparison appears in Mary Shelley's *Frankenstein*, when the creature weeps for the fate of the original inhabitants of North America. "Who would be free must first strike the blow," Byron wrote in *Childe Harold's Pilgrimage*, echoing Ray's "Heav'n ne'er made us slaves — man was born to live free." Ray's poem is unusual in imagining Liberty blossoming over Jefferson's grave, nineteen years before the event.

WAR,
OR A PROSPECT OF IT,
From recent instances of British Outrage.
BY WILLIAM RAY.

VOT'RIES of Freedom, arm!
   The British Lion roars!
Legions of Valor, take th' alarm —
   Rush, rush to guard our shores;

Behold the horrid deed —
   Your brethren gasping lie!
Beneath a tyrant's hand they bleed —
   They groan — they faint — they die.

Vet'rans of seventy-six,
   Awake the slumb'ring sword! —
Hearts of your murd'rous foes transfix —
   'Tis vengeance gives the word.

Remember Lexington,
   And Bunker's tragic hill;
The same who spilt your blood thereon,
   Your blood again would spill.

Ye who have seen your wives,
   Your children, and your fires,
To British ruffians yield their lives,
   And roast in savage fires; —

Our cities lost in flames, —
   Your mothers captive led;
Rise and avenge their injur'd names,
   Ye kindred of the dead.

But not Revenge alone,
   Should urge you to the field;
Let Duty lead you firmly on,
   And Justice be your shield,

Sure as we fail to join
    And crush our impious foes,
War, fire and sword, and death combine,
    And woes succeed to woes. —

Behold, with blushes red,
    The sea like blood appears;
Our streams are bridg'd with fancied dead.
    And brim'd with orphans' tears;

But Union can perform
    The wonders of a host —
Avert the danger, quell the storm,
    And drive them from our coast.

Unite, and side by side
    Meet vict'ry or your graves;
That moment we in War divide,
    That moment we are slaves.

July 20th, 1807.

1:37

Of the three poems by William Ray that Jefferson clipped, this is the most realistic. Ray articulated many of Jefferson's most controversial positions, such as his stance on the embargo. In this poem, he focused on British outrages during the Revolutionary War, using biblical imagery ("the wonders of a host") to describe the burning of women and children "in savage fires." Not revenge, but duty should be the "shield" to protect Americans from "impious foes." Unity alone can protect Americans from becoming slaves.

A NEW "HAIL COLUMBIA."

For the approaching Republican Jubilee.
[Anonymous]

I.

HAIL, Columbia! happy land!
Hail, ye patriotic band!
Who late oppos'd oppression's laws
And now stand first in freedom's cause;
Rejoice — for now the storm is gone,
Columbia owns her chosen son;
The bill of rights shall be our boast,
And Jefferson our fav'rite toast:
Ever grateful for the prize,
Let our voices reach the skies.

    Firm, united, let us be,
    Rallying round the sacred tree;
    May its leaves o'erspread the world,
    And tyrants from their thrones be hurl'd.

II.

See the Hamiltonian Feds,
How they hang their jaw-lock'd heads;
Moaning now their fallen chief,
In whom they hop'd to find relief —
Who with an army at command,
Thought soon to rule this happy land.
But now their hopes are all destroy'd,
Their wicked schemes are null and void,
The federal rats have left the ship,
The democrats will take a trip.

    Thro' the rough "tempest'ous sea,"
    We'll safely guide our liberty:
    Stop the leak, the rigging clear,
    And to a peaceful haven steer.

III.

Sound, sound the trump of fame,
Let Jefferson's great name,
Ring thro' the world with loud applause,
As the firm friend of freedom's cause;
Let ev'ry clime to freedom dear,
Now listen with a joyful ear;

With honest pride and manly grace,
He fills the presidential place—
The constitution for his guide,
And truth and justice at his side.
    Firm, united, let us be,
    Rallying round the sacred tree;
    May its leaves o'erspread the world
    And tyrants from their thrones be hurl'd

IV.

Republicans, behold your chief!
He comes to give your fears relief
The rock on which the storm has beat
Who brav'd the faction's deadly hate,
Now arm'd with virtue, firm and true,
Looks for support to heav'n and you.
When hope was sinking in dismay,
When glooms obscur'd Columbia's day,
He mourn'd his country's threaten'd fate,
But sav'd here 'ere it grew too late.

    The year of Jubilee is come,
    Restore ye Britian agents home;
    For we, in turn, will rule the roost
    And make Jefferson the toast.

1:38

In his first inaugural address, Jefferson stated that "we are all Republicans — we are all Federalists,"[32] but he did much to strengthen the Republican party ten years before he was elected as their representative. He was too shrewd to rejoice in seeing the Hamiltonian Feds "hang their jaw-lock'd heads" in public, but he clipped the poem in private. Jefferson must have also enjoyed a poem that associated him with the "bill of rights" and "freedom's cause."

23. A NEW SONG.

[Anonymous]

TUNE — "Anacreon in Heav'n, &c."

YE vot'ries of freedom, who firmly oppos'd,
Those measures which led to the brink of perdition,
Your foes are appall'd, for their plots are disclos'd,
We can now speak and print without fear of sedition —
    Come then, freemen, along,
    And join in my song;
We've sworn that we'll never to tyrants bow long,
That in union and harmony still we'll combine,
And kneel with devotion to liberty's shrine,

Methinks I see liberty's genius on high,
Escorted by shades of those heroes who dy'd
T'secure independence — she smiles — her bright eye
Sheds cheerfulness, happiness, harmony wide;
    Lo, her banners high wave:
    Fetters drop from the slave;
Arts, science, philosophy start from the grave,
Where long they had languish'd for close round were twin'd
The strong cords of king-craft and priest-craft combin'd!

See how her sweet influence enliven[s] the scene,
Triumphantly swells ev'ry breast with delight;
No longer her foes and oppressors are seen,
They have fled to the shadows and darkness of night,
    E'en "the chief who commands"
    Like "a rock" in quick sands,
Shrinks aghast at the touch of democracy's wand!
And cries, "I'm undone for e'er daring to 'twine,
The chains of oppression round liberty's shrine."
Hark, the echoes of joy, how they ring thro' the land!
Avaunt ye pale tyrants, 'tis freedom's strong voice!
On the hills of Columbia she fixes her stand,
And proclaims the glad tidings — and this is her choice;

Lo, Jefferson height,
Fill up bumpers, that's right;
Here's his health, we'll support him,
If needful, we'll fight;
But union and harmony wish to combine,
And kneel with devotion at liberty's shrine.

1:40/39

This nationalistic song is remarkable for its celebration of republican virtue as a semi-religious rite, in which votaries make offers to "liberty's shrine." Jefferson embodies the hopes of citizens who refuse to bow to tyrants. The shackles or "strong cords" of "king-craft and priest-craft" fall when the spirit of liberty chooses Jefferson as a moral leader who disperses "the shadows and darkness of night."

MAY ERIN BE FREE.

[Anonymous]

TUNE — "Let the toast pass."

A toast to the land where our forefathers dwelt —
    Dear Erin's the spot that I mean, sirs;
And a tear to the heroes whose blood has been spill'd,
    In fighting her rights to regain, sirs.
        CHORUS.
May Erin be free — and enjoy liberty,
All her sons and her daughters as happy as we.

Here's to the fair of the Emerald Isle,
    Alike faithful in peace and in danger;
Who in liberty's cause embarked with a smile,
    Unaw'd by the — *"Foe and the stranger."*
     Chorus — May Erin be free, &c.

And here's to the land where for shelter we fled;
    The assylum where truth knows no danger,
May the sons of Columbia ne'er feel woe, nor dread
    The arms of a traitor or a stranger.
     Chorus — May Erin be free, &c.

And here's to those friends here assembled around,
    And blessed by each good institution;
May this prove a blessing to *Erin's poor sons,*
    Who seek refuge from fell persecution.
     Chorus — May Erin be free, &c.

1:39

This poem, like the songs of Carolan, is one of several whose inclusion in the scrapbooks indicates Jefferson's interest in the fate of Ireland. Editors of American newspapers who were Irish, such as William Duane, saw Ireland's fate as similar to America's. The sentimental acknowledgment of fallen heroes ("a tear to the heroes whose blood has been spill'd") recalls Thomas Moore's poems and songs about Ireland, though he did not link America and Ireland until his views on Catholic emancipation and political reform became more radical.

Temple of the Muses.
A PATRIOTIC POEM.
[Anonymous]

The martial trumpet, hark, it sounds,
And all Columbia's shores alarms;
Its clangor, from her hill rebounds,
And rouses all her sons to arms.

Fir'd the call, a chosen band
Of youths rush forth, who nobly dare
In thick embattled ranks, to stand;
And brave the thunders of the war.

The kneeling son, his sire entreats,
For leave, to join and crush the foe;
The Patriot sire, his ardor greets,
Blesses the youth, and bids him go.

No fears maternal urge his stay,
Restraining him, from glory's call:
The matron sends her son away,
Secure, to conquer or to fall.

Yet ere he goes he seeks the fair,
One tender kiss, to give, and take;
The toils of war, then flies to share,
Life venturing for his country's sake.

The virgin turns a tearful eye,
To see her lov'd, brave youth depart:
Fear for his life excites a sigh,
While admiration fills her heart.

'Gainst men like these, what can avail,
Injustice, and oppression's force,
Vain is their fury, to repel,
The sons of freedom, in their course.

God of Columbia! from above,
Propitious on thy sons, look down:
May they to war, resistless move,
And victory all their efforts crown.

1:42

This poem describes the difficulties of sending a lover off to battle. Mothers and "virgins" participate in their country's cause by sending their sons to battle willingly: "The matron sends her son away, / Secure, to conquer or to fall . . . The virgin turns a tearful eye, / To see her lov'd, brave youth depart." Linda Kerber has described the role of women in the new republic in her groundbreaking book *Women of the Republic*; James and Alan Golden have shown how important the rhetoric of virtue (self-sacrificing motherhood, virginity) was to the success of the new republic (Columbia's sons "resistless move" in their support of freedom's cause).

FROM THE PORTFOLIO.
COLUMBIA's EAGLE.
[Anonymous]

LET England's flock boast his pow'r,
Let Gallia's Cock defiance crow;
Columbia's Eagle free, shall cow'r
To any foreign foe.
With equal ease, aloft she waves
The branch of PEACE, or shafts of War,
And wafts the fame
Of Freedom's name
To lands enslav'd and realms afar.

Once, could the Roman Eagle soar,
Beyond the reach of human eye;
But now, she plumes her wings no more,
No more invades the sky:
For Freedom fled, and with her bore
The Eagle's pow'r, the Eagle's sway;
Her wings are weak.
And dull her beak,
Her name no more shall strike dismay.

Not so Heaven's FAV'RITE bird, that wields
The weapons of Columbia's ire,
And every ear bought interest shields
From Mad Ambition's fire:
While Time rolls on the passing hours,
Her flight the world shall awe,
And widely spread
The Olive's shade,
To shelter Liberty and Law.

1:44

This poem offers a Federalist perspective on
war, describing the American eagle as a fallen
creature: "Her wings are weak. / And dull her
beak, / Her name no more shall strike dismay."

POEMS OF NATION

COLUMBIA'S PRIDE — HER LIBERTY.

[Anonymous]

Land of my Fathers — Freedom's Field,
  Thy sacred rights shall be maintain'd;
Columbia's sons will never yield,
  Or see thy spotless honor stain'd;
For He who gave us life gave thee,
Our country's pride — sweet LIBERTY.

With joy each freeman hears the sound,
  That calls to arms — to arms! ye brave;
The servile heart will not be found,
  That would not bleed, our rights to save:
For he who gave us rise, gave thee,
Our country's pride — sweet LIBERTY.

The cannon's music charm the ear,
  When freemen do for freedom fight;
Prepare! Columbia's Sons, prepare!
  We'll die before we'll yield our right;
For He who gave us life, gave thee.
Our country's pride — sweet LIBERTY.

Father above, in thee we trust —
  A band of *brothers* look to thee;
We own *thy power*, but know thee just,
  And trust that nature *made us free*!
Yes, He who gave us life, gave thee,
Our country's pride — OUR LIBERTY.

Martyrs to Freedom, view each heart,
We'll die or save the rights you've giv'n;
With these just rights we will not part,
Unless it be, to meet in Heav'n,
For He who gave us life, gave thee,
Columbia's pride — OUR LIBERTY.

1:44

Federalists accused the Republicans of mistaking license for liberty; they associated Republican celebration of liberty with the worst excesses of the French Revolution and viewed Republican "democracy" as an excuse for mob rule. As in previous poems that Jefferson clipped, this Republican celebration of "Columbia's pride" views liberty as a gift from God: "For He who gave us life, gave thee / Columbia's pride — OUR LIBERTY." At cer-tain points in the poem, God and the laws c nature are equivalent: "Father above, in the we trust — / A band of *brothers* look to thee / We own *the power*, but know thee just, And trust that nature *made us free!*" Soldier are martyrs whose self-sacrifice for the country in war takes on religious overtone ("Land of my Fathers — Freedom's Field, Thy sacred rights shall be maintain'd").

From the True American.
HETTY's HYMN,
OR AN ODE TO EMBARGO.
[Anonymous]
TUNE — "The Old Spinning Wheel."

"With a patriot's true zeal,
    How indignant I feel,
    While I turn my old wheel,
And reflect on the conduct of George & his lords;
    If they do not desist,
    All the girls will enlist,
    And will give them a twist,
That shall bind them for ever like monsters in cords.

CHORUS
"So we'll break off the trade,
    Which by tyrants is made
    To insult and degrade,
And to cut up our nation as lions eat prey:
    Independent we stand,
    In a free happy land,
    And the world we'll command,
For the voice of EMBARGO the world must obey.

"O, what language can speak,
    The late outrage and freak,
    On th'unarm'd Chesapaeake,
In demanding, and killing, American tars;
    War so wantonly wag'd,
    Has my nation enrag'd,
    And all hands are engag'd,
While young Jemmy, my sweet-heart, Leaves Venus for Mars —
    So we'll break off the trade, &c.

"If I part with my dear,
  He'll get murder'd I fear,
  (Then she dropt the big tear,
While kind Hetty o'erwhelm'd, made a sigh and a pause) —
  Ah! — but since it is so
  (She resum'd) let him go,
  For I'll never say no,
If he dies, let him die, in so glorious a cause.

"How I feel my blood rise,
  But pray tell me ye wise,
  What deep scheme you'll devise,
To prevent future outrage, and punish the past;
  Shall our youth fly aboard
  And with cannon and sword,
  Kill the man-killing horde,
And destroy their proud navy with terrible blast?

"Since they will be our foe,
  Let us strike them a blow,
  That shall lay the proud low,
And sequestrate their debts, from Americans due;
  Let us cast far away,
  The old treaty of Jay,
  For I heard Justice say,
Let the righteous go free, and the wicked pursue.

"Let us try to allure,
  The oppresss'd, and the pure,
  Their just rights to secure,
Thy sons, O Hibernia, we deem as our own;
  Ye brave patriots advance,
  For, now, now, is your chance,
  With Columbia, and France,
To revolt from a tyrant, and pull down his throne.

"Let us sell George no bread,
Till a famine has spread,
That shall strike his host dead,
Till disease and dismay shall have thinned their ranks,
We their trade can destroy,
Nor will purchase a toy,
Till they die for employ,
Till we break all their merchants and ruin their banks.

"It is Non-Intercourse,
That will drain their resource,
For they can't stand its force,
But our trade with the Indies impairs us alone;
I file this as my plea,
That our coffee and tea,
Which is brought over sea,
Have deprived half my sex, of the life-giving tone."

With such music my niece,
Well belabor'd the fleece,
Till she finished her piece,
And prepared each thread for the shuttle and loom:
May each true-hearted girl,
Give her wheel a good twirl,
And unite in their whirl,
Till they tell to proud Britain her merited doom.

1:45/46

The first decade of the nineteenth century has been described as a period of bitter rivalry between Republicans and Federalists; poetry served the function of airing their differences and grievances, and capturing the public imagination for one side or the other.

UNCLE JONATHAN.

From the POLITICAL OBSERVATORY.

AN ODE

FOR THE FOURTH OF JULY.

[Anonymous]

Columbia, Columbia! with songs and with mirth,
Salute the bless'd day of your national birth;
With accents melodious, and hearts of devotion,
Extol the fair goddesses, Freedom and Peace,
While, free from the ruin of war's dread commotion,
You rise to the summit of national bliss;
   Let gratitude rise
   To the God of the skies,
Who's granted you rulers so just and so wise.

Regard not the demagogue storming with rage,
Nor in the contention of parties engage;
But bravely oppose the fierce torrent of faction,
Unmov'd by the arts and intrigues of the vile,
While Liberty's enemies rave in distraction,
To see their cursed projects and base designs fail.
   Be virtue your guide,
   Let talents preside,
And safe in the haven of happiness ride.

The vot'ries of monarchy labour in vain
To rivet upon you fell tyranny's chain;
For long as your rivers flow into the ocean,
And annual verdure, your meadows adorn
Yea, e'en to the moment of earth's dissolution,
Your country shall florish, — shall shine as the morn.
   Fair Liberty's yours,
   While nature endures,
In spite of the efforts of envious pow'rs.

Columbia will never for conquest contend,
Her rights from invasion alone she'll defend;
No lust for dominion excites her ambition,
But rulers pacific and impartial laws,

Extort from all nations, who grudge her condition,
The unwilling tribute of fear and applause.
    In war's direful rage,
    Let Europe engage, —
Chaste peace shall embellish your history's page.

Shout, shout! sons of freedom! 'tis good to rejoice,
Chant praises to Heaven with heart, soul, and voice;
With grateful emotions remember the heroes,
Who fought, bled and di'd mid the thunder of Mars,
And purchased the blessings — the boon to which ye rose,
By quitting life here for a feat 'bove the stars:
    Till memory cease,
    Their fame shall increase, . . . [ms. breaks off]

I:47

This poem makes use of the key words *Liberty*, *virtue*, *talents*, and *happiness* to oppose the monarchical party of Federalists who would rely on class position to rule. The poet wishes to avoid the "contention of parties" and the "fierce torrent of faction," even as he characterizes the Federalists as "Liberty's enemies" and "vot'ries of monarchy." The speaker echoes Jefferson's first inaugural address by stressing the importance of avoiding involvement in European wars: "In war's direful rage, / Let Europe engage, — / Chaste peace shall embellish your history's page."

A New Song,

Tune — "Yankee Doodle."
[Anonymous]

LET Britain bo[a]st her naval power,
    And threaten how she'll tear us;
This much she must have learnt before,
    Her blustering cannot scare us.

Yankee Doodle — Jersey *Boys,*
    Will mock her menac'd dangers;
Though cannon roar with thund'ring noise,
    Their hearts to fear are strangers.

The fact is plain as A B C,
    Our wrongs must all be righted;
However else we disagree,
    In this we are united.

Yankee Doodle — all will join,
    Who boast of patriot blood, sir,
Their Freedom never to resign,
    Nor kiss a tyrant's rod, sir.

Should traitors vile our union mar
    They'll well deserve a lathering;
We'll pay them over first with tar,
    Then give their coats a feathering!

Yankee Doodle — look about —
    Conspiracy and treason,
With all their rascal rebel rout,
    Should be suppress'd in season.

Let Bunker's Hill and *T*renton tell,
 With York and Saratoga,
We lack not courage, strength nor skill,
 To scale the heights of glory!

Jersey Boys! — Make ready, then,
 Your muskets, pikes and rifles,
That when you're call'd to arms to run
 You be not stay'd in trifles.

1:47 / 46–1:48 / 47

Many versions of "Yankee Doodle" exist; this one is in the present, rather than the past tense, using the song for the purpose of marshaling warlike feeling against Britain. The song blithely assumes that the best way to unify the country is through warfare: "The fact is plain as A B C, / Our wrongs must all be righted; / However else we disagree, / *In this we are united.*"

AN ADDRESS to the LADIES.

[Anonymous]

Young Ladies in town, and those that live round,
    Let a friend at this season, advise you,
Since money's so scarce, and times growing worse,
    Strange things may soon hap and surprise you.

First then throw aside your high top-knots of pride,
    Wear none but your own country's linen,
Of economy boast, let your pride be the most.
    To shew clothes of your own make and spinning.

What if homespun they say, is not quite so gay
    As brocades; yet do not be in a passion:
For when its once known, that it's much worn in town,
    One and all will cry out "'Tis the fashion!!"

No more ribbons wear, nor in rich dress appear,
    Love your country much better than fine things.
Begin without passion, 'twill soon be the fashion
    To grace your smooth locks with a twine string.

These do without fear, and to all you'll appear
    Fair, charming, true, lovely & clever;
Though the times remain darkish, young men will be sparkish,
    And love you much stronger than ever.

1:48 / 47

This poem encourages women to support Jefferson's policy of embargo by wearing homespun clothes. "No more ribbons wear, nor in rich dress appear, / Love your country much better than fine things." Jefferson wrote a letter to his granddaughter Cornelia reproving the ladies of Williamsburg for resisting the embargo on British luxury.

THE EMBARGO. — A SONG.

Composed by Henry Mellen, Esq. of Dover,
and sung at the celebration of the 4th July

TUNE — "Come let us prepare."

DEAR Sirs, it is wrong
To demand a New Song,
I have let all the breath I can spare, go
With the Muse I've confer'd,
And she wont say a word,
But keeps laughing about the Embargo

I wish that I could
Sing in Allegro mood:
But the times are as stupid as Largo:
Could I have my choice,
I would strain up my voice,
'Till it snapt all the strings of Embargo.

Our great politicians,
Those dealers in visions,
On paper, to all lengths they dare go,
But when call'd to decide,
Like a TURTLE they hide,
In their own pretty shell, the Embargo.

In the time that we try,
To put out Britain's EYE,
I fear we shall let our own FAIR go;
Yet still we're so wise,
We can see the French eyes,
And then we shall like the Embargo,

A French privateer,
Can have nothing to fear:
She may load and may here or may there go,
Their friendship is such,
And we love them so much,
We let them slip thro' the Embargo.

Our ships all in motion,
Once whiten'd the ocean,
They sail'd and return'd with a Cargo;
Now doom'd to decay
They have fallen a prey
To Jefferson, worms and Embargo.

Lest Britain should take,
A few men by mistake,
Who under false colours may dare go;
We're manning their fleet,
With our Tars, who retreat
From poverty, sloth and Embargo.

What a fuss we have made,
About rights and free trade,
And swore we'd not let our own share go!
Now we can't for our souls
Bring a Hake from the shoals,
'Tis a breach of the twentieth Embargo.

Our Farmers so gay
How they gallop'd away,
'Twas money that made the old mare go;
But now she wont stir,
For the whip or the spur,
'Till they take of her clog, the embargo.

If you ask for a debt,
The man turns in a pet,
"I pay, sir? I'll not let a hair go;
"If your officer comes,
"I shall put up my thumbs,
And clap on his breath an Embargo."

Thus Folly destroys
A great part of our joys.
Yet we'll not let the beautiful fair go:
They all will contrive,
To keep commerce alive,
There's nothing they hate like Embargo.

Since rulers design,
To deprive us of wine,
'Tis best that we now have a rare go:
Then each to his post,
And see who'll do most,
To knock out the blocks of Embargo.

I:47–8

Henry Mellen opposed Jefferson's embargo, which Henry Adams described as more costly than war with Great Britain. Mellen was one of the few poets to bring a sense of humor to the task ("I wish that I could / Sing in Allegro mood: / But the times are as stupid as Largo: / Could I have my choice, / I would strain up my voice, / 'Till it snapt all the strings of Embargo"). His poem was clever enough to draw a refutation from Simon Pepperpot the younger. (see page 84).

Jefferson juxtaposed poems favoring and opposing the embargo. Mellen faulted it for allowing French commerce to flourish at the expense of American trade (stanza five): A high-minded policy designed to protect free trade had the ironic effect of stifling it. In better days, American ships "once whiten'd the ocean, / They skil'd and return'd with a Cargo" (stanza six). The author was extraordinarily forgiving of British impressments, which he describes ludicrously as "tak[ing], / A few men by mistake." The resistance to the embargo seems like the resistance to the Stamp Act, but this time citizens were resisting their own government.

Dumas Malone speculated about whether Jefferson saw this poem. "There is no way of knowing whether Jefferson himself read in the Port Folio or in a Boston paper the words of a song that was sung on July fourth in New England and was to find its way into later works of history."[33] Malone went on to say that "We must assume that in this period he based his judgment of public opinion on the written communications he is known to have received and must look for clues in his own correspondence."[34] Jefferson's scrapbook provides another source for determining what he read. The "discovery" of the poem in his clippings book suggests that he read it in the *Trenton American.*

Willliam Cullen Bryant, at thirteen years old, wrote a versified compilation of Federalist stanzas attacking Jefferson, as Malone pointed out, titled "The Embargo, or Sketches of Our Times."

> Go, wretch, resign the presidential chair,
> Disclose thy secret measures foul or fair,
> Go, search, with curious eye, for horned frogs,
> Mongst the wild wastes of Louisianian bogs;
> Or where Ohio rolls his turbid stream,
> Dig for huge bones, thy glory and thy theme;
> Go scan, Philosophist, thy **** charms,
> And sink supinely in her sable arms;
> But quit to able hands, the helm of state,
> Nor image ruin on thy country's fate.[35]

HENRY MELLEN *Esquire's smart Song*
"The Embargo,"
PARODIED BY
SIMON PEPPERPOT, *the younger.*

Now be at your posts, for the mighty man Sin
Stands watching the door, to let Fed'ralists in;
For something must rule them, no doubt a wise thing,
And where it the Devil, *they'd call him a* King

TUNE — "Come let us prepare."

Dear Sir, you are wrong
To tell lies in a song,
   And let all the filth you can spare go;
For the Muse is quite mad.
To view herself clad
   In falsehood about the Embargo.

Our wise politicians
In spite of divisions,
   To Johnny Bull won't let a hair go:
Tho' his friends wish to reign,
And their hoarse voices strain,
   To curse and blaspheme the Embargo.

The tories would twist
Till they steal all the grist,
   And cajole us as far as they dare go;
While like turtles, the feds
Still poke out their heads,
   And hiss at the prudent Embargo.

When Britain did try
To put out our eye,
   Behold she let one of her pair go;
So let us be wise,
And regard not their lies,
   And t'other we'll shut by Embargo.

The French we believe
Like the British deceive,
   They both want a smack at the cargo;
But our rulers, who saw
The extent of their maw,
   Have sav'd us the whole by Embargo.

Our ships, for a time,
Ride safe in our clime,
   Lest with Denmark, we lose ships and cargo:
They'd better decay,
Than be stolen away,
   By scoundrels who hate the Embargo.

Old Britain has slain
Our Tars on the main,
   On our land, the Lord knows, she don't dare go;
For when there she was beat,
She took to her fleet,

   As now when kept off by Embargo.
What a fuss do they make
About lobsters and hake,
   And swear we have let all the share go!
But we've pouts and sow fish,
A good Fed'ral dish,
   For those who oppose the Embargo.

Our farmers, so gay,
With pork, beef and hay
   To Europe will not let a hair go:
'Till she is so fair,
As to grant equal share,
   We'll stick to the prudent Embargo.

Whilst Eden's best stores
Enrich all our shores,

We'll venture to make the old mare go,
But Fed'ralists fret
And demand ev'ry debt,
   And father it all on Embargo.

Thus Tommy destroys
Intriguers chief joys;
   But to ruin will not let the Fair go;
For he will secure
Our damsels so pure,
   By keeping off rogues with Embargo.

When Fed'ralists dine
And are tipsey on wine,
   No wonder they call it a rare go;
They sigh for lost Posts,
Then knock for their Hosts,
   And take off their twentieth Embargo.

1:48–49

Though Jefferson lamented the lack of a uniquely American literature, political issues such as the embargo inspired one, complete with a vernacular ("They both want a smack at the cargo"), mobilized both for and against his policy. Jefferson's embargo policy, for example, spawned William Cullen Bryant' career as a poet.

PARODY.

[Anonymous]

Mr. PRINTER, — The "song" of which the following is a parody, was by Mr. T — given in large numbers to the post, to be distributed GRATIS among the inhabitants to the Eastward of Walpole. It was done, no doubt, to answer electioneering purposes; for such TRASH, it is well known, will have more influence upon the minds of some, than whole volumes of rational arguments, couched in the most elegant language. The federalists are very active — I hope the republicans are not less so.

Yours, U. P.

Dear Sirs, 'tis not "wrong" to new vamp a short Song,
Which came from one "stupid as Largo:"
The Feds have conferr'd, and can't reason a word,
So they only "laugh" at "the Embargo."

They "wish" that folks would all believe, a good mood,
As much falsehood as they "can let spare go:"
Could they have their choice, they would cry with one voice,
Slay Government with the "Embargo."

"Our great politicians, those dealers in visions,
On paper, to all lengths they dare go:"
They have oft prophesied, and a thousand times lied,
So now they condemn "the Embargo."

How warmly they "try to put out" Freedom's "eye," —
Ah! ye; and they'd have the whole "pair go:"
"Yet still we're so wise, we can see with our "eyes,"
So Feds will ne'er raise "the Embargo."

For our country so dear, they "have nothing to fear,"
For Britain's their land, and they'd "there go,"
If they by their noise could involve us in wars,
A thousand times worse than "Embargo."

Tho' "our ships all in motion once whiten'd the ocean,"
"And sail'd and return'd with a cargo:"
Yet when foreign decrees so infest all our seas,
We will preserve peace by "Embargo."

"What a fuss" Feds "have made about rights and free trade,"
And wish'd "we would not let our share go:"
But British EXCISE — it has made them more wise —
They prefer it to any "Embargo."

"Our farmers so say," who once "gallop'd away,"
And to the store "made the old mare go,"
Will shortly, in troth, learn to wear their own cloth,
And prosper, in spite of "th' Embargo."

A year or two hence ask a man for some pence —
He don't to the store for "a hair go" —
Therefore he rich grows — he can pay all he owes —
He has learnt to be wise by "th' Embargo."

Thus if "folly destroys" but our baubles and toys,
We are wise if we don't "let the fair go" —
But when Royal decrees shall once quit the high seas,
We'll all join and hate "the Embargo."

                                    UNUS PLEXIS.

1:50

This poem responds to Henry Mellen's counter-part, which appears in quotation marks throughout the text. It echoes other Republican poems by urging Americans to "wear their own cloth, / And prosper, in spite of 'th' Embargo.'" The note by U. P. refers to Walpole, New Hampshire, the site of Federalist activity.

EMBARGO & NAVY.

[Anonymous]

The TORIES dislike the EMBARGO, because
It keeps all our ships, crews, and cargoes at home;
Which they'd rather should gorge the insatiable maws
Of hungry sea-robbers that round the world roam.

The WHIGS answer NO — what we've got let us keep,
Till right is respected, and commerce is free;
Put our ships afloat now, they are gone at a sweep;
They are safer in port than they are at sea.

Then give us a Navy — the TORIES rejoin —
Our rights to assert and our trade to protect:
All the evils we feel and at which we repine,
Can fairly be trac'd to the Navy's neglect.
The WHIGS can retort — and have truth of their side —

A Navy can serve us no purpose at all;
Has not the experiment often been tried,
And do not the large navies swallow the small?
The Navies of *Holland*, of *France*, and of *Spain*,
Were larger than *we* could expect or equip;
Yet, *united*, their fleets could no footing maintain,
But, disgrac'd and defeated, abandon'd the deep.

The Navy of *Denmark*, respectably large,
In her harbors securely and peaceably lay;
Yet from Ships of the Line to a Custom-House barge,
To Britain it falls, "at one fell swoop," a prey.
Just so with *our* Navy it doubtless had been,
Had vanity led us a navy to build,
'Twould have heighten'd the triumphs of Ocean's proud
    Queen;
And blasted the laurels we won in the field.

A cheaper and safer defence, is, by far,
To exclude all their goods, all our products retain;
This will punish *them* worse than a seven years war,
Yet will injure *us* less than a single campaign.

1:49

A rallying point for both Federalists and Republicans was Great Britain's impressment of American soldiers. This poem rehearses the debate between Whigs and Tories on the desirability of an American navy. Until one was established, alliances with France and Spain were used by presidents as leverage against Great Britain.

EMBARGO.

There's knaves and fools and dupes & tools
 Debas'd enough to argue,
That every ill the people feel
 Is owing to *The Embargo.*

Does some loose tongue like clapper hung
 Delight in constant dinging:
The Embargo well supplies the bell
 Against which to be ringing.

Do party-men incline to pen
 A false and foolish farr'go,
No other theme so fruitful seem
 As *"Jefferson's d — d Embargo."*

To self and power would villains soar
 Mid uproar and confusion;
With hearts well-pleas'd, *the Embargo's* seiz'd
 To work the dire delusion.

Should Hessian Fly our wheat destroy,
 Or granaries crawl with wevil,
The Embargo's curst in language worst
 As source of all the evil.

Does wind or wave to watry grave
 Consign ship, crew and cargo,
'Tis chance but some, with visage grim,
 Ascribe it to *the Embargo.*

Does cold or heat or draught or wet
 Work hay or harvest's ruin,
'Tis made appear, as noon-day clear,
 'Tis all *the Embargo's* doing.

Or should our crops exceed our hopes,
    Right roundabout they dare go,
And in a trice the lessen'd price,
    Is charg'd upon *the Embargo*.

Should boat or ship lose tide or trip,
    By gale, or ice, or freshet;
The Embargo 'tis puts all amiss,
    And merrily they curse it.

Do vermin bold on trees lay hold,
    And make their limbs quite bare go,
'Tis ten to one the mischief done
    Is saddl'd on *the Embargo*.

Has drunken swab, or idle drab,
    Become forlorn and needy,
Both he and she will find a plea,
    "Embargo," always ready.

Is buck or blade bankrupt in trade,
    By sloth, or vice, or folly;
He's not to blame — the fault and shame
    Rest on *the Embargo* wholly.

Does some vile knave, his cash to save,
    Pay all his debts with paper;
"The Embargo laws" are made the cause,
    And loud he'll rant and vapor.

But tho' such knaves and fools and slaves
    Paint it a frightful scarecrow,
The good and wise, their arts despise,
    And cling to *the Embargo*.

They know it keeps from Pirate's grips,
    Our vessels, crews and cargoes;
Which were they lost, much more would cost
    Than half a-score Embargoes.

They know that this most punishes
    The nations that oppress us;
While it involves our injur'd selves
    In least and fewest distresses.

They know that war would cost us more
    Monthly than this does yearly;
While every blow some blood must flow
    From kin or friends lov'd dearly.

Then let who will, to work our ill,
    Against it lie and argue;
Columbia's Sons, in loudest tones,
    Will laud THE WISE EMBARGO.
                    JERSEY BLUE.

1:50

This poem strikes a balance in suggesting that "every ill the people feel / Is [not] owing to *The Embargo*." The author is aware of his trimming perspective, for he criticizes "party-men incline[d] to pen / A false and foolish farr'go." Jefferson may well have enjoyed the rational point of view the poet satirist adopts, depicting others as slaves to their emotions (stanza five). In various letters, he enjoyed hearty opposition as a sign of democratic health. For this reason, perhaps Jefferson would have enjoyed the passion of those who opposed the embargo, even though it was his own policy: "merrily they curse it." The utilitarian perspective wins out in the end: "They know that war would cost us more / Monthly than this does yearly; / While every blow some blood must flow / From kin or friends lov'd dearly." This poem nicely reverses Clausewitz's dictum that war is diplomacy by other means. Who, one would like to know, was "Jersey Blue"?

On a more personal note, Jefferson described the consequences of his own policies in a letter to Ellen Wayles Randolph on February 23, 1808: "You give a bad account of the patriotism of the ladies of Williamsburg who are not disposed to submit to the small privations to which the embargo will subject them. I hope this will not be general and that principle and prudence will induce us all to return to the good old plan of manufacturing within our own families most of the articles we need."[36]

Embargo — A New Song.
[Anonymous]

'Tis good for a freeman to know and discern,
The hinge upon which public measures may turn:
And reason and fact, and the right and the wrong,
Will not change their nature, tho' put in a song.
Let lyon and tyger contend, if they choose,
For similar objects, for similar views:
Our distance, thank God, is a thousand of leagues
From the focus of sight and the spot of intrigues.
Does any man ask what embargo be for?
Embargo is reason in lieu of a war.

Impetuous leaders high mettled and warm,
Disdain to expect the subsiding of storm:
But ours can restrain indignation by rule,
Provok'd by hot outrage, or insolence cool.
The pause, the privation, that congress employs,
Is reason and peace against fury and noise:
And patience exposed to indignity wild,
Is the mind of a man to the mind of a child.
Does any one ask what embargo be for?
Embargo is reason in lieu of a war.

The man half instructed, of timorous soul,
Sees possible peril that never may roll —
Robes dangers fantastic in vapory hue,
And magnifies those that are real and true.
On billows of spleen, on discouragement toss'd,
Instead of exertion, exclaims, we are lost:
The greedy and bold from a tempest hope pelf,
In love with distinction, and profit and self,
Does any man ask what embargo be for?
Embargo is reason in lieu of a war.

At the frown of the sordid, who sordidly think,
Impatient for traffic, on jeopardy's brink:
At the clamor of faction who uses the hour
Of pressure for seizing on-stations of power;

Firm rulers and people will equally mock,
In the castle of fortitude built on a rock.
Such, fixing a measure of safety for all,
No menaces shake, and no clamors appal.
Does any man ask what embargo be for?
Embargo is reason in lieu of a war.

When measures are green, unenacted by laws,
Doubts often are wise and aid liberty's cause,
But when our free Senate decisive enact,
Resistance to law is high treason in fact,
Then let us who cherish a system so free,
Make imps of sedition whoever they be;
Bid reason, derision, in aid of the rule,
Smite the lips of the scorner, and dum-found the fool.
Does any man ask what embargo be for?
Embargo is reason in lieu of a war.

RUSTICUS.

1:52

Jefferson's arrangement of these poems sug-gests that the arguments get better as one goes along. Here the points of all three pre-vious poems are resolved in the refrain: "Embargo is reason in lieu of a war." As a product of the Enlightenment, Jefferson uses rationality to avoid violence.

Song,

Of spunky Jonathan, who, from the walls of Lexington road, fired away all his ammunition, and then threw stones.

[Anonymous]

A Plague on those snivelling coxcombs, say I,
　　Who would sell for a *sixpence*, their freedom;
About poverty, ruin & hardship they cry,
　　And think that the People will heed 'em.

If they say we regard our own pockets alone,
　　'Tis quite on wrong ground that they argue,
We reckon the *public* advantage *our own*,
　　Not selfishly curse the *Embargo*.

To paint out *starvation* the knaves seize the pen,
　　And paper defile by the acre;
They'll whine *till their purpose is answer'd* and *then*,
　　We may starve and be hang'd for what *they care*.

To save *us* from starving, and hanging to boot,
　　I'm mistaken if *they* would so far go;
Number one, as I *guess*, is the principal root
　　Of this clamor about the *Embargo*.

When hungry I've fought, and when naked I've toil'd
　　For Freedom, the greatest of treasures:
No hardship could move me when Liberty smil'd,
　　I laugh'd at effeminate pleasures.

Shall I, who so often, mid danger & want,
　　Have gone, far as any man dare go,
Beneath lighter burthens now grumble and pant,
　　And shrink from the ills of *Embargo*?

When no pay I could get, to be sure I did stare,
　　'Twas hard — but we were independent.

All suffer'd — so, cheerfully I bore my share,
    'Twas *well lost* — so there was an end on't.

In *those* times, when *Tories* appeal'd to our wants,
    We soon did for feathers and tar go;
T'in the old soldier still, whom no suffering daunts,
    Not even the pinching Embargo.

I hold, that when storms that we cannot controul,
    Sweep with terrible fury the ocean;
'Tis better in port to make sure of the whole,
    Tho' we lose, for a while a proportion.

I like, when my country is thriving, the cash,
    For *money* ('tis said) *makes the mare go;*
But in base competition with Freedom, 'tis trash —
    So, *Huzza for the prudent Embargo!*

                                        1:52

This final poem paints the embargo as a patriotic act, one concerned with "public advantage." The poet prefers freedom to cash, ostentatiously proving his patriotism by refusing to dwell on financial losses incurred by "the prudent Embargo."

A Tickler for Timothy!

A NEW SONG. — Tune, Bow, Wow, Wow, &c.
By JACK "*nine thread*" RATLINE.

Sit down, neighbours all, and I'll tell a merry story;
About the "*Essex Junto*," and *Timothy* the *Tory*, —
Who about the Embargo, make such a noisy bluster,
But who in time of war, were all afraid to muster.

When *Timothy* was summon'd, to Lexington fam'd battle;
Where the cannon loud did roar, and the muskets did rattle,
He "*embargoed*" his regiment in great trepidation;
Thus devoting himself for the honor of the nation!

When WASHINGTON the brave had plan'd an expedition,
To attack Staten Island with his troops in good condition,
Then *Timothy* by sad "*mistake*" his "*swingle-trees*" mislaid, sir,
And La Fayette could not proceed for want of needful aid, sir.

When Boston was blockaded, the *tories* were so skittish,
Their country they deserted, and joined with the British;
But when the war was over, return'd and made their bow, sir,
And the yankies were so kind, they pardon'd them I vow, sir.

When safe in Boston landed, they strutted and look'd big, sir,
They were follow'd in their train, by each apostate whig, sir;
These *caballers* go together, "*the People's*" rights to damn, sir,
They form'd the "*Essex Junto*," and *Timothy's* their man, sir.

When "the People" did assemble to end all State confusion,
And establish well their rights, by a "Fed'ral Constitution:"
The "*Junto*" then pretended to respect the "*Rights of Man,*" sir,
For, to hide the *cloven foot* was a part of their plan sir.

In the year *"ninety two,"* when the French Revolution,
Had promis'd vassal'd man, an equal distribution;
"Equal Rights — Equal Laws" — then the *"Junto"* did exclaim, sir,
"Down with the *"Rights of Man"* — *"Equality's* our bane, sir.

When Britain with her navy, our commerce did attack, sir,
And stirred up the Indians, all through the country back, sir;
Then the *"Junto"* did exult, and loudly cried *"encore,"* sir,
Till Washington the sage, was near deafen'd by their roar, sir.

Then the Chief Justice *Jay*, was taken from his station,
And was sent to reconcile the haughty British Nation;
He made a famous Treaty, *"like the handle of a can,"* sir,
Which puzzled much our Washington and ev'ry other man, sir.

When matters did grow turbulent, and worked quite contrary,
And *Timothy*, O, strange to tell, was made State Secretary!
Then the *"Junto"* chuckled loud, for they very plainly saw, sir,
That all the *"loaves and fishes"* would soon enter in their maw, sir.

When the British captain, *Matson*, poor *Giles* did sorely flog, sir,
And to all his just complaints, only answer'd *"Yankee dog,"* sir,
Then *Timothy*, O shame, was this outrage justifying!
And oaths were thrown aside to make room for *Matson's* lying!

    . . .

When the warring powers of Europe, had got in such commotion,
That our commerce could not fail, unmolested on the Ocean;
When Britain gave out orders, to overhaul each cargo;
Then Jefferson the sage, recommended an Embargo.

Then the *"Junto"* went to work, to abuse administration,
They exercis'd their wits, and made much *botheration*:
Their factious presses groaned, with many a vile remark,
And ev'ry fed'ral puppy was call'd upon to bark, sir.

Then *Timothy* sat down, and wrote a long narration;
As he'd often done before to bamboozle the nation;
When *Patriots* oppose the laws and insurrection plan, sir,
Such *modern* "Roman virtue" must *secure* the *"Rights of Man."*

Now the *"Junto"* do intend to dictate in our election,
And have sent their emissaries to raise a disaffection;
NEW HAMPSHIRE's SONS will rally round their liberty and laws,
And leave the *"Essex Junto"* to support the British cause.

1:52–53

For this poet, the embargo became a test of man's patriotism and courage. Timothy the Tory is portrayed as a man who would not have aided Washington in supporting Lafayette. The "Essex Junto" refers to the Federalists who "betray" the American nation. The term was first applied (by John Hancock) to leaders who were residents of Essex County, Massachussetts, including George Cabot, John Lowell, Timothy Pickering, Theophilus Parsons, Stephen Higginson, Benjamin Goodhue, and Fisher Ames. The county's interests were commercial, and the term came to personify the business community's desire for a stronger federal government. Members of the Essex Junto were characterized by their resistance to the embargo, alleged intention to secede in 1808, open councils, suspected designs on the Hartford Convention, and stubborn opposition to the war. During Jefferson's administration, the term became synonymous with New England Federalism.

FOR THE VIRGINIA ARGUS.
ON THE BATTLE OF PRINCETON,
JANUARY 3, 1777.
A Song.
[Anonymous]

STERN winter scowl'd along the plain,
And ruthless Boreas urg'd amain
   His fierce impetuous course;
In ice the wat'ry regions bound,
—— The torrent's foaming rage confound
   And stop its boisterous force.

While hostile bands their rights invade,
Columbia's sons in tents were laid,
   And winter's blasts defied:
No foes appal, no dangers fright,
Whilst freedom's sacred cause they fight,
   And Washington's their guide.

While slumbers seal'd the hero's eyes,
He saw a God-like form arise,
   Like martial Pallas drest;
'Twas LIBERTY, celestial maid!
In all her golden charms array'd,
   The Goddess stood confess'd.

My son, she cried, the Gods above,
Thy country's sacred cause approve,
   And on the virtues smile;
Though proud oppression waste the land,
Yet freedom purchas'd by thy hand,
   Shall soon reward the toil.

Lo! where Britannia's banners rise,
In awful pomp, and brave the skies,
   Exulting o'er the land;

Her haughty legions soon shall feel,
The force of thine avenging steel
  And this thy chosen band.

Though veterans compose their train,
And ten-fold legions fill the plain,
  To martial deeds enur'd;
Undaunted rise and take the field,
For liberty shall lend her shield
  And victory her sword.

Up rose the chief, at the command
And strait conven'd his faithful band,
  Inspir'd by freedom's lore;
Egyptian darkness veil'd the night,
But liberty's celestial light
  Their footsteps went before.

Where Princeton rears the muses' seat,
In argus the hostile legions met,
  And fate upheld the scale;
Forth rush'd the blazing orb of light,
To add new glories to the sight,
  When freedom's sons assail.

Like Mars Columbia's hero stood,
Her haughty foes were drench'd in blood,
  Or shunn'd the doubtful fight;
Whilst Britons shame and grief confound,
Fair liberty the victors crown'd
  With honors ever bright.

Henceforth the grateful muse shall twine
Her annual wreath at freedom's shrine,
  The hero's brow to grace;

By whose victorious arm restor'd,
No more, she flies the hostile sword,
    But hails her native place.

And still with the revolving year,
A garland shall the muse prepare,
    To deck her Mercer's urn;
While freedom fills the trump of fame,
Columbia shall revere his name.
    His fate her sons shall mourn.

        1:61

Washington's success at the battle of Trenton on December 26, 1776, preceeded the battle of Princeton. Trying to build on his momentum et aware that enlistments expired on December 31, he persuaded his troops to xtend their tour for at least a month. By ttacking the rear flank of the British army on nuary 3, 1777, Washington gained enough of n advantage to rout the British from the positions they held in New Jersey. The poet compares Washington's victory to an act ordained by God. Washington's strategic encircling of Cornwallis's sleeping army helped ensure victory. The frozen roads made it possible to evacuate without noise, as did Washington's clever ruse of covering the wheels of the cannon with cloth.

THE EMBARGO.
A SATIRE.

BY A YOUTH OF THIRTEEN.

[William Cullen Bryant]

"When private faith and public trust are sold,
And traitors barter liberty for gold,
When fell corruption, dark, and deep like fate,
Saps the foundation of a sinking state;
Then warmer number glow thro' Satire's page,
And all her smiles are darken'd into rage;
Then keener indignation fires her eye,
Then flash her lightnings and her thunders fly."

ESSAY ON SATIRE.

LOOK where we will, and in whatever land,
Europe's rich soil, or Afric's burning sand;
Where the wild savage hunts his wilder prey,
Or art and science pour their brightest day;
The monster Vice appears before our eyes,
In naked impudence, or gay disguise.

But quit the lesser game, indignant MUSE,
And to thy country turn thy nobler views.
Ill-fated clime! condemn'd to feel th' extremes
Of a weak ruler's philosophic dreams;
Driv'n headlong on to ruin's fateful brink,
When will thy country feel, when will she think!

Wake, Muse of Satire, in the cause of trade,
Thou scourge of miscreants, who the Laws evade!
Dart thy keen glances — knit thy threat'ning brows,
And hurl thine arrows at fair Commerce's foes!

Much injur'd Commerce, 'tis thy falling cause,
Which, from obscurity, a stripling draws;
And were his powers but equal to his zeal,
Thy dastard foes his keen reproach should feel,

Curse of our Nation, source of countless woes,
From whose dark womb unreckon'd misery flows;
Th' EMBARGO rages, like a sweeping wind,
FEAR low'rs before and Famine stalks behind.
What words, oh Muse! can paint the mournful scene,
The saddening street, the desolated green;
How hungry labourers leave their toil, and sigh,
And sorrow droops in each desponding eye!

See the old Sailor from the ocean torn,
His element — sink friendless and forlorn!
His suffering spouse the tear of anguish shed,
His starving children cry in vain for bread!

The Farmer, since supporting trade is fled,
Leaves the rude joke, and cheerless hangs his head;
Misfortunes fall, an unremitting shower,
Debts follow debts — on taxes, taxes pour,
See in his stores his hoarded produce rot,
Or sheriff sales his profits bring to naught;
Disheartening cares in thronging myriads flow,
'Till down he sinks to *poverty* and woe!

Oh, ye bright pair, the blessing of mankind,
Whom time has sanction'd, and whom fate has join'd,
Commerce, that bears the trident of the main,
And Agriculture, empress of the plain;
Who, hand in hand, and heav'n directed, go,
Diffusing gladness through the world below;
Whoe'er the wretch, would hurl the flaming brand,
Of dire disunion — palsied be his hand;
Like Cromwell, damn'd to everlasting fame.
Let unborn ages execrate his name.
Dark is the scene, yet darker prospects threat,
And ills may follow, unexperienc'd yet!
Oh heaven, defend, as future seasons roll,
This western world from Bonaparte's control,

Preserve our freedom, and our rights secure,
While truth subsists, and virtue shall endure!

Lo, Austria crouches to the tyrant's stroke,
And Rome's proud states receive his galling yoke;
Kings fall before him — for his sway extends,
Where'er his all-subduing course he bends.
See Lusitania's fate — and shall we say,
Turn not our feet, that tread the self same way!

Must we with Belgia, and Helvetia mourn,
In vile subjection, abject, and forlorn?
Our laws laid prostrate, and our freedom fled,
Our independence, boasted valour dead?

We, who seven years erst brav'd Britannia's power
By heaven supported in the gloomiest hour;
For whom our sages plann'd and heroes bled,
Whom WASHINGTON, our pride and glory, led;
Till Heaven, propitious, did our efforts crown,
With freedom, commerce, plenty and renown!

When shall this land, some courteous angel say,
Throw off a weak and erring ruler's sway?
Rise, injur'd people, vindicate your cause,
And prove your love for Liberty and laws;
Oh wrest, sole refuge of a sinking land,
The sceptre from the slave's imbecile hand!
Oh ne'er consent, obsequious, to advance,
The willing vassal of Imperious France?
Correct that suffrage you misus'd before,
And lift your voice against a Congress' roar!

. . .

But vain are reason, eloquence and art,
And vain the warm effusions of the heart,
Ev'n while I sing, see Faction urge her claim,
Mislead with falsehood, and with zeal inflame,

Lift her broad banner, spread her empire wide,
And stalk triumphant, with a fury's stride,
She blows her brazen trump, and at the sound,
A motley throng obedient flock around;
A mist of changing hue, o'er all she flings,
And darkness perches on her dragon wings!

As Johnson deep, as Addison refin'd,
And skill'd to pour conviction o'er the mind,
Oh might some Patriot rise, the gloom dispel,
Chase errors mist, and break her magic spell!

But vain the wish, for hark! the murmuring meed,
Of hoarse applause, from yonder sheds proceed;
Enter, and view the thronging concourse there,
Intent, with gaping mouth, and stupid stare,
While in the midst their supple leader stands,
Harangues aloud, and flourishes his hands;
To adulation tunes his servile throat,
And sues, successful, for each blockhead's vote.
"Oh, where I made a rider in the land,
Your rights no man can better understand;
For the dear people, how my bowels yearn!
That such may govern, be your chief concern,
Then federal tyranny shall flee away,
And *mild democracy* confirm her sway."
The powerful influence of the knave's address,
In capers droll, the foolish dupes confess,
With horrid shouts the affrighted sky is rent,
And high in air their tatter'd hats are sent.

But should truth shine, distinguishingly bright,
And lay his falsehoods naked to the sight;
He tries new arts to bind their willing eyes,
Feeds with new flatteries, hammers out new lies;
Exerts his influence, urges all his weight,
To blast the laurels of the good and great;

Till reconfirm'd, the fools uphold him still,
Their creed, his *dictum*, and their law his will.

Now morning rises, borne on golden wings,
And fresh to toil the waking postboy springs;
Lo, trudging on his raw-boned steed, he hies,
Dispersing Suns, and Chronicles, and Spys;
Men un[i]formed, in rage for something new,
Howe'er unprincipled, howe'er untrue,
Suck in with greedy throat the gilded pill,
Whose fatal sweetness pleases but to kill
Wide, and more wide, the dire contagion flies,
Till half the town is overwhelm'd with lies.
Hence that delusion, hence that furious zeal,
Which wrong heads cherish, and which hot heads feel.

In vain Italia boasts her genial clime,
Her Rome's proud tower's, and palaces sublime:
In vain the hardy Swiss inur'd to toil,
Draw scant subsistence from a stubborn soil,
Both Doom'd alike, to feel, in evil hour,
The giant grasp of huge despotic power!
Touch not their shores, fair freedom is not there,
But far remote, she breathes Columbian air;
But here its temple totters to its fall,
Our rulers bowing to audacious Gaul!

Oh, let not prating history proclaim.
The foul disgrace, the scandal to our name!
Write not the deed, my hand! Oh, may it lie,
Plung'd deep and mantled in obscurity!
Forbid it, Heaven! that while true honour reigns,
And ancient valour glows within our veins:
(Our standard Justice, and our shield our God,)
We e'er should tremble at a despot's nod!

Oh! may the laurels of unrivall'd fame,
Forever flourish round your honor'd name!

Ye, who unthrall'd by prejudice or power,
'Termin'd stood in that eventful hour:
Tore the dire secret from the womb of night,
And bar'd your country's infamy to light!
Go boldly on, the deep-laid plot unfold,
Tho' much is known, yet much remains untold
But chief to thee our gratitude belongs,
Oh Pickering! who hast scann'd thy country's wrongs,
Whose ardent mind, and keen discerning eye,
Pierc'd the deep veil of Gallic policy;
And in whose well-timed labours, we admire,
The sage's wisdom and the patriot's fire!

Rise then, Columbians! heed not France's wiles,
Her bullying mandates, her seductive smiles:
Send home Napoleon's slave, and bid him say,
No arts can lure us, and no threats dismay;
Determin'd yet to war with whom we will,
Choose our own allies, or be neutral still.

Ye merchants, arm! the pirate Gaul repel,
Your prowess shall the naval triumph swell;
Send the marauders shatter'd, whence they came,
And Gallia's check suffice with crimson shame.
But first select, our councils to direct,
One whose true worth entitles to respect;
In whom concentrates all that men admire,
The sage's prudence, and the soldier's fire;
Who scorns ambition, and the venal tribe,
And neither offers, nor receives a bribe.
Who firmly guards his country's every right,
And shares alike in council or in fight.

Then on safe seas the merchant's barque shall fly,
Our waving flag shall kiss the polar sky;
On canvas wings our thunders shall be borne,
For to the west, or tow'rd the rising morn;

Then may we dare a haughty tyrant's rage,
And gain the blessings of an unborn age.

'Tis done, beloved the cheerful prospects rise!
And splendid scenes the startled eye surprise;
Lo! busy Commerce courts the prosperous main;
And peace and plenty glad our shores again!
Th'industrious swain sees nature smile around
His fields with fruit, with flocks his pastures crown'd.

Thus, in a fallen tree, from sprouting roots,
With sudden growth, a tender sapling shoots,
Improves from day to day, delights the eyes
With strength and beauty, stateliness and size,
Puts forth robuster arms, and broader leaves,
And high in air, its branching head upheaves.

Turn now our views, to Europe's ravag'd plains,
Where murd'rous war, with grim oppression reigns;
There long and loud the storm of battle roars,
With direful portent to our distant shores:
The regal robber, rages uncontroul'd,
No laws constrain him and no faith can hold;
Before his steps, lo, cow'ring terror flies,
And pil'd behind him, heaps of carnage rise!
With fraud or force, he spreads his iron sway,
And blood and rapine mark his frightful way!

Thus some huge rock of ice, on Greenland's shore,
When bound in frost the surges cease to roar,
Breaks loosen'd from its base, with mighty sweep,
And thunders horrid o'er the frozen deep!

While thus, all Europe rings with his alarms,
Say, shall we rush unthinking, to his arms?
No: let us dauntless all his fury brave,
Our fluttering flag, in freedom's gale shall wave,

Our guardian Sachem's errless shafts shall fly,
And terrors lighten from our eagle's eye!

Here then I cease, rewarded, if my song,
Shall prompt one honest mind, though guided wrong,
To pause from party — view his country's state,
And lend his aid to stem approaching fate!

2:62–2:64

The embargo was enacted on December 21, 1807. The composition of this 244-line poem followed the announcement of the passage on April 25, 1808, of the Third Embargo Act, a law that spelled out in detail the restrictive provisions Jefferson had put into effect; the poet wrote a lengthier version after January 9, 1809, when the final version of the Embargo Act was passed. "My father was a Federalist," Cullen later remembered, "and his skill in his profession gave him great influence in Cummington. . . . I had written some satirical lines apostrophizing the President, which my father saw, and, thinking well of them, encouraged me to write others in the same vein."[37] Bryant (like Thomas Moore) did not include this poem in his published works, though he acknowledged his authorship. This hard-hitting satire is in the tradition of Pope and Swift; Bryant was composing verses at the age of eight, and his training in Greek and Latin prepared him well for the task of lampooning Jefferson.

The editor omitted eighteen of the poem's most caustic lines; they follow "And lift your voice against Congress' roar" (see page 106). The omitted lines can be found in Thomas Mabbott's facsimile edition:

"And thou, the scorn of every patriot name,
Thy country's ruin, and her council's shame!
Poor servile thing! derision of the brave!
Who erst from Tarleton fled to Carter's cave;
Thou, who, when menac'd by perfidious Graul,
Didst' prostrate to her whisker'd minion fall;
And when our cash her empty bags supplied,
Didst meanly strive the foul disgrace to hide;
Go, wretch, resign the presidential chair,
Disclose thy secret measures foul or fair,
Go, search, with curious eye, for horned frogs,
Mongst the wild wastes of Louisianian bogs;
Or where Ohio rolls his turbid stream,
Dig for huge bones, thy glory and thy theme;
Go scan, Philosophist, thy **** charms,
And sink supinely in her sable arms;
But quit to abler hands, the helm of state,
Nor image ruin on thy country's fate!"[38]

HAIL LIBERTY.
[Anonymous]

HAIL Liberty! supreme delight,
   Thou idol of the mind;
Thro' every clime extend thy flight,
   The word range unconfin'd.

    The virtues of the just and brave,
      Exist alone with thee;
    Nature disdain'd to form a slave,
      Her birth right's Liberty.

Tho' all the Tyrants in the world,
   Conspire to crush thy fame;
Yet shall thy banners be unfurl'd,
   External be thy name.
        The virtues of, &c.

Then let mankind in one great band
   Of glorious unity,
Drive Despotism from each land,
   Or die for Liberty.
        The virtues of, &c.

Columbia's sons! how blest are ye
   Safe from tyrannic sway;
Maintain your rights, live ever free,
   Drive discord far away,
        The virtues of &c.

1:63

One of three poems Jefferson clipped
celebrating liberty.

AN ODE,

Composed for the BALTIMORE TYPOGRAPHICAL SOCIETY,

in Commemoration of American Independence,

July 4, 1808.

BY A MEMBER.

TUNE — "Dauphin."

While round the festive *board*
    The sons of FREEDOM through,
And bid her praises rise
    In patriotic song;
Ye Brethren of our Heaven born ART,
    Unite to hail the day
Let joy expand each patriot heart,
    Each tongue assist the lay.

CHORUS.
Arise, 'tis Freedom's natal morn,
    Ye sons of FAUST arise,
Forever swear to guard
    The dearly purchased prize.

Mankind in darkness grop'd
    Their blind and erring way,
Deep veil in Gothic *shades*
    With scarce a glimpse of day;
'Till Faust arose and bid our ART
    Illume their darken'd mind;
Then INDEPENDENCE fir'd the heart
    Which knowledge had refin'd.

CHORUS.
Arise, &c.

But long they fought in vain,
    To win the Heavenly prize;
Oppression's lengthen'd reign
    Their ardent wish denies.

'Till o'er our hard earn'd western soil,
   He dar'd his sceptre wield,
'Twas then our fires, with blood and toil,
   Gain'd FREEDOM and the field.

CHORUS.

Arise, &c.

Then smiling PEACE was ours,
   And every earthly bliss,
Till Europe's treach'rous pow'rs
   Betray'd us with a kiss.
But like our fathers, now we'll rise,
   Our birth right to maintain —
Swear by the God of earth and skies,
   No tyrant here shall reign.

CHORUS.

Arise, &c.

Then let the foe advance,
   The Press shall still inspire
To wield the massive lance,
   Or guide the vengeful fire;
And here we swear, when Freedom calls,
   We'll not refuse to die;
Thy foe shall lie beneath our *balls*,
His *columns* fall in *pye*.

CHORUS.

Arise &c.

Long o'er a foreign flag
   O'er tops Columbia's stripes,
We pledge our *picks* to arms
   To *balls* convert our *types*.
We'll never flinch, but give them *chase*,
   Display our mystic stars;
Our Eagle still shall hold his place,
   And hurl the shafts of Mars.

CHORUS.
Arise, &c.

Who threats with foreign rule,
 Our *shooting sticks* decry;
We'll have a *brush* with all,
 Before we take the *lie*
Well hath the *English!* yon's roar,
 French cannon we'll *compose,*
The form of tyranny *best o'er,*
 And *hot press* all our foes.

CHORUS.
Arise, &c.

Long may we keep the morn
 Which gave our nation birth,
And when at length our *form*
 Is finish'd here on earth,
Our *type* in *case* correctly *laid,*
 A face and *body* pure,
Which *set* in Heaven shall *stand display'd*
 Forever to endure.

CHORUS.

Then hail fair Freedom's natal morn,
 Let sounding paeans rise,
Today for us was born,
 The Goddess of the skies.

1:65 / 63

In this poem, the invention of movable type is a second day of independence. The colonists are the "sons of Faust," the necromancer who tried to turn base metals to gold. Goethe turned Faust into an Enlightenment figure in his Romantic drama, a man who turns his back on Gothic darkness and superstition (here represented as Europe).

Portrayed as Judas, Europe is not faithful to the United States; cannonballs are converted into paper bullets of the brain, or the lead of type ("To *balls* convert our *types*"). Other puns such as "hot press" bring the point home. The poet sees the foreign policy of England, the harassment of American shipping, as a second revolutionary cause that joins two generations: "like our fathers, now we'll rise, / Our birth right to maintain."

Ode to Liberty,

Commemorative of the thirty-second Anniversary of American Independence, celebrated at New Bedford, Fourth of July, 1808.

By Elihu Doty.

TUNE — "Ode to Science."

Daughters and Sons of Patriot Sires,
Attend the theme the music inspires!
A theme that calls forth all her fires,
   Joyful to greet the Annual Lay:
The Day that gave an Empire birth,
Let it resound through the whole earth,
Sacred to Freedom, and to mirth,
   And to thy sons, America!

CHORUS.

Hail Liberty, thou Good Supreme!
The wise man's wish, the patriot's theme?
On us in broad effulgence beam;
   With thy mild spirit fill our hearts!
From Eastern nations, plunged in war,
Thou to the Western world afar
Hast come; th'attendant on thy car
   Are Science, Virtue, and the Arts.

Heroes of Seventy-Six! we claim
Th' immortal honors of your fame,
Our breasts with glory to inflame,
   And urge us on to virtuous deeds:
Then shall no foe our land invade,
Or impious, dare the soil to tread,
"That's sacred to your relic's made."
   The tyrant, who attempts it, bleeds.
     Hail, Liberty, &c.

'Twas Freedom made the desert smile,
And sweeten'd our forefather's toil;
They deeply planted in our soil
    The TREE we celebrate this day:
Then let us, heart and hand, oppose
All foreign or domestic foes,
That dare by art, or dare by blows,
    To blight, or lop, or branch away.
      Hail, Liberty, &c.

The fairest tree the groves among,
Firm may it stand, and flourish long,
The envied theme of future song;
    While nations in its praise combine.
Now we our annual offerings bring,
Let joy through all our temples ring!
Let us with grateful rapture sing,
    And the whole earth in chorus join!
      Hail, Liberty, &c.

Let distant lands the echoes hear;
Th' oppressed smile, th' oppressor fear,
While we forever hold thee dear,
    Thee, Liberty, thou Sovereign Good!
Thou didst to us thy name reveal;
We own thy power, thy influence feel;
Behold us at thy altar kneel
    To seal the contract with our blood!
      Hail, Liberty, &c.

        1:65 / 63–1:66

---

fferson often represented his presidency as a
eturn to the spirit of '76. The tree of liberty is
epresented as planted in the soul of "our fore-
ther's toil." Thomas Moore attacked "That
aellic garbage of philosophy, / That nau-
ous slaver of these frantic times, / With

which false liberty dilutes her crimes!"[39] For
Republicans, however, the national cause took
on a religious meaning with patriots wor-
shiping at the altar of liberty: "Behold us at
thy altar kneel / To seal the contract with our
blood!"

SPANISH PATRIOTISM.
A PARODY.
[Anonymous]

The God, who rides upon the spheres,
With bright, angelic charioteers —
   Thus speaks in thundering voice: —
"Iberians! Hear th' Almighty Lord,
Maintain your birthrights — grasp the sword,
   Be this your happy choice."

The awful mandate spreads alarms,
An universal shout, TO ARMS —
   Is heard from sea to sea:*
They swear to front the haughty foe,
And let all *Hell*, and BONA know —
   Iberians† will BE FREE

* From the Mediterranean to the Atlantic.
† The ancient name of the Spaniards.

1:68

In 1808, Napoleon invaded Spain and placed his brother, Joseph Bonaparte, on the throne under the pretext of freeing the Spanish from Ferdinand VII. This poem suggests that true patriotism resides in resisting Napoleon. Byron's *Childe Harold's Pilgrimage* (canto one) treats the struggle of the Spanish to free their country from foreign oppressors.

PATRIOTIC ODES FOR THE YEAR 1808.
ODE I.

AN ADDRESS TO THE MUSE.
[Anonymous]

Goddess divine! by whom, in ancient times,
    All laws were given and lessons taught;
Inspir'd by whom, in *Greek* and *Gothic* climes
    Their sages sung, their heroes fought!
I now invoke thee to *Columbia's* shore!
Oh, come, and leave it never more!
Goddess of *poverty!* Who teachest those,
To whom thou dost their charms disclose,
    To love thee for *thyself* alone;
Who makest thy *favorites* glad, tho' void of cash,
And nobly scorn the glitt'ring trash;
    To me let all thy beauties then be known.
And let thy presence from this happy land
    The demon *avarice* expel;
The *virtues* (pure and hallowed band)
    Redeeming from his deadly sway,
Which misers, rogues, and usurers obey,
    And send him howling to his native hell.
Tho' here exists a money loving crew
    Of bank men, shavers, sharpers bold,
Voracious speculators not a few,
    And office hunters all a thirst for gold,
Tho' mean self-interest scorns to rule,
    With boundless sway,
While wealth (*with many*) dignifies a *fool*,
    Or makes the beams of honor 'round a *villain* play;
Yet *some* there are who love their *country* more
    Than *private interest, offices* or *pelf;*
Who do not *Mammon's deity adore,*
And are not govern'd by the love of *self.*
Thy voice, oh goddess, *others,* too, might turn,
And cause their breasts with patriot zeal to burn.
Come then, and aid me, while the lay
    Is dedicated to my country's cause;

Her *rights*, her *wrongs*, her *duties* to display,
    And justly praise the champions of her laws.
Now that her enemies, (with strength renew'd,)
    Are striving to destroy her,
To drive fair freedom from the earth,
Or slay her in the land which gave her birth,
    Oh! be my verse with energy endued,
      To lash with satire's scourge, the scoundrels who
      annoy her!
Now that a wise embargo (laid to save
    Her sons from *slavery*, and their wealth
From burial in an *Admiralty grave*,
To force our foes to do us right,
And victory secure without a fight.)
    The slaves of avarice still elude by stealth;
Now that they toil to serve a foreign state,
And pull our own down by the embargo's weight.
Now, Goddess, now, or never, help what's written
To free us from dependency on Britain;
Nor less, I pray thee, too, the verse advance,
Scouting submission to imperial France.
Instruct us how to shun them both,
    Relying on ourselves alone,
And using (nothing loath)
    No manufactures but our own.
Teach us of *Freedom* only to be *proud*,
    With *virtue* and *religion* to be blest,
    And trust to *Heaven* the rest.
'Tis done — the Goddess comes. From yonder cloud
Which opens, she reveals her glorious face,
And form refulgent with celestial grace.
I feel her spirit breathing thro' my heart,
And to Columbia *thus* her dictates I impart.

1:68

Written in the last year of Jefferson's presidency, this poem celebrates Republican virtues as Jefferson understood them: "Yet *some* there are who love their *country* more/ Than *private interest, offices*, or pelf." Jefferson's controversial policy of an embargo tested the patriotism of the merchant class. The poem suggests that the gods will reward America for resisting a mercantilist policy. All this was done, as the poet suggests, "to free us from dependency on Britain."

FOR THE VIRGINIA ARGUS.

PATRIOTIC ODES FOR THE YEAR 1808.

[Anonymous]

ODE IV.

TO THE ANGLO-FEDERALISTS.

Ye worthy friends of BRITAIN! 'tis said
That ye again are looking up to power;
That ye are must'ring all your forces dread
And lo! the perilous storm begins to lower?
In secret ye have met, a dark divan,
And form'd committees who in secret meet:
Thus have ye organized a subtle plan,
Throughout the states the *Demos* to defeat.
Such are your sanguine hopes; but much I fear,
Those hopes will vanish into empty smoke,
Already have ye labor'd many a year:
And still (as fast as form'd your bubbles broke!)
And us'd all arts, which *Satan's* aid supplied;
Your arch-foe, JEFFERSON to overcome:
But, while ye strive to mount, ye backward fall;
The PEOPLE will not listen while ye bawl;
Nor will they follow when ye beat the drum.
In *Massachusetts* ye have done *great things*:
Gain'd a majority by *rare finesse*!
Yet even from this no solid comfort springs;
That short liv'd triumph cannot *fix* success.
Me thinks, while *there* ye strut, and fume, and boast,
That for a little while ye rule the roast,
(Ah! soon to sink before the Sov'reign PEOPLE)
I see the frog who with them is in size
By swelling arose, or *Dwarf* ambition's rise,
On *tip-toe*, struggling hard to match a steeple!
Great were your hopes from *little* Aaron BURR;
And yet in vain was all *his* mighty stir.
'Tis true you sav'd him from th' insulted laws:
Yet his escape but little serv'd your cause
Could he indeed a *diadem* have won,
The federal reign of glory, had begun.
Your *second Bonaparte* then

With dukedoms had adorn'd his chosen men:
The mines of Mexico had given them gold:
And *Burr* had given them titles grand!
In splendour then each lordly *fed* had roll'd;
Princes and chiefs, and rulers of the land.
Alas! these golden hopes, too sweet to last,
Were fleeting at the morning's airy dream:
The cunning democrats your projects blast,
And still, alas! their party is supreme.
"Choice spirits" cannot reign, nor *"best of blood"*
Who scorn'd *"the dull pursuits of civil life."*
Here must they "vegetate" with sons of mud:
Forbid to mingle in the glorious strife.
"The spirit-stirring drum, ear-piercing fife,
Pride, pomp and circumstance of glorious war."
All now are lost! and (what they most abhor)
This vile EMBARGO cramps their energies!
Te quondam friends of order then arise!
Put on your strength; — one powerful effort make,
And by that effort ye may win the day.
Now is the time the citadel to take
Could but its sentinels the gates betray.
'Tis true their *honesty* is such,
To bribe them you may strive in vain;
And such their *wisdom*, that not much
Your artful tricks from them will gain.
Your only chance is *discord* to excite;
That, while they quarrel, you the gates may reach.
Divide and conquer then! *yourselves* unite,
And stick together *close as any beech*;
While they dispute for *Clinton* or *Monroe*,
And thus lie open to the fatal blow.
So thro' the world your victory may ring,
And *Demos* bow to *Cotesworth* or to *King*.

1:70

This poem exults in Jefferson's triumph over Aaron Burr, the second Bonaparte. The embargo tries the souls of Americans, separating the self-interested businessman from the noble patriot. Rufus King and Charles Cotesworth Pinckney were the Federalist candidates for president and vice president in 1800 and 1808, but were decisively defeated. King supported Hamilton's fiscal policy and the Jay treaty; he opposed the War of 1812.

For the Journal.

[BY PARTICULAR REQUEST.]

An **ODE** to the Constitution, for preserving the right
of sufferage to the *common* class of citizens — contrary to Snyder and his junto.

THE CONSTITUTION.

[Anonymous]

Let all be 'sham'd and troubled sore, that en'mies are to thee:
Let them turn back and suddenly ashamed let them be.

Behold! they in iniquity do travail, as in birth,
And mischief they conceived have, and falsehoods do bring forth.

And in their mouth there is no truth; their inward part is ill;
Their throat's an open sepulchre, their tongues do mischief tell.

But those that knew *thy* worth, in thee their confidence did place;
And thou hast safe preserv'd all those that lov'd and kept thy face.

And those that needy are, will not forgotten be of thee.
The expectation of the poor, will answer'd be by thee.

Thou know'st their folly and mischief and spite thou wilt repay;
The poor commits himself to thee; thou art the orphan's stay.

Thou judgest the fatherless, and those that are oppressed sore;
That man that is but sprung of earth, let him oppress no more.

Thine hand shall all those men find out, that enemies are to thee.
Yes, thy right hand shall find out those of thee that haters be.

When, for thy sake, to thee we fled, to us thou shew'd thy name:
Thy face we lov'd, and kept it safe, and have not suffer'd shame.

We will show forth thy wond'rous worth, that all mankind's offspring.
In the assemblies of this land, thy worthiness may sing.

The just and faithful thou did'st guide, for seventeen years past:
If we behave ourselves thou can'st, as long as time may last.

With treach'rous men you have not sat, nor with dissemblers gone;
The conduct of such men you hate, to sit with such you shun.

When all thine ENEMIES and FOES, most wicked persons grown,
To spoil thy FACE against thee rose; now they complain and MOURN.

And now e'en in October next, your head will lifted be
Above all those that were thy foes, about for to spoil thee.

For now thou art so stately grown, they fear to tell the truth;
For election sake alone, they say they won't abuse thy youth.

Believe them not, they mischief plot; power they want to have;
Put Simon Snyder in th'chair, a majority they'll have.

So trust not double-faced-men, that think and speak two ways;
If a majority they gain, they'll try to spoil thy rays.

Thou wast our strength and shield, our hearts upon thee did rely,
Thou art preserved safe, and we do joy exceedingly.

With ill men thou won't go away, that work deceitfully,
That speak fair words to men, whilst in their hearts do mischief lie.

And thou hast not enclosed us within the en'my's hand,
And by thy choice we have been made safe in this state to stand.

Thou can'st instruct us, and us teach the way that we should go,
And with the charms that are in thee, thou can'st direction show

Thou do'st the poor set free from him that is for him too strong:
The poor and needy, from the man that spoils and does him wrong,

False witness rose, and to thy charge gross falsehoods much they lay;
They, to the spoiling of thy face, with slander would repay.

And in thy trouble they rejoic'd; gathering themselves together;
Yes, discontents and scum of men did often 'gainst thee gather.

Thou thought it not, they would thee tare and quiet would not be,
And ignorant hypocrites at least, oft gnash'd their teeth at thee.

For a reward of this their shame, let them confounded be,
That in such manner ignorantly do try to dispoil thee.

Surely the wrath of fools unto thy praises do redound:
Thou to the remnant of their wrath can'st set restraining bound.

With whom thine hand shall 'stablish'd be, thine arm shall make him strong:
On him thy foe shall not exact, nor son of falsehood wrong.

A FRIEND TO THE CONSTITUTION.

1:72/69

Simon Snyder (1759–1819) served in the state house of representatives from 1797 to 1807 and served as speaker in 1804, 1805, and 1807. A strong supporter of Jefferson, Snyder was selected to unseat Governor McKean in 1805, but McKean won by forming a coalition with the Federalist party. Snyder served as governor of Pennsylvania for three terms, from 1808 to 1817.

(The following beautiful as well as spirited little
ODE, we copy from the *Northern Budget*, of *Troy*.
It possesses the spirit of Poetry — and answers to
the spirit of the times — or, at least, it breathes a
spirit which ought to pervade every American
breast.]

ENGLAND AND FRANCE.

[Anonymous]

OCEAN weeps at BRITAIN'S crimes,
Wafted o'er a thousand climes;
Ocean's surges stream with gore,
Dark and crimson to the shore.

From his blue, unfathom'd bed,
Regions of the shroudless dead,
Wakes the unrelenting strife —
Peals the closing dirge of life.

Billows mix with billows dire;
Ocean glows with mimic fire:
Deep beneath the mountain wave,
Millions plunge, to find a grave.

GALLIC valor scours the plain,
Heaps of heroes newly slain,
Erst with martial pride elate,
Swell the catalogue of fate.

Rearing his terrific crest,
Giant arm, and dauntless breast,
Europe's arbiter appears,
And victory's lofty standard rears.

He, for conquest and renown,
Mows the warlike phalanx down,
Valor's offspring yield their breath,
Gallant armies sink in death.

Pyrenees and *Alps* in vain
Strive his mad career to chain!
Close he girds his blood stain'd robe,
And plans the conquest of the globe.

Rise ye spirits of the deep!
NEPTUNE's ancient Sabbath keep;
Bid his wat'ry realms be free,
Whelm the TYRANT OF THE SEA.

Rise ye patriots! on the shore!
Bid the trump of Freedom roar:
Grasp her thunders in your hand,
Crush the TYRANT OF THE LAND!

CLEOS.

1:76/73–1:77/74

In this poem, France and England are equally
bloodthirsty. "Ocean weeps at Britain's crimes"
(line one), but the "Pyrenees and Alps in vain /
Strive [Napoleon's] mad career to chain!"

The following beautiful piece of composition was sung
in this city, at the celebration of the 4th of JULY.
Its origin is not known; its excellence it carries with
it. It was written for the 4th of MARCH, the 2nd era
of American Liberty — some slight alterations were
made to accommodate it to the 1st era, the occasion
on which we speak of its having been improved.

[Anonymous]

BRAVE Sons of Columbia! salute, this blest day,
Your JEFFERSON, rais'd to the Chair of the Nation;
With rapture the Statesman and Patriot survey —
The man of your choice, and your Freedom's salvation;
    And long may you find
    His immutable mind,
The foe of all tyrants and friend of mankind;
And ne'er may the Sons of Columbia deplore
The loss of their Freedom till time is no more.

When late the great WASHINGTON call'd to the skies
Exulting arch-angels the hero surrounding,
Bade weeping Columbia refrain from her sighs —
"Lo Jefferson lives!" from the heavens resounding,
    She heard the glad strain —
    Heav'n echo'd again,
"He lives and your charter of rights will maintain.
And ne'er shall the sons of Columbia deplore
The loss of their freedom till time is no more."

Again while proud Europe, in slaughter combin'd
With horrors of war, fills the world with commotion;
And tyrants the scourge and the curse of mankind,
Whelm nations in gore, and encrimson the ocean,
    Columbia! thy name
    The trumpet of fame
Shall sound thro' all seasons, our rights to proclaim:
And ne'er shall the sons of Columbia deplore
The loss of their freedom till time is no more.

May the gleam of our arms, like the beams of the sun,
Dispel the dark clouds of all future invasion,

Should slav'ry essay to rear tyrants a throne,
Or anarchy whelm in confusion the nation,
   Our freedom to save,
   The sword of the brave
Montgomery and Warren, would leap from the grave;
And ne'er shall the foes of Columbia deplore
The loss of their freedom, till time is no more.

The blood of your heroes has purchas'd the prize
Of liberty, glory, and rich independence:
The shade of your forefathers beam from the skies,
In smiling complacency, on their descendants.
   The blood of each wound,
   Cries aloud from the ground,
O ne'er let a foe to your freedom be found
And ne'er shall the sons of Columbia deplore
The loss of their freedom, till time is no more."

1:77/74

This poem underscores the tendency of American poets to attribute divine providence to the American experiment. "May the gleam of our arms, like the beams of the sun, / Dispel the dark clouds of all future invasion." If Jefferson felt that his election was a return to the spirit of '76, this poem represents the spirit of the past watching over future endeavors: "The shade of your forefathers beam from the skies."

[Anonymous]
[Editor's Introduction]

The two following songs are adapted to the Irish Music, of whose contemplated publication the public has been apprized.

The first air, *"my lodging is on the cold ground,"* in ancient times called the *"song of death,"* is solemn and martial: through it however there runs a vein of pathos, which has not often been surpassed.

An essay on the history and character of the Ancient Music of Ireland, is in a state of preparation. To render this more correct, as well as the collection of national airs, the Irish Gentlemen resident in America, are invited to forward to the proprietors of this Paper, the choicest sets of the finest of the airs in question, together with such copies of Gaellic or English Songs, as have survived.

1:88

This clipping gives early evidence of Jefferson's interest in Gaelic writings, showing that it continued through his presidency. As a young man, Jefferson shared his passion for Macpherson's *Ossian* with his guest at Monticello, the marquis de Chastellux. He never renounced his interest in finding an Anglo-Saxon bard like Homer.

O, *glory* thou shadow, thou sound far away,
Be thy shouts, and thy trumpets, and drums;
Thy gore dripping trophies, thy glittering array;
And all that from victory comes;

But all hail to the hero, who starts from the sleep,
Of friendship, retirement, and love;
Whose blade like the light'ning of Heaven destroys,
Yet, who sighs for his village and grove.

At the great call of nature, 'tis *glorious* to rise,
When tyranny rears his fell head:
Strike a blow, which shall sound through the earth and the skies;
Greatly live, or *nobly* join the great dead.

But in peace, when the banners of liberty wave,
Ah how sweeter than glory, is love:
How delicious its joys, to the just and the brave,
Midst the sports of the village and grove.

1:87

Jefferson avoided military confrontation as president, but many poems in his newspaper commonplace book celebrate martial valor.

[Anonymous]
TUNE — "Erin Go Brah."

Despair in her wild eye, a Daughter of Erin*
Appeared on the cliffs of the bleak rocky shore,
Loose in the winds flow'd her dark streaming ringlets,
And heedless she gaz'd on the dread surges roar;
Loud rung her harp in wild tones of despairing,
The time past away with the present comparing,
In soul thrilling strains deepest sorrows declaring
She sang Erin's woes — and her Emmet no more.

O Erin, my country, your glory's departed,
For tyrants and traitors have stabb'd thy heart's core;
Thy children have lav'd in the stream of affliction,
Thy Patriots have fled, or lie stretched in their gore:
Ruthless Russians now prowl thro' thy hamlet's forsaken
From pale hungry orphans their last morsels taken,
The screams of thy females no pity awaken.
Alas! my poor country — your Emmet's no more.

That brave was his spirit, yet mild as the Bramin;
His heart bled in anguish the wrongs of the poor,
To relieve their hard sufferings, he brav'd every danger,
The vengeance of Tyrants undauntedly bore;
E'en before him the proud titled villains in power,
Were seen, tho' in ermine, with terror to cower:
But ah! he is gone, he is fallen a young flower,
They murder'd my Emmet — my Emmet's no more.

*It is said that Mr. Emmet was engaged to be married to
a daughter of the celebrated Orator, Mr. Curran.

1:90 / 87

Jefferson clipped a number of poems set to Irish music, including "Shelah na Gira," sung by the blind bard Carolan, and "Boyne Water." This poem is the most political of the Irish verse he collected, treating the hero Robert Emmet (1778–1803), an Irish nationalist and revolutionary who, in 1800, planned a French-aided uprising in Ireland. This uprising took place in July 1803, when Emmet attempted to march on Dublin castle with one hundred men. Emmet's lawyer, Leonard MacNally, was in the pay of the British Crown, it was later discovered, and Emmet's stirring speech on the scaffold made him a political hero.

POEMS OF NATION

A Dead March

[Anonymous]
TUNE: "Though far beyond the mountains."

Thick night, in her dark mantle,
　　Enshrouds the bloody field;
And now to soft emotions
　　The baser passions yield.
Where death triumphant raged,
　　The sorrowing Hero goes,
To seek his slaughtered comrade
　　Amid his breathless foes.

Now silent moves the soldier
　　With solemn peace and slow,
To pay the last sad honours
　　To him in war laid low.
The Hero's manly sorrow,
　　In one expressive tear,
Excells the idle pageants,
　　That deck the soldier's bier.

Hark, the thundering volley,
　　The soldiers last farewell,
In loud repeated echoes,
　　Now sounds his mournful knell.
Light rest upon his bosom,
　　The cold sepulchral clay,
And there each gallant soldier,
　　A soldier's tribute pay.

Fresh wreaths of martial laurel
　　Shall shade the soldier's grave,
Who dies with arm uplifted,
　　His country's right to save.
Eternal honours rising,
　　With each renewed year,
In never fading glory,
　　Shall bloom forever there.

EDWIN.

1:113/112

This poem captures the struggle of a soldier to overcome "baser passions" that make him skeptical about war. Though he did not serve in the military, Jefferson valued those who did; Hamilton was Washington's aide-de-camp and enjoyed a special relationship with the first president that Jefferson could not share.

The Grave of Russel.

[Anonymous]

"Never did martyr with more lovely grace,
Part from a world unworthy to possess him!"
Haley.

The morn with mild splendour illumin'd the hill,
    And shed her pale radiance around the dark heath;
The lake was unruffled, the greenwood was still,
    The wind of the west had forgotten to breathe —

When lo! From the sky like an augur of light,
    The genius of ERIN, in glory array'd
Came — borne on a white passing cloud of the night,
    And stood on the spot where her RUSSEL was laid.

The voice of her harp that to sorrow was strung,
    Partook of the anguish that reign'd in her soul;
And while to its plaintive rais'd numbers she sung,
    Thus sad on her ear the sweet melody stole: —

"O! RUSSEL! enthron'd with the souls of the brave,
    Look down with mild eye from the regions of day:
'Tis Erin that calls thee, that kneels by thy grave,
    And kisses the turf that encloses thy clay,

The tear of affection for thee does it fall,
    And thine is the sigh that escapes from my breast;
Oh! could thy the strength of the mighty recall,
    And win back the souls from the realms of the blest.

For ever the torrent should stream from mine eyes,
    And sighs ever swelling employ my fond breath;
Until thy great spirit, restor'd from the skies,
    Should wake thy remains from the slumber of death!

I saw thee the prospect of ruin despise,
   And firm 'mid destruction thy progress pursue;
When oft would a tear at thy danger arise,
   And hide thy strong efforts a while from my view.

But, shade of the mighty! thine efforts remain,
   To arouse in my cause each degenerate son,
Their spirits recoil'd at the prospect of pain;
   They bow'd to their fears and the brave was undone!

Foul falsehood rejoic'd when *M'Donnel** had trac'd
   His name on the scroll thy destroyers unfurl'd;
Truth wept o'er the word that she wo'd have eras'd,
   And infamy published the tale to the world.

When treachery's triumph at length was complete,
   And death, the resource of the wretched, was near,
I heard thy bold accents — when highest his seat [illegible],
   They shook the proud heart of *Injustice* with fear!

Collected and calm, in the soul trying hour,
   Firm, was thy footstep, nor faltered thy breath;
Thou smild'st at the utmost exertion of power,
   Resign'st thy great spirit and triumph in death!

O RUSSEL! tho' high o'er thy mouldering dust,
   No sculptor has chissel'd thine actions in stone;
Nor rear'd the tall column, nor embolded the bust,
   To grace the green sod that embosoms my son,

Yet there will the muses in her sorrow recline,
   And cull sweetest flow'rers to strew on thy grave;
The bosom of Friendship thy name shall enshrine,
   And dwell with delight on the deeds of the brave,

Farewell, blessed spirit! the finger of fame,
   Has twin'd her fair chaplet thy brow to adorn;
In ages to come will she boast of thy name,
   And tell thy sad story to millions unborn."

She ceas'd to complain—and her harp's silent strings,
   No longer were swept to the numbers of woe;
But, rising from earth on the clouds' fleecy wings,
   She heav'd a fond sigh for her harp laid low.

*A physician in Belfast, once an intimate friend of *Thomas Russel's*, but from mercenary motives, in his practice as a physician, basely joined with others, in offering a reward for the apprehension of *Russel.*

1:114/113

.

This poem refers to the hanging (October 21, 1803) of the republican hero Thomas Russell, a member of the United Irishmen from 1791 to 1803. A spiritualist, Russell (spelled "Russel" in the poem) read Isaac Newton's *Observations upon the Prophecies of Daniel and the Apocalypse of St. John* (1733) for signs of Ireland's political destiny. He corresponded with Frances Dobbs, an Irish MP who opposed the Act of Union as anti-scriptural. Peter Linebaugh and Marcus Rediker's *The Many-Headed Hydra* treats Russell's career. Russell wrote a poem, published in 1797, about the defeat of the Gael ("The Fatal Battle of Aughrum"). He echoed the words of Thomas Paine in his verse. *The Rights of Man* sold forty thousand copies in Ireland — twice the figure it reached in England

POEMS OF NATION

Soldier's Song.
By T. G. Fessenden, Esq.

WHEN cannons roar, when bullets fly,
And shouts and groans affright the sky,
Amid the battle's dire alarms,
I'll think, my Mary, on thy charms,
    The crimson field, fresh proof shall yield,
      Of thy fond soldier's love;
    And thy dear form, in battle's storm,
      His guardian angel prove.

Should dangers thicken all around,
And dying warriors strew the ground —
In varied shapes should death appear,
Thy fancied form my soul shall cheer.
    The crimson field, fresh proof shall yield,
      Of thy fond soldier's love;
    And thy dear form, in battle's storm,
      His guardian angel prove.

And when loud cannons cease to roar.
And when the din of battle's o'er,
When safe return'd from war's alarms,
O then I'll feast on Mary's charms.
    In ecstasy, I'll fly to thee —
      My ardent passion prove:
    Left glory's field, my life I'll yield,
      To all the joys of love.

1:132/129

Fessenden's poem celebrates the soldier's heroism; he thinks of his lover, Mary, to "cheer" himself in the "din of battle." This poem appears on the same page as "The Fowler" and "A Persian Gazel," and does not appear to be included because of its focus on military themes. The reasons for Jefferson's juxtapositions of specific poems, based on knowledge of his aesthetic tastes and preferences, forms a fruitful avenue for future research.

To the President.
[Anonymous]

Thou Chief rever'd! while slander pours
Her venom o'er thy tranquil hours,
While many a rude unhallowed tale
The lustre of thy life assail,
E'en round thy virtues' calm retreat,
Would bid the warring passions beat
And, arm'd with *Party's* vengeful dart,
Strike the firm fortress of thy heart,
Unmov'd amid the mental strife,
Thy noblest *"answer is thy life."*
A Life, instructive wisdom's claim,
Enrich'd by deeds of deathless fame;
Wisdom an Angel seem'd to guide!
And *Deeds*, a grateful nation's pride!
That grateful nation early, known,
To claim thy dictates as her own,
When doubting — daring — to be free,
She caught th'inspiring words from thee;
Still shall her letter'd annals shine
With ev'ry brilliant act of thine,
And *Time's* impartial page declare
What thy unclouded glories were;
While *Falsehood* to her den shall fly,
Drink th'applauding strain, and *DIE.*

COLUMBIA.

1:171/166

In this poem, Jefferson appears as a man who dared America to be free ("That grateful nation early, known, / To claim thy dictates as her own, / When doubting — daring — to be free"). Jefferson's close election and eight-year term were both marked by the Republicans' fight for political legitimacy. Though Jefferson stated that "we are all Republicans — we are all Federalists"[40] in his inaugural address, the spirit of faction still threatened the nation "While slander pours / Her venom o'er thy tranquil hours." Jefferson instructed by his example: "Thy noblest 'answer is thy life.'" Blake portrayed Jefferson as a minor character in *America*, by contrast. "The builder of Virginia throws his hammer down in fear," focusing, instead, on "Washington, Franklin Paine and Warren, Allen, Gates, and Lee."[41]

Paper — A Poem.

Extracted from the Works of the late Dr.
BENJAMIN FRANKLIN.

SOME wit of old — when wits of old there were —
Whose hints show'd meaning whose allusions care,
By one brave stroke to mark all human kind,
Call'd clear blank paper ev'ry infant mind;
When still, as opening sense her dictates wrote,
Fair virtue put a seal, or vice a blot.

The thought was happy, pertinent and true;
Methinks a genius might the plan pursue.
I, (can you pardon my presumption) I —
No wit no genius, yet for once will try.

Various the papers, various wants produce,
The wants of fashion, elegance, and use.
Men are as various: and, if right I scan,
Each sort of paper represents some man.

Pray note the Fob — Half powder and half lace —
Nice as a band box, were his dwelling-place:
He's the *Gilt-paper*, which apart your store,
And lock from vulgar hands in the seritoire.

Mechanics, servants, farmers, and so forth,
Are *copy-paper* of inferior worth;
Less priz'd, more useful, for your desk decreed,
Free to all pens, and prompt to every need.

The wretch whom avarice bids to pinch and spare,
Starve, cheat and pilfer, to enrich an heir,
Is coarse *brown paper*; such as pedlars choose
To wrap up wares, which better men will use.

Take next the Miser's contrast, who destroys
Health, fame, and fortune, in a round of joys:
Will any paper match him? Yes, throughout,
He's a true *sinking-paper*, past all doubt.

The retail politician's anxious thought
Deems *this* side always right and *that* stark nought;
He foams with censure, with applause he raves —
A dupe to rumours, and a tool of knaves;

He'll want no type his weakness to proclaim,
While such a thing as *fools-cap* has a name.
The hasty gentleman whose blood runs high,
Who picks a quarrel if you step away,

Who can't a jest, a hint, or look endure:
What's he? What? *Touch-paper* to be sure.
What are our poets, take them as they fall,
Good, bad, rich, poor, much read, not read at all.

Them and their works in the same class
        you'll find;
They are the mere *waste-paper* of mankind.
Observe the maiden innocently sweet,
She's fair *white paper* an unsullied sheet;

On which the happy man whom fate ordains,
May write his *name*, and take her for his pains.
One instance more, and only one I'll bring;
'Tis the *great man* who scorns a little thing,

Whose thoughts, whose deeds, whose maxims are
        his own,
Form'd on the feelings of his heart alone:
True genuine *royal paper* is his breast;
Of all the kinds most precious, purest, best.

1:181/181

With a priggish, utilitarian perspective that irked such writers as D. H. Lawrence, Franklin admonished poets for wasting paper. Franklin's cynical humor shines forth in this inventive satire. Byron noted that poems wind up lining pastry shelves; Franklin did him one better: "What are our poets, take them as they fall, / Good, bad, rich, poor, much read, not read at all. / Them and their works in the same class you'll find; / They are the mere *waste-paper* of mankind."

For the PENNSYLVANIA HERALD.

MESSRS. CAREY AND CO.

If you think this humble tribute, to the merits of dr.
Franklin by a young hand, worthy a place in your
poet's corner, it is at your service.

When science seeks the good of all the race —
When heaven aspiring labour aids to trace
The mystic paths, whence flows all nature's laws,
And boldly mounts to the primaeval cause;
Where freedom mild, exalted justice dwell,
Strive in the human bosom to excell:
Whose country's woes (each meaner thought deprest)
Employ his care and fill alone his breast;
For him the muse shall prompt some bard divine —
For him the muse her choicest wreath shall twine —
For him Apollo's sons exert their art,
And by his bright example raise the heart
To glory's blest pursuits. — The trump of fame
Shall tell his virtues, and old FRANKLIN'S name.

C. B.

1:188/182

This poem on Franklin should be compared
with "Paper — A Poem," which Jefferson also
clipped and which this poem immediately follows in the notebook. Franklin preceded
Jefferson as ambassador to France, and
Jefferson noted that one could succeed
Franklin, but never replace him.[42]

EPIGRAM — PARODIED.
PAINE and THE DEVIL, a DIALOGUE.

Scene. — *A room in Lovell's hotel, at Washington.* —
The DEVIL *reading* PAINE's *third letter.*

Says SATAN to THOMAS, "I shrewdly suspect
You mean to disgrace our 'Republican' sect —
Or between you and me, you should manage things better,
Than such language to me in this impudent letter."

Says THOMAS to SATAN — half sneer and half smile,
"Who gives me the MATTER should furnish the STYLE;
But why you find fault I can scarcely divine,
For the GLORY is yours, tho' the 'labors' are mine.

'Tis yours to deceive with the *semblance* of *truth*,
Thou *prop* of my AGE, and thou *guide* of my YOUTH
But to prosper pray give me some farther supplies,
A set of new words, and a SET OF NEW LIES."

When Paine was in jail at *Paris*, his FRIEND was Secretary of
State here: but we do not find he ever made application to
ROBESPIERRE for his liberation: And yet we know that this
same friend, on another occasion, could send Dr. LOGAN on
an equally impertinent embassy to *Paris*.

2:4

This poem ridicules Thomas Paine, who was jailed by Robespierre. The poet insinuated that Jefferson never aided his friend Paine, though he had it in his power to do so. On March 18, 1801, Jefferson wrote to Paine to indicate that the United States had no interest in becoming entangled in French politics, but would provide Paine with passage back to America. Dr. George Logan, a Quaker, was sent by Jefferson on a peace mission to Paris. Jefferson thought Logan was the best farmer in Pennsylvania, and he was a leader in the Democratic Society.[43]

THE FEDERAL PUPPY.
[Anonymous]

An entertaining, pleasing story,
'Tis my design to lay before you,
The truth of which you cannot doubt sir,
It was as follows brought about sir,
A *federal* man of finest sense sir,
Thinking to show his consequence sir,
Went to a *Demo's* son to try sir,
A FED'RAL PUPPY for to buy sir,
Determin'd that the pretty creature,
Should be a *federalist* by nature,
Or he'd go back again and leave it,
Unless 'twas *federal* he'd not have it;
And when his errand he'd related;
Was told he'd be accommodated,
With one exactly to his liking,
Of *federalists* example striking.
He wish'd the boy to go and find one,
Who did, and brought the man a BLIND ONE!
And this, exclaim'd "the little creature,"
"Is a true FED'RALIST BY NATURE!"
Like federalists it still doth grope on,
For neither of its EYES ARE OPEN.

2:5

Jefferson must have enjoyed this poem, which depicts the Federalists as best represented by a man physically blind who gropes politically because "neither of its eyes are open." The term *puppy* was used in the late eighteenth century (by novelists such as Samuel Richardson in *Clarissa*) to describe a callow male.

Epigram by Thomas G. Fessenden.

Some wicked people in the nation,
Find fault with our administration;
But if the whole truth were unfurl'd,
They're not the worst men in the world:
They lack but two things, I suspect,
Viz. *honesty* and *intellect*.

2:6

Jefferson clipped several poems by Thomas Fessenden; he clearly kept an eye on the attacks of his adversaries, which may have contributed to his disgust with newspapers by the end of his second term. Born in Walpole, New Hampshire, Fessenden was friends with Joseph Dennie and Royall Tyler. He attended Dartmouth College from 1792 to 1796 and was class valedictorian. His verse reflects the Federalist perspective of Dennie's *Port Folio*, to which he contributed. William C. Spengemann has noted that Fessenden's "satirical poem *Democracy Unveiled* (1805) helped to inspire *The Embargo* (1808), the first published poem of William Cullen Bryant, and his verse narrative called 'Jonathan's Courtship' gave James Russell Lowell the model for his popular dialect poem 'The Courtin'."

IMPROMPTU.

[Anonymous]

Jefferson's resignation
Creates much consternation,
And a great paradox it is thought,
That a man of his power
Should in such an hour
Resign what's so eagerly sought.

Yet if we but attend
To the ultimate end,
And examine the cause with precision,
We shall find that the cause
Is the want of applause,
And the dread of the people's decision.
NO JEFFERSONIAN.

2:8

The description of this poem, "From a London paper," suggests the hostility of the British to Jefferson's administration. Jefferson developed an Anglophobia that distinguished him from Washington, Adams, Hamilton, and other Federalists. Jefferson's suspicion of English culture stemmed in part from his struggle to emulate the country estates of such men as Lord Spencer's Chiswick and his wounded pride (which he shared with Franklin) that the British regarded Americans as culturally inferior. Jefferson also experienced, firsthand, Colonel Tarleton's invasion of Monticello and endured a frosty reception in 1783 by George III, who turned his back on the two ministers from America (Adams and Jefferson) when they visited the Court of St. James after the conclusion of the war.[44] In turn, Jefferson's treatment of the British ambassador, Anthony Merry, threatened to devolve into an international incident in 1805.

THE REWARD OF MERIT.
A SATIRE.
[Anonymous]

AH me! what pangs ambition's steps await!
What mighty cares imbitter transient state!
When Disappointment whets her galling sting,
And sick'ning Envy waves her pallid wing;
When Jealousy her saffron robe displays,
And squints malign at MERIT's well-earned bays;
When great Revenge, that strides the lightning's flash,
A prey to conscience, smarts beneath the lash,
The wholesome lash, by honest Satire giv'n,
Satire, the scourge and minister of Heav'n.

. . .

Bid Observation ope her amber eyes,
Pierce to the centre, and explore the skies;
Search each close haunt that tyrant pow'r invades,
The peopled palace, and the sylvan shades;
Trace ev'ry action of this world of man,
And build experience but on Reason's plan;
Oft shall she find, beneath the cloak of pride,
Vile int'rest lurk, and rankling envy hide.
Oft shall she find, and tremble to behold!
A heart of meanness in an angel's mould.
Should'st thou by justice measure out thy days,
Correct bold vice, and give to virtue praise;
Should'st thou, weak man, by thy example strive,
The fire of emulation to revive;
Should all thy actions to one centre tend,
Thyself to worth, a patron, father, friend;
Should Science to thy eye unveil her stores,
And watchful [all] unbar her golden doors;
Should thirst of fame within thy bosom dwell,
Glow in thy soul, and prompt thee to excel,
Swift from her cave shall pale Detraction start,
Redoubled malice gnawing at her heart,
Shall on thy efforts cast a deadly foam,
And pluck thee down from Fame's aspiring dome;

Shall show how weak, how very weak his claim,
Who thinks on MERIT's base to build a name.

Turn to the Church, with eager footsteps run,
Weep, fast, and pray, and stile thyself her son,
Her loving son, by ancient Faith allied,
By duty warm'd, and by affection tied.
Implore her favor with unceasing care,
With lifted hands, and animated pray'r,
That from her ample cruise thou may'st derive
One little drop, to keep thy soul alive;
A scanty pittance, that thy soul may prove
The fond indulgence of maternal love.

    . . .

Canst [thou] devoid of manhood, waste thy prime,
Where e'en existence borders on a crime,
Enslav'd to Custom's arbitrary rule,
Labor the mill horse of a boarding-school,
To beat ideas in a dunce's brain? —
To match which, Hell, with her inventive train,
Demands whole ages! Can thy humble mind
Drudge on content, nor cast one look behind;
One ling'ring look, by sad reflection lent,
To mourn the time thy folly has mispent?

    . . .

As well may'st thou, frail mortal, think to find
One prevalent and universal mind.
As well may'st thou successfully explore,
Truth in a lie, or virtue in a whore:
For when, thro' ev'ry reign, and ev'ry age,
Thy care has search'd the biographick page;
Then shalt thou find, whilst blockheads block heads join,
To rule the state, and swell the priestly line.
Then shalt thou find, and curse thy fruitless search,
MERIT ne'er yet found favor with the CHURCH.
Would'st thou from poverty exemption claim,
And mount superior in the path of fame;
Would'st thou, secure, on Fortune's summit stand,
Nor fear her frowns, nor dread her fickle hand,

Fly to the GREAT! be prudent, and be wise,
And court the villain, Honor would despise.
Soften each act of cruelty and whim,
And praise whatever vice is found in him.
Then shall thy honest services find grace,
Where honest Virtue dares not show her face.
Then shall admiring lords, enraptur'd sit,
And well bred ladies wonder at thy wit.
Then shall preferment wait thy saintly brow.
"Room for his GRACE!" Merit, stand & bow!"

[TO BE CONTINUED.]

2:11A

A very interesting critique of the church and of education as a place where merit is not rewarded.

For the NATIONAL ÆGIS.
[Anonymous]

KIND reader, if you'll deign to hear,
I'll tell a tale that's something queer;
Where Monticello's summits rise,
In tow'ring columns to the skies,
There lives a man as fame relates,
Who makes great clamor in these States;
Some tell he's learned, just and wise,
While others say these tales are lies,
And call him idiot, knave and fool,
A sensual beast and party tool;
Yet this strange man ne'er says a word,
But moves like Cynthia* in her orb,
Regardless what his sland'rers say,
As if they held the moon at bay,
And now six years amid their prate,
He's guided safe our car of State,
While every year the lamp of fame,
Has caught new lustre from his name;
Yet fed'ral puppies yelp and bark,
And with the rest the mongrel Pack,
Who say that all is p[r]one to wrack,
He's play'd the D—l and turn'd up Jack,
In our last plot he's spoil'd the fun,
And Burr and all his host undone;
E'en *pious Strong*, alas! *poor Caleb*,†
His friends can hardly hold his tail up,
We fear in spite of all our care,
Next May will sweep him from the chair.
Then down we sink to grief and shame,
Unless oblivion hides our name,

---

* *Cynthia* was a name for the Greek moon goddess Artemis, given because Kynthos was the mountain on Delos on which she and her twin brother, Apollo, were born. Oddly, Jefferson's presidency is feminized, compared to "Cynthia in her orb."

†Caleb Strong was a Congregationalist from Massachussetts.

For fed'ralism when once 'tis o'er,
Like Irishman returns no more,
But chuses onward still to roam,
And fares the best where least 'tis known.

                              A SQUATTER.

                                        2:13

This poem is a fair measure of Jefferson's success
as president and his growing reputation. It also
describes at least one Federalist charge against
Jefferson, as "a sensual beast and party tool."

The Irish Drummer.
A TALE.
[Anonymous]

A soldier, so at least the story goes,
    It was in Ireland I believe,
    Upon his back was sentenced to receive,
Five hundred gentle cat-and-nine-tail blows;
Most sagely military law providing,
    The *back* alone shall suffer for *backsliding*.

Whether his crime was great or small,
Or whether there was any crime at all,
    Are facts which this deponent never knew;
But tho' uncertain whether justly tried,
The man he knows, was to the halberd tried,
    And hopes his readers will believe so too,

Suppose him then, fast to the halberd bound,
His poor companions standing silent round,
    Anticipating every dreadful smack;
While Patrick Donovan, from Wicklow county,
Is just preparing to bestow the bounty,
    Or *beat quick time* upon his comrade's back

Of Stories much we read in tales of yore,
    Of Zeno, Possidonius, Epictentus,*
Who, unconcern'd, the greatest torments bore,
    Or else these ancient stories strongly cheat us.

My hero was no Stoic, it is plain:
    He could not suffer torments and be dumb,
But roar'd, before he felt the smallest pain,

Zeno was a skeptic who wrote on logic, atomic theory, biology, ethics, literary style, oratory, poetry, the
heory of knowledge, and mathematics.

    Posidonius ("Possidonius") made some minor contributions to pure mathematics, where he is the
uthor of terms ("theorem") related to geometry.

    Epictetus (AD 55–135; spelled Epictentus in poem) was an exponent of Stoicism. He lived and worked
rst as a student in Rome, and then as a teacher with his own school in Nicopolis in Greece. His student
rrian compiled such works as the *Discourses* and the *Handbook*.

As if ten rusty nails had perc'd his bumb!
Not louder is the terror-spreading note,
Which issues from the hungry lion's throat,

When o'er Numidian* plains, in search of prey,
He takes his cruel, *life-destroying* way.
        The first two strokes, which made my hero jump,
Fell right across the confines of his rump;
On which he pitiously began to cry,
"Strike high! strike high! for mercy's sake, strike high!"

Pat, of a mild, obliging disposition.
Could not refuse to grant his friend's petition:
An Irishman has got a tender heart,
And never like to act a cruel part,
Pat gave a good example to beholders,
And the next blow fell on his comrade's shoulders!

Our suffering hero now began to roar
As loud, if not much louder than before;
At which Pat lost all patience, and exclaim'd
While his Hibernian face with anger flam'd,
"The devil burn you, can't your tongue be still?
There is no pleasing you, strike where one will."

2:20

An American newspaper included this humorous dramatic monologue about an Irish soldier who frustrates his officer, Patrick Donovan, by refusing to be satisfied with where he is whipped. The story had obvious resonance for American colonists, recently emancipated from British rule. This humorous tale, which recalls the opening scene of *Don Quixote*, depicts unequal relationships in a comic light, with a clear demo-cratic eye on the person who suffers the injury. Sheridan repeated this story in his speech on the Warren Hastings trial, turning the tale of the drummer into an account of colonial oppression of the Irish. Byron repeated a version of this story again in his Catholic emancipation speech, depicting the officer as British and the victim as Irish. The poet calls attention to the fictional nature of his own utterance ("It was in Ireland I believe").

---

* Under the Roman Republic and Empire, Numidia was a part of Africa north of the Sahara.

An ADDRESS,

Delivered by Mr. Hallam, at the Theatre, in Philadelphia, previous to an entertainment performed to the benefit of the American captives in Algiers.

In life's strange scene what incidents arise
To wound the virtuous and confound the wise!
From public guise, what private sorrow springs,
What devaluation from the state of kings!
The shame of nations, and the source of tears,
Behold! The barbarous triumph of Algiers,
See christian blood bedew the burning plains,
And friends to freedom languishing in chains!
See mighty Europe crouches to the law,
And one bold pirate keeps the world in awe.

In days of Yore with pious phrenzy fraught,
On Palestine's fam'd fields what myriads taught,
Their rival monarchs, partial views despite,
Glory their passion, and a tomb their prize.
Our modern system, fatally refin'd,
Corrupts the gen'rous ardor of mankind,
And jealous nations with the Turk allied,
Regain their virtue, and desert their pride.

Those veterans perhaps, whose patriot toil,
Gave independence to their native soil,
Lost in the sad vicissitudes of fate,
Call on their country to repay the debt.
Perhaps some father shakes the pond'rous chain,
His wretched offspring left to want and pain:
Whence are those groans, and whence that
    plaintive cry ——
Oh! Speed your bounty, or a wife must die:
And mark! Where heav'nly charity appears,
Corrects our errors, and dispels our fears:

Through the dark dungeon spreads a kindly ray,
And shields her children vot'ries from dismay:
With savage power the glitt'ring bribe succeeds,
And freedom from benevolence proceeds.

"When all our earthly bliss shall pass away,
This globe dissolve, and nature's self decay;
When guilt shall at impending judgment start,
And keen affliction wound the hard of heart;
Then white rob'd charity her friends shall chear,
And pay with interest what they lent her here."

Ye sons of liberty, attend the theme,
Indulge your feelings, and assert your fame:
Let sad experience paint the bondsman's woe,
And still be bless'd, while blessings you bestow.

2:33

This poem reflects one consequence of the
Barbary wars, when American shipmen were
taken captive in Algiers. One poet, William
Ray, published a volume based on his experiences as a prisoner of war in Tripoli.

Alexander's Feast: An Ode.
By Doctor Wolcot.

Timotheus now, in music handy,
   Struck up a tune call'd — Drops of Brandy;
The hero pulls out Thais to dance:
Timotheus now struck up a reel;
The couple skipp'd with nimble heel,
Then sat them down, and drank a quart of Nantz.

   Now did the master of the lyre
   On dancing exercise his fire.
He sung of hops at court, and wakes, and fairs;
He sung of dancing dogs, and dancing bears;
   He praised the minuet of Nan Cately,
   And lumps of pudding, and Moll Pately:
The king grew proud and soon began to reel,
A hopping inspiration seiz'd his heel.

   Bravo, bravo, the soldier croud
   In admiration cried aloud.
   The lady dances like a bold Thalestris,
And Alexander hops like Monsieur Vestris.
Again, so furiously they dance a jig,
The lady lost her cap, the hero lost his wig,
   The motley mob, behind, before,
   Exclaim'd encore, encore, encore.
   Proud of th' applause and justly vain,
      Thais made a curtsey low,
Such as court ladies make before the Queen.
      Alexander made a bow,
Such as the royal levee oft has seen,
   And then they danc'd the reel again.

   Of vast applause the couple vain,
   Delighted, danc'd the reel again:
      Now in, and now out,
      They skipp'd it about,

As tho' they felt the madness of the Moon;
Such was the power of Timothy and tune.
When the dub a dub, dub a dub drum,
In triumph behind 'em beat — Go to bed Tom.

And now in their ire,
Return'd from the fire,
In revenge for the Greeks that were dead,
The King and his punk
Got most horribly drunk,
And together went reeling to bed.

2:35

Jefferson exchanged four letters with Alexander I and accepted a gift of the emperor's bust, which he placed beside Napoleon's at Monticello. Educated in the principles of republicanism from his Swiss tutor, Frédéric-César de La Harpe, Alexander was viewed as an enlightened despot. "A more virtuous character man, I believe, does not exist," Jefferson informed William Duane of the *Aurora*, "nor one who is more enthusiastically devoted to better the condition of mankind."[45] There is a tension, then, between English representations of Alexander and American perceptions. Alexander signed the treaty of Tilsit with Napoleon, making them temporary allies against England. Wolcot's view of Alexander as a drunken monarch predominated in the American press in some quarters. In January 1804, the tsar made an effort to aid Americans captured when the frigate *Philadelphia* ran aground (October 31, 1803) and American prisoners were taken in Tripoli.

POEMS OF NATION

TO HENRY GRATTAN.

On his Voting with the Ministry of England,

For the Irish Insurrection Bill.

[Anonymous]

HARRY, honey, would you dish me,
For moulded leaves or stinking fishes fly
Or would you let pale *Spencer* mould you;
Or *Dog in Office pye crusts* hold you?
Or would you play the trick again,
And sell the rights of Irishmen?!
Tho' Liberty and Ormond scold,
And loudly say you are too old,
Tho' childhood is the lot of man,
Shake off the bauble if you can,
For, rest assured, *your drones* of State,
Are fast approaching to their fate,
Nor *Martial Law* nor *Peculation*,
Can hold the *Botches* in their station;
JOHN BULL looks fierce, his eyes are open,
His horns sharp, his heart unbroken;
His daughter *Liberty* quite merry."
His *prophet son* as brisk as SHERRY:
Both know the parties and the stealth,
That long have guarded JOHNNY's wealth,
They know the prowling *Peculation*,
They know the sanguine *Flagellators*,
They know who stopped the constitution
They know the time for retribution!
They hear the BULL for Justice roar,

And freedom echo round his shore
Crying, deadly vengeance I'll dispose,
On Foreign and Domestic Foes!
Buddhough-Stuokoane, July 29.

ENNOD.

2:60

Henry Grattan was an Anglo-Irish Protestant who supported Catholic emancipation. The poet regarded Grattan as a traitor for his support of the Irish Arms and Insurrection Bills (1807), which Grattan defended in a speech that was widely praised. In his maiden speech in the House of Commons (1805), he addressed an earlier question about his consistency to radical causes: "I call my countrymen to witness if in that business I compromised the claims of my country, or temporised with the power of England; but there was one thing which baffled the effort of the patriot and defeated the wisdom of the senate: it was the folly of the theologian."

HAM & TURKEY.

[Anonymous]

NAPOLEON one day took young JEROME aside,
And whisper'd, "As you have forsaken your bride,
"On purpose to please your imperial brother:
"For granting that favor I'll do you another.
"Though in face like a Jew, yet I know you love Pork,
"And as with the Prussians I've finish'd my work,
"I'll give you Westphalia, where you shall be King,
"Provided each year to my table you bring
"A Ham, fat and tender, of that country's breed,
"By way of a tribute — a small one, indeed."
Low bow'd royal Jerome, his whiskers he curl'd
"Dear brother," said he, "you, who've conquer'd the world,
"Have a right from your slaves what you please to command,
"So permit me the honor to slaver your hand,
"And to say, when my tribute you sit down to eat,
"Without TURKEY you'll find 'twill be still incomplete."
Well pleas'd at the hint — though in viands not nice —
BONEY jump'd up, and swore "he'd try hard for a SLICE."

2:39

Napoleon's brother, Jerome, was king of Westphalia. Jefferson enjoyed verse that mocked Napoleon, who viewed countries as dishes to be devoured. When he offered his brother the kingdom of Westphalia, Jerome had only to allude the Ottoman Empire's strategic importance (and especially that of Turkey's) before Napoleon set his eyes on that land as well.

EPISODE.

IN THE COLUMBIAD.
[Joel Barlow]

STORY. — Miss McCrea was betrothed to an English
Officer, and was on her way, escorted by her lover
to be married, when they were overtaken by a party
of Savages attached to Burgoyn's army — Two
chiefs dispute for the lady and are proceeding to
blows, when an old chief in order to prevent dis-
putes, kills her — The Officer who had been
driven off, returns with assistance and finds the
lady dead.

Her eyes, that stream'd and fill'd again with tears
Like gushing founts, which many a riv'let pour
And yet are full; she throws on either chief
Alternate, suppliant, while her sad laments
Plaintive and loud the sorrowing Champaigne fill.
Beauty so sad, so woeful, but enflam'd
The savage chieftains to possess her, more —
They interchange fierce glances, which denote
Bloody intentions, fix'd and deadly hate;
Thus, when desire enflames the horrid rage
Of two fierce lions on the burning tops
Of Atlas; or parch'd banks of Senegal;
They pace the Female round, growing in wrath:
A short and sullen roar; their jaws distent
By rage, their horrid teeth and tongues display'd;
Their tawny flanks lash'd by their sounding tails;
Their mains on end, the earth with fury paw'd,
Are dreadful preludes to their lordly strife.
At once the Indians loose their weeping prey:
Their angry eyeballs glare and in their hands
Two missile Tomahawks shone; then had been sought
A combat, which if action bodily,
If physical exertion ought to gain
Warlike repute; had rais'd the victor's name
High as Achilles, or the fabled strength
Of Hercules: the fame of which had liv'd
Long as tradition oral, and perhaps,

Snatch'd from oblivion by the genial care
Of polish'd climes, whose records more exact
Written exist; had down the stream of time
Sail'd proud, immortal in the sacred arks
Of history and of song; had not the chiefs,
The Elders interpos'd, but chiefest, ONE —
Deep skill'd in savage politics, named OMAI:
He fearing that the interests of the tribe
Would suffer by this contest of the chiefs,
Snatches a Tomahawk and with savage zeal,
Seizes the lovely, trembling, guiltless cause
Of this disunion: and inhuman strikes
The iron deep, into her panting breast.
Her beauteous limbs relax'd, she falls alone
Like [t]o a Roe, whose comely side the spear
Of hunter pierces: Wonder seiz'd the tribe,
The rival chiefs resign their rage to weep.
And even the prudent ruffian felt his soul
Assail'd by pity. On her ivory breast,
The gash appears, as if a stream of blood
Had thaw'd a wound upon the virgin snow.

2:87

The sixth book of Joel Barlow's poem was perhaps most effective as literature, if not as history. Here he began to demonize the British and to paint his epic poem in the broad strokes of good and evil that Milton assumed in *Paradise Lost*, when Michael opposed Satan and the rebel forces. The last few lines of the poem also recall Macpherson's *Ossian*, which eroticized ("ivory breast") political conflict. This poem influenced Blake's *America*, which surprisingly made scant mention of Jefferson and treated Washington, Hamilton, Franklin, Warren, and Allen as major figures in the Revolutionary War.

AN ACROSTIC.

[Anonymous]

G O to the tomb where WASHINGTON now lies,
E ach deed important of his life review,
O 'er all his actions search with argus'* eyes,
R etire to pause — and make thy record true.
G o tell the world unrival'd is his fame,
E nroll'd in immortality his name.

W hen foreign legions landed on our shore,
A nd sought to ravage o'er this peaceful land,
S ome pitying Angel on swift pinions bore
H eaven's fav'ring mandate to our martial band;
I nspir'd them to protect pure freedom's laws,
N am'd our lov'd Hero to the tented field,
G ave WASHINGTON to gain the glorious cause,
T o guard our Rights and force the foe to yield;
O n justice bent, his sword obedient drew,
N one felt its weight, but own'd, its mercy too.

2:138

Jefferson clearly enjoyed this acrostic on George Washington's name. The third president's delight in witty epigrams on political figures is a striking feature of this scrapbook.

---

* Argus was the dog from Greek mythology who had many eyes.

A VERY ANCIENT CHINESE ODE

Translated into English by John Collegins, esq.

Quoted in the Ta Hio of Confucius.

(. . . [from a manuscript] preserved in the Bodleian Library)

The following ode has been translated into Latin by *Sir William Jones*, who informs us in his Treatise on the second classical book of the Chinese, that the Ode is taken from the 1st Vol. of the Shi King. "It is a panegyrick (says he) on Vucan. Prince of Guey, in the province of Honang, who died near a century old, 756 years before the birth of Christ. The Chinese poet might have been cotemporary with Homer and Hesiod, or at least must have written the Ode before the Iliad and Odyssey were carried into Greece by Lycurgus."

See how the silvery river glides,
And laves the fields bespangled sides!
Hear how the whispering breeze proceeds
Harmonious through the verdant reeds!
Observe our prince thus lovely shine!
In him the meek ey'd virtues join!
Just as a patient carver will
Hard ivory model by his skill,
So his example has impress'd,
Benevolence in every b[re]ast.
Nice hands to the rich gem, behold,
Impart the gloss of burnish'd gold:
Thus he in manners goodly great,
Refines the people of his state.
True lenity, how heavenly fair!
We see it, while it threatens, spare!
What beauties in its open face!
In its deportment — what a grace!
Observe our prince thus lovely shine!
In him the meek ey'd virtues join!
His mem'ry of eternal prime,
Like truth defies the power of time!

2:161

Following the Enlightenment tradition of Montesquieu, whose *De l'Esprit des Lois* drew on the manners and mores of many countries, Jefferson drew on the wisdom of Confucius for his own ideas about political leadership. This clipping is significant, in part, because no book by Confucius appears in Jefferson's library.[46] Jefferson, like the editors of this newspaper, used Homer as the gauge by which to measure other literary efforts.

TO VIRTUE.
[Anonymous]

WHAT tho' beneath a humble roof,
I live, and die, unknown to fame!
From courts and cities far aloof,
And Great ones ne'er pronounce my name.

Though soon, beside some lonely heath,
I'm lodg'd, mid undistinguish'd dead,
With not a friend to weep my death,
Nor place a marble at my head; —

Yet, VIRTUE! thou shalt make me blest,
Thy hand shalt lead, thy arm sustain;
And *life*, with thee shall lack no rest,
And *death*, with thee shall give no pain!

2:163

In an 1819 letter to William Short outlining the philosophy of Epicurus, Jefferson described virtue as "the foundation of happiness," and "utility" as "the test of virtue."[47] American political leaders such as Washington and Jefferson stressed the importance of virtue in the preservation of any republic. "The essence of virtue is in doing good to others," Jefferson wrote to Adams in 1816, "while what is good may be one thing in one society, and its contrary in another."[48]

POEMS OF NATION

THE DEATH OF W. WALLACE,

The maintainer of the Liberties of Scotland.

FROM SOUTHEY.

Joy, joy in London now!
He goes, the rebel Wallace goes to death,
At length the traitor meets the traitor's doom,
Joy, joy in London, now!

He on a sledge is drawn,
His strong right arm unweapon'd and in chains,
And garlanded around his helmless head
The laurel wreath of scorn.

They throng to view him now
Who in the field had fled before his sword,
Who at the name of Wallace once grew pale,
And faltered out a prayer.

Yes, they can meet his eye,
That only beams with patient courage now;
Yes, they can gaze upon these manly limbs
Defenceless now and bound.

And that eye did not shrink
As he beheld the pomp of infamy;
Nor did one rebel feeling shake these limbs
When the last moment came.

What tho' suspended sense
Was by their damned cruelly revived,
What tho' ingenious vengeance lengthen'd life
To feel protracted death;

What tho' the hangman's hand
Graspt in his living breast the heaving heart —
In the last agony, the last sick pang,
Wallace had comfort still.

He call'd to mind his deeds
Done for his country in the embattled field;
He thought of that good cause for which he died,
     And that was joy in death!

Go Edward, triumph now!
Cambria is fallen, and Scotland's strength is crush'd;
On Wallace, on Llewellyn's mangled limbs
     The fowls of heaven have fed.

Unrivalled, unopposed,
Go, Edward, full of glory to thy grave!
The weight of patriot blood upon thy soul,
     Go, Edward, to thy God!

The Scottish poem, in twelve books, entitled *"The
life and acts of sir William Wallace,"* says,
     Monteith him sold, and that o'er well was known.
     Scotland he freed, and brought it from thirlage,
     And now in heaven he has his heritage,
     Whereof we have right steadfast confidence,
     Since for his country he made so great defence.

2:165

This poem, marked by sarcasm and bitterness, contrasts the noble courage that marked the Scottish hero William Wallace's life with the curious and craven spectators in London who observe his death. The death of Wallace (1272–1305) might have been the fate of the signers of the Declaration of Independence as well if they had not been successful.

ON THE DEATH OF LORD NELSON.
By the Hon. C. J. Fox.

In death's terrific icy arms
    The brave illustrious Nelson lies:
He's free from care and war's alarms,
    Sees not our tears, nor hears our sighs.

Cold is the heart where valor reign'd
    Mute is the tongue that Joy inspir'd
Still is the arm that conquest gain'd,
    And dim the eye that glory fir'd.

Too mean for him a world like this
    He's landed on the happy shore,
Where all the world partake of bliss,
    And heroes meet to part no more.

2:165

dmiral Nelson died on October 21, 1805, in the battle of Trafalgar, and this poem appeared in the *Morning Post.* The poet suggests that a happier world awaits Nelson after death, where "he's free from care and war's arms." Nelson's death inspired a number of egies, including one by the husband of Georgiana, duchess of Devonshire, a close friend of Fox. Though Fox and Lady Georgiana opposed the policies that placed Nelson in opposition to Napoleon, they distinguished between party politics, the product of ambition, and national politics, the measure of patriotism.[49]

TO GEN. KOSCIUSKO.

By Peter Pindar.

O THOU, whose wounds from Pity's eye
Could force the stream and bid her sigh,
   That God-like valor bled in vain —
Sigh that the land which gave them birth
Should droop its sorrowing head to earth,
   And groaning curse the Despot's chain!

Her beams around shall glory spread,
Where'er thy star thy steps shall lead,
   And Fame thy ev'ry deed repeat:
Each heart in suff'ring Virtue's cause
Shall swell amid the loud applause,
   And raptur'd catch a kindred beat.

In Fancy's eye, thy friend the Muse
Thy bark from wave to wave pursues,
   With fondest wish to join the way,
To view the shore where Freedom reigns,
(An exile long from British plains)
   And blesses millions by her sway.

While thou, in Peace's purple vale,
Fair Freedom, Fame and Health shall hail,
   At ease reclin'd amid the shade —
Britannia's wail will wound thy ear;
And lo! I see thy gen'rous tear
   Embalms her laurels as they fade.

2:167

Kosciusko was a hero of the Polish resistance to Napoleon; he also fought in the American War of Independence. In this poem, Pindar (John Wolcot) portrayed England as a country where Freedom has been "an exile long from British plains." Kosciusko enjoyed Pindar's poetry and visited John Wolcot in London to tell him so. Jefferson hoped that Poland would be as successful as the United States had been in throwing off the oppressor's yoke. "May heaven have in store for your country a restoration of the blessings of freedom and order, an you be destined as the instrument it will use fo that purpose. But if this be forbidden by fate, hope we shall be able to preserve here a asylum where your love of liberty and disinte ested patriotism will be forever protected an honored," Jefferson wrote to Kosciusko in 179 "General Kosciusko is as pure a son of libert as I have ever known," he wrote to Horat Gates in 1798, "and of that liberty which is go to all, and not to the few or the rich alone."

An elegy on Gen. Alexander Hamilton.
By Wm. Hewit.

A sable cloud enshrouds Columbia's head!
   Faint droops the Laurel round her martial brow!
Her fav'rite son! her Hamilton! — is dead. —
   See, o'er his tomb compatriot heroes bow.

*Mourn patriot band, who for your country bled,
   "In times that tried mens' souls," the foe to brave,
Your chief laid low! ne'er from fair freedom fled,
   Let Soldiers tears embalm the Hero's grave.

Mourn! Columbia mourn! the Statesman is no more,
   Whose fiscal talents raised thy infant name,
Thro' shoals, thro' storms, thy fragile barque he bore,
   And proudly moored her on eternal fame.

Brilliant in genius, learned without shew,
   In goodness first, to purchase honest fame
Such Hamilton! great Washington did know,
   Tho' dead! has left behind, a death-less name.

* Hic manus, ob patriam, puguando, vulnera patsi. — *Virg.* — Alluding to the Cincinnati [a society of veterans of the American Revolution that was banned, at Jefferson's encouragement, for an elitism and exclusivity inappropriate to a democratic country].

2:170

This poem begins by describing the cloud that enwraps Columbia's head (stanza one). Hamilton's "fiscal talents" steered the United States "through storms." Hamilton was Washington's aide-de-camp during the American Revolution, and secretary of the treasury before he was killed in a duel by Aaron Burr. Jefferson would hardly agree that he was "learned without shew," but Hamilton was one of the most successful lawyers of his day in New York, who earned a fortune, in part, by defending New York Tories who had lost their estates.[51] Hewit quoted Paine's lines after the defeat of a Virginia branch of the militia in December 1776 when he wrote a pamphlet titled *The American Crisis*: "These are the days that try men's souls. The summer soldier and the sunshine patriot will, in this crisis, shrink from the service of their country; but he that stands it *now* deserves the love and thanks of man and woman." Paine followed the Virginia battalion in their retreat from New York to New Jersey, which inspired these lines.

The Slave.

[R. Anderson]

From Poems, now in the Press,
by R. Anderson of CARLISLE,
ENGLAND.

Torn from every dear connection,
    Forc'd across the yielding wave,
The Negro, stung by keen reflection,
    May exclaim, man's but a slave!

In youth, gay hope delusive fools him,
    Proud her vot'ry to deprave;
In age, self-interest over-rules him,
    Still he bends a willing slave.

The haughty monarch, fearing reason
    May her sons from *ruin* save,
Of traitors dreaming, plots and treason,
    Reigns at best a sceptr'd slave.

His minion, honesty would barter
    And become *corruption's* knave;
Won by *ribband*, *star*, or *garter*,
    Proves himself *ambition's* slave.

Yon *patriot* boasts a pure intention,
    And of RIGHTS will loudly rave,
'Till silenc'd by a *place* or *pension*,
    Th' *apostate* sits a courtly slave.

In pulpit perch'd, the pious preacher,
    Talks of conscience wond'rous grave
Yet not content, the tithe-paid teacher
    Pants to loll a mitr'd Slave.

The soldier, lur'd by sounds of glory.
    Longs to shine a hero brave;
And, proud to live in future story,
    Yields his life, to fame a slave.

Mark yon *poor* miser o'er his treasure,
　　Who to want a mite ne'er gave;
He, shut out from peace and pleasure,
　　Starves, to avarice a Slave.

The lover, to his mistress bending,
　　Pants, nor dares her hand to crave;
Vainly sighing, time misspending,
　　Wisdom scorns the fetter'd Slave.

Thus dup'd by fancy, pride or folly,
　　Ne'er content with what we have;
Toss'd 'twixt hope and melancholy,
　　Death at last sets *free* the slave.

2:191

Anderson's Shakespearean poem cleverly shows the Negro's moral superiority over those who enslave him. His tormentors prove themselves to be slaves of gold. Each stanza, like Jacques's seven ages of man speech in *As You Like It*,[52] shows man to be a dupe, even as he thinks himself master of his fate. Even haughty monarchs, who fear traitors, reign at best a "sceptr'd slave." Byron's *Don Juan* created the same trope in canto five: "Most men are slaves, none more so than the great, / To their own whims and passions and what not. / Society itself, which should create / Kindness, destroys what little we had got. / To feel for none is the true social art / Of the world's stoics — men without a heart."

By 1802, Callendar had moved to Virginia; he had begun editing the *Richmond Recorder*, and turned against Jefferson and the Republicans. "It is well known," he wrote, "that the man *whom it delighteth the people to honor*, keeps, and for many years past has kept, as his concubine, one of his own slaves. Her name is SALLY." The story that Jefferson maintained a sexual relationship with his slave Sally Hemings and fathered a number of her children has been in circulation ever since.[53] Thomas Moore helped to perpetuate it in his *Epistles* of 1806, and visitors to Monticello, such as Francis Wright and Francis Trollope, grappled with the contradictions posed by Jefferson's ownership of slaves.[54] Federalists resented the three-fifths clause of the Constitution, which gave southerners, through their slaves, additional representation in Congress.[55] "Great men can never lack supporters, / Who manufacture their own voters," Thomas Green Fessenden wrote in 1806 in *Democracy Unveiled*.

TRUE FREEDOM.
by Cowper.

HE is the Freeman, whom the TRUTH makes free,
And all are slaves beside. There's not a chain
That hellish foes, confed'rate for his harm,
Can wind around him, but he casts it off
With as much ease, as Sampson his green withes,
He looks abroad in to the varied field
Of nature; and, though poor perhaps, compared
With those whose mansions glitter in his sight,
Calls the delightful scen'ry all his own;
His are the mountains, and the vallies his,
And the resplendent rivers; his t'enjoy,
With a propriety that none can feel,
But who, with filial confidence inspir'd,
Can lift to heav'n an unpresumptuous eye,
And, smiling, say "my father made them all."
Are they not *his* by a peculiar right,
And by an emphasis of interest *his*,
Whose eye they fill with tears of holy joy,
Whose heart with praise, and whose exalted mind
With worthy thoughts of that unweary'd love
That plann'd, and built, and still upholds a world
So cloath'd with beauty, for rebellious man?
Yes — ye may fill your garners, ye that reap
The loaded soil, and ye may waste much goods
In senseless riot; but ye will not find,
In feast or in the chase, in song or dance,
A liberty like his, who unimpeach'd
Of usurpation, and to no man's wrong,
Appropriates nature as his Father's work,
And has a richer use of yours than you.
He is indeed a Freeman — free by birth
Of no mean city, plann'd or e'er the hills
Were built, the fountains open'd or the sea,
With all his roaring multitude of waves.
His freedom is the same in every state;
And no condition of his changeful life.
So manifold in cares, whose ev'ry day

Brings its own evil with it, makes it less:
For he hath wings that neither sickness, pain,
Nor penury, can cripple or confine:
No nook so narrow, but he spreads them there
With ease, and is at large. The oppressor holds
His body bound; but knows not what a range
His spirit takes, unconscious of a chain;
And that to bind him is a vain attempt.

                                        2:192

Jefferson juxtaposed Cowper's celebration of religious freedom with Anderson's view of man as a "scepter'd slave." Cowper wrote poems like "The Task" in brief moments of respite from the effects of a gloomy Calvinism, which led him to the brink of sanity on more than one occasion.

PART TWO

Poems of FAMILY

Thomas Jefferson had six children by Martha Skelton, two of whom survived infancy. Jefferson's two surviving daughters were Martha (Patsy) and Mary (called Pol or Polly in France, and Maria after the family's return). After ten years of marriage, Jefferson's wife died on September 6, 1782, having given birth to Lucy Elizabeth. Lucy died two years later when Jefferson was in France. Jefferson's other daughter Mary died in 1804 at twenty-six, leaving two children, Francis, age three, and an infant, Maria Jefferson, who did not survive past a few months.[1] During the years he compiled this clippings book, Jefferson had seven grandchildren by his daughter Martha: Anne Cary, Thomas Jefferson, Ellen Wayles, Cornelia, Virginia, Mary, Benjamin Franklin, and

James Madison. Born after he left the White House, Meriwether Lewis (1810), Septimia Anne (1814), and George Wythe (1818) completed the picture. "I have compared notes with Mr. Adams on the score of progeny," Jefferson wrote to Abigail Adams, "and find I am ahead of him, and think I am in a fair way to keep so. I have 10½ grandchildren, and 2¾ great-grand-children; and these fractions will ere long become units."[2]

Before examining the poems that make up this section, it seems worth exploring Jefferson's domestic life in greater detail, for the poems Jefferson clipped sometimes weave a fantasy that had little relation to the grittier circumstances that marked his own life. During his years in France, for example, he noted that "conjugal love having no existence among them, domestic happiness, of which that is the basis, is utterly unknown" in contrast with "the tranquil, permanent felicity with which domestic society in America blesses most of it's inhabitants."[3] In 1786, he informed Lucy Ludwell Paradise that family life in America was "infinitely more replete with happiness than . . . in Europe."[4] What was the basis for this assessment?

Jefferson married a widow, Martha Wayles Skelton, and brought her to the mountain of Monticello on a snowy evening for their honeymoon. They inhabited a one-room brick house at the edge of the South Pavilion, enjoying a half-finished bottle of wine they found "on a shelf behind some books."[5] Martha, who played the harpsichord, may have preferred the six-foot, red-haired Jefferson to other suitors because of his violin playing and love of music. Little is known of her because Jefferson destroyed papers related to their ten years of marriage. Her son from John Wayles died before she married Jefferson, though he presumably intended on helping her raise him.

As noted above, Jefferson had six children by Martha Wayles Skelton, two of whom survived infancy, and one of whom survived him. On September 6, 1782, Martha died of complications that arose from giving birth to Lucy, who died two years later (October 13, 1784). Jefferson mourned his wife for six weeks, and was prostrate with grief. At the time Jefferson's wife died, he had retired from his position as governor of Virginia, drafted *Notes on Virginia*, and looked forward to a life of retirement. "Before that event my scheme of life had been determined," he wrote of his wife's death in December. "I had folded myself in the arms of retirement, and rested all prospects of future happiness on domestic and literary objects. A single event wiped away all my plans and left me a blank which I had not the spirit to fill up."[6]

On her deathbed, Martha asked her husband that he not remarry, for she did not want her children brought up by another woman. Jefferson consigned his daughter Maria to the care of Frances Eppes, and traveled with his daughter Martha to France, where he served as ambassador. After the death of

Lucy, he sent for his youngest daughter to accompany him. Upon his return to the United States in 1789, Martha became engaged to Thomas Mann Randolph, Jr., her third cousin.[7] Though Jefferson thought the odds fourteen to one "that in marriage she will draw a blockhead," he was pleased with her choice and described her future husband as "a young gentleman of genius, science, and honorable mind."[8] They married on February 23, though Martha's loyalties remained, predominantly, to her father.[9] Jefferson's first grandchild, from this union, was born on January 13, 1791. He called the girl Anne Cary, a name that belonged to both sides of the family.

On October 13, 1797, Mary married John Wayles Eppes, the eldest of Uncle and Aunt Eppes's children. "I now see our fireside formed into a group," he wrote to Martha, "no one member of which has a fibre in their composition which can ever produce any jarring or jealousies among us. . . . In order to keep us all together . . . I think to open and resettle the plantation of Pantops for them."[10] He also gave Maria some advice, which is reflected in several of the poems gathered in his newspaper clippings book: "[H]armony in the marriage state is the very first object to be aimed at . . . a husband finds his affections wearied out by a constant string of little checks and obstacles."[11] Though Jefferson had hoped his daughter would settle near Monticello, the newlywed couple accepted Eppes's father's gift of a plantation near Bermuda Hundred. For this reason, and because of her own sense of diminishment compared with Martha, Mary did not become as close to her father.[12]

During the years he served as president, when he was clipping these poems, Martha served as hostess at the White House on only two occasions: from mid-November 1802 to January 1803; and from December 2, 1805, through May 1806.[13] When Jefferson returned to Monticello, she had reason to complain that he was distracted by official duties and could not attend to his grandchildren. Jefferson reminded his family of his public duties, but the truth is that he saw his family on a limited basis until his retirement from the presidency in 1809. The poems that appear in this collection seem to be as much about an ideal unrealized as one he actually enjoyed. "Despite the pain and the sorrow, perhaps because of them," Merrill Peterson has written, "he came to prize domestic felicity above any other and would have gladly traded worldly fame for a larger portion of it."[14] Domesticity was a part of the two-sphere system of life in Virginia, however. Jan Lewis argued that Jefferson used his daughters as "replacements for their departed mother (and) the handmaidens of their father's happiness: their primary function in life was to make him happy. No wonder both would later tell their father that they loved him above all; that is exactly what he had trained them to do."[15]

Whatever its origins, Jefferson's dedication to his extended family was unwavering. References to a clippings book, kept by his granddaughters or by Jefferson himself, surface continually in the family correspondence.[16] "Whenever an opportunity occurred, he sent us books," his granddaughter Virginia Trist remembered, "and he never saw a little story or piece of poetry in a newspaper, suited to our ages and tastes, that he did not preserve it and send it to us; and from him we learnt the habit of making these miscellaneous collections, by pasting in a little paper book made for the purpose any thing of the sort that we received from him or got otherwise."[17] Jefferson continued to discuss poetry in his correspondence, advising his granddaughters to "strengthen your memory by getting pieces of poetry by heart."[18] He instilled values in his granddaughters, guiding their intellectual and social development. They came to share his love of literature through the scrapbooks they kept. The process exemplifies the Romantic theories of education Wordsworth described in the closing lines of *The Prelude* (1801), published during the first year of Jefferson's presidency: "what we have loved, / Others will love, and we will teach them how."[19] The emphasis was not on mastering an abstract body of knowledge, but on doing so in a way that was personally meaningful.

In the last year of his term as president, Jefferson wrote a charming letter to his granddaughter Cornelia Randolph, on December 26, 1808, which underscores the scrapbooks the family compiled as a bridge between generations. "I congratulate you, my dear Cornelia, on having acquired the valuable art of writing. How delightful to be enabled by it to converse with an absent friend as if present! To this we are indebted for all our reading; because it must be written before we can read it. To this we are indebted for the Iliad, Aeneid, the Columbiad, Henriad, Dunciad, and now, for the most glorious poem of all, the Terrapiniad, which I now inclose to you. This sublime poem consigns to everlasting fame the greatest achievement in war ever known to ancient or modern time: in the battle of David and Goliath, the disparity between the combatants was nothing in comparison to our case."[20] Unfortunately, the "Tarrapiniad" has proved difficult to locate,[21] but the poem may have linked the turtle with Jefferson's embargo policy of nonengagement.

Jefferson wrote moving letters to his granddaughters, but his notion of domesticity has left him open to criticism. Even sympathetic biographers such as Dumas Malone acknowledged that Jefferson could sometimes be an overbearing father: "if Patsy had been less aware of her father's limitless kindness, she might have found some of his exhortations rather hard to bear."[22] Several of his letters suggest that he had a narrow view of women (even for his time), as if they existed solely to comfort men. "When Jefferson rhapsodized about the happiness of home, he assumed that his daughters would always love him;

he never had to worry about earning their love," Jan Lewis has written.[23] Jefferson certainly considered this complaint during his own lifetime by clipping poems that addressed it. In "Woman's Hard Fate," for example, the speaker stated:

> How wretched is poor Woman's fate!
> No happy change her fortune knows:
> Subject to Man, in ev'ry state;
> How can she then be free from woes?

The poem then enumerated women's woes.

> In youth, a Father's stern command,
> And jealous eyes, control her will:
> A lordly Brother watchful stands,
> To keep her closer captive still.

> The tyrant Husband next appears,
> With awful and contracted brow:
> No more a Lover's form he wears;
> Her Slave's become her Sov'reign now.[24]

With his sense of eighteenth-century balance[25] and complementarity, however, Jefferson included "The Answer." The "father's stern command" of the first poem became "a father's tender love" in the second.

> How happy is a Woman's fate!
> Free from care, and free from woe;
> Secure of Man in ev'ry state,
> Her Guardian-god below.

> In youth, a Father's tender love,
> And well-experienc'd eye,
> Refrain her mind, too apt to rove,
> Enamour'd with a toy.

> Suppose her with a Brother blest —
> A Brother, sure, is kind:
> But in the Husband stands fondest,
> The Father, Brother, Friend.[26]

Jefferson could preach in patriarchal tones in letters to his daughters, but he obviously had a more empathetic side that allowed him to sympathize with the role Virginian society assigned them, even as he accepted the status quo.

Often it was a satirist such as John Wilmot (Peter Pindar) who seemed most adept at getting this balance right. Jefferson collected seventeen poems by Wilmot (more than by any other poet), poems that treat both public and private life. He may well have appreciated Wilmot's hard-hitting commentary on Great Britain, though he also collected jeu d'esprits such as "Conscience"[27] and "The Owl and the Parrot," where the political message was subsumed, as in La Fontaine. With worldly wisdom, not to say weariness, "The Owl and the Parrot" painted a portrait of the benefits and drawbacks of marriage. The Parrot "had all she wanted — meat & drink, — washing & lodging — full enough, I think," but soon found that the Owl she married did not satisfy her wishes. Jefferson recognized that both genders could be dissatisfied with the sacrifices they made to enter the golden cage of matrimony.

Some of the poems in this collection challenge Aristotle's golden mean, and may surprise Jefferson's critics, such as the proto-feminist poem "Women,"[28] written, ironically enough, by the young radical and future Tory, Robert Southey. The last line — "Perhaps with justice you this creed advance / Had women wit, puppies could stand no chance" — is interesting because Jefferson followed eighteenth-century usage (as in Richardson's *Clarissa*, for instance) in referring to inexperienced men as "puppies," whose company should be avoided.[29] Jefferson respected accomplished women, as his friendship with Maria Cosway proves, and as the sheer volume of his clippings by Williams, Opie, Barbauld, and others suggests. Though his *Literary Commonplace Book* includes a number of misogynist passages gleaned from classical writers — reflecting, perhaps, his difficult relationship with his mother — Jefferson's mature collection is more wistful, dwelling on the pleasures of romantic love. He thought enough of his daughters' intellect to insist that they read Cervantes in the original, and of his granddaughters' to encourage them to start their own libraries.

Jefferson admired women not only as a father, but also as a man. Some of his selections are lascivious and libertine, celebrating a woman's kiss or the pleasures of romance. These qualify as sentimental or even domestic poems, however, for they describe the pleasures of courtship, the thrill of the pressing hand. For Jefferson, libertinism is closely related to such courtship rituals. As in the poem by Peter Pindar, pleasant feelings flow from being in love. But there was a darker side. "A Brief Epistle on Courtship" seemed to revisit the discomfort Jefferson must have faced in wooing his previously married wife, Martha Wayles Skelton. Perhaps his own shyness kept him from becoming, once again, "anxious to obtain a wife."[30] The conclusion to this poem provides a fitting coda to Jefferson's epistolary romance with Maria Cosway:

> I would not wish my notions to be known;
> But truly, I have thought, the ills that wait
> On Courtship, are so numerous and so great
> 'Tis better far — to let the thing alone.

And Jefferson did "let the thing alone," until the age of twenty-nine, when he married an experienced wife who was also a widower with a son. That Jefferson had a sense of humor about the strange mixture of eros and sentimentality that fueled his relationships with women seems clear by his appreciation of such Sternian poems as "On a Long Nose." In this poem, a person with a long nose was described as a "Narcissist"; for Sterne, however, the long nose indicated sexual prowess.[31] Jefferson's purchase of Sterne's Sermons, in 1765, was "one of the earliest book transactions recorded in Jefferson's life."[32] A month before leaving for France, Jefferson ordered the five-volume complete works of Sterne; he owned a copy of *Sentimental Journey* as early as 1768, purchasing pocket-sized editions of Sterne in 1789 for his journey through Italy, and in 1804, as president.[33]

Jefferson enjoyed Sterne's and Moore's erotic sentimentality, but was not led into the kind of public avowal of libertinism that marked Byron's literary emulation of Moore in such works as *Fugitive Pieces*. A poem titled "The Affectionate Heart," pasted in the clippings book twice, shows Jefferson's interest in cultivating affectionate feelings toward others that had no erotic charge at all.

> Let the great man his treasure possessing,
> Pomp and splendour forever attend:
> I prize not the shadowy blessing,
> I ask the affectionate friend.[34]

Cottle's late-eighteenth-century nod to friendship recalled one reason why Jefferson described the post of presidency as not "enviable, as it affords little exercise for the social affections . . . the heart would be happier enjoying the affections of a family fireside."[35] Poetry, by contrast, exercised the human heart. Cottle's affectionate relationship with Coleridge was, in large part, responsible for Coleridge's success as a poet in Bristol, and then nationally. Cottle was a crucial resource for Coleridge, encouraging his efforts and publishing his first verse, and Dennie did much to help Coleridge's reputation in the United States.

Attracted to poets such as Cottle, Jefferson enjoyed the limitless claims that anonymous newspaper versifiers might make for the human heart.

> What is fame, bidding envy defiance,
> The idol and bane of mankind,
> What is wit, what is learning or science,
> To the heart that is steadfast and kind?[36]

If friendship was based on reciprocal affection, libertine desire subordinated one gender to the other. Women, to remain a blessing to men, should not become pedants or pedagogues, as Moore suggested in "When Time, who steals our years away":

> Never mind how the pedagogues profess,
> You want not the antiquity's stamp;
> The lip, that's so scented with roses
> Oh! Never must smell of the lamp.[37]

Thomas Moore's poem continued in this vein, celebrating the intoxication of sexual attraction.

> Old Chloe, whose withering kisses
> Have long set the loves at defiance,
> Now, down with the science of blisses,
> May fly to the blisses of science.[38]

The anti-intellectual tone of Moore's poems recalls Wordsworth's "The Tables Turned," where he instructed William to "close thy books": "Come forth into the light of things, / Let nature be your teacher." Something of the same strain occurs in Moore's poem, written only a few years after, though Moore casts his argument in more libertine and perhaps self-interested terms than Wordsworth:

> But for *you* to be buried in books,
> Oh, Fanny, they're pitiful sages,
> Who could not in *one* of your looks,
> Read more than in *millions of pages*[39]

Visitors to Monticello return with handbags that state I CANNOT LIVE WITHOUT BOOKS, but Jefferson clearly hoped women could live without them, especially when they complicated his epicurean philosophy by being "buried" in them.

As the witticism on paper suggests, Jefferson did not collect poetry for purely aesthetic reasons: In some ways, this collection reads like an autobiography of his polymath mind, showing his love of women, gardening, wine drinking,[40] segars,[41] and retirement. In some poems, such as "Conjugal Love,"[42] Jefferson managed to fuse political and erotic sentiments.

> What, though no grants of royal donors,
> With pompous titles, grace our blood? —
> We'll shine in more substantial honours:
> And, to be noble, we'll be good.

Jefferson apparently took pride in cutting out a poem that included an emotion so appropriate to the Republican party: "The rich, the great, shall think, and wonder, / How they respect such little folk." Even a poem such as *Mirror for Magistrates* could reinforce this thought.

Jefferson's interest in how the domestic and the political could be linked is not surprising in a man who foregrounded the pursuit of happiness as a public and private right. Jefferson deliberately juxtaposed two poems on contentment that make reference to these two spheres. The first is titled "To Content."[43]

> Falsely we think that change of place,
> Or alter'd circumstance, can please,
> Can from the soul its canker chace,
> When Discontent's the dire disease
> In vain the wretch his native land
> Forsakes, and seeks a foreign sky;
> Care follows to the distant strand,
> He never from himself can fly.

The second stanza of "In Praise of Content"[44] mirrors Jefferson's comments to his daughter after he retired from the presidency.

> With passions unruffl'd, untainted with pride,
> By reason my life let me square,
> The wants of my nature are cheaply supply'd
> And the rest are but folly and care.

Though previously consigned to oblivion, "On Content" has been recently attributed, mistakenly, to Nathaniel Hawthorne, who copied the poem in his own commonplace book.[45] This link between Jefferson and Hawthorne's literary tastes is suggestive, and borne out by their shared fascination with Thomas Green Fessenden's work. When Hawthorne wrote his moving account of Fessenden's life, he humanized Fessenden by describing his domestic environment and avoiding references to his political satires as beyond the scope of the *American Spectator*.

Perhaps the most significant theme that unites poems in this section is the eighteenth-century theme of retirement. It is almost as if Jefferson was indulging in the fantasy of retirement at the very moment when he was most fully embroiled in affairs of state. Monticello represented Jefferson's idealization of what retirement might offer him; poems such as "The Mansion of Rest" and "The Pleasure of Retirement"[46] reflect this ideal. What distinguishes the poems Jefferson collected from other eighteenth-century poems on the topic is their focus on sanguine hopes, as in the poem "To-morrow":

> In the downhill of life, when I find I'm declining,
> May my life no less fortunate be;
> Than a snug elbow chair can afford for reclining,
> And a cot that o'er looks the wide sea,
> With an ambling pad poney to pace o'er the lawn,
> While I carrol away idle sorrow;
> And blithe as the lark that each day hails the dawn,
> Look forward with hope for *to-morrow*.

It is easy (if ahistorical) to consider Jefferson's taste in verse as unfortunate. Yet these poems articulate sentiments he expressed in his letters to his granddaughters and gave him fortitude to bear the travails of everyday life.

> Let the base traitor heap up gold;
> The price of his dear country sold,
> By perfidy made great.[47]

With the embargo, as with the American Revolution, mercenary motives were often at odds with his republican virtues. Jefferson's policy of embargo with Great Britain required self-sacrifice from American citizens. In his own life, Jefferson held public office for so long that he ended up in considerable debt Monticello was sold on the auction block on July 22, 1828.[48] Perhaps a poem such as "The Pleasure of Retirement" consoled him with the thought of private benefits for the public sacrifices he made.

Wordsworth's *Michael* thought the sheepfold he built with his son, Luke would be "a kind of permanent rallying point for their domestic feelings."[4]

Jefferson's poems on the domestic affections, which include his retirement poems, serve a similar function. That poetry was not peripheral to Jefferson's life seems clear. During his wife's final illness, Jefferson traded lines from *Tristram Shandy* with her. His wife wrote, "Time wastes too fast: every letter I trace tells me with what rapidity life follows my pen, the days and hours of it are flying over our heads like clouds of [a] windy day never to return — more every thing presses on — ." When she became too weak to go on, Jefferson continued Sterne's lines: "and every time I kiss thy hand to bid adieu, every absence which follows it, are preludes to that eternal separation which we are shortly to make!" Rhys Isaac noted that "Thomas kept that scrap of paper, wrapped around a lock of Martha's hair till the end of his days; it was almost the only writing by Martha he did not deliberately destroy."[50] Sterne's *Tristram Shandy*, like the poetry Jefferson collected, allowed him to communicate with members of his family in times of duress.

When he was on his own deathbed, Jefferson directed his daughter Martha to several poems he had written, which helped him communicate his feelings for her. At least one of them was preserved:

> A Death-bed Adieu from Th. J. to M. R.
> Life's visions are vanished, its dreams are no more;
> Dear friends of my bosom, why bathed in tears?
> I go to my fathers, I welcome the shore
> Which crowns all my hopes or which buries my cares.
> Then farewell, my dear, my lov'd daughter, adieu!
> The last pang of life is in parting from you!
> Two seraphs await me long shrouded in death;
> I will bear them your love on my last parting breath.[51]

Greek and Christian images of the afterlife jostle for supremacy in this fascinating poem. Charon brings Jefferson's soul across the river Styx and Acheron only to be greeted by Christian "seraphs," presumably his wife and daughter. Jefferson's occlusion of the feminine ("I go to my fathers") is as interesting as the nautical and monarchical metaphors emphasized through enjambment ("I welcome the shore / Which crowns all my hopes or which buries my cares"). Providing two competing figurative representations of the afterlife ("crowns" or "buries"), Jefferson faces the implications of his philosophical skepticism with courage.

CHARM FOR ENNUI.
A MATRIMONIAL BALLAD;
By William Hayley, Esq.

Ye couples, who meet under love's smiling star,
Too gentle to skirmish, too soft e'er to jar:
Tho' cover'd with robes, from joy's richest tree,
Near the couch of delight lurks the damon Ennui.

Let the muse's gay lyre, like Ithuriel's bright spear,
Keep this fiend, ye sweet brides, from approaching your ear
Since you know the squat toad's infernal *spirit*,
Never listen, like Eve, to the devil Ennui.

Let no groom of your hall, no shade of your bower,
Make you think you behold this malevolent power;
Like a child in the dark, what you fear you will see;
Take courage — away flies the phantom Ennui.

O trust me, the powers both of person and mind,
To defeat this sly foe, full sufficient you'll find;
Should your eyes fail to kill him, with keen repartee
You can *sink* the flat boat of th'invader Ennui.

If a cool *non-chalance* o'er your sposa should spread,
For vapours will rise e'en on Jupiter's head,
O ever believe it from jealousy free!
A thin passing cloud, not the fog of Ennui.

Of tender complainings, though love be the theme,
O beware, my sweet friends! 'tis a dangerous scheme;
And tho often 'tis try'd, mark the *pauvre mari*
Thus by kindness enclos'd in the coop of Ennui.

Let confidence rising, such meanness above,
Crown the discord of doubt in the music of love;
Your *duette* shall thus charm in the natural key.
No sharps from vexation, no flats from Ennui.

But to you, happy husbands, in matters more nice,
The muse, tho' a maiden, now offers advice;
O drink, not so keen your bumper of glee;
E'en Extacy's cup has some dregs of Ennui.

POEMS OF FAMILY

Though love for your lips fill with nectar his bowl,
Though his warm bath of blessings inspirit your soul,
O swim not too far on Rapture's high sea,
Lest you sink, unawares, in the gulph of Ennui.

Impatient of law, passion oft will reply,
"Against limitations I'll plead till I die;"
But Chief Justice Nature rejects the vain plea,
And such culprits are doom'd to the gaol of Ennui.

When husband and wife are of honey too fond,
They're like poison'd carp at the top of a pond;
Together they gape o'er a cold dish of tea,
Two muddy sick fish in the net of Ennui.

O Indolence most, ye mild couples, beware!
For the myrtles of love oft hide her soft snare;
The fond doves in her net from his pounce cannot flee,
But the ark in the morn 'scapes the demon Ennui.

Let cheerful good humour, the sunshine of life,
With smiles in the maiden, illumine the wife;
And mutual attention, in equal degree,
Keep Hymen's bright chain from the rust of Ennui.

To the graces together, O fail not to bend,
And both to the voice of the muses attend;
So Minerva for you shall with Cupid agree,
And preserve your chaste flame from the smoke of Ennui!

1:80/77

Hayley was a generous man who helped Cowper and corresponded with Blake. The poem works through a series of oppositions (tuned/flat; clouds/clear skies; bright chain/rust; bright flame/smoke), mixing neoclassical references to Minerva and Cupid with allusions to Eve and contemporary secular language, comparing "Nature" to a pompous "Chief Justice." *Minerva* is another name for Athena, goddess of Justice. Eve listened to the devil "Ennui" (like a squat toad whispering in her ear) with disastrous results. The ninth stanza vividly portrays a quarreling couple as "poison'd carp at the top of a pond."

Jefferson warned his daughter about the dangers of Ennui as the most potent challenge to happiness. Hayley's rather cynical poem balanced the sentimental verse ("The Wedding Ring") that also appears in this collection.

PARNASSIAN SHRUBBERY.

... *"With sweetest flow'rs enrich'd,*
From various gardens cull'd with care."

THE LADIES' MAN

AN EXTRACT.

[Anonymous]

Not all the favors Coquettes shew,
And smiles the Fop is heir to,
Could tempt me to become a Beau,
And feel as Beaux appear to.

No malice, no Envy inspires
    The Bard his advice to disclose;
The favors a *Fopling* acquires,
    Will never disturb my repose.

Though *sad*, he must always seem *gay*;
    Though *restless*, appear at his ease;
Must *talk* when he's nothing to say,
    And *laugh* when there's nothing to please.

Must never look shy nor afraid,
    Approve of nonsensical *chatter*,
And smile at whatever is said,
    Good, bad, or indifferent, no matter.

If Nancy says, *"Croesus** was poor,"
    'Tis his to say *"yes,"* and agree;
Or Charlotte, "two three's are but four,"
    "Correct, Ma'am, just four they must be."

Should Susan remark, "it is *hot*,"
    His answer must be — "it is so;"
If Mary observes, "it is not,"
    To *her* he consents, and says *"no."*

---

* Croesus was the last king of Lydia (560–546 BC) whose affluence made his name a byword for wealth.[52]

Would any dispense with his mind,
    Bow, wheedle, sigh, whimper and pray;
And *hoodwink'd*, be led by the blind,
    To *such* I have only to say —

Quit *Paley*, and study to *please*,
    Read *Chesterfield's* system of laws —
And then you must *balk* at your ease,
    In the *sunshine* of *female* applause.

                  1:82/79

Accused of libertinism in his own lifetime,[53] Jefferson clipped poems that parody such behavior. William Paley and Lord Chesterfield's works appear in Jefferson's library.[54] Paley's book is filled with sound, moral advice; Chesterfield's letters to his son were proverbial for their cynicism. The poem pits true merit against mere foppery.

The author of this poem offered a personal perspective on libertinism. The widower who built Monticello and counted the peas in his garden may have balked at maintaining silence when corrected. "If Nancy says, '*Croesus* was poor,' / 'Tis his to say '*yes*,' and agree; / Or Charlotte, 'two three's are but four,' / 'Correct, Ma'am, just four they must be.'" He could not "balk" at his ease "in the sunshine of female applause."

The Female Auctioneer.
By Mr. Upton.

WELL, here I am, and what of that?
Methinks, I hear you cry;
Why, I am come and that is pat,
To *sell*, if you will *buy*:

   A *Female Auctioneer* I stand,
Yet, not to seek for self:
Ah! No! the *lot* I have in hand,
Is now to *sell myself!*
     And I'm going, going, going, going!
      Who bids for me?

   Ye *Bachelors*, I look at you:
And pray don't deem me rude;
Nor rate me either *Scol'd* or *Shrew*,
A *Coquette*, or a *Prude*:

   My *hand* and *heart* I offer fair,
And should you *buy* the *lot*,
I swear I'll make you e'er my care,
When *Hyman* ties the *Knot*.
     And I'm going, going, going, going!
      Who bids for me?

   Tho' some may deem me pert or so,
Who deal in idle strife;
Pray, where's the *girl*. I wish to know,
Who'u'd not become a Wife?

At least, I own, I really would
In spite of all alarms;
Dear Batchelors, now be so good —
Do take me to your arms;
    For I'm going, going, going, going!
        Who bids for me?

1:83

.

In this comic poem, a woman desires marriage enough to take the drastic step of auctioning herself off: "Pray, where's the *girl*. I wish to know, / Who'u'd not become a Wife?" The question may not have been entirely rhetorical — women enjoyed more freedom after marriage than before. Maria, Jefferson's youngest daughter, seemed to enjoy the freedom that came from her marriage to John Wayles Eppes. Unlike Martha, her oldest sister, she chose to live at some remove from her father's vigilant eye.

A SQUINT AT THE LADIES.

Parodied from the Sporting Magazine.

[Anonymous]

Beauty there's something to hide and reveal,
There's a thing which we Decency call;
The Ladies of *Lynn* may show a great deal,
But the Ladies of *Boston* show all!

The taste of the men we know to be such,
That exposure will appetites pall;
Low tuckers I think display quite too much,
But the Ladies of *Boston* show all!

Dear girls, while your features enrapture each heart;
Complain not your power is too small;
The Graces' attraction we're charm'd with a part,
But the Ladies of *Boston* show all!

Mary had suitors wherever she came,
Her shape was so tastefully small;
Her ankle to view set my blood in a flame,
But at *Boston*, the show would be — ALL!

The tip of the elbow below the white cuff,
Makes my heart bounce as tho' 'twas a ball;
Such sweet little sights are pleasant enough,
But the Ladies of *Boston* show all!

Tho' you wish to enchant — this lesson should strike
Lasses fair, brown or black, short or tall;
Be content in shewing 'tis all that we like,
But for God's sake, dear girls, don't show all!!

SQUINTISSIMO.

Lynn, Sept. 1806

1:84/81

Women's dress had become increasingly revealing. This poem registers the puritan anxiety that attended this change. The poet contrasts Mary's taste in showing only her ankle with the ladies of Boston who "show all!" Implicit is a contrast between manners appropriate to the city and the country.

ADVICE.

[Anonymous]

Says young Damon, one day, to his prudent old Sire,
"Sir, to rise in the world is my warmest desire;
"Pray, then, how shall I quickest, and best, become great,
"And command much respect, Sir?" — *"Why, get an estate."*
"What will make me at dinners, and spouting clubs, summus,
"And make wiltings adore and applaud me, Sir?"— *"Nummus"*
"Should a widow attract by her beauty and sense,
"Pray what arguments first should I use?" — *"3 per cents."*
"But, young Delia I long in these arms to enfold:
"What will gain me her love and affection, Sir?"— *"Gold."*
"What will dive into closets, and secrets unlock,
"And discover intrigues and cabals, Sir?" — *"Bank Stock."*
"Will aught make me support whate'er Ministers mention,
"And give them my vote, right or wrong?" —*"Yes, a pension."*
"Suppose some disorder should ruin my health,
"What will bring me relief in my misery?"— *"Wealth."*
"As to spend all I gain, should I prove such a ninny
"What will cure all my ills in this world, Sir?"— *"A penny."*
"But if nothing is left, then you might as well stay,
"Charon won't take you, e'en to the De'el, without pay."

Shakespeare appears to have been of the same opinion.
    "O the charity of a penny cord!
    "It sums up thousands in a trice:
    "You have no true debtor and creditor but it —
    "Of what's past, is, and to come, 'tis the discharge."
                Cymb. Act 5. Se. 4

                      1:85/82

efferson's increasing indebtedness may have ed him to view this poem ruefully, for he was orced to start a nail factory to defray expenses ecause of his extended public service and the xpenses he incurred in building Monticello. ive years after leaving the presidency, he sold is books to the Library of Congress. At his eath, his Monticello estate was auctioned off. In his case, getting an estate was really no solution, though it did help foster the perception of him as "great" during his lifetime. While the poem surveys various forms of wealth, it proceeds ironically from the wealth of an estate to the absurd idea that a penny will cure the "ills in this world."

The Old Wedding Ring.

[Anonymous]

I SEE, my dear, your wedding token
Is grown so thin, 'tis almost broken,
   By days of service told;
Its alter'd form and weaken'd frame
Whispers that we shall be the same:
   In short — we're growing old.

'Tis now just two and twenty years,
Since with alternate hopes and fears
   Our beating bosoms heav'd:
When at the altar's sacred base
This golden pledge of fond embrace
   Was given and receiv'd.

Then was it polish'd, bright and neat,
Its form a circle quite complete,
   Stamp'd with the mark of truth:
So to the newly wedded pair
Each prospect seemed bright and fair;
   The fond ideas of youth.

But we have found and others must,
That joys are only joys on trust;
   That troubles will accrue.
Still you and I should not complain,
For though we've had our share of pain,
   We've had our pleasures too.

Can we forget those happy days,
When oft we join'd in sports and plays,
   Our infants to delight?
Or when we turn'd the instructive page,
Forming them in maturer age
   "To do the thing that's right?"

This was the solace and the balm
Of early life; and still the charm
   Maintains its gladd'ning powers:
Though growing now to men's estate,
We see them come with hearts elate
   To cheer our social hours.

As for this ring, we'll lay it by,
A new one shall its place supply,
   And this no more adorn;
Except on days of festive note,
When your new gown and my best coat
   For compliment are worn.

1:87/84

For this writer, love and especially marriage are
marked by public display. A new ring is purchased and the old one laid aside, "Except in
days of festive note," when the couple will wear
their best gown and coat "for compliment."

KISSING.
By Peter Pindar, Esq.

When we dwell on the lips of the lass we adore,
    Not a pleasure in nature is missing;
May his soul be in Heaven, he deserv'd it I'm sure,
    Who was first the inventor of kissing.

Master Adam, I very well think was the man,
    Whose discovery will ne'er be surpass'd,
Well, since the sweet game with creation began,
    To the end of the world may it last!

1:87/84

Peter Pindar posits Adam as the "first inventor
of kissing." By avoiding the moral aspects of
creation as described in Genesis, Pindar portrays the Garden of Eden as a place where "the
sweet game with creation began."

SONG

FROM THE GERMAN.

[Anonymous]

WHAT feels the soften'd bosom,
　　The gentler virtues sway,
Best suits the muse's favour,
　　And breathes the sweetest lay.
While sympathy awakens
　　Attention's ready ear,
And spreads the soft infection,
　　And prompts the pleasing tear.

Let poets sing of heroes,
　　And all the pomp of war,
And such as pant for glory
　　Attend with eager ear;
Be mine an humbler triumph,
　　My theme the rural plain,
My boast, the simple numbers
　　That charm the village swain.

And would my blooming Daphne,
　　But lend her ear the while,
And one kind look wou'd deign me,
　　And one approving smile; —
I'd envy not the poet,
　　Though wreathes adorn his brow,
And envy not the hero,
　　That bade his numbers flow.

　　　　　　　　　　1:95/92

Jefferson celebrated rural life as a subject that "charm[ed] the village swain." The poet casts himself in the role of Apollo, who pursued Daphne until she turned into a laurel tree to escape him. Love is a "soft infection," in this poem, which gives a slightly darker coloring to the image of Cupid shooting Apollo with his dart: "Two diff'rent shafts he from his quiver draws; / One to repel desire, and one to cause."[55]

MODESTY.
[Anonymous]

SERENE is the morning, the lark leaves his nest,
    And sings a salute to the dawn;
The sun with his splendor illumines the east,
    And brightens the dew on the lawn.

While the sons of debauch to indulgence give way,
    And slumber the prime of their hours,
Let us, my dear Mary, the garden survey,
    And make our remarks on the flow'rs!

The gay color'd tulip observe as you walk,
    How splendid the gloss of its vest!
How proud! and how stately it stands on its stalk,
    In beauty's variety drest.

From the rose, the carnation, the pink and the clove
    What odours delightfully spring!
The breeze wafts a richer perfume to the grove,
    That brushes the leaves with its wing.

Apart from the rest in her purple array,
    The violet humbly retreats;
In modest concealment she peeps on the day,
    Yet none can excel her in sweets.

So humble, that though with unparallell'd grace,
    She might e'en a palace adorn;
She oft in the hedge hides her innocent face,
    And grows at the foot of the thorn.

1:96/93

In "The Tables Turned," Wordsworth wrote "Let Nature be your Teacher!"[56] — a sentiment that also finds expression in this poem. Mary and the poet enjoy the pleasures of the morning while "the sons of debauch" nurse a hangover and "slumber the prime of their hours." (Jefferson himself took pride in rising with the sun and bathing his feet in ice water.) Nature's flowers, particularly the rose and carnation, give delightful "odours" in spring; these showy flowers contrast with the humble violet that "peeps on the day, / Yet none can excel her in sweets."

Ellen Coolidge remembered how Jefferson involved his grandchildren in planting in his garden after his retirement:

"I remember the planting of the first hyacinths and tulips, and their subsequent growth. The roots arrived labeled, each one with a fancy name. There was "Marcus Aurelius" and the "King of the Gold Mine." . . . Eagerly and with childish delight, I studied this brilliant nomenclature, and wondered what strange and surprisingly beautiful creations I should see arising from the ground when the spring returned; and these precious roots were committed to the earth under my grandfather's own eye, with his beautiful grand-daughter Anne standing by his side, and a crowd of happy young faces, of younger grandchildren, clustering round to see the progress, and inquire anxiously the name of each separate deposit."[57]

THE BUTTERFLY'S BALL and
THE GRASSHOPPER's FEAST.
[William Roscoe]

COME, take up your hats, and away let us haste
To the Butterfly's ball, and the Grasshopper's feast;
The trumpeter Gadfly has summoned the crew,
And the revels are now only waiting for you.

On the smooth shaven grass, by the side of a wood,
Beneath a broad oak, which for ages had stood,
See the children of earth, and tenants of air,
To an evening's amusement together repair.

And there came the Beetle, so blind and so black,
Who carried the Emmet, his friend on his back;
And there came the Gnat, and the Draggon-fly too,
With all their relations, green, orange, and blue.

And there came the Moth, with her plumage of down,
And the Hornet, with jacket of yellow and brown,
Who with him the Wasp, his companion, did bring,
But they promis'd, that ev'ning, to lay by their sting.

Then the sly little Dorm[o]use peep'd out of his hole,
And led to the feast his blind cousin, the Mole;
And the Snail, with her horns peeping out of her shell,
Came, fatigued with the distance, the length of an ell.

A mushroom the table, and on it was spread
A water dock leaf, which their tablecloth made,
The viands were various, to each of their taste,
And the Bee brought the honey to sweeten the feast.

With steps more majestic the Snail did advance,
And he promised the gazers a minuet to dance;
And they all laugh'd so loud, that he drew in his head,
And went, in his own little chamber, to bed.

Then, as ev'ning gave way to the shadows of night,
Their watchman, the Glow-worm, came out with his light:
So home let us hasten, while yet we can see,
For no watchman is waiting for you, or for me!

1:96/93

Jefferson sent this poem to Ellen Coolidge to start her collection on March 1, 1807. "I send for Cornelia a little poem, the grasshopper's ball, to begin her collection. The Yankee story is for yourself." Roscoe's poem illustrates a close attention to nature that must have been as delightful to Ellen's sister Cornelia as it was to Jefferson himself. Jefferson also believed in his granddaughter's talents, noting that one day she would write books of her own.

This poem, by a poet from Liverpool, broke new ground in having no moral attached, unlike Anna Barbauld's *Lessons for Children*.

FROM THE PORT FOLIO.

[Anonymous]

AT a time when the pretty song of

> "Shepherds, I have lost my love,
> Have you seen my Anna."

was sung by every chambermaid; some wit, eager to satirize the *Grecian* style of dress, then introducing by the ladies, wrote a diverting parody which began

> "Lovers, I have lost my *waist*,
> Have you seen my *body?*"

As the ladies now discard all dress, except a kind of longer *chemise*, we present them with the following parody; and sincerely hope, that it may persuade them as the winter approaches, to purchase more flannel, and fewer muslins.

> Doctors, I have lost my health,
>   Where, O where's my vigour?
> No faithless swain, no act of stealth,
>   Reduc'd me to this figure.
>
> Plump and rosy was my face,
>   And graceful was my form,
> Till fashion deem'd it a disgrace
>   To keep my body warm.
>
> I sacrific'd to modish whim,
>   (What belle can ere forsake it?)
> To make myself genteel and slim
>   I stript me almost naked.

And naked thus I must remain
Till Fashion weds with Reason,
God grant they may united reign,
Before the frosty season.

1:96/93

In France, Madame de Recamier popularized the wearing of muslin; in England, Georgiana Spencer set impractical fashions for several decades, many of which found their way to the United States (the Spencer cap, for example). The taste for fashion and luxury was associated with England; in this poem, following fashion is compared, playfully, to losing one's reason: "Till Fashion weds with Reason, / God grant they may united reign, /

Before the frosty season." London satirists admonished Lady Georgiana, a great trend-setter in England, for wearing clothes that did not protect her from the cold.

Like "The Ladies Man," which takes the male point of view, this poem shows how foolish women enjoy the company of libertines, and dress in such a way as to attract them, "till Fashion weds with Reason."

ADDRESS TO MY SEGAR.

[Anonymous]

COMPANION of my leisure hours,
Sweet soft'ner of my care;
Court thy kind solacing aid,
Thou fragrant, *sweet Segar.*

To thee I'll constantly apply,
For thou art better far,
To soothe my cares, than fickle friends,
Thou fragrant, *sweet Segar.*

When troubles press, or friends deceive,
Or foes their hate declare;
One quaff of thy sweet incense cures,
Thou fragrant, *sweet Segar.*

When discontent prevails at home,
Abroad destructive war;
Thy kind exhilarating fumes
Cure all, thou *sweet Segar.*

With thee I can enjoy my friend,
And thou art better far,
Than pompous hall, or drawing room,
Thou fragrant, *sweet Segar.*

'Tis thou that lullest all my cares,
Drive on thy fiery car;
Perfume my cot with odors sweet,
Thou fragrant, *sweet Segar.*

Should wife's olfact'ry nerves reject,
And curse thy incens'd air;
Then, gently breathe thy sweet perfumes,
Thou fragrant, *sweet Segar.*

1:93–1:97/94

Though he did not smoke cigars and objected to growing tobacco, Jefferson cultivated pleasure in a country known for its puritanism, which is, perhaps, one of the most endearing things about him. Jefferson's epicurean philosophy may well be tied to his sanguine temperament, his optimism, and his belief in the "pursuit of happiness." He clipped poems praising cigars, potatoes, and violets, and others mocking snuff, bad razors, and other threats to domestic peace. He took a minute interest in the private lives of Americans, linking this to the pursuit of virtue in the new republic.

The following verses are quite sufficient to vindicate Mr. Moore's pretentions to genius. He is addressing a very young lady, who is supposed to have expressed her regret that she was not profoundly skilled in science and literature. [Port Folio.]

[Thomas Moore]

Never mind how the pedagogues profes[s],
    You want not the antiquity's stamp;
The lip, that's so scented with roses
    Oh! never must smell of the lamp.

Old C[h]loe, whose withering kisses
    Have long set the loves at defiance,
Now, down with the science of blisses,
    May fly to the blisses of science.

Young Sappho, for want of employment,
    Alone o'er her Ovid may melt,
Condemn'd but to read of enjoyment,
    Which wiser Corinna had felt.

But for *you* to be buried in books,
    Oh, Fanny, they're pitiful sages,
Who could not in *one* of your looks,
    Read more than in *millions of pages*.

Astronomy finds in your eye,
    Better lights than she studies above,
And music must borrow your sigh,
    As the melody dearest to love.

In ethics, 'tis you that can check
    In a minute their doubts and their quarrels,
Oh! shew but that mole on your neck,
    And 'twill soon put an end to their morals,

Your Arithmetic only can trip
    When to kiss and to count, you endeavor,
But eloquence glows on your lip,
    When you swear that you'll love me forever.

Thus you see what a brilliant alliance,
    Of arts is assembled in you.
A course of more exquisite science,
    Man never need with to go through.

And ah! if a fellow like me,
    May confer a diploma of hearts,
With my lip thus I seal your degree,
    My divine little Mistress of Arts!

                           1:98/95

Joseph Dennie's introduction to Moore's
poem indicates the high regard he had for the
Irish poet.

THE AFFECTIONATE HEART.

By Joseph Cottle.

Let the great man his treasures possessing,
Pomp and splendor forever attend:
I prize not the shadowy blessing,
First — the affectionate friend.

Though foibles may sometimes o'ertake him,
His footsteps from wisdom depart;
Yet, my spirit shall never forsake him,
If he own the affectionate heart.

Affection! thou soother of care,
Without thee unfriended we rove:
Thou canst make e'en the desert look fair,
And thy voice is the voice of the dove.

Mid the anguish that preys on the breast,
And the storms of morality's state:
What shall lull the afflicted to rest,
But the joys that on sympathy wait?

What is Fame, bidding Envy defiance,
The idol and bane of mankind;
What is wit, what is learning, or science,
To the heart that is stedfast and kind?

Even genius may weary the sight,
By too fierce and too constant a blaze;
But affection, mild planet of night!
Grows lovelier, the longer we gaze.

It shall thrive when the flattering forms
That encircle creation, decay:
It shall live mid the wide-wasting storms,
That beat on undistinguish'd away.

Then time, at the end of his race,
Shall expire with expiring mankind:
It shall stand on its permanent base;
It shall last 'till the wreck of the mind.

1:102/100

The fifth stanza of this poem aptly summarizes Jefferson's philosophy. In his letters to Maria Cosway on the head and the heart, Jefferson sought a balance between both human qualities. Surrounded by intelligent but contentious politicians in Washington, Jefferson preferred the company of sentimental friends. "Even genius may weary the sight, / By too fierce and too constant a blaze; / But affection, mild planet of night! / Grows lovelier, the longer we gaze." Wit and learning are nothing compared with "the heart that is stedfast and kind."

A great promoter of Wordsworth and Coleridge, Cottle displayed the qualities he celebrated in this poem. He once supported Coleridge's wife and children while Coleridge traveled in Malta.

The readers of *Love and Reason*, a ballad, by
Mr. Moore, and lately printed in the Port
Folio, will be pleased, as I persuade
myself, with the subjoined poem entitled
The Nursing of Love. Here, too, the poor
child arrives at an untimely end, but not
through the means of that terrible bug-
bear, Reason.

THE NURSING OF LOVE.
[W. Spencer]

Lapp'd on Cythera's golden sands,
    When True Love first was born of earth;
Long was the doubt what fost'ring hands
    Should tend and rear the glorious birth.

First Hebe claim'd the sweet employ:
    Her cup, her thornless flow'r, she said,
Would feed him best with health and joy,
    And cradle best his cherub-head.

But anxious Venus justly fear'd
    The tricks and changeful mind of youth;
Too mild the seraph, Peace, appear'd;
    Too stern, too cold, the matron, Truth.

Next Fancy claim'd him for her own;
    But Prudence disallow'd her right;
She deem'd her Iris-pinions shone
    Too dazzling for his infant sight.

To Hope awhile the charge was giv'n,
    And well with Hope the cherub throve;
Till Innocence came down from Heav'n,
    Sole guardian, friend, and nurse of Love!

Pleasure grew mad, with envious spite,
    When all preferr'd to her the sound;
She vow'd full vengeance for the slight,
    And soon success her purpose crown'd.

The traitress watch'd a sultry hour,
        When pillow'd on her blush-rose bed,
Tir'd Innocence, to slumber's pow'r
        One moment bow'd her virgin head;

Then Pleasure, on the thoughtless child,
        Her toys and sugar'd poisons prest;
Drunk with new joy, he heav'd, he smil'd,
        Reel'd, sunk — and died upon her breast.

The above is a translation, and, as you need
not be told, from a modern poet: I regret
that I cannot give you the author's name. It
is very possible that we have here the parent
of Love and Reason, which seems to be neither more nor less than an illustration of
one of the thoughts: Too cold, too stern, the
matron, Truth.

1:108/106

Juxtaposed with Thomas Moore's "Love and Reason," William Spencer's "The Nursing of Love" shows that Innocence is the true guardian of love, which Pleasure can destroy. Fancy, Prudence, and Hope prove to be less competent caretakers. This poem uses allegory to give a Christian coloring to Pagan myth — innocence seems to be a metonymy for virginity. The poem thus corrects the libertinism of Thomas Moore, which earned him critical reviews in England but not, surprisingly enough, in the United States. Spencer wrote a translation of Burger's "Leonora," which Jefferson also clipped.

A Ballad
By Th. Moore, Esq.

THOU hast sent me a flowery band
    And told me 'twas fresh from the field;
That the leaves were untouch'd by the hand,
    And the purest of odours would yield.

And indeed it is fragrant and fair;
    But if it were handled by thee,
It would bloom with a livelier air,
    And would surely be sweeter to me.

Then take it, and let it entwine
    Thy tresses, so flowing and bright;
And each little flow'ret will shine
    More rich than a gem to my sight.

Let the odorous gale of thy breath,
    Ambalm it with many a sigh;
Nay let it be wither'd to death
    Beneath the warm noon of thine eye.

And instead of the dew that it bears,
    The dew dropping fresh with the tree;
On its leaves let me number the tears
    That affection has stolen from thee!

1:109/107

If love is a jargon of compliments, as Byron suggested, Moore certainly mastered the vernacular. While Francis Jeffrey of the *Edinburgh Review* thought his lyrics too sensuous and (therefore) unmanly, Moore succeeded despite the Scottish lawyer's censures. Moore was not simply a poet who wrote during the Romantic period, after all, but one who incarnated its values: Irish nationalism, Catholic emancipation, and licentious love poems refined by sensibility.[58] When he performed at the pianoforte, he was every bit the Romantic poet: Men wept and women swooned, as Moore himself noted, somewhat immodestly, in his own *Journal*. Charming, yet touchy and quick to anger, Moore fought a duel with Jeffrey because of the latter's review of Moore's *Epistles, Odes, and Poems*, which appeared in 1806, and challenged Byron to a duel for mocking Moore's duel with Jeffrey in *English Bards*.

Song in Praise of Women.
[Anonymous]

Oft through trackless desarts straying,
 Unattended, unsupply'd:
Sorrow on my bosom preying,
 Comfort to my heart deny'd?
Man would treat a fellow creature,
 Now with friendship, now disdain:
But o'er woman's gentle nature
 Pity ever seem'd to reign.

Hearts with charity o'erflowing,
 Touch'd at sorrow's plaintive tale;
Lips, a soothing balm bestowing
 When the stings of woe assail;
No ungen'rous pride opposes
 Pity, with unkind delay;
But the female hand uncloses,
 Bounteous, as the op'ning day.

Form'd from nature's choicest treasures,
 Virtues all in her unite;
Life's short path she strews with pleasures,

Goddess of supreme delight!
Homely fare to me be given,
Sweet the limpid stream will prove,
Earth will be a little heaven,
With the woman that I love.

1:109/107

Jefferson continued to clip poems celebrating domestic life despite the death of his wife in 1782: "Earth will be a little heaven, / With the woman that I love." There is considerable pathos in Jefferson's being wedded to an ideal he could no longer achieve, but it is partly explained by the doctrine of the two spheres, which assigned women a domestic and men a worldly function. Jefferson's letters to his daughters from the White House suggest that he viewed them as "hearts with charity o'er-flowing," an alternative to the "ungen'rous pride" that characterized political life. Clipping poems in the White House allowed Jefferson to transport himself back to Monticello.

Through the verse he sent to his granddaughters and their visits to the White House, he continued the domestic life he enjoyed with his wife for ten years before her death in 1782. Martha visited the White House only twice, once with Mary from mid-November 1802 until January 1803; and a second time from December 2, 1805, until May 1806.[59] After ten years of married life, Jefferson cultivated a close relationship with his daughter Martha and his granddaughters, who became part of his extended family. Jefferson's obedience to his wife's wishes that he not remarry may well have increased his children's affection and protective feelings toward him.

POEMS OF FAMILY

SONG.

[Sir Charles Sedley]

Phyllis, men say that all my vows
    Are to thy fortune paid;
Alas, my heart he little knows,
    Who thinks my love a trade.

Were I of all these woods the lord,
    One berry from thy hand
More real pleasure would afford,
    Than all my large command.

My humble love has learnt to live
    On what the nicest maid,
Without a conscious blush, may give
 ·   Beneath, the myrtle shade.

                  1:109/107

In this poem, the speaker denies that he is a bounty hunter ("my heart he little knows, / Who thinks my love a trade") by stating that one berry from his beloved would mean more to him than all the lands he presumably stands to inherit by marrying her. The lascivious yet restrained subject matter of stanza three is as libertine, in its own way, as anything written by Moore.

Americans were a nation of newspaper readers by the early 1800s. Foreign visitors commented on the volume of newspaper print consumed by Americans. Irish and Scottish editors used their papers to educate readers, teaching them to read poetry and instructing them on how to enjoy it. "[T]he secret charm of a song, is to be admired for the delicacy of its thought, and the easy grace of its diction," this editor noted. If newspapers formed imagined communities for their readers, they also made them lifelong learners, in some cases replacing formal instruction.

A GLEE:

SUNG AT THE SOMERSET HOUSE LODGE OF MASONS.
Written by G. Dyer.
Set to music by R. Spotforth.

Lightly o'er the village green
Blue-ey'd Fairies sport unseen,
Round and round in circles gay —
Then at cock-crow flit away:
Thus, 'tis said, tho' mortal eye
Ne'er their merry freaks could spy,
Elves for mortals lisp the pray'r —
Elves are guardians of the Fair;
    Thus, like Elves, in mystic ring
    Merry Masons drink and sing.

Come then, brothers, lead along
Social rites and mystic song!
Tho' not Madam, Miss, or less
Could our mist'ries ever guess,
Nor could even learn'd Divine
Sacred Masonry define,

Round our Order closed we bind
Laws of love to all man!
    Thus, like Elves, in mystic ring
    Merry Masons drink and sing.

Health then, to each honest Man,
Friend to the Masonic plan!
Leaving Parsons grave to blunder,
Leaving Ladies fair to wonder,
Leaving THOMAS still to lie,
Leaving BETTY still to spy,
Round and round we push our
    Glass —
Round and round each toast his
    Lass
    Thus, like Elves, in mystic ring,
    Merry Masons drink and sing.

1:109/108

This poem documents Jefferson's interest in freemasonry. He cut five Masonic songs from newspapers and wrote a letter defending the society of the Illuminati from Abbe Barruel's intemperate attacks.[60] Washington and Monroe were Masons. Jefferson, who was as skeptical about evangelical religion as he was about mysticism, did not join this fraternal order. As an architect, he might have commented in interesting ways on the Masons' view of architecture as a metaphor for man's moral development.

The Weeping Mother.
A TRUE TALE.
[Anonymous]

IN tears I'll bathe my bonny bairn,
　　And press him to my bleeding heart;
And underneath yon moss-clad cairm,
　　We shall be laid, nae maer to part.

How fondly did a mother's breast,
　　Thy lengthen'd term of years presage,
To cheer her through life's dreary waste,
　　And shield her in declining age.

Thy ruddy cheeks, that glow'd yestre en,
　　Are new in death's pale liv'ry clad:
Cold are thy lips, and closed thy een,
　　And ilk a dimpling smile is fled.

Oh! wrap me and my bonny bairn,
　　Into a sheet as white as snaw,
And lay us underneath yon cairn,
　　Where sorrow's blast shall nae mair blaw,

Three days she raved in wild despair,
　　While floods her pallid cheeks did lave;
And aye she cried for evarmair,
　　Oh! lay me in my Willy's grave.

Indulgent heaven beheld her woe,
　　And sent the friendly mandate forth,
Which laid the Weeping Mother low,
　　With Willy in the clay cold earth.

1:112/111

"The Weeping Mother," a Scottish poem, depicts the grief of a woman who wishes to die alongside her child. She has her wish granted after three days. The poem is sentimental and slightly less bracing than Wordsworth's "The Thorn," which depicts a woman who is accused of murdering her child, or "Leonora," which also treats a woman's compulsion to join her lover, even if dead. "The Weeping Mother" may reflect Jefferson's grief over the loss of several children in infancy: Lucy Elizabeth (first); Lucy Elizabeth (second), who lived beyond her first year, Jane Randolph, and an unnamed son.

Mutual Love.
[Anonymous]

WHEN on thy bosom I recline,
Enraptur'd still to call thee mine,
   To call thee mine for life;
I glory in the sacred ties
Which modern wits and fools despise,
   Of husband and of wife.

One mutual flame inspires our bliss —
The tender look, the melting kiss,
   E'en years have not destroy'd;
Some sweet sensation, ever new,
Springs up and proves the maxim true,
   That love can ne'er be cloy'd.

Have I a wish! 'tis all for thee —
Hast thou a wish? 'tis all for me;
   So soft our moments move,
That angels look with ardent gaze,
Well pleas'd to see our happy days,
   And bid us live — and love,

If cares arise, (and cares will come)
Thy bosom is my softest home,
   I lull me there to rest,
And is there aught disturbs my fair?
I bid her sigh out all her care,
   And lose it in my breast.

I:112/III

The rationalist path Jefferson pursued in other areas of his life might have led him to become cynical about love, like Voltaire in *Candide*. This poem celebrates an ideal of marriage that Jefferson never surrendered. Twenty years after his wife's death, when he had lived most of his life as a bachelor, Jefferson cherished the company of his granddaughters and took pains to ensure that Martha lived close to Monticello.

POEMS OF FAMILY

THE OLD MAN's COMFORTS,
AND HOW HE GAINED THEM.
[Robert Southey]

YOU are old, Father William, the
    young man cried,
    The few locks that are left you
      are grey
You are hale, Father William, a
    hearty old man,
    Now tell me the reason, I pray.

In the days of my youth, Father
    William replied,
    I remember'd that youth would
      fly fast,
And abus'd not my health and my
    vigor at first,
    That I never might need them at
      last.

You are old Father William, the
    young man cried,
    And pleasures with youth pass
      away,
And yet you lament not the days
    that are gone,
    Now tell me the reason, I pray:

In the days of my youth, Father
    William replied,
    I remember'd that youth could
      not last;
I thought of the future, whatever I
    did,
    That I never might grieve for the
      past.

You are old, Father William, the
    young man cried,
    And life must be hastening away;
You are cheerful and love to con-
    verse upon death!
    Now tell me the reason, I pray.

I am cheerful, young man, Father
    William repli'd
    Let the cause thy attention
      engage —
In the days of my youth I remem-
    ber'd my God!
    And he hath not forgotten my
      age.

1:124

The tactless speaker in Southey's poem inspired Lewis Carroll's parody:

> "You are old, father William," the young
>   man said,
> "And your hair has become very white;
> And yet you incessantly stand on your
>   head —
> Do you think, at your age, it is right?"
> "In my youth," father William replied to
>   his son,
> "I feared it would injure the brain;
> But now that I'm perfectly sure I have none,
> Why, I do it again and again."

Jefferson stressed the importance of leading a moderate, orderly life and might have said, without irony, that "I thought of the future, whatever I did, / That I never might grieve for the past." Jefferson recommended constant employment to Martha as the best antidote to ennui. "Determine never to be idle," he wrote in 1787. "No person will have occasion to complain of the want of time who never loses any. It is wonderful how much may be done if we are always doing."[61]

SEDUCTION.

[Anonymous]

On one parent stalk, two white roses were growing,
    From buds just unfolded, and lovely to view!
Together they bloom'd, with the same sunbeam glowing,
    And anointed at night by the same balmy dew.

A spoiler beheld the fair twins, and, unsparing,
    Tore one from the stem, like a gay victim drest,
Then left its companion, his prize proudly bearing,
    To blush for an hour, ere it died on his breast.

But, ah, for the widow'd one — shrivell'd and yellow,
    Its sleek silver leaves lost their delicate hue;
It sicken'd in thought — pin'd to death for its fellow,
    Rejected the sun-beam, and shrunk from the dew.

Then where, ruthless spoiler! ah, where is thy glory?
    Two flow'rs strewn in dust, that might sweetly have bloom'd,
A tomb is the record which tells thy proud story,
    Where beauty and love are untimely confirm'd.

1:125/122

The speaker's reference to a plucked flower as "widow'd" places this poem firmly in the sentimental tradition. Jefferson mourned his wife in a manner reminiscent of the description of the flower: "But, ah, for the widow'd one — shrivell'd and yellow, / Its sleek silver leaves lost their delicate hue; / It sicken'd in thought — pin'd to death for its fellow, / Rejected the sun-beam, and shrunk from the dew." The poem also portrays an earlier episode in Jefferson's life, that of the "ruthless spoiler" who would destroy the happiness of a married couple. There may be some self-rebuke in Jefferson's decision to clip this poem. He flirted with the wife of his neighbor, John Walker, thus compromising their friendship; charges of improper conduct resurfaced when he ran for president.

In Praise of CONTENT.

[Anonymous]

No glory I covet, no riches I want,
  Ambition is nothing to me;
The one thing I beg of kind heaven to grant,
  Is a mind independent and free.

With passions unruffl'd, untainted with pride,
  By reason my life let me square,
The wants of my nature are cheaply supply'd,
  And the rest are but folly and care.

The blessings which providence freely has sent
  I'll justly and gratefully prize,
While sweet meditation and cheerful content,
  Shall make me look healthy and wise.

How vainly, thro' infinite trouble and strife,
  Do many their labours employ;
Since all that is truly delightful in life,
  Is what all, if they will, may enjoy.

1:136/133

This didactic poem suggests Jefferson's stoic outlook on life: A person achieves contentment by rejecting materialism ("no riches I want"), pride, and passion, and by remaining "unruffled" by life's vicissitudes ("with passions unruffl'd, untainted with pride"). The speaker praises content by finding "delight" in life. Nathaniel Hawthorne copied the first and third verses of this poem in his journal and labeled it "Moderate Views" on February 13, 1817. This poem has been mistakenly attributed to Hawthorne himself.[62]

The Mansion of Rest.

[Anonymous]

I TALK'D to my flattering heart,
    And I chid its wild wandering ways;
I charg'd it from folly to part,
    And to husband the best of its days;
I bade it no longer admire
    The meteors that Fancy had drest:
I whisper'd, 'twas time to retire,
    And seek for a *Mansion of Rest.*

A Charmer was list'ning the while,
    Who caught up the tone of my lay:
Oh come then, she cried, with a smile,
    And I'll shew thee the cause and the way:
I follow'd the witch to her home,
    And vow'd to be always her guest:
"Never more, I exclaim'd, will I roam,
    "In search of the *Mansion of Rest.*"

But the sweetest of moments will fly;
    Not long was my fancy beguil'd,
For, too soon I confess'd with a sigh,
    That the Syren deceiv'd, while she smil'd;
Deep, deep did she stab the repose
    Of my trusting and innocent breast,
And the door of each avenue close
    That led to the *Mansion of Rest.*

Then Friendship entic'd me to stray,
    Thro' the long magic wiles of romance,
But I found that he meant to betray,
    And shrunk from the sorcerer's glance;
For Experience has taught me to know,
    That the soul which reclin'd on his breast,
Might toss on the billows of woe,
    And ne'er find a *Mansion of Rest.*

Pleasure's path I determin'd to try,
　　But Prudence I met in the way,
Conviction flash'd light from her eye,
　　And appear'd to illumine my day;
She cried, as she shew'd me a grave
　　With nettles and wild flowers drest,
O'er which the dark cypress did wave,
　　Behold there the *Mansion of Rest*.

She spoke, and half vanish'd in air;
　　For she saw mild Religion appear,
With a smile that would banish Despair,
　　And dry up the penitent tear;
Doubts and years from my bosom were
　　driven,
　　As pressing the cross to her breast,
And pointing serenely to Heaven,
　　She shew'd me the MANSION OF REST.

　　　　　　　　　　1:146/142

To-morrow.

[Anonymous]

In the downhill of life, when I find I'm declining,
  May my life no less fortunate be;
Than a snug elbow chair can afford for reclining,
  And a cot that o'er looks the wide sea,
With an ambling pad poney to pace o'er the lawn,
  While I carrol away idle sorrow;
And blithe as the lark that each day hails the dawn,
  Look forward with hope for *to-morrow.*

With a porch at my door both for shelter and shade
  As the sunshine or rain may prevail;
And a small spot of ground for the use of the spade,
  And a barn for the use of the flail;
A cow for my dairy, a dog for my game,
  And a purse when my friend wants to borrow:
I'll envy no nabob his riches or fame,
  Nor the honors that wait him *to-morrow.*

From the bleak northern blast may my cot be completely
  Secur'd by a neighboring hill:
And at night may repose steal on me more sweetly
  By the sound of a murmuring rill.
And while peace and plenty I find at my board,
  With a heart free from sickness or sorrow,
With my friend shall I share what *today* may afford
  And let them spread the table *to-morrow.*

And when I at last must *throw off* this frail cov'ring
    Which I've worn for three-score years and ten,
On the verge of the grave I'll not seek to keep hov'ring,
    Nor my thread wish to spin o'er again.
But my face in the glass I'll serenely survey,
    Nor repine at each wrinkle or furrow;
As this *old worn out stuff, which is threadbare to-day,*
    May become *everlasting* TO-MORROW.

1:146/142

Jefferson juxtaposed "The Mansion of Rest" with "To-morrow," a poem that expresses the conceit of retirement less abstractly. At a time when plastic surgery is so prevalent and acceptance of aging so rare, the fourth stanza provides an interesting if somewhat idealistic view of how one might face "each wrinkle or furrow."

The Tear.
[Anonymous]

On beds of snow the moon-beam slept,
    And chilly was the midnight gloom;
When by the damp grove *Ellen* wept,
    Sweet maid! it was her lover's tomb.

A warm tear gushed, the wintry air
    Congeal'd it, as it flowed away;
All night it lay an ice-drop there,
    At morn, it glittered in the ray.

An angel, wandering from her sphere,
    Who saw this bright, this frozen gem,
To dew-eyed Pity brought the tear
    And hung it on her diadem.

1:141 / 142

Jefferson clipped several poems with this title. In "The Tear," the speaker views grief as pleasant. Moore's uplifting and sentimental verse — not to mention his talent — made him the great favorite of American newspaper editors. This poem first appeared in *The Poetical Works of the Late Thomas Little, Esq.*[63] Adding pathos, however fictional, to his verse collection, Moore assumed the persona of Thomas Little, whose life was cut short at twenty-one.

THE BOTTLE.

By Hugh Kelly.

WHILE the bottle to humour and social delight
    The smallest assistance can lend,
While it happily keeps up the laugh of the night,
    Or enlivens the mind of a friend;
O let me enjoy it, thou bountiful pow'r!
    That my time may deliciously pass!
And should care ever think to intrude on the heart,
Scare the haggard away with a glass.

But instead of a rational feast of the sense,
    Should Discord preside o'er the bowl,
And Folly, Debate or Contention commence,
    From too great an expansion of soul:
Should the man I esteem, or the friend of my heart,
    In the ivy feel nought but the rod;
Should I make fair Religion a profligate jest,
    Or daringly sport with my God:

From my lips dash the poison, O merciful Pow'r!
    Where the madness or blasphemy hung,
And let ev'ry word, at which Virtue should low'r,
    Parch quick on my infamous tongue —
From my sight let the cause be eternally driv'n,
    Where my reason so fatally stray'd,
That no more I may offer an insult to Heav'n,
    Or give man a cause to upbraid.

1:127/124

Jefferson began a vineyard at Monticello under
the direction of Philip Mazzei. This poem, by
an English playwright and journalist, suggests
the value of drinking in moderation, as a form
of "social delight."

WOMEN.
[Anonymous]

The cautious fool is frightened but to find
A female gifted with a spark of mind,
The dart of wit opposed to folly's shield.
Compels him trembling from the routed field.
He seeks for those, if such there well can be,
Beneath him sunk in folly one degree;
That women should be fools you seem to think,
Like purblind owls on reason's sunshine blink.
Perhaps with justice you this creed advance —
Had women wit, puppies could stand no chance.

1:130/127

Many of the poems in Jefferson's newspaper clippings book praise women and mock men, noting that "puppies" (young, inexperienced, or unintelligent men) who are threatened by a woman's superior intellect don't deserve that woman's attention. Perhaps Jefferson's perspective as a protective father altered his views as a student at William and Mary, when he copied several misogynist passages from Aeschylus, Euripides, Virgil, Milton, and other writers in his literary commonplace book.[64] "Now the race of women by nature loves scandal," Jefferson wrote in this book, "and if they get some slight handle for their gossip they exaggerate it, for they seem to take a pleasure in saying everything bad of one another."[65]

Conjugal Love.
[Anonymous]

AWAY — let nought of love displeasing,
    My Winifreda, move your care;
Let nought delay the heav'nly blessing —
    Nor squeamish pride, nor gloomy fear.

What, though no grants of royal donors,
    With pompous titles, grace our blood? —
We'll shine in more substantial honours:
    And, to be noble, we'll be good.

Our name, while virtue thus we tender,
    Will sweetly sound, where'er 'tis spoke:
The rich, the great, shall think, and wonder,
    How they respect such little folk.

What, tho' from fortune's lavish bounty
    No mighty treasures we possess? —
We'll find, within our pittance, plenty;
    And be content, without excess.

Still shall each returning season
    Sufficient for our wishes give;
For we will live a life of reason:
    And that's the only life to live.

Thro' youth and age, in love excelling,
    We'll hand in hand, together tread;
Sweet-smiling peace shall crown our dwelling,
    And babes, sweet-smiling babes, our bed.

How should I love the pretty creatures,
    While round my knees they fondly clung;

To see them look their mother's features,
    To hear them lisp their mother's tongue.

And when with envy, time transported,
    Shall think to rob us of our joys,
You'll, in your girls, again be courted;
    And I'll go wooing in my boys.

1:135 / 132

This poem distills Jefferson's philosophy (and the three sections of this book) for it views family, love, and democratic ideology as inextricably combined. Here the poet sees domestic love as the seat of virtue. The family is a model for democratic politics as well, for though this family has "no grants of royal donors," its members achieve their nobility through acts of virtue ("to be noble, we'll be good"). The speaker implicitly rejects British luxury by stating their plan to "be content, without excess." The poem's most original sentiment occurs in the final stanza when the couple cheats old age by wooing lovers vicariously through their children: "You'll, in your girls, again be courted; / And I'll go wooing in my boys."

"Harmony in the married state is the very first object to be aimed at," Jefferson wrote to Maria. "Nothing can preserve affection uninterrupted but a firm resolution never to differ in will and a determination in each to consider the love of the other as of more value than any object whatever on which a wish has been fixed."[66]

POEMS OF FAMILY

On Content.

[Anonymous]

FALSELY we think that change of place,
  Or alter'd circumstance, can please,
Can from the soul its canker chace,
  When Discontent's the dire disease.

In vain the wretch his native land
  Forsakes, and seeks a foreign sky;
Care follows to the distant strand,
  He never from himself can fly.

The weak, the avaricious mind,
  That wastes its time in anxious thought,
Vast wealth to hoard, shall sadly find,
  With gold contentment is not bought.

Content, a gem but rarely found,
  Amid the splendour of a crown,
She shuns Fame's noisy trumpet's sound!
  Too copious draughts the blessing drown.

But in the humble cot she lies;
  Though seasons various changes bring,
Though Nature round her droops and dies,
  Her preference makes it constant spring.

1:136 / 133

As befits a man who wrote about the pursuit of happiness, Jefferson took interest in a poem that stresses its elusive quality. Happiness cannot be found in travel or in the pursuit of gold. Romantically, the poet finds it in Nature's "humble lot." Novels of sensibility, such as *Emma; or, the Unfortunate Attachment*, by Georgiana, duchess of Devonshire (1773), contrast the fashionable life of London with the contentment to be found in a humble cot. Though he spent four years in France, Jefferson never tired of praising the virtues of his native Virginia.[67] He could be critical of the shoddy architecture there but would have agreed, with Emerson and Schopenhauer (Jefferson's contemporary), that travel is no cure for melancholy. "Falsely we think that change of place, / Or alter'd circumstance, can please." In a letter to Peter Carr, Jefferson wrote that "travelling makes men wiser, but less happy."[68]

The Way to Keep Him.
[Anonymous]

ATTEND all ye fair, and I'll tell you the art,
　　To bind ev'ry fancy with ease in your chains;
To hold in soft fetters the conjugal heart,
　　And banish from hymen his doubts and his pains.

When Juno accepted the cestus* of love,
　　At first she was handsome; she charming became;
With skill the soft passion it taught her to move,
　　To kindle at once, and to keep up the flame.

'Tis this gives the eyes all their magic and fire;
　　The voice melting accents; impassions the kiss;
Confers the sweet smiles that awaken desire,
　　And plants round the fair each incentive to bliss.

Thence flows the gay chat, more than reason that charms;
　　The eloquent blush that can beauty improve;
The fond sigh, the fond vow, the soft touch that alarms;
　　The tender disdain — the renewal of love.

Ye fair, take the cestus, and practise its arts;
　　The mind unaccomplish'd — mere features are vain;
Exert your sweet powers — you conquer all hearts,
And the lover, joys, & *graces shall walk in your train.*

                                        1:136 / 133

This poem suggests that a successful marriage depends upon maintaining one's charm. Juno, to whom Zeus was so often unfaithful, seems like a poor model for a woman intent on keeping her husband's interest, and yet Juno was the goddess of marriage and protector of women.

---

*A cestus was the girdle of Venus, fashioned by her husband Vulcan, to keep her faithful. When she dallied with Mars, the girdle fell off and became a symbol of woman's irresistible attraction.[69]

The Tomb of My Fathers.

[Anonymous]

Subdued by misfortunes, and bow'd down with pain,
I sought on the bosom of peace to recline;
I hied to the home of my fathers again,
But the home of my fathers no longer was mine.

The look that spoke gladness and welcome was gone;
The blaze that shone bright in the hall was no more;
A stranger was there with a bosom of stone,
And cold was his look as I enter'd the door.

'Twas his, deaf to pity, to tenderness dead,
The falling to crush, and the humble to spurn;
But I staid not his scorn — from the mansion I fled,
And my beating heart vow'd never more to return.

What home shall receive me! one home yet I know;
O'er its gloomy recess, see the pine branches wave!
'Tis the Tomb of my fathers! the world is my foe,
And all my inheritance now is a grave.

'Tis the Tomb of my fathers! the grey moisten'd walls,
Declining to earth, speak aloud of decay;
The gate off its hinge, half opening calls.
"Approach, most unhappy, thy dwelling of clay!"

Alas! thou sole dwelling of all I hold dear,
How little this meeting once anger'd my breast!
From a wanderer accept, oh my fathers! this tear,
Receive him, the last of his race, to your rest.

1:141 / 137

Jefferson's interest in the poetry of Macpherson finds expression in this poem, in which a romantic and solitary figure portrays himself as "the last of his race." Many of Macpherson's heroes, including Fingal, are the last of a group of Scottish and Irish heroes who fought for the honor of their country or clan. What makes this poem Romantic is the picturesque details of ruin, "the grey moisten'd walls," provided by the speaker.

The Days That Are Gone.
[Anonymous]

THE sun was departed, the mild zephyr blowing,
    Bore over the plain the perfume of the flowers;
In soft undulations the streamlet was flowing,
    And calm meditation led forward the hours:
I struck the full chord, and the ready tear started,
I sung of an exile forlorn broken harted,
Like him, from my bosom all joy is departed,
    And sorrow has stol'n from the lyre all its powers.

I paus'd on the strain, when fond mem'ry tenacious,
    Presented the form I must ever esteem;
Retrac'd scenes of pleasure, alas, how fallacious!
    Evanescent all, all, as the shades of a dream.
Yet still, as they rush'd through oppres'd recollection,
The silent tear fell and the pensive reflection,
Immersed my sad bosom in deeper dejection,
    On which cheering hope scarcely glances a beam.

In vain into beauty all nature is springing.
    In vain smiling spring does the blossoms unfold;
In vain round my cot the wing'd choristers singing,
    When each soft affection is dormant and cold.
E'en sad as the merchant, bereav'd of his treasure,
So slow beats my heart, and so languid its measure,
So dreary, so lonely, a stranger to pleasure,
    Around it affliction her mantle hath roll'd.

But meek resignation supporting the spirit,
Unveils a bright scene to the uplifted eye:
A scene, which the patient and pure shall inherit,

Where hearts bleed no more, and the tear shall be dry,
There souls, which on earth in each other delighted,
By friendship, by honor, by virtue united,
Shall meet, and their pleasure no more shall be blighted,
But perfect and pure as their love be their joy.

1:143/139

Jefferson clipped another poem with this title for his literary commonplace book. In this version of "The Days That Are Gone," the speaker overcomes his melancholy at the arrival of spring by imagining a heaven free of pain ("where hearts bleed no more, and the tear shall be dry"). The first two stanzas recall Francesca's comment, in the fifth canto of Dante's *Inferno*: "There is no greater pain, than to remember happy times in misery."

Landscape. — Mrs. Jones will sing the
following beautiful Swiss Song of
DULCE DOMUM! SWEET HOME!
COMPOSED AND SUNG BY MR. BRAHAM.

Deep in a vale a cottage stood,
Oft sought by Trav'lers weary,
And oft it prov'd the blest abode
Of Edward and of Mary.

For her he'd chase the mountain
    goat,
O'er Alps and Glaciers bounding,
For her the Chamois he would
    shoot,
Dark horrors all surrounding.

But evening came, he sought his
    home,
While (anxious lovely woman!)
She hail'd the sight, and every night
  The cottage rung
    As they sung
Oh! Dulce, Dulce Domum.

But soon alas! this scene of bliss
Was chang'd to prospects dreary,
For war and honor rous'd each
    Swiss,
And Edward left his Mary.

To bold St. Gothard's height he
    rush'd
'Gainst Gallia's foes contending,
And by unequal numbers crush'd
He died his land defending.

Thy evening comes! — he sought
    not home
While she (distracted woman!)
  Grown wild with dread,
  Now seeks him dead,
  And hears his knell
  That bids farewell
To Dulce, Dulce Domum.

1:143/139

Like Burger's ballads, Braham's song depicts the mental distraction of a woman who loses her heroic lover in battle, in this case "'Gainst Gallia's foes contending." Like Macpherson's poetry, which Jefferson admired, Braham's lyric celebrates nationalism and the pathos of lost causes: "by unequal numbers crush'd / He died his land defending." Wordsworth depicted such heroines less dramatically, in "The Maid of Buttermere," which Jefferson also clipped. John Braham was the most popular tenor of his day; he later worked with Isaac Nathan, who composed music for Byron's *Hebrew Melodies* (1814).

LINES ON FRIENDSHIP.
[Anonymous]

WHAT warms the soul, what cheers the heart,
Is FRIENDSHIP'S renovating tie;
Yes, this can social joy impart,
And wipe the tear from sorrow's eye.

This wakes the feelings of the soul,
It bids the noble passions rise,
And makes our days with rapture roll:
Such heavenly bliss in FRIENDSHIP lies!

FRIENDSHIP is what we all admire;
Yet often nothing but a name;
Will kindle, burn, and soon expire,
Just like a meteor's empty flame.

Have you a FRIEND? a fair one cried,
Have you a FRIEND in time of need?
Yes — I with earnestness replied,
Says she, then you've a FRIEND indeed.

Where real FRIENDSHIP is possess'd,
It is a blessing to mankind,
It soothes affliction's troubled breast,
And elevates the sinking mind.

Thus private friends who dwell in love,
Are taught to feel another's woe,
To raise their thoughts on things above,
And live in friendship here below.

(Freemans' Friend.)

1:125

Jefferson's sociability is well known; his most recent editors count fourteen thousand letters, incoming and outgoing, during his retirement.[70] A constant stream of visitors came to Monticello. "I find friendship to be like wine," he wrote to Benjamin Rush in 1811, "raw when new, ripened with age, the true old man's milk and restorative cordial."[71] In this poem, friendship improves those lucky enough to enjoy its "renovating tie."

Jefferson's correspondence is one of the most prolific of any former president; thirty-two volumes cover his correspondence from 1760 to 1801. More than two hundred years later, the letters Jefferson wrote while president are just beginning to be edited for the twentieth and twenty-first centuries.

Constancy in Death.

A Song, sung by a Hindu Woman, on the point of being burned with her Husband: — translated from the Hindu language, and originally published in Calcutta.

[*Republican Farmer.*]

HASTE! haste! with speed the sacred pile
    Prepare, which shall my form consume,
And death in Cassah's arms I'll smile,
    And joyful meet so blest a doom,
With him a life of love I've past;
    With him a death of love I'll die;
On his cold corpse my body cast,
    In his dear arms all pain defy.

When Cassah liv'd, with throbs of joy
    I saw love sparkle in his eyes:
Nought could our happiness destroy,
    While soft we heav'd love's tender sighs;
Endearing smiles, and kindest deeds
    Still made us bless each happy day,
But ah! No joy in life succeeds
    To me, if Cassah be away.

No more to gaze on his lov'd charms,
    To be no more his faithful care,
The object of his fond alarms,
    The partner of his frugal fare;
Detested thought! with joy I mount
    The sacred pile by me prepar'd,
I joyful die on love's account,
    And Brama shall my zeal reward.

In the fair form of spotless doves
    Should Brama chuse we still may live.
Wander o'erjoy'd through verdant groves,
    And in new beauteous shapes revive;

Then light the pile, dissolve this frame
 Of human woe, of human care;
Since still our souls shall be the same!
 On wings of love we'll mount in air.

She said — and strewing flowers around,
 O'er joy'd as on her bridal day,
Heard the last fatal music sound
 Which warn'd her Brama to obey.
Then mounting on the funeral pile,
 With look serene she welcom'd death,
Embrac'd her Cassah with a smile,
 And in his arms resign'd her breath!

1:144/140

"Constancy in Death" provides an exoticized portrait of suttee, in which a Hindu woman proves her dedication to her husband by destroying herself when he dies. In Hinduism, Brahma is the Absolute, which is impersonal. The Brahmins claimed Brahma as the founder of their religious system.[72] Years after this poem was written, Byron penned *Sardanapalus*, which depicts a young Greek slave who destroys herself on a funeral pyre rather than live without the Assyrian king who had captured her. Byron was more equivocal about love in *Don Juan*. "Love, constant love, has been my constant guest,"[73] the narrator stated. Goethe and Madame de Staël wrote eloquently on suicide, the heroism and ethics of which occasioned much debate during the period known as literary romanticism (1780–1830).

Woman's Hard Fate.
By a Lady.
[Anonymous]

HOW wretched is poor Woman's fate!
    No happy change her fortune knows:
Subject to Man, in ev'ry state;
    How can she then be free from woes?

In youth, a Father's stern command,
    And jealous eyes, control her will:
A lordly Brother watchful stands,
    To keep her closer captive still.

The tyrant Husband next appears,
    With awful and contracted brow:
No more a Lover's form he wears;
    Her Slave's become her Sov'reign now.

If, from this fatal bondage free,
    And not by Marriage-chains confin'd;
If, blest with single life, she see
    A Parent fond, a Brother kind.

Yet Love usurps her tender breast,
    And paints a phoenix to her eyes:
Some darling Youth disturbs her rest;
    And painful sighs in secret rise.

Oh cruel Power's, since you've design'd,
    That Man, vain Man, should bear the sway,
To slavish chains, add slavish mind,
    That I may thus your will obey.

1:144/141

Jefferson juxtaposed a woman in India who willingly died with her "Cassah" with a Western view of "woman's fate," which saw marriage as a form of enslavement. Yet Richardson's *Clarissa* came very close to describing marriage in precisely the terms that this poet did, especially in the second stanza. Linda Kerber has noted how the laws of coverture, which date to Blackstone, made women virtual slaves in late-eighteenth-century America.[74] "A married woman had no independent control of her property. Since republican theory emphasized that the right to participate in the management of a political unit stemmed from the ownership of property, the denial of political rights to women seemed quite natural," Kerber noted. [75]

The Answer.
By a Gentleman.
[Anonymous]

HOW happy is a Woman's fate!
    Free from care, and free from woe;
Secure of Man in ev'ry state,
    Her Guardian-god below.

In youth, a Father's tender love,
    And well-experienc'd eye,
Refrain her mind, too apt to rove,
    Enamour'd with a toy.

Suppose her with a Brother blest —
    A Brother, sure, is kind:
But in the Husband stands confest,
    The Father, Brother, Friend.

'Tis Man's to labour, toil, and sweat,
    And all his care employ,
Honor, pow'r, or wealth to get:
    'Tis Woman's to enjoy.

But look we on those halcyon days,
    When Woman reigns supreme;
While supple Man his homage pays,
    Full proud of her esteem.

How duteous is poor Strephon's love!
    How anxious is his care,
Lest e'en the zephyrs breathe too rough,
    And discompose the Fair!

Then say not, any Pow'rs ordain,
    That Man should bear the sway:
When Reason bids, let Woman reign;
    When Reason bids, obey.

1:144/141

In this piece, the poet counters the lady of the previous poem by finding husbands to be the perfect amalgamation of "Father, Brother, Friend," all seen in idealistic terms. Men toil so women can be happy, the complacent narrator concludes. Is it significant that the man gets the last word?

Ode to Modesty.

NYMPH of the downcast eye,
  Sweet blushing MODESTY,
Whose mien supplies the music of the tongue;
  Thy charms were still delay'd,
  Thy beauties unportray'd,
Though Fancy pencil'd while the Muses sung!

  More lovely to my sight,
  Than morn's returning light,
That wakes the lowly dew encumber'd rose,
  Or, mingling into day,
  With bright and purer ray,
Its mellow lustre o'er the landscape thrown.

  O thou, the more admir'd
  When seeming most retir'd —
Who far from pomp and grandeur lov'st to dwell:
  Thou who art oft'ner seen
  Upon the village green,
Or in the cottage, or the humbler cell!

  Come, sweet nymph, and bring with thee
  Thy sister, dear SIMPLICITY.

Come, gentle exile of Patana's shore,
  And draw the veil by Fashion rent aside;
Forbid each eye promiscuous to explore
  Those latent beauties Nature meant to hide.

Illume the cheek that recently display'd
  At once the lily's and the morning's glow:
E'en in thy absence, health begins to fade;
  And, see! the crimson yielding to the snow.

And when thou com'st more grateful than the spring,
   Crown'd with green garlands, after winter's reign,
With all thy blessings this instruction bring,
   And let the moral echo round the plain:

"Those charms so fair were more lovely still,
   If obvious only to the mental eye:
Those beauties, form'd the ravish'd heart to thrill,
   Expos'd to all, will soon that power deny.

Those smiles, so open to the vulgar sight,
   Were soon unheeded as the mid-day beam:
That bosom gives more exquisite delight
   Conceal'd, and throbbing but in fancy's dream.

Arabia's perfumes, lavish'd on the breeze,
   Soon grew familiar to the sated sense;
And each attempt that Beauty makes to please,
   Devoid of Modesty, but gives offence.

The leafy fruit, that toil to reach demands,
   Acquir'd, a richer recompence bestows;
And the rude thorn, that guards from vulgar hands,
   But gives a higher value to the rose.

1:163

Ellen Wayles Randolph received this poem from her grandfather on July 20, 1805, and thanked him for it in a letter of July 20, 1805: "I am very much obliged to you for the Poetry you sent me and think it all very Pretty, particularly Little John and the Ode to Modesty."[76] "Little John" does not appear in Jefferson's scrapbook. That same month, Jefferson's daughter Martha requested that he purchase Anna Letitia Barbauld's *Lessons for Children from Four to Five Years Old* (1780, 1798, 1801).[77] It would be difficult to find a poem that better summarizes the qualities Jefferson valued in a woman: "O thou the more admir'd / When seeming most retir'd." His letters to his daughters stress the importance of modesty, which Jefferson heightened to a national characteristic. If American men were expected to be optimistic, self-reliant, and resourceful, American women were clean, modest, and simple in their tastes. "But be you from the moment you rise till you go to bed as cleanly and properly dressed as at the hours of dinner or tea," Jefferson wrote to Martha on December 22, 1783. "A lady who has been seen as a sloven or slut in the morning, will never efface the impression she then made with all the dress and pageantry she can afterwards involve herself in. Nothing is so disgusting to our sex as a want of cleanliness and delicacy in yours. I hope therefore the moment you rise from bed, your first work will be to dress yourself in such a stile as that you may be seen by any gentleman without his being able to discover a pin amiss, or any other circumstance of neatness wanting."[78]

"Mirror for Magistrates."
Wrote above two hundred years ago.
[Anonymous]
[in pencil, in Jefferson's hand,
"As good now as when it was written"]

WHAT doth avail to have a princely place,
A name of honour, and a high degree;
To come by kindred of a noble race.
Except we princely, worthy, noble be!
The fruit declares the goodness of the tree
Do brag no more of birth, or lineage then;
For virtue, grace and manners make the man.

1:193/184

Jefferson seems to have admired the democratic sentiments expressed in this passage from *Mirror for Magistrates*, a collection of English Renaissance poems that dates to 1560. On his own tomb, he chose to be remembered for the Declaration of Independence, the Statute of Religious Freedom in Virginia, and the founding of the University of Virginia rather than for the political offices he held, including the presidency. For Jefferson, nobility of manner was more important than "a noble race," though his admiration of Macpherson suggests that he admired the latter as well.

SEAT OF THE MUSES.
VERY USEFUL LESSONS.
[Anonymous]

IN clothes, be fashion crazy to excess,
And show your great capacity for dress;
Of powders and perfumes, employ a store,
Smell as no creature ever smelt before:
With heavy loads of lace, profusely glare,
And make the thoughtless mob with wonder stare.
Then all your finery to your mistress show,
And boldly claim the title of a *Beau.*

    Let folly even on your actions wait.
And nonsense be the subject of your prate;
Before your mistress like a monkey skip;
Let no occasion to be silly, slip;
Turn on your heel just like a school-boy's top,
And prove yourself a most egregious *Fop.*

    Sometimes a trifling story may prevail,
But be yourself the hero of your tale.

    Tell her, on such a time, by way of joke,
How many men you beat, and lamps you broke:
How hob'ling watchmen compass'd you around,
Oppress'd by numbers, how they made you roar,
And laid you welt'ring in your common gore;
Before the constable how bold you stood.
Defied his power and swore yourself a *Blood.*

    How, before justice you appear'd next day,
Who made you fairly all expences pay;
Then curse his worship and your horrid luck,
And think yourself a most engaging *Buck.*

1:191/185

By pasting this poem and the preceding "Extract from the 'Mirror for Magistrates'" on the same page, Jefferson contrasted the foolish philosophy recommended in "Very Useful Lessons" with the sound advice offered in "Mirror for Magistrates." Though both poems are English, Jefferson associated British luxury with monarchical corruption. Beau Brummell and Georgiana, duchess of Devonshire, were the arbiters of fashion in London and, often, of outrageous dress. Brummell popularized the modern tuxedo, showing restraint where others, the Macaronis, did not. Georgiana wore ostrich feathers so high she needed to sit down in carriages to travel to a fashionable party. The terms *fop*, *blood*, and *buck* were synonyms, sometimes used interchangeably to describe effeminate men excessively concerned with appearances. Lady Georgiana made subtle distinctions among such types in her novel *The Sylph* (1779).

The Farmer's Creed,

By Sir John Sinclair, President of the
Board of Agriculture (in England).

Let this be held the Farmer's Creed —
Of Stock seek out the choicest breed,
In peace and plenty let them feed.
Your land sow with the best of seed,
Let it not dung nor dressing need,
Enclose and drain it with all speed —
And you will soon be rich indeed.

1:191/185

This poem appears in Jefferson's notebooks directly under the satire "Very Useful Lessons." "The Farmer's Creed" contrasts the virtuous farmer with the citified gentleman. In *Notes on the State of Virginia*, Jefferson described farmers as "God's chosen people if ever he had a chosen people."[79]

GOOD CONSAILE, of Chaucer, *Who was born in 1328, and died in 1400*, Attempted in Modern English, from Adelburg, author of philological essays on the English Language. Dr. Kippis has also given it a place in the Biographia Britannica.

THE POET'S LAST ADVICE.

Fly from the crowd, and be to virtue true,
    Content with what thou hast, tho' it be small.
To hoard brings hate; nor lofty thoughts pursue,
    He who climbs high, endangers many a fall.
Envy's a shade that ever waits on fame,
    And oft the sun that rises, it will hide;
Trace not in life a vast expensive scheme,
    But be thy wishes to thy state ally'd.
Be mild to others, to thyself severe;
So truth shall shield thee, or from hurt or fear.

Think not of bending all things to thy will,
    Nor vainly hope that fortune shall befriend;
Inconstant she, but be thou constant still,
    Whate'er betide, unto an honest end.
Yet needless dangers never madly brave,
    Kick not thy naked foot against a nail,
Or from experience the solution crave,
    If wall or pitcher strive which shall prevail;
Be in thy cause, as in thy neighbor's, clear,
So truth shall shield thee, or from hurt or fear.

Whatever happens, happy in thy mind
    Be thou, nor at thy lot in life repine,
He 'scapes all ill, whose bosom is resigned,
    Nor way, nor weather will be always fine.
Besides, thy home's not here, a journey this,
    A Pilgrim thou; then hie thee on thy way,
Look up to God, intent on heavenly bliss,
    Take what the road affords and praises pay;
Shun brutal lust, and seek thy soul's high sphere;
So truth shall shield thee, or from hurt or fear.

1:18

This is the second of two poems Jefferson clipped that draw advice from fourteenth-century poets. In the first stanza, Chaucer endorsed the self-restraint and simplicity of lifestyle that Jefferson advocated but to which he did not always adhere.

Sensibility.

[Anonymous]

SOON as the smiles of Youth disclose
The radiance of the budding rose,
O fount of Beauty! fount of joy!
Enchanting Sensibility!*
'Tis thine, with every mental charm
The Virgin's breathing mien to warm:
Thine, o'er her native bloom to throw
Of sentiment the living glow;
Or make that radient bloom appear
Lovelier, when moistened with a tear.
The charming air of Modesty,
Love's sweetest smile and melting eye
Are thine; and thine the livelier glance
That darts divine Intelligence;
The blushes thine, that tinge the cheek,
And o'er the trembling bosom break;
Thine is each sweetly-pensive grace,
And thine the passion-breathing face,
O fount of Beauty! fount of Joy!
Enchanting Sensibility!

The lovelier than the dewy rose,
That on the robe of Summer blows:
The Nymph who dares thy graces
    scorn,
Shall sigh in solitude forlorn;
Her smile no living radiance show,
Her heart no throb of rapture know,
No flower shall deck her early bier;
Her grave shall drink no gen'rous tear;
No Daughter for a Guardian mourn,
No weeping Lover clasp her urn.

1:173/166

* Sensibility is here intended to represent that exquisite moral sense,
  which is the Soul of female Beauty.

Sterne's narrator in *A Sentimental Journey Through Italy and France* exhibited keen sensibility, and Jefferson admired this work so much that he traveled with it in his breast pocket while visiting the south of France.[80] By the time Jane Austen penned *Sense and Sensibility* (1811), the term *sensibility* was ripe for satire, especially for those who claimed this quality as an excuse for selfish behavior. Austen's Marianne, for example, could hardly be described as evincing "the charming air of Modesty."

The Pleasure of Retirement.
[Anonymous]

HAPPY the man, whose country seat
Affords a pleasing, calm retreat
   Beneath its shady bow'rs:
No heavy cares of public life;
No noisy parties' clam'rous strife,
   Disturb his peaceful hours.
Ambition dwells not in his breast,
No sting of envy breaks his rest;
   No grief corrodes his mind;
No fierce desires of gold controul,
Or sway the dictates of his soul,
   To heav'n's decrees resign'd;
With empty titles let the great,
And all the useless pomp of state,
   Perpetuate their name:
Peace and contentment fills his cot,
And healthy temp'rance crowns his lot,
   Tho' unadorn'd by fame.
Let others to preferment climb,
By daring some atrocious crime,
   And rule the subject state.
Let the base traitor heap up gold;
The price of his dear country sold,
   By perfidy made great.
He lives beneath his humble home,
More blest than in the gilded dome,
   Where guilt torments the breast.
To him, retirement joy affords,
Fair competence supplies his board,
   And virtue makes him blest.

1:169

This poem stresses the pleasure of retirement by pointing out that neither care, strife, ambition, nor envy attends it. The poet's use of anaphora drives the point home: "No heavy cares . . . No noisy parties . . . No sting of envy . . . No grief."

Home.
[Anonymous]

When evening flings her dusk[e]y shade,
   O'er days departing close:
When labor drops the pen or spade,
   For pleasure, or repose.

With hasty steps and gladsome heart,
   I seek my much lov'd home;
A cot that boasts no builder art,
   An unaspiring dome.

Yet there the virtues with their train,
   Of docile joys resort;
There health and peace and freedom reign,
   Fair exiles from a court.

When heard the scrapings of my feet,
   What transports stir within!
Affection pipes her welcome sweet,
   A pleasing, tuneful din.

My children fly to share my kiss;
   A little artless group!
There centred is a mother's bliss
   And all a father's hope.

My loving partner in her turn,
   Anticipates desire —
And oft, as if it would not burn,
   She trims the blazing fire.

Consciously she now displays
   The dish and cleanly platter,
And when excuse for aught she prays,
   Contentment cries "no matter."

Thus round the soul endearment twines,
  With stronger faster hold —
Yet hymen's lamp still higher shines,
  And charms still new unfold.

As thus connubial pleasures rise;
  To gild my dear abode,
To heaven lift my grateful eyes,
  And thank a bounteous God.

1:175/169

Jefferson clipped several poems treating home as a subject. While president, Jefferson regretted the time he spent away from Monticello, which was never completed to his satisfaction during his lifetime. "It is in the love of one's family only that heartfelt happiness is known," he wrote to Mary Jefferson Eppes on October 26, 1801. When he did return for visits, Martha complained that she could barely spend "one sociable minute with him" because of the people vying for his attention. Her father, she noted, was "always in a crowd, taken from every useful and pleasing duty to be worried with a multiplicity of disagreeable ones which the entertaining of such crowds of company subjects one to in the country."[81] Jefferson responded by saying that visits to Monticello were "evidences of the general esteem which we have been able [sic] all our lives trying to merit."[82]

POTATOES,

The ground apple of Ireland is proverbially dear to Irishmen. If, however, the people of that country discover a peculiar partiality for this valuable esculent it is rather, we imagine, because the soil is peculiarly suitable for it, and that it grows there to the greatest perfection, than from any traditional or national regard for it, as has sometimes been alleged. In truth wherever this wholesome and nutritive root has been cultivated to any purpose it has been esteemed; and, we believe, the inhabitants of Britain and America scarcely place a less value on it than those of Ireland. In the following stanzas, from an Irish paper, the writer has done ample justice to his subject, at once evincing that he is no contemptible poet and no indifferent friend to potatoes. — N. Y. Daily Adv.

ODE ON POTATOES.
[Anonymous]

WHERE lies sterling taste in eating?
　In the costly French ragout?
I say No, but in Potatoes;
　What my gentle friend, say you?

Sordid Epicures may glory,
　In the joys their feast afford;
May Contentment and Potatoes,
　Ever spread my humble board.
　　. . .
O thou honest Irish sirloin!
　How I chuckle when I see
Social on the table smoking,
　Hot Potatoes stand by thee!

Here, ye nauseous frog destroyers,
　Here the feasts of health behold;
Feed on these, ye wiser Irish,
　If ye covet to be old.

Happiest produce are Potatoes,
  Of Hibernia's happy Isle;
The support of toiling millions,
  And the glory of her sail.

These refin'd to snowy whiteness,
  With Munditia's bosom vie,
Please at once her nicest palate,
  And delight the wand'ring eye.

These, in bread, in pie, or pudding,
  Scallop'd, roasted, boil'd excel;
All their uses, all their value,
  Not the Muse herself can tell.

Never may those virtuous Irish,
  Who their King and Country serve,
Never may they want Potatoes
  Who those noble roots deserve.

1:179/172

Jefferson's interest in gardening is well known. "The greatest service which can be rendered any country is to add an useful plant to its culture," he wrote, "especially a bread grain; next in value to bread is oil."[83] In this he followed Swift, who stated that "whoever could make two ears of corn or two blades of grass to grow upon a spot of ground where only one grew before, would deserve better of mankind and do more essential service to his country than the whole race of politicians put together."[84] Jefferson smuggled Piedmont rice from Italy in 1787, for the benefit of Edward Rutledge in rice-growing South Carolina in what one historian has described as "agricultural espionage."[85] Jefferson's interest in Irish culture extended to music, literature, and food.

Address to a Husband.
[Anonymous]

WHEN thou, O man, the lovely Fair can find,
Whose manners soft with mental grace is join'd,
Her form be such as fancy shall approve,
Her breast replete with gentleness and love.

O take her to thy home, thy arms, thy heart,
Let nought but death the nuptial tie dispart;
She is thy sweetest bosom friend, thy wife,
Ordain'd by Heav'n, the noblest balm of life.

As mistress of thy house, confess her sway,
And thus instruct thy servants to obey;
Let no imperious airs, nor peace annoy —
She shares thy grief, and let her share thy joy.

Let reason guide, when from her faults reprove,
And may such admonition flow from love;
Trust all thy secrets to her gentle breast,
And there repose thy anxious cares to rest.

And oh, when fell disease exerts its power,
And sad affliction darkens every hour;
When pallid sickness o'er her cheeks is spread,
And the fair train of rosy charms is fled:

When all her beauties languish in her eyes,
And tales of tenderness hang on her sighs:
Oh let affection's sympathetic glow
Soothe all her pangs and mitigate her woe.

Be all attention, every aid impart,
With sweet endearments raise her drooping heart;
Watch 'round her couch, anticipate each want,
And ere she forms a wish, her wishes grant.

1:194/185

Though men had legal power over their wives, "Address to a Husband" encourages them to "confess her sway" and avoid "imperious airs": "ere she forms a wish, her wishes grant." Like "Three Things a Good Wife Should Be Like,"[86] this poem refers to woman's "sway," a word that means something like "influence," and used by Byron in *Sardanapalus*: "Which she once sway'd — and thou mightst sway. / I sway them."[87] The word can be traced to Alexander Pope's *Moral Essays*. Pope noted women's "love of pleasure / and love of sway"; "In men, we various ruling passions find; / In women two almost divide the kind; / Those only fix'd, they first or last obey. / The love of pleasure, and the love of sway."[88]

POEMS OF FAMILY

LINES,

Addressed to a Young Lady Shortly
after her marriage.
[Anonymous]

Let not my friend, tho' now a wife,
    Bid all her cares adieu;
Comforts there are in married life,
    And there are crosses too.

I do not wish to mar your mirth
    With an ungrateful sound,
But know that perfect bliss on earth
    No mortal ever found.

Your prospects and your hopes are great,
    May God those hopes fulfil!
But you will find in every state
    Some difficulties still.

The rite which lately join'd your hands,
    Cannot insure content;
Religion forms the strongest bands,
    And love the best cement.

A friendship founded on esteem;
    Life's battering blast endures;
It will not vanish as a dream,
    And such I hope is yours.

But yet God's daily blessing crave,
    Nor trust your youthful heart;
You must Divine assistance have
    To act a prudent part.

Though you have left your parent's wing,
    Nor longer ask its care,
It is but seldom husbands bring
    A slighter yoke to wear.

They have their humours and their faults,
    So mutable is man;

Excuse his foibles in your thoughts,
   And hide them if you can.

No anger nor resentment keep,
   Whatever is amiss,
Be reconciled before you sleep,
   And seal it with a kiss.

Or if there's a cause to reprehend,
   Do it with mild address;
Remember he's your dearest friend,
   And love him ne'er the less.

Tis not the way to scold at large
   Whate'er proud reason boast,
For those their duty best discharge,
   Who condescend the most.

Mutual attempts to serve and please
   Each other will endear;
Thus may you bear the yoke with ease
   Nor discord interfere.

Thus give your tender passion scope,
   Yet better things pursue,
Be Heaven the object of your hope;
   And lead him thither too.

Since you must both resign your breath,
   And God alone knows when;
So live that you may part at death
   To meet with joy again.

And may the Lord your ways approve,
   And grant you both a share
In His redeeming saving love,
   And providential care.

1:193/186

Like the previous poem, which admonishes a man to be prepared for his wife's charms to flee and to nurse her when she becomes ill, this poem represents, with depressing realism, the "crosses" that attend married life. Religion is needed, "Divine assistance," for "It is but seldom husband's bring / A slighter yoke to wear." Love, we learn, is "the best cement." Jefferson wrote numerous letters advising his daughters on the proper attitude they should display toward their husbands to sustain a marriage. Newspapers often linked advice to husbands with advice to wives; the subject formed a popular genre during Jefferson's presidency.

The CHOICE of a WIFE.

To —— ——, Esquire.

WHENEVER, my friend, you chance to find,
A female who attracts your mind,
   Your choice awhile suspend;
Examine nearly first her heart,
If uncorrupt, if free from art,
   To that, be sure attend.

For beauty soon familiar grows,
Or fades, as hourly fades the rose,
   Frail tenant of decay;
But virtue, life's extremest length,
Will never droop, but gather strength,
   With each succeeding day.

This is the beauty worth your care,
And not the cheek, the lip, the hair,
   The eye, the teeth, the mein [sic];
If no deformity disgrace,
You'll soon think that a lovely face,
   Where truth and honor reign.

Be then the purpose of her heart,
Whom of yourself you'd make a part,
   Confirm'd and well inform'd;
In all things moral and Divine,
The virtues more attractive shine
   By true devotion warm'd.

These virtues still have least allay,
And best will bare the strict assay,
   That on religion grow;
Others to fear, or interest yield,
Or shrink and meanly quit the field,
   When storms of passion blow.

Let no vain, superstitious fear,
Create imaginary cares,
  For those who mean the best;
Who've only honest ends in view,
Will carefully those ends pursue,
  And leave to Heav'n the rest.

If gratitude her bosom swell,
If there kind, gen'rous pity dwell,
  Meekness and manly sense;
If no desire for dress or play,
Can lead her steady heart away,
  Fear not her innocence.

Fair virtue[,] honor, candor, truth,
Alone maintain the charms of youth,
  Through every stage of life;
These with new lustre ever glow,
And every day, new charms bestow,
  Upon the friend, the WIFE.

Those light the lamp of pure desire,
Those form the clear, celestial fire,
  Bright flame of lasting love;
While practised look, and airs and smiles,
And art, that thoughtless man beguiles,
  But flashes — meteors prove.

                              1:197/188

The poet, anxious to separate libertine from "pure desire," argues that attention to virtue, not beauty, will make for the proper choice of a wife: "This is the beauty worth your care, / And not the cheek, the lip, the hair." Mr. Palmer learned this lesson the hard way in Jane Austen's *Sense and Sensibility*. "His temper might perhaps be a little soured by finding, like so many others of his sex, that through some unaccountable bias in favour of beauty, he was the husband of a very silly woman."[89]

THE WIDOW.

By Richard B. Davis, late of New-York.

Fair mourner, lingering near the ground
   Where mortals rest in awful sleep,
Why dost thou turn the parting step
   So oft, and still return to weep?

Chill the unwholesome dews descend;
   The moon pours down a sickly light;
Nor will thy unprotected charms
   Avert the dangers of the night.

Then why among these drear abodes
   Pensive and sad wilt thou remain;
Thus fond to court the gloomy shade,
   Seeking society with pain?

'Tis sympathy demands, whose heart
   Has learnt to feel, and hopes to sooth,
That look, that sign to yonder tomb
   Too well disclose the mournful truth.

Yes, there the marble marks his grave,
   Come nearer — still — forgive my sighs;
Yes, here, I scarcely can repeat,
   My friend, my all, my husband lies.

Here manly worth and ardent love,
   And generous youth lie low beneath
The pressure of the mouldering earth,
   And own thy victory, O death!

When long affection lately crown'd,
   Exulted in the blissful hour,
Contagion breath'd the poison'd air,
   And blasted hope, thy fairest flower.

The sun, descending, saw him gay,
   Inhaling health with purest breath;

The rising morn illumed a scene
　Of mourning, agony and death.

Sad friendship o'er his couch reclined,
　Affection ceased not to deplore;
Grief call'd him back with frantic voice;
　He hear'd it not — he was no more.

1:198/189

This conversation poem (a genre Wordsworth and Coleridge helped popularize shortly before Jefferson's presidency) shows a woman grieving for her husband, whose precipitate death leads the bereaved widow to take the listener to his grave site to explain his virtues. Jefferson promised his wife he would not remarry after her death, obeying her wish that her children not be raised by a stepmother. As she lay dying in September 1782, she and Jefferson wrote out several lines from Laurence Sterne's *Tristram Shandy* that described the pathos of her condition. "Time wastes too fast: every letter I trace tells me with what rapidity life follows my pen, the days and hours of it are flying over our heads like clouds of [a] windy day never to return — more every thing presses on — ."[90]

Answer to the question, What is Happiness?
[Joseph Brown Ladd]

'TIS an empty fleeting shade,
By imagination made;
'Tis a bubble, straw or worse;
'Tis a baby's hobby horse;
'Tis a little living clear;
'Tis ten thousand pounds a year!
'Tis a title, 'tis a name;
'Tis a puff of empty fame,
Fickle as the breezes blow:
'Tis a lady's YES or NO!
And, where the description's crown'd,
'Tis just *no where* to be found.

2:3

The author of the Declaration of Independence thought the pursuit of happiness one of the goals of human endeavor, though this poem ironizes such rhetoric. The poet's use of anaphora propels the reader to the inevitable, cynical conclusion, which lands, like a thunderclap, after a list of the vanity of human wishes: "'Tis just *no where* to be found." Perhaps the pursuit of happiness interested Jefferson as much as its attainment.

EPIGRAM.
THE PRUDENT HUSBAND.
[Anonymous]

Dick's wife was sick, and pos'd to doctor's skill,
Who differ'd how to cure th'invet'rate ill.
Purging the one prescrib'd: No quoth the other,
That will do neither good nor harm, dear brother;
Bleeding's the only thing — 'twas quick reply'd,
That's certain death — But since we differ wide,
'Tis fit the husband chuse by whom abide.
"He no great skill," cries *Richard* "by the rood!
"But He think *bleeding's* like to do most good."

2:6

Bleeding, often by leeches, was standard medical practice to cure fevers ("*Bleeding's* the only thing"), though patients did not welcome such a sanguinary prescription. The "prudent" husband of this poem seems to take sadistic pleasure in following the doctor's advice, more interested, as he is, in hastening his wife's death than curing her of her ailment.

EPIGRAM.
[Anonymous]

What recompense, my lady wife,
    For all my faults, can I bestow you?
I only liv'd a rakish life —
    A thousand debts of love I owe you.

"Pay one my lord — 'tis all I mind."
"Name it thou dear forgiving creature.["]
"Only, my lord, you'll be so kind
Speedy to pay the — *debt of Nature*.["]

                    2:8

Once again, Jefferson shows his sense of balance by including an unforgiving wife to match her homicidal husband. The prudent husband who wishes for the death of his wife as "like to do most good" finds his counterpart in a woman who wishes that her husband, a rake and spendthrift, would "recompense" her by paying "the debt of nature."

CASH.

BY WILLIAM RAY.

Wise moralists in vain have told
How sordid is the love of gold,
   Which they call filthy trash;
Thou stranger to these eyes of mine,
Ten thousand virtues still are thine,
   Thou all-sufficient CASH!

Tho' thy intrinsic worth be small,
Yet, money, thou art all in all —
   Tho' transient as a flash,
In passing just from hand to hand,
The earth is at thy sole command —
   It gravitates to CASH.

Possess'd of thee, we may defy
Not death itself — but very nigh,
   For when the tyrant's lash
Is felt (and ah 'twas felt by me*)
It *did* — it *will* the vassal free —
   Then who despises CASH?

By nature void of ev'ry grace,
If thou hast (reader! view thy face)
   But this cosmetic wash;
'Twill whiten and improve the skin —
Thy monkey-nose, thy cheeks, thy chin;
   Are beautified by CASH.

And tho' your mental pow'rs be weak,
(To you who money have I speak)
   Ne'er fear to cut a dash;
For men of genius and sense,
If *poor*, will make a *poor* defence
   Against the man of CASH.

Or should you for the basest crimes,
Become indicted fifty times,
   This settles all the hash;
For bills which leave the poor no hope
T' escape the dungeon, or the rope,
   Are cancell'd, all, by CASH.

Nay 'twill be found that money can
The grovelling beast transform to man,
   Tho' diff'rent natures clash;
For 'tis a fact beyond dispute,
The miser's far beneath the brute —
   A lump of living CASH.

And yet what crowds around him wait —
Behold him cloth'd in pow'r and state —
   The garter, star and sash;
Fools fly before the potent nod
Of him whose flesh, whose soul, whose God,
   Whose heav'n itself is CASH.

But, sons of Plutus, lest you go,
To those infernal *mines* below,
   Where teeth are said to gnash,
Give to the needy — bribe the grave —
O, if you wish your souls to save,
   Be gen'rous of your CASH.

*Mr. Ray was one of the American prisoners
in Triopoli; and is now preparing a poem on
that subject.

2:14–2:15

Jefferson, though rarely cynical about
courtship, might have admired Ray's realism:
"Thy monkey-nose, thy cheeks, thy chin; / Are
beautified by CASH."

THE DEXTEROUS EVASION.
[Anonymous]

THE doctor was just on the very last stair,
Tow'rds the room of his son when of damsels a pair,
    Escap'd by the opposite door:
Whilst the youth had just time to lay hold of a book,
And in it (assuming a sanctified look)
    He began most intensely to pore.

When the doctor beheld him, cried he, overyjoy'd,
"To see you, dear Richard, so wisely employ'd,
    Your affectionate father much pleases;
But what, were you reading? — your Blackstone?" —
    "Why, no sir,
Twas only beguiling an hour or so, sir,
But with what?" — "Why some *fugitive pieces.*"

2:15

The pun on "pieces," with its carnal reference to
women, caps the humor of this bawdy poem.

FROM THE EVENING FIRESIDE.

The following epistle on courtship was read the other evening in a social little circle much to our amusement. At our separating, I requested a copy, which its fair possessor kindly granted me. No author's name was attached to it, and therefore hoping no evil will arise from its publication, I send it for insertion in your "Fire-sides". It has already furnished a small company with much innocent diversion; you may, if you please, extend it to a large one — Yours, AMICUS.

A BRIEF EPISTLE ON COURTSHIP.

DEAR FRIEND,
   I've had a thought or two of late
Respecting courtship, and I seem inclin'd,
To let thee know a little of my mind,
About that awkward purgatorial state.

If, haply anxious to obtain a wife,
Some seeking youth should try thy hand to gain;
I know thou would's not trifle with his pain;
Nor waste in courtship half the morn of life.

How blest mankind, if all the race were so!
What doubt and fear, what risque of limbs and life,
By land and water, to obtain a Wife,
Some poor afflicted mortals undergo!

What nameless pangs the wretched mortal proves
Who, sadly smitten, tries in vain to find
A proper method to unfold his mind;
Or hint his wishes to the maid he loves!

An aching heart with brazen front to hide —
With outward smiles to veil internal woe —
With stammering tongue propound the *yes* or *no*,
To do all this — and more — and be denied.

An, lo! if once denied, though e'er so clever,
Wide spreads the rumor of the soul defeat;
In council dire the female despots meet
And doom the wretch to singleness forever!

In amorous ditties, if he mourn his doom,
The luckless scrawl, produced in evil hour,
Proof of *his* folly and the *fair one's* power,
Is borne in triumph round the tittering room.

I would not wish my notions be known;
But truly, I have thought, the ills that wait
On Courtship, are *so numerous* and *so great*
'Tis better far — to let the thing alone.

2:15

Jefferson seems not to have recovered from his difficulties finding a wife. The sixth stanza of this poem represents marriage as an institution controlled by "female despots" who can doom a "wretch to singleness forever." To fall in love is to risk writing "amorous ditties" which women mock by passing it "round the tittering room." Courtship reveals "the *fair one's* power." In England, during the Regency period, poets recorded a similar imbalance. Burke described the late eighteenth century as the age of powerful women. "To meet a cabinet minister," wrote Miss Berry, "one had to go to Madame de Stael's."[91] Byron noted the need to please the "loveliest oligarchs of our gynocracy" who governed English life in the Regency period,[92] and compared Lady Melbourne's power over him to that of "the Ottoman family to the faithful, they frequently change their rulers, but never the reigning race."[93]

POEMS OF FAMILY

During his presidency, Jefferson minimized the pageantry of office, greeting the British ambassador (scandalously) in courduroys and slippers. Despite his democratic sincerity, he continued to receive correspondence that addressed him as "His Excellency." A. J. Laird donated Jefferson's scrapbooks to the University of Virginia, describing it as "one of the relicks of its supposed Author."

His troubles all were ended here be-
low.
Loud hallelujahs now dwell upon his
tongue,
While all the saints in glory join the
song.
Let us but live like him, and like
him die,
Then we, like him, shall dwell with
Christ on high:
Let us but live a life of faith and love,
And we again shall meet our friend
above:
And if we meet upon that happy
shore,
No dire disease, or death, shall part
us more.

CHARACTERS.

Death of General Montgomery.

The hero's death was as his life sublime
Proudly he lies along the ensanguined plain
So great, so fair that all the standers by
Resign their terrors of the grisly King
Thinking death lovely. Thus the travell'd sage
Beneath the ruin of triumphal arch
Feels such a sacred phrenzy as he views
The awful monuments of other times
That scarcely doth he wish the venerable pile
Restor'd to order.

Death of General Warren.

He died as if he studied all his life
Most firmly, proudly, nobly how to die.
The grace of native worth yet in his face
Lies cold as if unwilling to depart:
And such heroic sufferance shone throughout
His bold and marked outline; that in vain
Raphael or natures Angelo had striven
To catch him dying; Sculptors in vain
Even he whose magic chisel struck to life
Mirmillo dying.

For the NATIONAL ÆGIS.

INVOCATION TO HEALTH.

COME, thou lovely, blooming maid,
Thy genial influence impart;
Come, in rosy charms array'd,
To ease an anguish'd heart.

Sweet are the aromatic flowers,
That summer strews around the plain;
And sweet the gently falling showers,
The soft descending rain.

Sweet are the beauties of the grove,
The silent, shadowy retreat,
Where silvan swains their notes of love
On oaten reeds repeat.

But what are groves and blooming flowers,
Or songs that sorrow's self beguiles?
But what are soft, descending showers,
Without thy cheering smiles?

In vain for me creation blooms,
In vain for me from opening flowers;
On Zephyr's wing the sweet perfumes
Come floating thro' my bowers.

The gentle streams meander
In silence through the wood;
Along their banks I wander,
And gaze upon the flood.

But all that once delighted,
Looks desolate and drear:
I grope like one benighted;
Till thou, O Health, appear.

Not showers to larks so pleasing,
Nor sunshine to the bee;
Not sleep to toil so easing,
As thy dear smiles to me.

THE MAID OF THE GROVE.

POETRY.

FRIENDSHIP.

THE sun is grateful to the op'ning rose;
For, bless'd not with its smiles, her lustre goes;
Bedew'd with Nature's tears she droops her head,
And fades and dies upon oblivion's bed.
So Friendship to the mind each joy imparts;
Without its aid existence were in vain;
It e'er delights to dwell in generous hearts,
And where 'tis found, no selfish thought can reign.
Then come, blest Friendship! ever in my mind
Proclaim thy power—thy transports let me feel,
In adverse fortune be a solace kind,
For thou alone the wounds of fate can heal—
For thou alone canst sooth each anxious thought,
Subdue our sorrows, and calm patience give;
For from thy blest example we are taught
Those golden rules for which we ought to live.
Depriv'd of Friendship what is human life?
A wretched void—a desert of despair,
Within whose limits dwell eternal strife,
Soul-cank'ring grief, and misery and care!

Edward Young and Thomas Gray popularized the genre of "graveyard poetry," a mood evoked by "Scenes of My Youth," a poem on mutability. Jefferson did not paste poems into this collection wily-nily, but arranged them according to theme and topic. Anna Seward's poem seems to answer the first two, by considering the dangers of indulging one's grief. The oak leaf in Jefferson's scrapbook can still be found in the Alderman Library at the University of Virginia; it is placed on a page that includes one of the few references to "a tender mother [who] strove/To keep my happiness in view."

I can ... but reme ... such things were,
And ... ngst f ... us to me. ...

... once ... ear,
... wont ... ger he ... y ;
... daw ... o closing day.
... pale sorrow ...
A shade o'e ... your beaut ...
And robs the ... ents ...
That scatter'd ... su ...
While, still, to ... ight ... ca ...
Reflection tells ... *Such things were.*

Twas here a ... nder mother strove
To keep m ... happiness in view ;
I smil'd bene ... th a parents, love,
That soft ... ompassion ever knew ;
In whom th ... virtues all combin'd,
On whom I could with faith rely,
To whom my heart and soul were join'd
By mild ... affection's primal tie ;
Who sm ... es in heaven, exempt from care,
Whilst ... remember—*Such things were.*

Twas here (where calm and tranquil rest
O'e ... pays the peasant for his toil)
Tha ... first in blessings, I was blest
With growing friendship's open smile,
My friend far distant doom'd to roam,
... low braves the fury of the seas ;
... fled his happy peaceful home,
His little fortune to increase ;
... hile bleeds afresh the wound of care,
... hen I remember—*Such things were.*

Twas here, e'en in this blooming grove,
I fondly gaz'd on Laura's charms.
Who blushing, own'd a mutual love,
And melted in my youthful arms.
Tho' hard the soul-conflicting strife,
Yet fate, the cruel tyrant, bore
Far from my sight the charm of life,
The lovely maid whom I adore.
It fills my soul with tender care,
When I remember—*Such things were.*

Here first I saw the morn appear,
Of guiltless pleasure's smiling day ;
I met the dazzling brightness here,
Here mark'd the soft declining ray ;
Behold the skies, whose streaming light,
Gave splendor to the parting sun,
Now lost in sorrow's sable night,
And all their mingled glories gone.
Till death in pity end my care,
I must remember—*Such things were.*

TO CLARA.

Say, did I trespass on the hallowed calm,—
... e melancholy sabbath of the mind,
That soothes the wound ... d heart like heavenly
balm,

... s the feeling breast with bliss refin'd ?
... nsive daughter of the tuneful nine,
Has frolick joy forever fled thy breast ?
Ah yes ! a bosom, too exalted thine,
Too soft to harber such a boist'rous guest.

But I have bid the whirl of pleasure roll,
Have ope'd my bosom to the tide of joy ;
Bid youth's fierce a; ries rage without control,
Nor ever dream'd the nectar'ous draught
would cloy.

Bright fancy dipt her brush in rainbow dyes,
And ting'd each scene with ever varying hues;
While the fond heart, too feeling to be wise,
Hail'd each delusion reckless of abuse.

Yet soon these days of pleasures bland were
past,
Pale sorrow soon my bosom did employ ;
And sad misfortune speedily o'ercast
Those halcyon scenes of undiminished joy.

Attachments unreturned too quickly rent
My youthful heart with agonizing cure :
And when the tide of grief tumultuous spen',
'Twas in the stagnant waters of despair.

Oh then, perchance, thy heart to pity prone,
Can feel for such a suffering wretch as me :
Yes thou wilt sigh for sorrows not thine own,
And I be blest with heaven-born sympathy.

JULIO.

SONNET.

BY ANNA SEWARD.

Short is the time the oldest being lives,
Nor has longevity one hour to waste :
Life's duties are proportion'd to the haste
With which it flows away ;—each day receives
Its task ; that, if neglected, surely gives
The morrow double toil.—Ye who have pass'd
In idle sport the days that fled so fast,
Days, that nor grief recals, nor care retrieves,
At length be wise, and think, that of the part
Remaining in that vital period given,
How short the date, and as the prospect start,
Ere to the extremest verge your steps be driv'n !
Nor let a moment unimprov'd depart,
But view it as the latest trust of heaven !

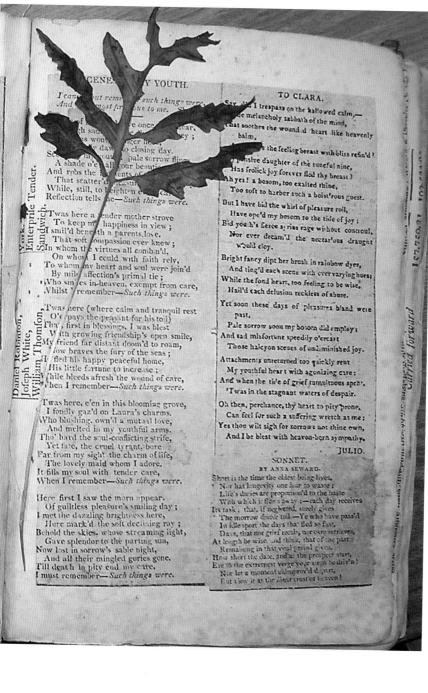

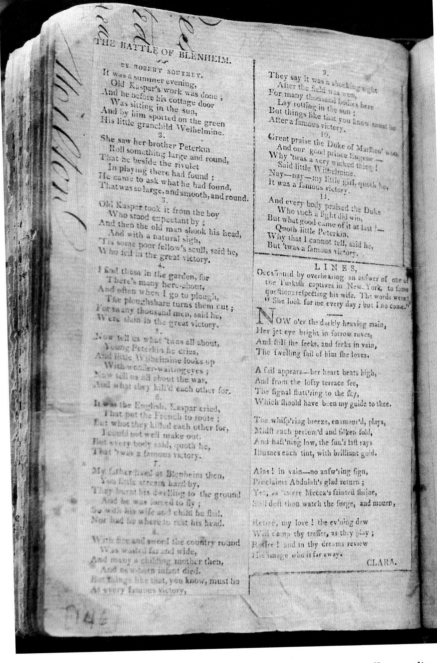

THE BATTLE OF BLENHEIM.

BY ROBERT SOUTHEY.

It was a summer evening,
 Old Kaspar's work was done;
And he before his cottage door
 Was sitting in the sun,
And by him sported on the green
 His little grandchild Wilhelmine.

2.

She saw her brother Peterkin
 Roll something large and round,
That he beside the rivulet
 In playing there had found;
He came to ask what he had found,
 That was so large, and smooth, and round.

3.

Old Kaspar took it from the boy
 Who stood expectant by;
And then the old man shook his head,
 And with a natural sigh,
'Tis some poor fellow's scull, said he,
 Who fell in the great victory.

4.

I find them in the garden, for
 There's many here-about,
And often when I go to plough,
 The ploughshare turns them out;
For many thousand men, said he,
 Were slain in the great victory.

5.

Now tell us what 'twas all about,
 Young Peterkin he cries,
And little Wilhelmine looks up
 With wonder-waiting eyes;
Now tell us all about the war,
 And what they kill'd each other for.

6.

It was the English, Kaspar cried,
 That put the French to route;
But what they kill'd each other for,
 I could not well make out.
But every body said, quoth he,
 That 'twas a famous victory.

7.

My father lived at Blenheim then,
 Yon little stream hard-by,
They burnt his dwelling to the ground
 And he was forced to fly;
So with his wife and child he fled,
 Nor had he where to rest his head.

8.

With fire and sword the country round
 Was wasted far and wide,
And many a childing mother then,
 And new-born infant died.
But things like that, you know, must be
 At every famous victory,

9.

They say it was a shocking sight
 After the field was won,
For many thousand bodies here
 Lay rotting in the sun;
But things like that you know must be
 After a famous victory.

10.

Great praise the Duke of Marlbro' won
 And our good prince Eugene —
Why 'twas a very wicked thing!
 Said little Wilhelmine.
Nay—nay—my little girl, quoth he,
 It was a famous victory.

11.

And every body praised the Duke
 Who such a fight did win,
But what good came of it at last?—
 Quoth little Peterkin.
Why that I cannot tell, said he,
 But 'twas a famous victory.

LINES,

Occasioned by overhearing an answer of one of
the Turkish captives in New-York, to some
questions respecting his wife. The words were:
"She look for me every day; but I no come."

NOW o'er the darkly heaving main,
Her jet eye bright in sorrow roves,
And still she seeks, and seeks in vain,
The swelling sail of him she loves.

A sail appears.—her heart beats high,
And from the lofty terrace see,
The signal flutt'ring to the sky,
Which should have been my guide to thee.

The whisp'ring breeze, enamour'd, plays,
Midst each perfum'd and silken fold,
And hast'ning low, the sun's last rays
Illumes each tint, with brilliant gold.

Alas! in vain—no answ'ring sign,
Proclaims Abdalah's glad return;
Yet, as 'twere Mecca's sainted shrine,
Still dost thou watch the surge, and mourn,

Retire, my love! the ev'ning dew
Will camp thy tresses, as they play;
Retire! and in thy dreams review
His image who is far away.

CLARA.

Robert Southey's "Battle of Blenheim" is one of several poems Jefferson clipped
commemorating famous battles. Robert Southey, Byron's great nemesis, appealed
to Jefferson for his moving, if sentimental, treatment of patriotism and domesticity

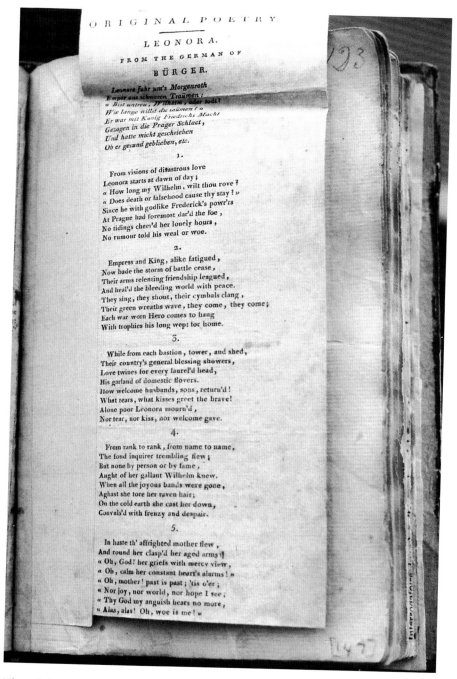

LEONORA.

FROM THE GERMAN OF

BÜRGER.

Leonore fuhr um's Morgenroth
Empor aus schweren Traümen :
« Bist untreu, Wilhelm, oder todt?
Wie lange willst du saümen ?»
Er war mit König Friedrichs Macht
Gezogen in die Prager Schlact,
Und hatte micht geschrieben
Ob er gesund geblieben, etc.

1.

From visions of disastrous love
Leonora starts at dawn of day ;
« How long my Wilhelm, wilt thou rove ?
« Does death or falsehood cause thy stay ? »
Since he with godlike Frederick's powr'rs
At Prague had foremost dar'd the foe ,
No tidings cheer'd her lonely hours ,
No rumour told his weal or woe.

2.

Empress and King, alike fatigued ,
Now bade the storm of battle cease ,
Their arms relenting friendship leagued ,
And heal'd the bleeding world with peace.
They sing, they shout, their cymbals clang ,
Their green wreaths wave, they come, they come ;
Each war worn Hero comes to hang
With trophies his long wept for home.

3.

While from each bastion, tower, and shed,
Their country's general blessing showers,
Love twines for every laurel'd head,
His garland of domestic flovers.
How welcome husbands, sons, return'd !
What tears, what kisses greet the brave!
Alone poor Leonora mourn'd ,
Nor tear, nor kiss, nor welcome gave.

4.

From rank to rank, from name to name,
The fond inquirer trembling flew ;
But none by person or by fame ,
Aught of her gallant Wilhelm knew.
When all the joyous bands were gone,
Aghast she tore her raven hair;
On the cold earth she cast her down,
Convuls'd with frenzy and despair.

5.

In haste th' affrighted mother flew ,
And round her clasp'd her aged arms ;
« Oh, God! her griefs with mercy view ,
« Oh, calm her constant heart's alarms ! »
« Oh, mother! past is past ; 'tis o'er ;
« Nor joy, nor world, nor hope I see ;
« Thy God my anguish hears no more ,
« Alas, alas! Oh, woe is me ! »

Though he admired Homer and Virgil, Jefferson also collected gothic poems, like Burger's Romantic "Leonora," which appeared in several English translations and at least one American newspaper. Too large to appear in the collection, the clipping was folded over to fit the book.

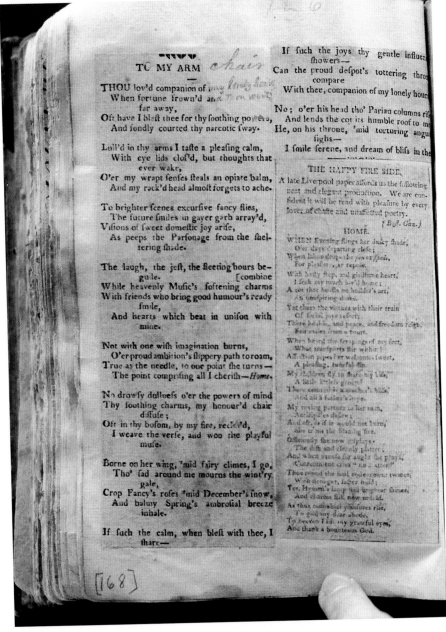

Meticulous in all his endeavors, Jefferson penciled in the missing word "chair" and portions of the first stanza from the original newspaper clipping, "To my Arm[chair]." The "pleasure of retirement" was one of Jefferson's favorite themes, taken, in part, from the Greek and Roman writers such as Cicero whom he admired. In his letters, he wrote continually of his desire to return to Monticello and enjoy his own happy fireside.

THE PLEASURE OF RETIREMENT

HAPPY the man, whofe country feat
Affords a pleafing, calm retreat
   Beneath its fhady bow'rs :
No heavy cares of public life ;
No noify parties' clam'rous ftrife,
   Difturb his peaceful hours.
Ambition dwells not in his breaft,
No fting of envy breaks his reft ;
   No grief corrodes his mind ;
No fierce defires of gold controul,
Or fway the dictates of his foul,
   To heav'n's decrees refign'd ;
With empty titles let the great,
And all the ufelefs pomp of ftate,
   Perpetuate their name :
Peace and contentment fills his cot,
And healthy temp'rance crowns his lot,
   Tho' unadorn'd by fame.
Let others to preferment climb,
By daring fome atrocious crime,
   And rule the fubject ftate.
Let the bafe traitor heap up gold ;
The price of his dear country fold,
   By perfidy made great.
He lives beneath his humble home,
More bleft than in the gilded dome,
   Where guilt torments the breaft,
To him, retirement joy affords,
Fair competence fupplies his board,
   And virtue makes him bleft.

Sir Henry Wotton,

In his character of a *happy life*, has the following beautiful ftanzas :

How happy is he born and taught
  That ferveth not another's will ;
Whofe armour is his honeft thought,
  And fimple truth his utmoft fkill.

Whofe paffions n t his mafters are,
  Whofe foul is ftill prepar'd for death :
Untied unto the world by care,
  Of public fame or private breath.

Who envies none that chance doth raife,
  Nor vice hath ever underftood ;
How deepeft wounds are given by prai e,
  Nor rules of ftate, but rules of good.

Who hath his life from rumours freed,
  Whofe confcience is his ftrong retreat ;

Whofe ftate can neither flatterers feed,
  Nor ruin make oppreffors great.

Who God doth late and early pray
  More of his grace than gifts to lend,
And entertains the harmlefs day
  With a religious book or friend.

This man is freed from fervile bands
  Of hope to rife, or fear to fall :
Lord of himfelf, tho' not of lands ;
  And having nothing, yet hath all.

HOME.

When evening flings her dufkey fhade,
  O'er days departing clofe ;
When labor drops the pen or fpade,
  For pleafure, or repofe.

With hafty fteps and gladfome heart,
  I feek my much lov'd home ;
A cot that boafts no builders art,
  An unafpiring dome,

Yet there the virtues with their train,
  Of focial joys refort ;
There health and peace and freedom reign,
  Fair exiles from a court.

When heard the fcrapings of my feet,
  What tranfports ftir within !
Affection pipes her welcome fweet,
  A pleafing, tuneful din.

My children fly to fhare my kifs ;
  A little artlefs group !
There centred is a mother's blifs,
  And all a father's hope.

My loving partner in her turn,
  Anticipates defire—
And oft, as if it would not burn,
  She trims the blazing fire.

Confcioufly fhe now difplays
  The difh and cleanly platter,
And when excufe for aught the prays,
  Contentment cries " no matter."

Thus round the foul endearment twines,
  With ftronger fofter hold—
Yet hymen's lamp ftill brighter fhines,
  And charms ftill new unfold.

As thus connubial pleafures rife,
  To gild my dear abode,
To heaven I lift my grateful eyes,
  And thank a bounteous God

THE STORM.

ON the lone cliff, that hides its savage brow
   Within the bosom of each threat'ning
     cloud,
I listen'd for the ship-bell's sound,
The merry seaman's laugh the labouring oar ;
I look'd for vales, with blooming flowrets
     crown'd ;
But all were fled. The wind blew cold and
    loud :
No footstep mark'd a wanderer on the shore,
The waves with anger rent the rock below.
Shivering I saw the tumbling bark a wreck,
Sink 'midst the fury of the boiling waves,
Poor hapless sailors' cold untimely graves,
Their knell the sea birds' melancholy shriek.
Perhaps some female at this very hour,
Chill'd by the grasp of fear, upbraids the wind,
And racks with busy thought the brooding mind,
As on the window beats the midnight show'r.
But half the world, unknown to thought or care,
Secure in costly domes, lie hid in sleep,
Deaf to the moanings of the troubled air,
Or shrieks of death that issue from the deep.

ADDRESS TO HOPE.

THOU welcome guest, where sorrow reigns,
Thou soother of corroding pains,
   To thee each lyre I bend ;
Thou who canst quell the rising sigh,
Can wipe the tear from sorrow's eye,
   And prove to grief a friend.

The heart oppress'd with woes, in thee
The cheering balm of comfort see,
   A balm by Heaven design'd,
To keep the spirits from despair,
To soothe the heart oppress'd with care,
   And ease the troubled mind,

Away then every anxious fear,
Come balmy Hope, my spirits cheer,
   And waft my soul on high ;
Where the pure limpid streams of love

Descend in Heavenly showers above,
   Though dim to human eye.

Though clouds now gather o'er my head,
And comfort seems forever fled,
   Yet will I not despair :
For the bright sun may rise once more,
Though with less lustre than before,
   To brighten every care.

And when about to quit this scene,
Where grief and sorrow intervene,
   May thou triumphant rise :
That as my soul shall take its flight,
I may ascend to worlds of light,
   Above the etherial skies.

               MARIA.

ON HOPE.

THOU bid'st me hope—Alas ! can hope
   Restore content, long lost ;
Or safely guide the shatter'd bark,
   That's on the ocean tost ?

When anguish tears the tortur'd soul,
   And heaves the pent-up sigh,
And sad reflection makes the tear
   Stand trembling in the eye ;

Think'st thou, that hope's delusive power
   Can ought of joy impart,
To calm the tumults of my mind,
   Or ease a breaking heart ?

Ah ! no, my friend ! too oft has hope
   My flatter'd sense deceiv'd ;
She glittering prospects oft has shewn,
   Too oft have I believ'd.

CANZONET.

FLOWERS are fresh, and bushes green,
   Cheerly the linnets sing,
Winds are soft, and skies serene ;
Time however, soon shall throw
         Winter's snow
O'er the buxom breast of Spring.

Hope that buds in lover's heart,
   Lives not through the storm of years !
Time makes love itself depart,
Time and scorn congeal the mind,
        Looks unkind
......affection's warmest tears !

Time shall make the bushes green,
   Time dissolve the winter's snow ;
Winds be soft, and skies serene,
   ...... sing their wonted strain :
            But again
Blighted love shall never blow.

Jefferson wrote an original poem on hope, one of his favorite subjects. On the same page, he pasted the more despairing "The Grave," which perhaps shows Jefferson's taste for antithesis and complementarity.

THE GRAVE.

[A rich vein of morality runs throughout the following production]—

THERE is a calm for those who weep,
A rest for weary Pilgrims found;
They softly lie, and sweetly sleep,
    Low in the ground.

The storm that wrecks the winter sky,
No more disturbs their deep repose,
Than summer ev'ning's latest sigh,
    That shuts the rose.

I long to lay this painful head
And aching heart beneath the soil,
To slumber in that dreamless bed
    From all my toil.

For Misery stole me at my birth,
And cast me helpless on the wild;
I perish—O my mother Earth!
    Take home thy child.

On thy dear lap these limbs reclin'd,
Shall gently moulder into thee;
Nor leave one wretched trace behind,
    Resembling me.

Hark!—a strange found affrights mine ear!
My pulse—my brain runs wild—I rave!
Ah! who art thou whose voice I hear?
    "I am THE GRAVE!

"The GRAVE, that never spake before,
Hath found at length a tongue to chide:
O listen!—I will speak no more:
    Be silent, Pride!

"Art thou a WRETCH, of hope forlorn,
The victim of consuming care?
Is thy distracted conscience torn
    By sell despiar?

"Do foul misdeeds of former times
Wring with remorse thy guilty breast?
And Ghosts of unforgiven crimes
    Murder thy rest?

"Lash'd by the furies of the mind,
From wrath and vengeance wouldst thou flee,
Ah! think not, hope not, Fool! to find
    A friend in me.

"By all the terrors of the tomb,
Beyond the power of tongue to tell!
By the dread secrets of my womb!
    By Death and Hell!

"I charge thee LIVE!—Repent and pray;
In dust thine infamy deplore;
There yet is mercy!—go thy way,
    And sin no more.

"——Art thou a MOURNER?—Hast thou
    known
The joy of innocent delights?
Endearing days forever flown
    And tranquil nights?

"O LIVE?—and deeply cherish still
The sweet remembrance of the past:

"Art thou a WANDERER?—Hast thou seen
O'erwhelming tempests drown thy bark?
A shipwreck'd sufferer hast thou been,
    Misfortune's mark!

"Tho' long, of winds and waves the sport,
Condemn'd in wretchedness to roam,
LIVE!—thou shalt reach a sheltering port,
    A quiet home.

"To FRIENDSHIP didst thou trust thy fame,
And was thy Friend a deadly foe,
Who stole into thy breast to aim
    A surer blow?

"LIVE!—and repine not o'er his loss,
A loss unworthy to be told:
Thou hast mistaken sordid dross
    For Friendship's gold.

"Go, seek that treasure, seldom found,
Of power the fiercest griefs to calm,
And soothe the bosom's deepest wound
    With Heavenly balm.

"—In WOMAN hast thou plac'd thy bliss,
And did the Fair One faithless prove?
Hath she betray'd thee with a kiss,
    And sold thy love?

"LIVE!—'twas a false bewild'ring fire;
Too often Love's insidious dart
Thrills the fond soul with sweet desire,
    But kills the heart.

"A nobler flame shall warm thy breast,
A brighter Maiden's virtuous charms!
Blest shalt thou be, supremely blest,
    In beauty's arms.

"——Whate'er thy lot—whoe'er thou be—
Confess thy folly, kiss the rod,
And in thy chast'ning sorrows see
    The hand of GOD.

"A bruised reed he will not break;
Afflictions all his children feel;
He wounds them for his mercy's sake,
    He wounds to heal.

"Humbled beneath his mighty hand,
Prostrate his Providence adore:
'Tis done!—Arise! he bids thee stand,
    To fall no more.

"Now, Traveller in the vale of tears!
To realms of everlasting light,
Through Time's dark wilderness of years,
    Pursue thy flight.

"There is a calm for those who weep,
A rest for weary Pilgrims found;
And while the mouldering ashes sleep,
    Low in the ground,

"The Soul, of origin divine,
GOD's glorious image, freed from clay,
In Heaven's eternal sphere shall shine;
    A star of day!

"The SUN is but a spark of fire,
A transient meteor in the sky,
The Soul, immortal as its Sire,
    "SHALL NEVER DIE."

Poet's Department.

THE DEATH OF W. WALLACE,
The maintainer of the Liberties of Scotland,
FROM SCOTTISH.

Joy, joy in London now !
He goes, the rebel Wallace goes to death,
At length the traitor meets the traitor's doom,
Joy, joy in London, now !

He on a sledge is drawn,
His strong right arm unweapon'd and in chains,
And garlanded around his helmless head
The laurel wreath of scorn.

They throng to view him now
Who in the field had fled before his sword,
Who at the name of Wallace once grew pale,
And faltered out a prayer.

Yes, they can meet his eye,
That only beams with patient courage now ;
Yes, they can gaze upon those manly limbs
Defenceless now and bound.

And that eye did not shrink
As he beheld the pomp of infamy ;
Nor did one rebel feeling shake these limbs
When the last moment came.

What tho' suspended sense
Was by their damned cruelty revived,
What tho' ingenious vengeance lengthen'd life
To feel protracted death ;

What tho' the hangman's hand
Graspt in his living breast the heaving heart—
In the last agony, the last sick pang,
Wallace had comfort still.

He call'd to mind his deeds
Done for his country in the embattled field ;
He thought of that good cause for which he died,
And that was joy in death !

Go Edward, triumph now !
Cambria is fallen, and Scotland's strength is
crush'd ;
On Wallace, on Llewellyn's mangled limbs
The fowls of heaven have fed.

Unrivalled, unopposed,
Go, Edward, full of glory to thy grave !
The weight of patriot blood upon thy soul,
Go, Edward, to thy God !

The Scottish poem, in twelve books, entitled
"*The life and acts of sir William Wallace,*"
says,
Monteith him sold, and that o'er well was known.
Scotland he freed, and brought it from thirlage,
And now in heaven he has his heritage,
Whereof we have right stedfast confidence,
Since for his country he made so great defence.

ON THE DEATH OF LORD NELSON.

BY THE HON. C. J. FOX.

In death's terrific icy arms
  The brave illustrious Nelson lies :
He's free from care and war's alarms,
  Sees not our tears, nor hears our sighs.

Cold is the heart where valor reign'd
  Mute is the tongue that Joy inspir'd
Still is the arm that conquest gain'd,
  And dim the eye that glory fir'd.

T___ ____ for him a world like this !
  He's landed on the happy shore,
Where all the world partake of bliss,
  And heroes meet to part no more.

ELEGY.

In vain this tear, lamented maid is shed :
  In vain this breast may sorrow for thy
  doom ;
The pang of woe can never reach the dead,
  Or pierce the sad recesses of the tomb.
Yet, sacred shade, the tributary sigh,
  Which friendship pays, in tenderness, re-
  ceive ;
It is the lot of excellence to die,
  And must be natures privilege to grieve.
The tender bosom is no longer warm,
  That cheek must blush no wand'rous gra-
  ces more ;
For death alas ! has triumphed over a form
  Design'd to conquer all the word before.
But here reflection easily may find
  The short duration of the human state ;
Since all the noblest virtues of the mind
  Can ne'er exempt us from the stroke of fate.

Jefferson collected a number of elegies of political heroes famous in his day: the
Scottish revolutionary figure William Wallace, the British naval commander Lord
Nelson, and American statesmen such as Washington, Hamilton, and Burr. Jefferson
was very much concerned with how he would be remembered by posterity and
encouraged the poet Joel Barlow to write an account of his presidency.

REMONSTRANCE to WINTER.

BY J. MONTGOMERY.

AH! why, unfeeling *Winter!* why,
Still flag's thy torpid wing?
Fly, melancohly Season, fly,
And yield the year to *Spring*.

Spring---the young cherubim of love,
An exile in disgrace,
Flits o'er the scene, like Noah's dove,
Nor finds a resting place.

When on the mountain's azure peak,
Alights her fairy form,
Cold blow the winds----and dark and bleak,
Around her rolls the storm.

If to the valley she repair
For shelter and defence,
Thy wrath pursues the mourner there,
And drives her weeping thence.

She seeks the brook---the faithless brook,
Of her unmindful grown,
Feels the chill magic of thy look,
And lingers into stone.

She woos her embryo flowers in vain,
To rear their infant heads;---
Deaf to her voice her flowers remain
Enchanted in their beds.

In vain she bids the trees expand
Their green luxuriant charms;---
Bare in the wilderness they stand,
And stretch their withering arms.

Her favourite birds, in feeble notes,
Lament thy long delay;
And strain their little stammering throats,
To charm thy blasts away.

Ah! *Winter*, calm thy cruel rage,
Release the struggling year;
Thy power is past, decrepid Sage!
Arise and disappear.

The stars that graced thy splendid night
Are lost in warmer rays;
The Sun, rejoicing in his might
Unrolls celestial days.

Then why, usurping *Winter*, why
Still flags thy frozen wing?
Fly unrelenting tyrant; fly---
And yield the year to *Spring*.

LE MALADE IMAGINAIRE.

AH! woe is me, on my sick couch reclining,
In dreary solitude condemn'd to stay;
Ah! woe is me, in grief of heart repining,
Chearless my night, and unendear'd my day.

Ah! woe is me, poor wretch, no pity gaining,
No pity, from the vacant noisy throng;
Ah! woe is me, to senseless walls complaining,
In happy health while others bound along.

Ah! woe is me, in melancholy sadness,
Counting the minutes, hours, and days go by,
No friend, no mistress, to relieve my sadness,
Or blandly smile in soothing sympathy.

In sympathy---ah no! they yield it never,
While the warm blood leaps high in my vein,
So from themselves their minds they cannot sever,
To sigh for sickness, when they feel no pain.

In vain for me, so brightly gleams the morning,
In vain for me the opening flow'rs expand,
In vain for me, with halcyon smiles adorning,
Spring dresses Nature with her rosy hand.

Ah! mock not me, ye sunbeams gaily flaunting,
I have no joy to see you look so fine;
Your laughing radiance seems most bitter taunt-
ing,
While I on wretched couch am doom'd to pine.

Ah me! that genial gale no joy diffuses,
With nervous tremours shook, despair'd I lie,
Shadow of hope, my shrunken heart refuses,
And in itself retir'd, prepares to die.

Ah! farther take those flowers, so gaily bloom-
ing,
It joys not me to see them look so bright;
Me, whom the hand of Death is swiftly dooming,
To fade forever in eternal night.

Shut out the garish Sun!---the light is anguish---
Exclude the day, and darkly let me think;
Ah! now---I feel---Death comes---I faint---I lan-
guish,
Together in the yawning grave we sink!

Ye spectres pale, your slender figures bending,
There in the gloom---haste, hasten on, I lay;
Ah! now I see your bony arms extending---
I come, thou grisly King---a willing prey!

TO THE ROSE IN JUNE.

Prepare sweet Rose! thy balmy treat
And all thy vivid charms display,
For lo! the anxious zephyrs wait,
To waft their fragrant draught away.

And lo, the fond expectant Bee,
Now wanders o'er the flow'ry plain,
And searches every plain for thee,
And longs to meet his rose again.

And hark, the minstrels of the grove,
For thee exert their vocal powers,
Mirth, beauty, melody and love,
Invoke thee to adorn their bowers.

Then bid the blushing leaves expand,
In all thy birth-day beauty drest;
Prepare to grace Lavina's hand.---
Prepare to bloom upon her breast.

And when thy tints begin to fade,
And when thy fragrant charms decline,
Then teach the amiable maid,
That beauty's reign resembles thine.

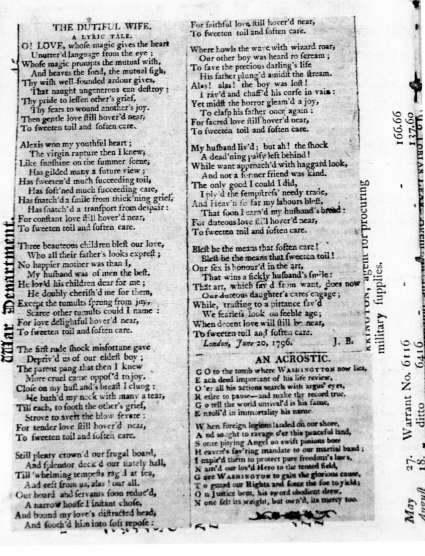

Jefferson admired Washington for his statesmanship rather than for his military prowess, though this "acrostic" is clearly pasted on War Department letterhead. Joseph Dennie accused Jefferson of hypocrisy in shedding tears for Washington at his funeral.

TO LORENZO.

Sighs the dark spirit of the wind,
Or, is't the sound of human woe!
Still, on my list'ning ear, it steals
And soft and sad the numbers flow.

Mourner unknown who breath'st the strain!
Thy strain awakes a kindred sigh:
For, I have felt thy ev'ry pain,
Have seen affection's fond hopes die.

Yet there is one—one bitter pang—
One woe supreme, I ne'er have known,
If aught, beside, thy mis'ry cause
Still bless thy fate, and cease to groan.

Thou hast not watch'd, the sinking eyes,
Of her, the idol of thy soul:
Nor, mark'd the last faint flutt'ring pulse
As, soft to Heav'n, the s,irit stole.

Thou hast not, o'er her lowly grave
Hung, in affection's speechless spell:
While, all unheard, the midnight breeze,
Lent to thy sighs, its mournful swell.

Thou know'st not this—then raise thine eye,
And, greet the loveliest beam of eve:
Patience and time, the care shall bring:
And, thou shalt surely, cease to grieve.

Tho' sorrow now, has clos'd thy heart,
Soon shall benigner signs prevail:
Then thy sick soul, to health, restor'd
Shall taste the fragrance of the gale.

Yes! thou shalt walk, in nature's train,
Her vast magnificence explore
Where, heaves the wildy swelling main,
Encroaching, on the shrinking shore.

Or humbler—join my pensive lay
To ev'ning's star, or Cynthia's beam,
While, all forgotten, day's dull cares
Fade, as the traces of a dream.

CLARA.

NATURE AND MAN.

NATURE renews her charming scenes,
Her hills, her dales, her lawns and greens;
But Man's gay summer once being o'er,
His cheerful spring returns no more!
The sun declines, and yields to night,
But the next morning shines most bright:
Not so with Man!—when once he dies,
His sun is set—no more to rise!

FOR THIS GAZETTE.

The following introductory address, written by the Rev. Dr. William Staughton, was delivered by one of the Young Ladies belonging to Mr. William Moulder's Academy, on the evening of his exhibition.

WHEN the mighty CREATOR, pursuing his plan,
From the dust of the ground had constructed a Man,
He nerv'd with firm vigour his arm;
All the animals round their great master confess'd
His countenance courage undaunted express'd,
The heart of a lion beat bold in his breast
And he still mocks the voice of alarm.

But in Woman's formation well pleas'd we beheld,
Soft features receiv'd from a delicate mould,
To her no wild passions belong;
With arms like the lily that graces the lawn,
With cheeks like the rose, or the meek-rising dawn,
With a heart palpitating, a timorous fawn,
All her energies lie in her tongue.

And yet would you think it, of this precious boon,
Stern man, or ill cuak m will rob us full soon,
Unless our own cause we espouse;
Narcissa hears often commended her mien,
Her easy address and her gait like a Queen,
But she's told 'tis enough that a female be seen,
She must always be still as a mouse.

No, Gentlemen! pardon our boldness to night,
We humbly come forward asserting a right
That nature has fairly confer'd;
You smile at the notes the sweet mocking bird brings,
No moments are heavy when Philomel sings,
And can you approve these irrational things,
And deny to a female a word.

Semiramis brought Babylon lasting renown,
The maid of Orleans on Charles plac'd a crown,
And historians give them their due;
But to no such achievements these bosoms aspire,
From the pile of the Hero, we borrow no fire,
No, generous audience! all we desire,
Will be found in a plaudit from you.

Should the fluttering heart make the memory fail,
And the dialogue mar, or disfigure the tale,
I know you will kindly excuse;
You, Mothers and Sisters, were once young as we,
Let soft recollection provide us a plea,
Yes, yes, the wet eye, at this moment I see,
Will not the sought favour refuse.

While we labour to speak with correctness and grace,
And cadence and emphasis skilfully place,
New ardours arise in our breast;
The footsteps of virtue we'd daily pursue,
And to parents still render obedience due,
O may Heaven shed its favours on us and on you,
And make us eternally blest.

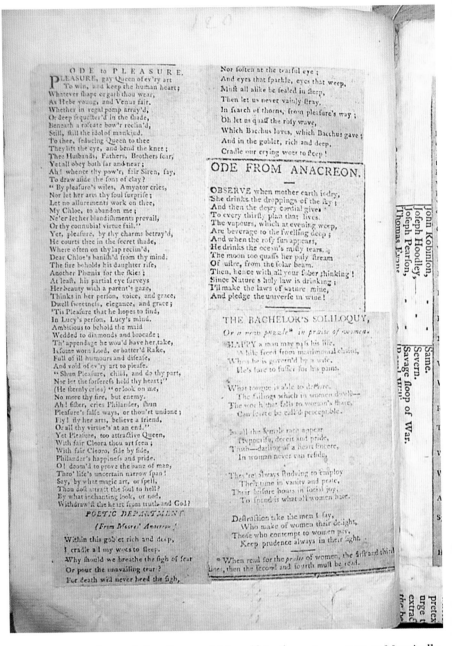

Jefferson kept a bust of Hamilton and himself in the entranceway at Monticello, informing his guests that they stood "opposed in death as in life." "I know I have been the object of uniform opposition from Mr. Jefferson, from the first moment of his coming to the City of New York," Hamilton wrote to George Washington.

AN ELEGY,
Occasioned by the
DEATH of Gen. HAMILTON.

The following Elegy was written in Scotland, soon after the arrival of the intelligence of the unhappy event, which it commemorates. In order to enter fully into the views of the author, it will be necessary to call to mind a leading distinction between free and despotic governments, viz: That the latter, for the most part, ensure tranquility, but subvert liberty—whereas the former preserve liberty but frequently interrupt tranquility.

Oppress'd, enfeebl'd, overwhelm'd with woe,
While lamentation thro' Columbia reigns,
With lingering steps behold the mourners go
To lay in earth their Hamilton's remains.

Loud tolls the bell—and messenger of grief,
Columbia's sons in sable garb attend,
From daily labor snatch a short relief
And o'er the relics of their hero bend.

But not on pageants does his fame rely,
Far nobler signs his fun'ral praises speak,
Ingenuous sorrow streams from every eye,
And heartfelt sadness dwells on every cheek.

Well might Columbia her forebodings tell,
When evil fortune this affliction gave,
Well might she tremble, when the hero fell,
Who sunk her glory in an early grave.

Rarely, 'mid this defect of virtue's light,
Such shining merit can our thoughts engage,
The dazzling splendour overpowers the sight
And leads remembrance to a classic age.

When first invited from her old retreats,
Exulting Freedom cross'd the Atlantic wave,
With joy she view'd her scarce-expected seats,
And independence to Columbia gave.

Awhile, delighted Freedom there remain'd,
But soon her dwelling unprepar'd she found,
Sprung from the land where civil discord reign'd,
And hovered doubtful on the wilds around.

Her wrath to soften and allay her fear,
Prone on the beach the hero oft would stand,
With outstretch'd arms, implored the goddess near,
And reconcil'd her to his native land.

Thrice trembling Freedom her alarms disclos'd
When civil contests dubious she survey'd,
And thrice the youth his counsels interpos'd,
Her flight suspended and her fears allay'd.

Full oft he stemm'd the democratic flood
That rules impetuous thro' Columbia's state,
And oft the fury undismayed withstood
Of public faction and of private hate.

Oft Freedom saw him quell intestine broils,
Saw her bright fabric rear'd by him alone,
The goddess smil'd propitious on his toils
And soon she fill'd an adamantine throne.

Drawn by the ties of gratitude and love,
Her wing celestial freedom sure shall spread
With care maternal every harm remove,
And anxious guard her benefactor's head.

Deceitful prospect! ah! 'twas vain to trust
That liberty her dearest child would save,
'Twas Freedom's self that laid him in the dust,
And dug her champion an untimely grave.

Shall freedom then be banished from below,
Back to the regions whence at first she came?
Shall the fond tears herself has taught to flow,
On earth extinguish her aspiring flame?

Sons of Columbia! will it not be feared
On earth the goddess shall conclude her reign,
With the same hand that pluck'd the fruits he reared,
And laid your hero lifeless on the plain!

From the bright mansions of eternal joy,
Where shines around him an imperial day,
And nought but mortal doubts his ear annoy,
Methinks I hear the martyr's spirit say:

Thrice-hallowed Freedom, only sovereign good
On whose bright altar of celestial plan
I oft aspired to immolate my blood,
Thou blest protection of defenceless man!

Tho' no succeeding annalist shall tell
In thy defence I found a glorious grave,
Tho' lull'd by soft security I fell,
Beneath the shelter of the shield it gave.

John Hemings was the master carpenter at Monticello and the younger brother of Sally Hemings; he crafted a Campeachy chair from a New Orleans design (based, in turn, on a chair designed in the Mexican province of Campeche). John Hemings was one of only five slaves that Jefferson freed in his will of March 1826.

Extract from the " MIRROR for MAGISTRATES,
Wrote above two hundred years ago.

WHAT doth avail to have a princely place,
A name of honour, and a high degree ;
To come by kindred of a noble race,
Except we princely, worthy, noble be!
The fruit declares the goodness of the tree.
Do brag no more of birth, or lineage then ;
For virtue, grace and manners make the man.

This selection from "Mirror for Magistrates" is one of three poems that includes Jefferson's own penciled emendation.

ON A LONG NOSE.
[Anonymous]

Heavens! what a nose! Forbear to look,
Whene'r you drink, in fount or brook;
For, as the fair Narcissus died
When hanging o'er a fountain's side,
You too the limpid water quaffing;
May die, my worthy sir, with laughing.

2:15

Jefferson's reading of *Tristram Shandy* inspired a bawdy reference to noses in a 1787 letter to Maria Cosway: "At Strasbourg I sat down to write to you. But for my soul I could think of nothing at Strasbourg but the promontory of noses, of Diego, of Slawkenburgius his historian, and the procession of the Strasburgers to meet the man with the nose. Had I written you from thence it would have been a continuation of Sterne upon noses."[94] In book four of *Tristram Shandy*, Sterne described a stranger who arrived in Strasbourg and created chaos because of the hugeness of his nose. Everyone wishes to see it, and the women to touch it.[95] The reference, most critics agree, is to the male anatomy. This subject, and its erotic significance, reappears in a clipping Jefferson chose to include in his scrapbook. Halliday's *Understanding Jefferson* stressed Sterne's importance as a clue to understanding Jefferson's erotic imagination.

A COMPLIMENT.
[Anonymous]

What is a compliment? It is a thing
Compos'd of pretty words, to charm fine girls;
It is a homage paid to vanity,
But, which our better judgement disapproves;
It is a fine drawn speech, made up of wit,
But sometimes void of common sense; it is
A monstrous favorite of flatterers,
It courts anticipation's powerful charms,
And suits the shallow grin of self-conceit:
It is a present proffer'd to fancy,
Which she accepts with queenlike pomp and pride;
No friend to frankness, rather shy of truth,
Bestow'd where it expects a smart return
Of ditto, to indemnify the breath,
Spent in the fine formation of itself;
In short, 'tis what we ever like to hear,
But what we sometimes ought to disbelieve.

ARION.

East Sudbury, August 30, 1805.

2:17

Jefferson knew the danger of flatterers and was unusually receptive to those who criticized his policies, as biographers have pointed out. His correspondence is remarkably free of unctuous praise, for he viewed compliments as "a homage paid to vanity / but, which our better judgement disapproves." "I like a person who points out a mistake just as much as one who teaches me a truth, because, in effect, a corrected mistake is a truth," Jefferson wrote in *Notes on Virginia*, quoting Buffon.[96]

CURE FOR BAD RAZORS.

[Peter Pindar]

A FELLOW in a market town,
Most musical cried Razors up and down,
   And offered twelve for eighteen pence;
Which certainly seem'd wond'rous cheap,
And for the money quite a heap,
   As ev'ry man would buy with cash and sense.

II.

A country bumpkin the great offer heard,
Poor hodge! who suffer'd with a broad black beard,
   That seem'd a shoe brush stuck beneath his nose,
With cheerfulness the eighteen pence he paid,
And smiling to himself in whispers said,
   "This rascal stole the Razors I suppose.

III.

"No matter, if the fellow be a knave,
"Provided that the Razors shave,
   "It certainly will be a monstrous Prize:"
So home the Clown with his good fortune went,
Smiling in heart and soul content,
   And quickly soap'd himself to ears and eyes.

IV.

Being well lather'd from a dish or tub,
Hodge began with grinning pain to grub,
   Just like a hedger cuttin' furze:*
'Twas a vile Razor — then the rest he tried,
All were imposters — ah! Hodge sigh'd,
   "I wish my eighteen pence within my purse."

V.

In vain to chaice his beard, and bring the graces,
He cut, and dug, and winc'd, and made wry faces
   Razors! a mortal confounded dog,
Not fit to scrape a hog;
Brought blood, caper'd, danc'd, and swore;
   And blam'd each Razor's body o'er and o'er.

---

* Furze is one of the first flowering plants of spring.

VI.

Hodge sought the fellow, found him, and begun,
"Perhaps master Razor-rogue, to you, 'tis fun,
    "For folks to flea themselves alive;
"You rascal for an hour have I been grubbing,
"Giving my scoundrel whiskers here a scrubbing,
    "With Razors just like oyster knives,
"Sirrah, I know you, you're a knave,
"To cry up Razors that can't shave."

VII.

"Friend," quoth the Razor-man, "I'm no knave,"
"As for the Razors you have bought,
"Upon my honor I never thought,
"That they would shave."

VIII.

"Not think they'd shave," quoth Hodge,
    With wond'ring eyes,
And voice not much unlike an Indian yell
"What were they made for then you dog?" he cries

IX.

"Made!" quoth the fellow with a smile,
"They were made to sell."

X.

The Razor man found he was overtaken,
The cure, sold by PACKWOOD, sav'd his bacon;
Said "take a whet on *Packwood's Strop* a while,
"Thou then shalt shave in a superior stile."

                                TURN OVER.

2:21

This poem reflects the American values of the hard-bargaining businessman who appears in works as diverse as Benjamin Franklin's *The Way of Wealth* and Melville's *The Confidence Man*. Victims of shoddy workmanship and zealous advertising can empathize with this eighteenth-century American told that the razors he purchased were made for selling.

THE OWL AND THE PARROT.

By Peter Pindar.

An Owl fell desp'rately in love, poor soul;
  Sighing and hooting in his lonely hole —
A Parrot, the dear object of his wishes,
Who in her cage enjoy'd the loaves & fishes;
    In short, had all she wanted — meat & drink, —
    Washing & lodging — full enough, I think.

Squire Owl most musically tells his tale;
  His oath's, his squeezes, kisses, sighs, prevail;
  Poll cannot bear, dear heart, to hear him grieve,
  So opes her cage, without a "by your leave:"
They're marry'd — go to bed with raptur'd faces,
Rich words, & so forth — usual in such cases.

A day or two pass'd amorously sweet —
  Love, kissing, cooing, billing all their meat:
At length they both fell hungry. "What's for dinner?
    "Pray, what have we to eat, my dear?" quoth Poll?
    "Nothing, by all my wisdom!" answered Owl —
"I never thought of *that*, as I'm a sinner!
    "But, Poll, on something I shall put my pats: —
    "What say'st, thou, deary, to a dish of rats?"

"*Rats! Mister* Owl; d'ye think that I'll eat rats?
    "Eat them yourself, or give them to the cats,"
Whines the poor bride, now bursting into tears.
    "Well, Polly, would you rather dine on mouse?
    "I'll catch a few if any in the house:
"Thou shalt not starve, love — so dispel thy fears."

"I won't eat rats, I won't eat mouse — I won't;
    "Don't tell me of such dirty vermin — don't.

"O that within my cage I had but tarry'd!"
  "Polly," quoth Owl," "I'm sorry, I declare,
  "So delicate, you relish not our fate: —
"You should have thought of that before you marry'd."

2:21

This humorous poem portrays marriage as a cynical quest for good cuisine. When the dishes run out and the owl proposes "a dish of rats," Polly reveals her true colors. The Parrot goes to bed with the Owl only to discover he is not the provider she took him for. Was this a warning to Jefferson's daughters not to marry beneath them and give up a splendid cage; or, as is more likely, was it a humorous and philosophical reflection on the "connubial bliss" his daughter already enjoyed in contrast with these self-seeking animals?

POEMS OF FAMILY

CONSCIENCE.
By Peter Pindar.

CONSCIENCE, a terrifying little sprite,
That bat-like winks by day and wakes by night;
Hunts thro' the heart's dark hole each lurking vice,
As sharp as weasels hunting eggs or mice;
Who, when the lightnings flash, and thunders crack,
Makes our hair bristle like a hedge-hog's back;
Shakes, ague-like, our hearts with wild commotion
Uplifts our saint-like eyes with dread devotion:
Bids the poor trembling tongue make terms with heaven,
And promise miracles to be forgiven:
Bids spectres rise, not very like the graces,
With goggling eyes, black beards, and Tyburn* faces;
With scenes of glowing brimstone, scares,
Spits, forks, and proper culinary wares
For roasting, broiling, frying, fricasseeing,
The soul, that sad offending little being,
That stubborn stuff of salamander† make,
Proof to the fury of the burning lake.

2:22

In a letter to his daughter, Jefferson praised "conscience" as a moral guide to all our actions. "If ever you are about to say any thing amiss or to do any thing wrong, consider before hand," he wrote to Martha. "You will feel something within you which will tell you it is wrong and ought not to be said or done: this is your conscience, and be sure to obey it. Our maker has given us all, this faithful internal Monitor, and if you always obey it, you will always be prepared for the end of the world."[97] This clipping of a poem by Peter Pindar shows that Jefferson could also have a sense of humor about the subject.

---

*Tyburn was the gallows in London where criminals were executed.
†The salamander was thought to be impervious to fire.

Tooth-Ache.
[Anonymous]

A man there was who fortune's blessings quaff'd,
　And sure had known no reason to complain,
Had not dame *Nature* as she view'd the draught
　Made his poor *teeth* too sensible of pain.

Sometimes it would the form of *grandeur* take,
　Swelling his cheeks to a majestic size;
And oft it would assume a meaner make,
　And like a *bruiser* close up both his eyes.

In short, in every shape that *tooth-ache* owns,
　He luckless felt and knew it still the same,
And midst a useless burst of speaking groans,
　Had tried all recipes that art could name —

Had stew'd his chops in vinegar and ginger,
　With mustard blister'd them, the pain to check,
And when provok'd by too severe a twinger,
　Had ate red hot *wild turnips* by the peck.

Galen had call'd and *Esculapius* too,
　To try their mental and their manual force;
But nought avail'd which they could say or do,
　They broke the teeth, & left the sufferer worse.
To *Time* and *Patience* then was left the cure,
Whose motions, tho' but slow, are always sure.

One day this man entirely free from pain,
　Rambling on horseback, o'er a neighboring hill,
　Fancied he heard, in accents wild and shrill,
The voice of anguish flit across the plain.

He tho't he guess'd the cause — with eager haste
　He spurr'd his courier to a gallop's speed;
And as o'er fence and wall the sound he chas'd,
Soon gain'd the house from whence it did proceed.

There as he stop'd, a woman he espied,
  Whose wailings added to the general clatter;
So springing from his horse he breathless cried,
  "La! help us — say, good woman, what's the matter?"

My son, she screech'd, by a most cruel fall,
  Has broke his legs, no comfort can the youth take:
"Poh! said the man," (remounting) is that all? —
  "I really tho't the fellow had the tooth ache."

2:22

Dentistry being what it was in the late eigh- his retirement, and once thought a bout of
teenth century, the speaker of this poem diarrhea would bring him to an early grave in
prefers a broken leg to a toothache. Jefferson 1800, though he lived past eighty.[98]
suffered from migraines, which ceased during

The Spirit of Contradiction.
FROM LA FONTAINE.

A woman sauntering near a river's brink,
From thought, or thoughtlessness, or drink,
   No matter which, fell in it —
And, as the story goes,
She ended quickly all her earthly woes,
   Was drown'd, to speak more plainly, in a minute.

Soon as her spouse the tidings knew,
Swift as an arrow to the spot he flew,
   The corpse to find and the last duties pay:
Friend, cried he, with tearful eyes.
If you know where my poor Peggy lies,
   Tell me, I pray.

Seek *down the stream*, said one — Ah, no,
Quoth he, I'd better *upwards* go —
   The wife on whom I doated,
Was so obstinate a jade,
That, by the mass, I'm much afraid,
   She *against the stream* has floated.

2:22

A spouse who, even after death, "swims upstream" would seem to exemplify the spirit of contradiction. Jefferson disliked open disagreement. In his letter to his grandson, Thomas Jefferson Randolph, he advised that "it was one of the rules which, above all others, made Doctor Franklin the most amiable of men in society, never to contradict any body. If he was urged to announce an opinion he did it rather by asking questions, as if for information, or by suggesting doubts. When I hear another express an opinion which is not mine; why should I question it? His error does me no injury, and shall I become a Don Quixote, to bring all men by force of argument to one opinion? If a fact be misstated, it is probable he is gratified by a belief of it, and I have no right to deprive him of the gratification."[99]

The Litigiouscals,
or Balancing the Scales — A Fable.
[Anonymous]

THOSE who, in suits of law engage,
May find employment for an age,
And, though success their cause attend,
Most sure are losers in the end;
For never maxim better hit,
Than this, that law's a boundless pit,
In law there's but a whit to choose
Twixt those who win, or those who lose.
The plaintiff by fatigue, and toil,
May get his will, his neighbor foil,
But mid the bustle, and the clash,
It is the lawyer gets the cash.
Two cats, one day, by chance, did meet
Within a pantry's lone retreat;
And in their plunder, took a cheese,
Which they bore off with greatest ease,
To some sequester'd place, where they,
In quiet, might enjoy their prey;
But here a circumstance arose,
Which interrupted their repose;
How to divide, their contests were,
Lest each should have the greatest share.
At length agreed by either side,
They choose a third one to decide;
And, for this all important end,
Their voices in a monkey blend.
Elate on bench the monkey sat,
With wig on head, and scollop'd hat,
Nor much unlike, did he appear,
To modern judges in the chair.
The judge, with deepest wisdom fraught,
Commands a ballance [sic] to be brought,
That he might, at exactest rate,
Deal out to each his share by weight.
The cheese being split, the ballance hung,
In either scale, the cheese was slung;

And then the judge, with care surveys,
Each scale, and sees which one outweighs,
And from the greater takes a piece,
To make it ballance with the less;
But hard to make the scales agree,
He nibbles half the cheese away.
Mean while the cats, impatient eye
The monkey's policy, and cry,
"Come give yourself no further pain,
'Tis near enough, we won't complain."
"No," quoth the monkey, "no, not so,
I being judge, must justice do."
Then nibbles this then t'other one,
Until the cheese was wholly gone,
So suffer all, who fly to law —
Nothing is left that's worth a straw.

2:23

As in "The Owl and the Parrot," "The Litigiouscals" uses a fable to point out the nefarious practice of a monkey who eats an entire cheese to determine which piece is bigger. The cats soon regret taking their case to this monkey judge.

The following is extracted from a new piece called *The Honey Moon*, just published by Long-worth, New York, price 2s. 6d. It abounds with much genuine wit and humour, and ranks, no doubt, among the first of modern productions. Although the author, TOBIN, whose death must ever be esteemed an infinite loss to the literary world, has borrowed most of his characters; yet he has not done it in a tame submissive manner — but in that gentlemanly style of one who borrows his friend's equipage, conscious he can any time return as good or better. Mr. Tobin, however, would not condescend to be under obligations to a less genius than Shakespeare's. I have made this extract and the preceding remarks that you may, if you please Mr. Printer, insert them in your paper, believing they will afford some amusement to your readers, and because I think the work possesses uncommon merit.   *N.Y.D. Adv.*

—— A woman *tam'd*,
With words? why, then he must invent a language
Which yet the learned have no glimpses of,
Fasting and faitigation may do something;
I've heard that death will quiet some of them;
But words? mere words? cool'd by the breath of man.
He may preach tame a howling wilderness;
Silence a full-mouth'd battery with snow-balls;
Quench fire with oil; with his repelling breath
Pull back the northern blast; whittle against thunder:
These things are feasible — but still a woman
With the nine parts of speech —
     Count. — You know him not.
     Rolando — I know the lady. Well, it may to him
Be easy, gentlemanly recreation. —
But as I hope to die a batchelor,
I'd rather come within a windmill's sweep,
Or pluck the lighted fuse from a bomb,
Which to say truth, she mostly does resemble,
Being stuff'd full of all things mischievous,
Than parley with that woman.
Could he discourse with fluent eloquence
More languages than Babel sent abroad,

The simple rhetorick of her mother tongue
Would pose him presently; for woman's voice
Sounds like a fiddle in a concert, always
The shrillest, if not loudest, instrument.

2:23

This is one of several poems that portray women as ungovernable, despite the patriarchal laws that denied them property and the vote. Her voice is "always / the shrillest, if not loudest, instrument." This epistolary introduction (perhaps ironized by the editor who published it) is ludicrously overblown. As he sends the poem in for consideration, the writer comments on the "genuine wit and humour" of the piece which must rank "among the first of modern productions."

POEMS OF FAMILY

From the Task.
By Cowper.

VIRTUE and vice had bound'ries in old time
Not to be pass'd. And she that had renounc'd
Her sex's honor, was renounc'd herself
By all that priz'd it; not for prud'ry's sake.
But dignity's, resentful of the wrong.
'Twas hard perhaps on here and there a waif
Delirious to return, and not receiv'd,
But was an whoesome rigor in the main,
And taught th'unblemish'd to preserve with care
That purity, whose loss was loss of all.

2:30

A good example of how Jefferson expressed interest in English notions of virtue: "she that had renounc'd / Her sex's honor, was renounc'd herself." Jefferson did not offer his daughters advice about flirtation and courtship, but he did pay careful attention to their appearance; see his letter to his daughter Martha in the comments on "Ode to Modesty."

Impromptu on the Young Roscius.
By Dr. Busby.

Dame NATURE, the Drama's great Mother, tho't fit
To display in an Actor her zenith of wit:
To the work she replied, saying, "Mortals, obey —
A GARRICK I send, all your passions to sway."
Yet, great as this wonder, she fain wou'd do more:
But how, since her gifts were exhausted before?
"Happy thought!" she exclaimed, and exultingly smil'd!
"What I wrought in a MAN, I'll produce in a CHILD."

2:33

Young Roscius was a child actor who took London by storm in the early nineteenth century. David Garrick helped make Shakespeare the most revered playwright in England by acting leading parts, organizing jubilees in his honor, and making his grave site a shrine.

A MATRIMONIAL THOUGHT.
By Matthew Bramble, Esq.

IN the blithe days of honey moon,
    With Kate's allurements smitten,
I lov'd her late, I lov'd her soon,
    And call'd her dearest kitten. —
But now my kitten's grown a cat,
    And cross like other wives,
O, by my soul my honest Mat,
    I fear she has nine lives!

2:35

One of many poems Jefferson clipped that treat the crossness of wives after marriage, when a kitten is "grown a cat." To take any of these poems out of context would distort the picture that emerges by reading the collection in the glory of its juxtapositions (see appendix two).

FROM THE HIVE.
SATIRE ON SNUFF.

[Anonymous]

'TWAS said of old, that angry Jove,
Sent down Pandora from above,
Loaded with ills of ev'ry size,
The Gods could in their wrath devise.
But dearest girls, I've often thought
That SNUFF was all the vixen brought:
It spoils each pleasure — causes strife,
And sets at variance, man and wife.
But their assertions won't avail,
So take the following woeful tale.

Old Belms travell'd void of strife
Along the middle vale of life,
Poor man! he needs, must have a wife,
A wife — a thing, to say no worse,
To some a blessing, some a curse.
A wife he got — the honey moon
Was sweet, no doubt, but over soon.

One day, as in his chair he sat,
With wife engag'd with pleasant chat,
He saw meandering down her lip
Enough to give good Job the hip,
Then peevish humor seiz'd the man,
And in this wife his plaints began! —

"When e'er I wish with jocund heart,
To dally with my better part,
Or take a harmless kiss or so,
As married people often do;
Each warm embrace at once to stop,
Appears an ugly tawny drop,
Which Snuff and something else compose,
Depending from thy yellow nose,
And trust me, wife, however fine,
Might once have been this skin of thine,

There's now about it dust enough,
Without the help of hated Snuff —
So foul a practice pray give o'er,
Nor force me to rebuke thee more."

Of good advice the usual fate,
This I serv'd but to exasperate,
And make his loving wife endeavour
To claim her nose more full than ever.

From that day forth, ye Gods! what squabbles!
What petty harms — what trifling troubles!
But of sufficient force t'annoy,
And blast each bud of home-bred joy.

Columbian maids attend the strain,
Nor let the well meant song be vain;
To keep the stream of life serene,
Be ever modest, neat, and clean.

2:41

Another poem titled "Snuff" precedes this one. Where indulging a taste for cigars exasperates wives, snuff, which gives women runny noses, disgusts the men. The poet urges a return to balance: "To keep the stream of life serene, / Be ever modest, neat, and clean." George Washington included a book on hygiene as part of his guide to American conduct, based on an older European etiquette work.

ADDRESS TO MY SEGAR.

[Anonymous]

Companion of my leisure hours,
Sweet softner of my care;
I court thy kind solacing aid,
Thou fragrant sweet Segar.
    To thee, I'll constantly apply,
For thou art better far,
To soothe my cares, than fickle friends,
Thou fragrant, sweet Segar.
    When troubles press, or friends deceive,
Or foes their hate declare;
One quaff of thy sweet incense cures,
Thou fragrant, sweet Segar.
    When discontent prevails at home,
Abroad destructive war?
Thy kind exhilarating fumes
Cure all, thou sweet Segar.
    With thee, I can enjoy my friend,
And thou art better far,
Than pompous hall, or drawing room,
Thou fragrant, sweet Segar.
    'Tis thou that lullest all my cares,
Drive on thy fiery car;
Perfume my cot with odours sweet,
Thou fragrant, sweet Segar.
    Should wife's olfact'ry nerves respect,
And curse thy incens'd air;
Then, gently breathe thy sweet perfumes,
Thou fragrant, sweet Segar.

2:41

This is the second of three poems Jefferson clipped on this subject; another, in the mock-heroic style, is titled "The Segar" ("O Muse! . . ."). This version celebrates the virtues of escape and regards the cigar as a panacea for troubles: "When discontent prevails at home, / Abroad destructive war? / Thy kind exhilarating fumes / Cure all, thou sweet Segar." Jefferson's newspaper clippings book seems to have performed similar functions of escape and consolation.

A letter from Hickory Cornhill, Esq. to his friend in the country.

SINCE you beg me to write how I pass of my time,
I will try my dear friend, to inform you in rhyme.
And first, all the morning, the debates I attend
Of the folks who our laws come to make or to mend:
Where sometimes I hear much fine declamation,
'Bout Judges and Bridges and Banks and the Nation,
But last night my amusement was somewhat more new,
Being asked to a party of ladies at loo,
Oh! then, my dear friend, what splendour was seen,
Each dame that was there was array'd like a queen!
The camel, the ostrich, the tortoise, the bear,
And the kid might have found, each his spoils on the fair,
Tho' their dresses were made of the finest of stuff,
It must be confest they were scanty enough;
Yet nought that this saving should their husbands avail,
What they take from the body they put in the tail.
When they fit, they so tighten their clothes that you can
See a lady has legs just the same as a man,
Then stretch'd on the floor were their trains all so nice,
They brought to my mind Esop's council of mice.
'Ere tea was serv'd up, they were prim as you please,
But when cards were produc'd all was freedom and ease.
Mrs. Winlow, our hostess, each lady entreated,
To set the example, "I pray ma'am be seated —
"After you, Mrs. Clutch — Well, if you insist;
"Tom Shuffle, sit down — You prefer loo to whist"
"I'm clear for the ladies — come Jack, *take a touch*,
"I'll *jump* Mrs. Craven, and you Mrs. Clutch."
Around the green board they now eagerly fix,
Two beaux and four ladies composing the six;
When I could but admire that choice occupation,
Which call'd forth such bright and refined conversation.
"First, ladies determine what shall be the loo,
My dear Mrs. Clutch, we will leave it to you."
"*One* and *one*, you know, Fribble, I think the best game:"
"I always knew madam, our tastes were the same."

"Come, shuffle, throw round and let's see who's to deal,
"I cannot tell why, but I already feel, —
"Stay, there's a knave, — "as if to-night I should win,
Well, Mr. Shuffle, you are dealer, begin."
"Is that the trump card? Then I cannot *stand*."
"And I must *throw up* — Let me look at your *hand*.
Come take a *cross-hop*" — "No" — "What do you say?"
"I'll *see you*, Shuffle, if I have but a tray.
"Play on, Mrs. Crutch, for I know 'twas a *stump*;"
"Ace of spades" — "I take it" — "You're *off* with a trump,"
"No indeed: but I've notic'd whenever you *flood*,
"If I was before you, I always was *loo'd*.
"And there's Mrs. Craven, she *threw up* the knave,
"I know I did, ma'am, but I don't play *to save*" —
"Come, ladies, *put up* don't be *bashful* and shy."
"I'm already *up*" — "So am I" — "So am I;"
"Say, Mrs. Inveigle" — "Oh! Is it a spade?"
"I *stand*" — "So do I" — "After two I'm afraid."
"And I'll *make a third*" — "Well *here's for the money*,"
Tho' I don't win the Pool, I'm sure of the *poncy:*
"Here is another" — "Which of these must I play?"
"Why, *keep a good heart*." — Oh? you've *thrown it away*."
And thus they go on, *checking, stumping and fleeting*,
With much other jargon that's not worth repeating,
Till at length it struck twelve, and the winners propose,
That the loo which was "up," the sitting should close.
On a little more sport tho' the losers were bent,
They could not withhold their reluctant assent.
Mrs. Craven, who long since a word had not spoke,
Whose fears gave a smile to the fly equivoque,
Nor, like an old mouser, for watching her prey:
Now utter'd the ominous sound of "I play."
And *swept* the grand loo, thus proving the rule,
That the still sow will ever draw most from the pool.
Tho' much had been lost, yet now this had done,
The devil of one would confess she had won.
But soon I discover'd it plain could be seen,
In each lady's face what her fortune had been.
For they frown if they lose, and then if they win,
The dear creatures betray it, as sure, by a grin.

POEMS OF FAMILY

Mrs. Craven, whose temper seem'd none of the best,
Quite sooth'd by her luck; thus the circle addrest
"Ladies and gentlemen, on Monday with me,
"You'll remember you are all engag'd to take tea;
"But don't stay after six, for I horribly hate,
"When I'm to play loo, to defer it so late.
"I expect the Dash eagles and mean to invite
"The Squabs from the countey with old Col. Kite,
"And I think, Mr. Cornhill, 'tis high time that you,
"Should, like the town beaux, join the ladies at loo."
I thank'd her and told her that one day I might
Deserve such an honor — then wished a good night,
So I hied to the Eagle, resolving to send,
A sketch of this night-scene to you, my dear friend.
                                         H.C.
Richmond, Jan. 6, 1806.

                                              2:46

This poem provides an interesting perspective on card-playing habits among Americans. Written in the form of a verse epistle, the poem includes several puns that reflect, negatively, upon the speaker. Through such devices, the poet highlights the card players' reckless conduct, materialism, and debased values (she "threw up the knave," "I don't play to save"; "here's for the money"; "you've thrown it away").

THE JUG OF RUM.

By Philip Freneau.

WITHIN these earthen walls confin'd
The ruin lurks of human kind;
More mischiefs here united dwell,
And more diseases haunt this cell,
Than ever plagu'd the Egyptian flocks,
Or ever curs'd Pandora's box.

Within these prison-walls repose
The seeds of many a bloody nose;
The chattering tongue, the horrid oath —
The fist for fighting, nothing loth;
The passion quick no words can tame,
That bursts like sulpher into flame;
The nose with diamond growing red,
The bloated eye — the broken head!

   Forever fastened be that door —
Confined within a thousand more
Destructive fiends, of horrid shape,
Even now are plotting an escape.
Here only by a cork controul'd,
And slender walls of earthly mould,
In all their pomp of death reside,
Revenge that ne'er was satisfied —
The tree that bears the deadly fruit
Of murder, maiming, and dispute;
Assault that innocence assails,
The images of gloomy jails.
The giddy thought on mischief bent,
The midnight hour in folly spent —
All these within this jug appear,
And Jack, the hangman, in the rear!

   Thrice happy he, who early taught
By nature, whene'er this poison sought;
Who, friendly to his own repose,
Treads under foot this worst of foes —

He, with the purling stream content,
The bev'rage quaffs which nature meant;
In Reason's scale his actions weigh'd,
His spirits want no foreign aid —
Not swell'd too high, nor sunk too low,
Placid his easy minutes flow;
Long life is his, in vigor pass'd,
Existence welcome to the last,
A spring that never yet grew stale —
Such virtue lies in Adam's ale!

2:53

First published in *The Daily Advertiser* on February 1, 1791, this poem was reprinted in more than twenty-five papers in Burlington (Kentucky), Newark, and other cities, sometimes as "The Jug of Whiskey."[100] "The ardent wines I cannot drink, nor do I use ardent spirits in any form," Jefferson wrote. "Malt liquors and cider are my table drinks, and my breakfast is tea and coffee."[101]

Advice to Young Women.
[Anonymous]

DETEST disguise; remember 'tis your part
By gentle fondness to retain the heart.
Let duty, prudence, virtue, take the lead,
To fix your choice: — but from it ne'er recede.
Abhor coquetry; — spurn the shallow fool
Who measures out dull compliments by rule,
And, without meaning, like a chattering jay;
Repeats the same dull strain throughout the day.
Are men of sense attracted by your fate?
Your well turn'd figure, or their compound grace?
Be mild and equal, moderately gay;
Your judgment rather than your wit display.
By aiming at good breeding strive to please,
'Tis nothing more than regulated ease.
Does one dear youth among a worthy train,
The best affections of your heart obtain?
And is he reckon'd worthy of your choice?
Is your opinion with the general voice?
Confess it then; nor from him seek to hide
What's known to every person else beside.
Attach him to you; in a generous mind,
A lively gratitude expect to find
Receive his vows; and by a kind return,
Affection's blaze will e'er the brighter burn:
Disdain duplicity — from pride be free:
What every woman should, you then will be.

2:54

Jefferson enjoyed this poem enough to clip it twice.[102] He reflected the values of Pope and other Augustan writers in collecting so many didactic poems: "Be mild and equal, moderately gay; / Your judgment rather than your wit display." Jefferson viewed courtesy as "artificial good humor":[103] "at good breeding strive to please, / 'Tis nothing more than regulated ease."

POEMS OF FAMILY

THREE THINGS
A GOOD WIFE SHOULD BE LIKE;
Which three things she should not be like.
[Anonymous]

A wife domestic, good and pure,
Like SNAIL should keep within her door;
But *not* like SNAIL, in silver'd track,
Place all her wealth upon her back.

A wife should be like ECHO true,
And speak, but when she's spoken to;
But *not* like Echo — still be heard,
Contending for the final word.

Like a TOWN CLOCK a wife should be —
Keep time and regularity;
But *not* like CLOCKS — harangue so clear,
That all the town her voice might hear.

Young man! if these illusions strike —
She, whom as bride you'd hail,
Must just be *like*, and just *unlike*
An ECHO, CLOCK, and SNAIL.

2:56

Though the humor of "Three Things" may well be lost on present readers, the poet works the similes of echo, clock, and snail to represent the perspective of an "imperious" husband, in a manner that recalls Julia's spouse in Sheridan's *School for Scandal*.

DRUNKENNESS CURED.

[Anonymous]

INSTANCE FIRST.

A FARMER once, on English ground,
Who, often, in his cups was found;
At ale-house, on a certain day,
Rememb'ring he had mown his hay,
Beheld a thunder storm, on high,
Threat'ning a torrent from the sky.
Quick he return'd with deep concern,
To save his fodder for the barn:
Indeed so great had been his haste,
He scarce had sip'd a common taste.
His little son, a lad of merit,
Who oft had viewed him steep'd in spirit,
In great surprise, cri'd "mamma see,
A miracle, a prodigy;
Pappa's come home, with decent spunk,
To save his *hay, and he is not drunk.*"
    The farmer felt the observation,
    And gain'd a thorough reformation.

INSTANCE SECOND.

A planter in a southern state,
(No matter on what day or date)
Repeating oft the cheering drop,
Had almost burnt his heart strings up.

One night he thro' his parlour door,
Could hear his kitchen in a roar;
And having gratified his ear,
Resolv'd to see as well as hear;
So thro' the key-hole sought to know,
What pleas'd his laughing negroes so.
CUFF he beheld, with mighty glee,
In attitude of mimicry;
Exposing every look and motion,
Occasioned by the pois'nous potion;

Indeed 'twas clear the tawny elf
Acted as MASSA did himself.
At which the grinning company
Cried, "MASSA'S self de berry he."

The planter saw its proper force,
And grew a sober man of course.

2:65

Like smoking cigars and taking snuff, the consumption of alcohol could lead to domestic discord. This poem shows a father correcting his bad habits when his son unwittingly reproves him for drinking. This simple poem is in many ways more clever, because less didactic, than Freneau's rhetorical exercise.

The second "instance" provides insight into the behavior expected of plantation owners and their slaves who sometimes satirized them; his reform refers to his manners and politeness (in this case, to drinking), though not to the institution of slavery itself.

THE TEST OF CONJUGAL LOVE.
[Royall Tyler]

Deprendi miserum est. — Hor. Sat.

On his fever-burnt bed, quick gasping for breath,
　　Lay Strephon, convulsed with pain,
While the wind in his throat shook the rattle of death,
　　The hot blood rag'd through the swoln vein,

Large drops of cold sweat on his forehead did stand,
　　The lustre was dim'd in his eye;
While the chill of his feet, and the chill of his hand,
　　Pronounc'd that poor Strephon must die.

His neighbors all wept, and his kindred all cried,
　　With handkerchiefs held to each eye,
While a boy and a girl sobb'd aloud on each side,
　　To think that their father must die.

But who can describe the fond grief of his wife,
　　Her shriekings, her tears and despair,
When she vow'd that same hour should end her own life,
　　And tore off by handfuls her hair.

O Death! thou fell monster, in anguish she rav'd,
　　O spare my dear husband, oh spare,
Throw thy ice dart at me, let my husband be sav'd,
　　Or I sink in a whirl of despair.

Oh how shall I live when my husband is dead?
　　Or why this loath'd life should I save? then haste,
Then haste, welcome death, and take me in his stead,
　　Or I'll go with my love to the grave.

The wind whistl'd high the old mansion about,
　　And rock'd like a cradle the floor,
When Death in the entry stood knocking without,
　　With his knuckle of bone on the door.

And he bursted the lock, and the door open'd wide,
    And in the slim spectre slow strode,
And he rattl'd his jaws, and he rattl'd his side,
    As over the threshold he trod.

Who's here, cried the spectre, who calls loud for me?
    Who wants Death? the thin spectre then said,
Why, who? cried the wife, why, who should it be?
    But the gentleman there on the bed?

2:73

Though Jefferson was sentimental, as his clipping of "Constancy in Death" suggests, he
could also be cynical and realistic about human
nature. He appreciated wit, even if it came
from a Federalist's pen, like Royall Tyler's.

Sir Henry Wotton, in his character of a *happy life*, has the following beautiful stanzas:

HOW happy is he born and taught,
 That serveth not another's will;
Whose armour is his honest thought,
 And simple truth his utmost skill.

Whose passions not his masters are,
 Whose soul is still prepared for death:
Untied unto the world by care
 Of public fame or private breath.

Who envies none that chance doth raise;
 Nor vice hath ever understood;
Whose deepest wounds are given by praise,
 Whose rules of state are rules of good.

Who hath his life from rumours freed,
 Whose conscience is his strong retreat;
Whose state can neither flatterers feed,
 Nor ruin make oppressors great.

Who God doth late and early pray
 More of his grace than gifts to lend,
And entertains the harmless day
 With a religious book or friend.

This man is freed from servile hands
 Of hope to rise, or fear to fall;
Lord of himself, tho' not of lands;
 And having nothing yet hath all.

2:112

Jefferson's notion of happiness is suggested by what John Stuart Mill called "negative liberty," freedom from the constraints of others. This poem is also typical of Jefferson's selection of poems on the domestic affections in that it praises a life free of materialism: "And having nothing yet hath all."

HOME.

An Extemporary Effusion on returning HOME,
after an absence of some weeks.
[Anonymous]

When *business* calls or *friends* invite me,
  And I am forc'd abroad to roam,
No objects that I meet delight me
  Like those which I have felt at HOME.

Tho' sure to find luxuriant dainties,
  And lodge beneath some splendid dome,
Still, still my sorrowful complaint is,
  That I am far, alas, from HOME.

Tho welcom'd with unfeign'd caresses,
  And *liking* all, nay *loving some;*
Much, much I fear my look expresses,
  That spite of all *I'm not at* HOME.

What tho' my friends, the hours to vary,
  For me select the curious tome!
Of verse and prose I soon grow weary,
  Not Pope amuses while from HOME.

What tho' to urge my stay's exerted
  The eloquence of Greece and Rome!
My steady purpose, not diverted,
  Still resolutely leads me HOME.

Tranquil gates again receive me,
  Once more our truant wanderer's come;
From future *calls* kind fate relieve me,
  And ne'er again I'll quit my HOME.

2:115

When Jefferson received a poem from his daughter, Maria, he quoted Ossian. "[Receiving your letter] was, as Ossian says, or would say, like the bright beams of the moon on the desolate hearth. Environed here in scenes of constant torment, malice and obloquy, worn down in a station where no effort to render service can aver any thing, I feel not that existence is a blessing but when something recalls my mind to my family or farm. This was the effect of your letter, and it's affectionate expressions kindled up all those feelings of love for you and our dear connections which now constitute the only real happiness of my life."[104]

The FIRST LESSON

OF A FATHER TO HIS SON A YEAR OLD.

[Anonymous]

Boy, love your mother! — she with tearful eye
    Reads the slow progress of thy op'ning mind,
Removes the cause of every infant sigh,
    And by her practice lures thee to be kind.

Boy, love thy mother! calm her beating heart,
    That throbs affectionate with care for thee;
Compose her anxious breast with playful art,
    Press her soft lips, and prattle at her knee.

Boy, love thy mother! — Let thy lisping tongue,
    In broken accents, charm her wond'ring ear,
And, when again upon her bosom hung,
    Say, Oh, Mamma! I love, I love you dear.

Boy, love thy mother! the reflected rays
Will beam new lustre o'er thy father's days.

2:177

Jefferson was a single parent who took a
minute interest in his daughters' education
and the emotional life of his grandchildren, as
this poem suggests.

THE DUTIFUL WIFE.

A LYRIC TALE.

[Anonymous]

O! LOVE! whose magic gives the heart
    Unutter'd language from the eye;
Whose magic prompts the mutual wish,
    And heaves the fond, the mutual sigh,
Thy wish well-founded ardour gives,
    That naught ungenerous can destroy;
Thy pride to lessen other's grief,
    Thy fears to wound another's joy.
Then gentle love still hover'd near,
To sweeten toil and soften care.

Alexis won my youthful heart;
    The virgin rapture then I knew,
Like sunshine on the summer scene,
    Has gilded many a future view;
Has sweeten'd much succeeding toil,
    Has soft'ned much succeeding care,
Has snatch'd a smile from thick'ning grief,
    Has snatch'd a transport from despair:
For constant love still hover'd near,
To sweeten toil and soften care.

Three beauteous children blest our love,
    Who all their father's looks exprest;
No happier mother was than I,
    My husband was of men the best.
He lov'd his children dear for me;
    He doubly cherish'd me for them,
Except the tumults sprung from joy,
    Scarce other tumults could I name:
For love delightful hover'd near,
To sweeten toil and soften care.

The first rude shock misfortune gave
    Depriv'd us of our eldest boy;
The parent pang that then I knew

More cruel came oppos'd to joy.
Close on my husband's breast I clung;
    He bath'd my neck with many a tear,
Till each, to sooth the other's grief,
    Strove to avert the blow severe:
For tender love still hover'd near,
To sweeten toil and soften care.

Still plenty crown'd our frugal board,
    And splendour deck'd our stately hall,
Till whelming tempests rag'd at sea,
    And rest from us, alas! our all.
Our board and servants soon reduc'd,
    A narrow house I instant chose,
And bound my love's distracted head,
    And sooth'd him into soft repose:
For faithful love still hover'd near,
To sweeten toil and soften care.

Where howls the wave with wizard roar,
    Our other boy was heard to scream;
To save the precious darling's life
    His father plung'd amidst the stream.
Alas! alas! the boy was lost!
    I rav'd and chass'd his corse in vain:
Yet midst the horror gleam'd a joy,
    To clasp his father once again:
For sacred love still hover'd near,
To sweeten toil and soften care.

My husband liv'd; but ah! the shock
    A dead'ning palsy left behind!
While want approach'd with haggard look,
    And not a former friend was kind.
The only good I could I did,
    I ply'd the sempstress' needy trade,
And Heav'n so far my labours blest,
    That soon I earn'd my husband's bread:
For duteous love still hover'd near
To sweeten toil and soften care.

Blest be the means that soften care!
    Blest be the means that sweeten toil!
Our sex is honour'd in the art,
    That wins a sickly husband's smile:
That art, which sav'd from want, does now
    Our duteous daughter's cares engage;
While, trusting to a pittance sav'd
    We fearless look on feeble age;
When decent love will still be near,
To sweeten toil and soften care.

                J. B.

London, June 20, 1796.

                2:138

A woman who loses two children still values her husband, whom she nurtures after he succumbs to a palsy. "Happiness in the married state is the very first object to be aimed at," Jefferson wrote to Maria. "Nothing can preserve affection uninterrupted but a firm resolution never to differ in will and a determination in each to consider the love of the other as of more value than any object whatever on which a wish has been fixed."[105] It would be interesting to consider whether this poem, signed only J. B., was written by a man or a woman.

POEMS OF FAMILY

HOSPITALITY.

[Anonymous]

—— THERE is a certain hospitable air
In a friend's house, that tells me I am welcome.
The porter opens to me with a smile —
The yard dog wags his tail, the servant runs,
Beats up the cushion, spreads the couch, and says,
"Sit down, good Sir," 'ere I can say I'm weary.

2:149

Jefferson was famous for his hospitality. So many visitors came to Monticello that he built Poplar Forest as a retreat from the prying eyes that watched him. "Jefferson's willingness to hang shutters between the portico columns of Monticello — somewhat like fitting the entrance of the White House with awnings — indicates the extent to which he would go for privacy."[106] When Martha complained that her father had no time for his family when he returned to Monticello, he wrote that "these visits [of guests] are evidences of the general esteem which we have been able all our lives trying to merit." He also warned Maria, who was reluctant to visit him in Washington, not to avoid society. Before becoming vice president, he explained, after he retired from his position as secretary of state under Washington, he too had "remained closely at home, saw none but those who came there, and at length became very sensible of the ill effect it had upon my mind, and of it's direct and irresistible tendency to render me unfit for society, and uneasy when necessarily engaged in it."[107]

ON RECEIVING A NOSEGAY
FROM A LIBERTINE.

[Anonymous]

This rose, true emblem of frail life,
   How beauteous doth it bloom;
But pluck'd by thy untimely hand,
   To wither in its noon.

You gather'd it to please my eye,
   And gave it with a smile;
Ah! tell me, did deception lie
   Beneath it to beguile.

If so . . . believe me when I say,
   Your art is all in vain;
For I from virtue never stray,
   For pleasures bought with pain.

Though great your wealth, and rich in store,
   Unenvied shall you be;
I covet peace . . . I ask no more . . .
   Pray, does it wait on thee?

Can you think on things now past
   Pleas'd with the deeds you've done?
Does nothing say . . . these will not last,
   Nor whisper what's to come?

Oh let reflection seize your breast,
   Where barb'rous discord dwells!
No more in vicious paths be press'd,
   Return . . . and all is well.

Then would I scorn the censurous world,
   And all its agents too;
With thee . . . my all . . . I'd pass my hours,
   With nought but heaven and you.

I'd smooth the brow of gloomy care,
And bless thee with each breath;
Drive from thy pillow black despair,
And cheer the hour of death.
                    VILLAGE GIRL.

2:154

This moving poem describes a woman rejecting the "nosegay" (or collection of flowers) she receives from a man who wishes to "beguile" her. She offers instead to "smooth the brow of gloomy care" and "cheer the hour of death" for him whom she loves more deeply than the unsettled and discordant heart of a libertine, who knows no "peace." This poem neatly reverses Marvell's "To His Coy Mistress"; as a poem about libertinism, it also might be compared to "The Dexterous Evasion," which Jefferson clipped.

THE GALLANT SKATER.

[Anonymous]

GLIDEWELL, the pride of skaters bold,
　　When on the ice a heart he drew,
To MARY said — "That heart, so cold,
　　Belongs, my love, to none but you."

O! rather call that heart your own,
　　Emblem of lovers insincere;
For scarcely shall an hour have flown,
　　Ere it shall change and disappear.
　　　　　　　　　　VON THAW.

2:155

Jefferson seems to have clipped this poem as a
companion piece to "On Receiving a Nosegay
from a Libertine." In this poem, the man gets
the final word.

THE WOUNDED MIND.
TO A FRIEND . . . BY MR. PRATT.

TO all the ills of varying life,
To public and to private strife,
To loss of pleasure, comfort, wealth,
And e'en that loss of losses . . . health;
To these, the suff'rer man's resign'd;
To all things but A WOUNDED MIND.

But foul Detraction's felon breath
Is sharper than the sting of Death,
And serpent Envy's aspic tongue,
Whose venom in the dark is flung,
What suff'rer is to these resign'd?
For these produce A WOUNDED MIND.

Oh! for such poisons slow and sure,
Say, what can minister a cure?
What potent herb, or mental balm,
'Midst these the suff'rer man can calm?
What healing med'cine can he find
To anodyne A WOUNDED MIND?

Yes, there's a time! and one alone,
And that, my injured Friend's your own:
The God, the God within the breast
Shall charm the suff'rer man to rest:
Thus was by Heav'n itself assign'd
A TRIUMPH for THE WOUNDED MIND.

2:168

This poem suggests that God alone can cure mental illness. The poem that follows it implies that nature is the best cure. Jefferson does not seem to have addressed the issue of George III's insanity, though poems by Byron ("The Vision of Judgment") and Shelley ("England in 1819") treated it more than a decade later.

STANZAS.

[Anonymous]

HAVE you not in some valley seen,
Of sweetest hue, of loveliest mien,
A Lily, distant from the tread
Of Sheep, or grazing Oxen — fed
By Zephyr's gentlest gales; the sun
His beams refreshing shed upon —
And nourish'd by the shower?
Have you not joyful view'd such flower,
And bid it live its little hour?

Have you not, too, some Virgin's eye,
Rising from "careless infancy,"
Delighted mark'd? The lovely form
And mind, hurt by no "pit'less storm,"
Each virtue op'ning with the day,
Beauteous, innocent and gay.
Have you not sigh'd to Heav'n a prayer
(Protecting from the world's wide snare)
To guard this blossom with its kindest care.

Ah! have you too, beneath the weight
Of poverty, mark'd virtue's seat,
Seen Genius mourn, abject, forlorn,
Depress'd beneath the proud one's scorn,
And have you felt the kindling glow,
That mitigates a brother's woe?
In spite of all the dull may say,
Or preach, or teach — Their rules away,
Thou art of Virtue taught, and own'st its
            truest sway.

2:168

Jefferson balanced Pratt's poem on the wounded mind with a poem about how contemplating nature and family ties helps one overcome adversity. Wordsworth's "I Wandered Lonely as a Cloud" was inspired by Wordsworth's own depression of spirits. For Pratt, as for Wordsworth, nature and family lessen pain, so "the kindling glow, / . . . mitigates a brother's woe."

POEMS OF FAMILY

MORAL AND NATURAL BEAUTY.

[Anonymous]

SWEET is the voice that soothes my care,
 The voice of love, the voice of Song;
The lyre that celebrates the fair,
 And animates the warlike throng.

Sweet is the counsel of a friend,
 Whose bosom proves a pillow kind,
Whose mild persuasion brings an end
 To all the sorrows of the mind.

Sweet is the breath of balmy spring,
 That lingers in the primrose vale;
The woodlark sweet, when on the wing
 His wild notes swell the rising gale.

Sweet is the breeze that curls the lakes,
 And early wafts the fragrant dew,
Through hovering clouds of vapour breaks,
 And clears the bright etherial blue.

Sweet is the bean, the blooming pea,
 More fragrant than *Arabia's* gale
That sleeps upon the tranquil sea,
 Or gently swells th'extended sail.

Sweet is the walk where daisies spring,
 And cowslips scent the verdant mead;
The woodlands sweet where linnets sing,
 From every bold intruder freed.

But *far more sweet* are virtuous deeds;
 The hand that kindly brings relief,
The heart that with the widow bleeds,
 And shares the drooping orphan's grief.

The PIOUS and HUMANE, here rise
With liberal hands and feeling heart:
And chase the tears from sorrows eyes,
And bid each anxious woe depart.

2:170

This is one of several poems in which the poet seeks connections between moral and natural beauty. The theme had become popular enough for Byron to lampoon the tendency, offering a similar catalog of "sweet" things, only to reverse himself by saying, "Sweet is the unexpected death of some old lady. . . ."[108]

The VOWS of LOVE.
[Anonymous]

SWEET is the summer's musky breath,
That lightly sweeps the flow'ry heath;
Sweet is the song young nature charts,
In lovelorn youth's romantic haunts;
Sweet is the cheerful cowslip's mien,
Quick rising from her couch of green!
And sweet at day's delightful dawn
The fresh rose-bud upon its thorn.
But tho' so sweet the various flow'rs
That flaunt in spring's embroider'd bowr's,
Or richly scent the summer grove,
Yet sweeter is the vows of love.

But with the flow'rs the fickle gale,
Shall quickly leave the blooming vale;
The woodland song shall cease its charms,
When nature sinks in winter's arms.
And when the cold north chills the sky
The cowslip on her stem shall die,
And shrinking from the first keen blast
To earth the lovely rose be cast;
So transient, tho' so sweet shall prove,
Ye trusting maids — the vows of love.

2:171

Jefferson clipped a second poem exploring sweetness as a trope (and placed them in sequential order, on successive pages), noting that the vows of love are as transient as they are sweet. The first lines of the two poems are similar enough for Jefferson to have clipped them, perhaps, for that reason. They contrast, markedly, with the poem on suicide that fol- lows. Once again, Jefferson showed his interest in complementarity: He chose extreme emotional states and juxtaposed them with poems about opposing sentiments. If the juxtaposition had any purpose, it might well have been to show how the classical bal- ance of Jefferson's mind competed with his romantic impulse.

On Suicide.

[Anonymous]

WHEN fate, in angry mood, has frowned
   And gather'd all his storms around,
The sturdy Romans cry:
"The great, who'd be releas'd from pain,
"Falls on his sword, or opens a vein,
   "And bravely dares to die."

But know, beneath life's heavy load,
In sharp affliction's thorny road,
   'Midst thousand ills that grieve;
Where dangers threaten, cares infest,
Where friends forsake, and foes molest,
   'Tis braver far — to live!

2:173

Suicide preoccupied Goethe (*Sorrows of Young Werther*) and Madame de Staël ("On Suicide"). For Enlightenment intellectuals drawn to neo-classicism, Roman stoicism represented suicide as a form of virtue (choosing the moment of one's death). The second stanza of this more conventional poem offers the tradi-tional interpretation of suicide as a sin in the Judeo-Christian religion.

MY MOTHER.

[Anonymous]

Who fed me from her gentle breast,
And hush'd me in her arms to rest,
And on my cheek sweet kisses prest?
                My Mother.

When sleep forsook my open eye,
Who was it sung sweet lullaby,
And rock'd me that I should not cry?
                My Mother.

Who sat and watch'd my infant head
When sleeping on my cradle bed,
And tears of sweet affection shed?
                My Mother.

When pain and sickness made me cry,
Who gaz'd upon my heavy eye,
And wept for fear that I should die?
                My Mother.

Who dress'd any doll in clothes so gay,
And taught me pretty how to play,
And minded all I'd got to say?
                My Mother.

Who ran to help me when I fell,
And would some pretty story tell,
Or kiss the place to make it well?
                My Mother.

Who taught my infant lips to pray,
To love God's Holy Book and Day,
And walk in wisdom's pleasant way?
                My Mother.

And can I ever cease to be
Affectionate and kind to thee
Who was so very kind to me,

>   My Mother.

Ah! no the thought I cannot bear,
And is God pleased my life to spare,
I hope I shall reward thy care,

>   My Mother.

When thou art feeble, old and grey,
My healthy arm shall be thy stay,
And I will soothe thy pains away.

>   My Mother.

And when I see thee hang thy head,
'Twill be my turn to watch thy bed,
And tears of sweet affection shed.

>   My Mother.

For God who lives above the skies,
Would look with vengeance in his eyes,
If I should ever dare despise,

>   My Mother.

>   2:177

"There is reason to believe that Jefferson's relationship with his mother was strained," Joseph Ellis has noted, "especially after his father's death, when, as the eldest son, he did everything he could to remove himself from her supervision."[109] Jefferson mentioned her once in a letter, describing her death in March 1776, and again, briefly, in his autobiography, *Anas.*[110] Jefferson had occasion to observe both of his daughters as mothers and had the highest respect for motherhood, calling it the "key-stone in the arch of matrimonial happiness" in a letter to Martha (see the note to "The Mother to Her Child," page 327).

MY DAUGHTER.
[Anonymous]

HOW was my aching bosom torn.
With doubts and fears upon that morn,
When thou, first pledge of love, were born —
> My Daughter!

But oh! how sweetly was I blest,
When soft thy Mother's hand I prest,
And saw thee sleeping on her breast —
> My Daughter!

Each day I held thee in my arms,
The thought e'en now my bosom warms,
To gaze upon thy infant charms —
> My Daughter!

And when baptismal rites to share
Thy careful nurse her charge did bear,
How ardent was thy Father's pray'r —
> My Daughter!

Full well remember'd is that day,
When in thy pretty prattling way,
Mama thou first didst seem to say,
> My Daughter!

Oft too, in infant playfulness,
Thy little hand my face did press;
Oh! then how fondly would I bless
> My Daughter!

If sickness made thee droop thy head —
How oft I stole, with cautious tread,
To watch thy slumbers and thy bed —
> My Daughter!

Well pleas'd I trac'd thy growth of thought,
And mark'd, with joy, how quick was caught
Each lesson that thy Mother taught —
                    My Daughter!

If e'er — as it would sometimes be —
My face look'd grave, thou'dst climb my knee,
And strive to make me share thy glee —
                    My Daughter!

And when thy voice I heard thee raise,
In singing simple sacred lays,
Thou seem'dst an angel hymning praise —
                    My Daughter!

The beauties thus I saw increase
In tranquil innocence and peace;
And may such blessings never cease,
                    My Daughter!

But now, the days of childhood fled, —
Sweet happy days! I view, with dread,
The dangers that are round thee spread,
                    My Daughter!

More fatal than the Siren's song,
The crafty Flatt'rer's wily tongue
Will strive to make thy youth go wrong,
                    My Daughter!

Pleasure will hold her charms to shew,
And Fashion tempt thee to pursue
Her dangerous follies — ever new —
                    My Daughter!

But oh! let Virtue be preferr'd,
Hold firm the lessons you have heard,
And ever love God's holy word,
                    My Daughter!

These precepts in remembrance bear,
And Heaven will have thee in its care,
And shield thee from each worldly snare,
                    My Daughter!

Then I, with all a Father's pride,
May see thee happy as a Bride,
With blooming Children by thy side,
                    My Daughter!

And when this dear delight is mine,
Oh! let me Earth for Heaven resign,
And there expect in Bliss Divine,
                    My Daughter!

                                        2:185

This poem charts a father's concern for his daughter as he tries to steer her away from "Fashion" and "dangerous follies." She can redeem herself, compensate her father for his tender care for her when a child, only through marriage, "with blooming children by her side."

THE WIDOW.
[Robert Southey]

COLD was the night wind, drifting fast the snow fell,
Wide were the downs and shelterless and naked,
When a poor wanderer struggled on her journey
      Weary and way sore.

Drear were the downs, more dreary her reflections,
Cold was the night wind, colder was her bosom!
She had no home, the world was all before her,
      She had no shelter.

Fast o'er the bleak heath rattling drove a charriot,
"Pity me!" feebly cried the poor night wander.
"Pity me, strangers!" left with cold and hunger
      Here I should perish.

"Once I had friends, — but they have all forsook me!
Once I had parents, — they are now in heaven!
I had a home once — I had once a husband —
I am a widow poor and broken hearted!"
Loud blew the wind, unheard was her complaining,
      On drove the chariot.

On the cold snow she laid her down to rest her;
She heard a horseman — "Pity me," she groaned out;
Loud was the wind, unheard was her complaining,
      On went the horseman.

Worn out with anguish, toil and cold, and hunger,
Down sunk the wanderer — sleep had seized her senses;
There, did the traveller find her in the morning,
      God had released her.

              SOUTHEY.

              2:191

Composed in Bristol, Southey's "The Widow" (1795) belongs to his radical period, when he wrote *Wat Tyler* (1794) and *Joan of Arc* (1796). By depicting the suffering incurred by a woman whose husband has died (presumably in a recent war), Southey acted in opposition to the tradition of celebrating British war heroes in such paintings as Benjamin West's *The Death of General Wolfe*. The cause of the woman's widowhood remains unmentioned, which gives the poem its sentimental power. Stanzas 4 and 5 differ from other published versions of the poem.

TO MY INFANT ASLEEP.

(1804.)

[Anonymous]

Sleep on, sweet babe, for thou canst sleep,
   No sorrows send thy peaceful breast,
Thy pensive mother wakes to weep,
   Depriv'd by grief of balmy rest!

May Angels watch around thy bed,
   Thee safe from ev'ry ill defend:
May Heaven's unnumber'd blessings shed,
   And be thy never-failing friend!

Sleep on, sleep on, my baby dear;
   Thy little heart, from sorrow free,
Knows not the anxious cares that tear
   Thy mother's breast, sweet babe, for thee.

Soft be thy slumbers, Sorrow's child!
   Serene and tranquil be thy rest;
Oft have thy smiles my pains beguil'd,
   And sooth'd my agitated breast!

Thine infant tongue has never known
   A father's name; nor can thine eyes
Recal to mind the graceful form
   That low in Death's embraces lies!

But I in thee delight to trace
   That form, so tenderly belov'd!
To picture, in thy smiling face,
   His image, far from earth remov'd?

His pious cares thou canst not share,
   Nor can he guide thy tender youth,
Or guard thee from each hurtful snare,
   Or lead thee in the paths of truth!

The sad yet pleasing task be mine,
     To Virtue's ways thy mind to form,
To point to thee those truths divine,
     Which in the Gospel are made known.

With Reason's dawn thou shalt be taught
     Thy father's God betimes to know;
The wonders he for us hath wrought,
     Shall be thy mother's task to show.

Each rising and each setting sun
     Thy little hands in prayer shall raise,
And early shall thine infant tongue,
     Be taught to lisp thy Maker's praise!

                                   2:202

This is one of a series of poems that touch upon very personal subjects. It is striking to think of Jefferson taking the time to remember his years as a father of infants while negotiating treaties and bargaining with Napoleon over the Louisiana Purchase. Jefferson's wife gave birth to six children, only two of whom survived past the age of three. Maria, Jefferson's second daughter, died while Jefferson was in office. Like his wife, she suffered from complications resulting from childbirth. Coleridge's "Frost at Midnight" also addresses a sleeping infant, watched over by an anxious father.

THE MOTHER TO HER CHILD.
[Anonymous]

Welcome, thou little dimpled stranger,
    O! welcome to my fond embrace;
Thou sweet reward of pain and danger,
    Still let me press thy cherub face.

Dear source of many a mingled feeling,
    How did I dread, yet wish thee here!
While hope and fear, in turns prevailing,
    Serv'd but to render thee more dear.

How glow'd my heart with exultation,
    So late the anxious seat of care,
When first thy voice of supplication
    Stole sweetly on thy Mother's ear.

What words could speak the bright emotion
    That sparkled in thy Father's eye,
When to his fond paternal bosom
    He proudly press'd his darling boy!

Oh! that thou may'st, sweet babe, inherit
    Each virtue to his heart most dear;
His manly grace, his matchless merit;
    Is still thy doating Mother's prayer.

While on thy downy couch reposing,
    To watch thee is my tender toil;
I mark thy sweet blue eyes unclosing,
    I fondly hail thy cherub smile.

Smile on, sweet babe, unknown to sorrow,
    Still brightly beam thy heavenly eye;
And may the dawn of every morrow
    Shed blessings on my darling boy.

2:202

Dumas Malone describes Jefferson's capacity for manipulation and taking pains with a subject. As a single parent forced to play the role of mother and father, Jefferson cultivated a tenderness toward his daughters that was unusual, especially for a man as occupied with public affairs as he was. At times it seems that Jefferson used his scrapbook to create, imaginatively, the familial ideal he could not enjoy in the White House. When news of Martha's pregnancy reached Jeffferson in Philadelphia, he wrote on February 9, 1791:[111] "Your two last letters are those which have given me the greatest pleasure of any I ever received from you. The one announced that you were become a notable housewife, the other a mother."

PART THREE

Poems of
ROMANTIC LOVE

At William and Mary College, Thomas Jefferson kept a literary commonplace book (1763) that provides the best evidence of his literary interests as a young man. The most frequently quoted author is Lord Bolingbroke, whose rational materialism and religious skepticism characterized Jefferson's views throughout his life.[1] Featured prominently in this same collection are the works of Greek and Roman poets such as Homer, Horace, Ovid, Cicero, and Virgil, as well as English and Scottish poets including Macpherson, Pope, Milton, Akenside, Young, and Thomson. In drama, Jefferson quoted from Euripides and Sophocles, and from plays by Rowe, Otway, and Shakespeare. Many of the entries are melancholy in nature, reflecting the interest in graveyard poetry that Thomas Gray helped to popularize. When his close friend Dabney Carr died, Jefferson chose for the epitaph a passage taken from Nicholas Rowe[2] that was first recorded in this book. When his wife was dying, Jefferson again turned to his literary commonplace book to communicate with her, writing out a passage from Laurence Sterne. He chose a passage from Homer for her gravestone: "Nay if even in the house of Hades the dead forget their dead, yet will I even there be mindful of my dear comrade."[3] Poetry helped Jefferson come to terms with the ineffable.

The newspaper clippings book of 1801–1808 formed a second chapter in the history of Jefferson's literary tastes. Here he emerged as a collector of Romantic verse, if not as America's first Romantic president. Perhaps this taste for Romantic ballads, doggerel, and light satire was another aspect of his multi-faceted personality and corrects the much-labored view of him as a strict neo-classicist. Neoclassicism was a public mantle of good taste donned by both Federalists and Republicans. Ellen Coolidge maintained this persona when she recalled her father reading "the classics" during his retirement years at Monticello.[4] But there was a private self as well, and Jefferson was more senti-mental in his literary tastes than his grandchildren, protective of his reputation, were willing to remember. Perhaps the Jefferson who traveled by ship to France with a copy of Cervantes's *Don Quixote* on board; who took an extended vaca-tion through the south of France with Sterne's *Sentimental Journey* in his breast pocket; who wrote suggestive letters to Maria Cosway that allude to Sterne's dissertation on noses in *Tristram Shandy*[5] — perhaps this Jefferson was America's first erotic liberal, a decade ahead of Lord Byron. Maybe!

In his diary of 1813, Lord Byron famously rated Moore, Campbell, and Rogers higher on the scale of Parnassus than Wordsworth, Southey, and Coleridge.[6] This has sometimes been taken as a sign of his poor judgment, but Jefferson's newspaper clippings book suggests that he shared Byron's mixture of neoclassical theory and Romantic praxis. One looks in vain for "Tintern Abbey" among Jefferson's newspaper clippings. In its place, however, one finds Moore's "Anacreontic Verses," Campbell's "To Caroline," and Scott's "Lay of the Last Minstrel." Byron would have approved.

When he was only fourteen, Byron read Thomas Little, the pen name assumed by Thomas Moore. At the age of fifty, Jefferson clipped more than ten poems by this same author. Byron praised Rogers and Campbell, and Jefferson clipped Rogers's "Farewell" and "A Sketch of the Alps at Day-Break," along with Thomas Campbell's "To the Evening Star," "Hohen Linden," "Exile of Erin," and four other poems. Both Byron and Jefferson denounced George III: "He has plundered our seas, ravaged our coasts, burnt our towns, and destroyed the lives of our people,"[7] Jefferson wrote. More than forty years later, surveying the history, Byron echoed Jefferson's opinion: "He ever warred with freedom and the free / Nations as men, home subjects, foreign foes, / So that they uttered the word 'Liberty!' / Found George the Third their first opponent."[8] Byron's poem was a direct response to Robert Southey's fatuous "A Vision of Judgment," which described George III's apotheosis in heaven as if Southey were an eyewitness. Jefferson admired the younger Southey's "The Oak of Our Fathers" and his poem on retirement, "The Old Man's Comforts," which express values of home and hearth. Southey had even planned on emigrating to the United States and starting an ideal community on the banks of the Susquehanna River.[9]

Jefferson maintained an interest in the poetry of foreign countries and clipped translations by William Jones. Hafiz appears prominently as do poems on Africa, such as Fanny Holcroft's "The Madagascar Mother." Though he did not anticipate Madame de Stael's celebration of German Romanticism, Jefferson clipped Oberon's "Wieland," placing it next to his poem celebrating Scottish patriotism: "The Death of Wallace." Jefferson's Enlightenment values — comparative and encyclopedic in scope, struggling to present poetic effusions in a dispassionate way — could be inferred simply from the arrangement of the poems in the newspaper clippings book, and the wide range of translated languages he included: German, Portuguese, Chinese, Spanish, French.

What led Jefferson to admire James Macpherson but take no notice of Byron and his contemporaries, Shelley and Keats? To begin with, Byron, Shelley, and Keats had not written much between 1800 and 1808, when Jefferson compiled this book. But there were other reasons he never alluded to them later in life, either — or to Blake, Coleridge, or Wordsworth. Jefferson's literary tastes were shaped by his classical education. The preferences he showed in architecture match his literary preferences. While Jefferson could warm to the romantic verse he read in the newspapers, he organized such verse according to neoclassical doctrines of propriety, arranging them by subject ("Spring" appears next to "Remonstrance to Winter"). There is something vaguely Aristotelian about Jefferson's project, as if he could tame the excesses of the poems he clipped by placing them in the proper category.

Jefferson's classical tastes were leavened by his appreciation for poems that were prototypically Romantic. As a college student, Jefferson already admired Edward Young, whose "Night Thoughts" had a profound influence on William Blake. Blake parodied figures obsessed with human rationality (Urizen), or slave owners like "Bromion" in "Visions of the Daughters of Albion." On the other hand, Blake sympathized with the American experiment and alluded directly to Thomas Jefferson in his poem "America" ("The builder of America throws his hammer down in fear"[10]). Jefferson enjoyed "Lines Written at

Midnight" or "Lines Written on the Bank of a River," which betray neoclassical restraint and decorum, though later in life he had much in common with the Romantic aesthetic enunciated by Wordsworth in his preface to *Lyrical Ballads* (1800). Like Wordsworth and Coleridge, Jefferson valued the language of everyday life. In fact, Wordsworth and Coleridge published their second edition of *Lyrical Ballads* that included Wordsworth's preface, a year before Jefferson was sworn in as president. Jefferson's American "Revolution of 1800" coincided with an English literary transformation.[11]

Like several poets he admired, Jefferson bridged the gap between neoclassicism and Romanticism. Concerned that the American dialect would be dismissed as barbaric, Jefferson was Romantic in his view of language, but used neoclassical references to make his case. "Has the beautiful poetry of [Robert] Burns, or his Scottish dialect, disfigured it?" he asked of the English language. "Did the Athenians consider the Doric, the Ionian, the Aeolic, and other dialects, as disfiguring or as beautifying their language? Did they fastidiously disavow Herodotus, Pindar, Theocritus, Sappho, Alcæus, as Grecian writers? On the contrary, they were sensible that the variety of dialects, still infinitely varied by poetical license, constituted the riches of their language, and made the Grecian Homer the first of poets, as he must ever remain, until a language equally ductile and copious shall again be spoken."[12] Like Wordsworth, Jefferson respected the vernacular; like Alexander Pope, however, he saw Homer as the first of poets and Greek as the model for what a language should be, "ductile and copious."

Jefferson, who was the author of an *Essay on the Anglo-Saxon Language* (October 1798), wrote intelligently about accentual as opposed to syllabic methods of scanning poetry ("Thoughts on Prosody," 1786), later reversing his opinions but showing an impressive attention to topics he first read about in the rhetoric books of Thomas Sheridan and Lord Home.[13] Jay Fliegelman has argued, persuasively, that these books on rhetoric influenced Jefferson's writing of the Declaration of Independence,[14] which was meant to be read aloud. Little wonder that Jefferson's interest in the oral tradition of the ballads, popularized by James Macpherson and Walter Scott, continued while he served as president and collected newspaper clippings.

Though seemingly random, then, the poems in this section share several traits that justify the label of Romantic. They are often rural songs or ballads, done in imitation of a medieval form. Others engage in social protest, exoticize American Indians, or exhibit an Orientalist interest in Persia ("An Ode from Hafiz"; "A Persian Song of Hafiz"). Many of the poems Jefferson collected exhibit a sensuousness of description not found in neoclassical verse. Campbell's "To Caroline" and Rogers's "Farewell" are both sentimental, with an intensity that prefigures Romanticism. Several others — "Dawn," by Miss Owenson; "Night" by Charlotte Smith — treat distinct times of the day, but do so in ways that lean toward pathetic fallacy, draping the natural landscape with human emotions. James Thomson began this trend in *Seasons*, but Charlotte Dacre and other poets took the observation of nature in a more personal and psychological direction.

A number of the poems Jefferson admired celebrate nationalism, a romantic theme, especially Scott's "Breathes There the Man" and Royall Tyler's versification of a passage from Ossian. Just as Scotland's literary heritage was being buttressed by James Macpherson's scholarly researches and Scott's "Lay of the Last Minstrel" (not to mention the verse of Burns), so, too, was Germany's native language made "literary" by Burger, who exploited its cadences in "The Lass of Fair Wone." Germany became the hothouse for superstitious tales of Gothic coloring, more than a decade before Madame de Stael urged Germans to eschew the neoclassicism of France in her work *De L'Allemagne* (1813).

The poets in Jefferson's collection wrote from a strong sense of place, an important Romantic theme. The newspaper clippings book's apparent randomness is belied, then, by the coteries that helped produce it. One of these — in Walpole, New Hampshire — was professedly neoclassical, and attracted bright young lawyers from Harvard and Dartmouth just starting their careers. Royall Tyler, Joseph Dennie, and Thomas Green Fessenden (as well as Samuel Hunt, Roger Vose, and Samuel West) met at the Crown Anchor tavern in Walpole before Dennie began his Tuesday club in Philadelphia.[15] English writers, like the Federalists who emulated them, had coteries of their own. In London, William Hayley ("A Matrimonial Ballad") was a patron of Blake and Cowper, while Samuel Rogers, Thomas Campbell, and Robert Merry published poems ("The Pleasures of Hope"; "The Pleasures of Memory"; "Pains of Memory") in a volume aptly titled *Bouquet*. In Bristol, Joseph Cottle published Southey, Wordsworth, and Coleridge, and Cottle's "The Affectionate Heart" appears no less than three times in Jefferson's collection. In 1802, Robert Anderson began an Edinburgh clique and cultivated the poetic work of Anne Bannerman and Thomas Campbell. Jefferson collected six poems by Thomas Campbell, who became far more famous than Anderson or Bannerman, but his career might not have prospered at all if Anderson had not introduced him to London publishers. Several women writers knew each other well, including Mary Robinson, Helen Maria Williams, Anne Seward, and Charlotte Dacre. Three or four poets (Pye, Scott, Spencer, Dacre) contributed translations of

"The Lass of Fair Wone" and "Leonora" and formed a coterie of rivals, struggling to capture a new market in London for German ballads.

While Federalist poets such as John Quincy Adams mocked Jefferson for exoticizing American Indians, the sentiment was genuine enough, as his clipping of "An Elegant Morceau, by a Caimerian Indian," reveals. Jefferson shared Rousseau's tendency to view Asians, Persians, and American Indians as noble savages, and he appears not to have applied such idealism to the Negroes on his own plantation in *Notes on the State of Virginia*. One cannot conclude, simply because "Sadi the Moor," "A Persian Gazel," and "Bryan and Pereene" appear in this collection, that Jefferson cultivated diversity for its own sake, nor that he was an abolitionist. Edward Said observed that Orientalism arose, in part, from the "textual attitude" toward Eastern nations that books fostered: In this way culture became the handmaiden of imperialism. Yet Jefferson's inclusion of poems such as "The Madagascar Mother" shows how he was prepared to change his views by reading other texts. He did this in at least two ways. First, authors with whom he shared his views on one subject often set his mind in new directions on another. Jefferson's admiration for William Godwin, for example, who opposed George III's trials for sedition, may have led him to read Fanny Holcroft's abolitionist poetry more attentively. The reverse could also prove true. In scouring Federalist newspapers and finding verse by Thomas Moore, Amelia Opie, and others, he inevitably read articles hostile to his administration. What began as a literary project for his granddaughters broadened his political awareness. Jefferson showed an increasing interest in this newest literary trend, Romanticism, which Federalists at first embraced and then abandoned because of its democratic tendencies.

Jefferson was nowhere more democratic or Romantic than in his fascination with ballads and folk music. Percy's *Relics* helped to popularize an interest in native songs in the eighteenth century, while Burns's Scottish songs fanned the flames. Thomas Moore's *Irish Melodies* went into many editions, some of which were purchased by Jefferson's granddaughters. As late as 1814, Byron, in *Hebrew Melodies*, was still capitalizing on the market created by Moore's success. The significance of this trend is shown by the fact that "Leonora," a ballad, went into seventeen editions in a single year.[16] In 1796, J. T. Stanley, William Taylor, H. J. Pye, W. R. Spencer, and Walter Scott published competing translations. That great master of the ballad form, Samuel Taylor Coleridge, wrote "Rime of the Ancient Mariner" and then "Christabel," which Scott heard before writing "Lay of the Last Minstrel." Jefferson clipped three sections of Scott's narrative poem, along with James Grainger's melodramatic, Gothic, and extremely popular "Bryan and Pereene."

Given the Greek revival and the interest in popular songs that occurred during Jefferson's presidency, it is no wonder that "Anacreon" Moore was one of Jefferson's favorite poets. "Moore embodied that mythical ideal of the romanticists, the national bard," Howard Mumford Jones has explained. "Moore did not merely 'belong' to the romantic period; he incarnated it. Moore presented in his small person the union of music and verse, of folk tradition and courtly accomplishment of which the age had read in Ossian, in Scott, in novel and historical romance. . . . Hundreds who turned a deaf ear to Wordsworth listened, enraptured, to Moore; thousands to whom Shelley was a filthy atheist learned of tyranny and nationalism from the persuasive Irishman."[17]

Thomas Jefferson shared Joseph Dennie's admiration for the poetry of Thomas Moore, a taste he may well have acquired by reading the *Port Folio*, for Moore's verse appeared frequently in that Federalist organ. In fact, Jefferson even clipped Joseph Dennie's prose introductions. "We will not delay the pleasure that our friends of sensibility and taste will derive from the following, by an expression of our own opinions or feelings. — Before a Grecian temple, we will erect no clumsy porch, but introduce at once the admiring connoisseur."[18] Dennie's comparison of Moore's poems to a Grecian temple would not have been lost on the architect of Monticello, yet it is a somewhat odd description for a man who "incarnated" the Romantic age. Yet the epithet was not misplaced. Moore appeared before the world as the translator of Anacreon, after all, and it was with anacreontic drinking songs that Jefferson padded his newspaper clippings book. Yet Jefferson also admired Moore's more Romantic productions, including "Invisible Girl," "Lake of the Dismal Swamp" (a Gothic poem set in Norfolk, Virginia), "Love and Reason," and several rondeaus. While Moore provided epigraphs from Martial and other Roman poets — though he wrote dedicatory epistles critical of the United States — he came to see that the political future was with America, however objectionable he had found it at age twenty-four. Moore's ambivalent position, succored by Joseph Dennie and collected by Thomas Jefferson, indicates how literary tastes were shared by Federalists and Republicans and began to change during Jefferson's presidency, when political parties became more divided.

While much has been written on Jefferson's classicism, then, a strong case can be made for his interest in Romantic poetry. The source for this paradox can be found even in as classical a structure as Monticello, as Malcolm Kelsall has recently shown. Though it is true that Jefferson drew on Palladian models, he kept Monticello in a constant state of construction. Though not quite a Romantic ruin, Monticello surprised visitors by its unfinished state. Frequently, a roof was missing; the cramped stairs and the dome room revealed the eclectic tastes of their proprietor,[19] his preference for fragmentary forms. As Isaac Jefferson noted, Thomas Jefferson built and tore down the house "six or seven times" over a period of "forty years."[20] He kept a pile of books on the floor, picking up one and putting down another, as he built a "pleasure dome" at Monticello, which was like Kubla Khan's Xanadu, a perpetual fragment, a "miracle of rare device."[21] Like the home he constructed, then, this selection of Romantic poetry indicates Jefferson's wide, sometimes contradictory visions for the new republic.[22]

———

In fact, Jefferson's Romantic predilections are one reason he came under attack: He was not classical *enough*. Thomas Green Fessenden contrasted writers who followed the neoclassical style of Goldsmith, Cowper, and Pope with the sentimental verse of the Della Cruscan school (Robert Merry, Mary Robinson); Fessenden argued that sentimentality, in writing, led to a corruption of feeling, opening the way for precisely the type of demagoguery Jefferson used to get elected.

> With politicians, wise as Solon,
> With Preacher, Hermit, Spondee, Colon
> . . . . And strives to make each rhyming elf
> As pure a writer as himself.
> And bids instructed taste to scorn
> The sound of Della Crusca's horn;
> But swift to Elysian fields elope,
> Hearkening to poetry and Pope;
> > Now, courteous reader, since awhile
> > To sing in Della Cruscan style,
> > By frolick Fancy born along,
> > We've stemmed the Cataract of Song;
> > > (Della Crusca's "Cataract of Light").

Colon and Spondee were the adopted names of Joseph Dennie and Royall Tyler, who contributed prose and poetry to the *Port Folio*. Their opposition to Della Crusca was as political as it was aesthetic, for Robert Merry penned many an ode to the National Assembly and Gallic freedom, while Fessenden, like Anne Seward, considered French revolutionary politics an infection. Where Merry's compassion led him to sympathize with the politically oppressed, Tyler and Dennie found that such an emotional approach to politics led to sloppy writing and thinking.[23]

Though Jefferson admired Pope, his collection of Romantic verse suggests that he embraced many of the poets of the Della Cruscan school, along with their French politics. Robert Merry's "The Wounded Soldier" appears, along with Mary Robinson's "The Beggar." When he did clip poems by Federalist poets, he chose their most sentimental passages, such as Royall Tyler's "Versification of a Passage from Ossian" or "Seduction" by Thomas Fessenden (why Federalists occasionally wrote such verse would be the subject of another essay).

In fact, if there is a unifying theme in this section of Jefferson's collection, it would be sentimentality. "Caroline" by Thomas Campbell and "To Mary in Heaven" by Robert Burns fit this category, as do "The Old Beggar" by Mary Robinson and "Hymn to Content" by Anna Barbauld. Burns's poem may have consoled Jefferson on the loss of his daughter Maria during his second term in office. Jefferson's Orientalism was also sentimental. He collected "A Persian Gazel by Hindley," "A Persian Song, of Hafiz," and several odes by Hafiz. Royall Tyler wrote three odes to Hafiz, while Joseph Dennie's *Port Folio* printed ten translations of Hafiz odes by Baron Revizki.[24] If Dennie read Hafiz's poems as products of the Greek revival ("this poet has all the agreeableness and vivacity of Anacreon, with the softness and charms of Sappho"), however, Jefferson seemed more willing to see such works on their own terms. He collected an ancient Chinese ode (included in the Poems of Nation section) and a poem about a Hindu woman's suttee, which romanticizes a woman's devotion to her husband (as Byron romanticized a Greek slave's devotion to her Assyrian captor in *Sardanapalus*). Jefferson compared two sentimental translations of the story of *Yusef and Zuleika* by Sir William Jones, which Byron would later use in Jami's version for *The Bride of Abydos* (1813). Four years later, without ever visiting India, "Anacreon" Moore, another poet Jefferson admired, turned his pen to Orientalism in *Lallah Rookh*.

Romantic celebrations of sentimentality made slavery a natural subject. If American New Englanders such as Joseph Dennie, Royall Tyler, and Thomas Fessenden criticized the American slave trade, they were not alone. Amelia Opie ("The Negro Boy's Tale"), Lady Morgan, and Rosa Matilda ("The Poor Negro Sadi") were equally appalled. The rise of the sentimental novel, specifically Mackenzie's *Man of Feeling* (1771), helped to make the plight of the slave a popular topic for verse. In "The Slaves, an Elegy" (1792), Robert Merry made use of the varied punctuation and capitalization popularized by Sterne to emphasize the injustice of the institution, and to juxtapose freedom and tyranny.

> If late I paus'd upon the Twilight plain
> Of Fontenoy, to weep the FREE-BORN BRAVE;

Sure Fancy now may cross the Western Main,
And melt in sadder pity for the SLAVE.

Lo! where to yon PLANTATION DROOPING GOES,
The SABLE HERD of Human Kind, while near
Stalks a *pale* DESPOT, and around him throws
The scourge that wakes — that punishes the Tear.[25]

Attracted to a sentimental politics, Jefferson was also torn between his conscience and two hundred inherited slaves that made up a large part of his wealth as a Virginia planter. "I tremble for my country when I reflect that God is just; that his justice cannot sleep forever," he wrote in *Notes on the State of Virginia*.[26] He invoked the "Almighty" in this fragmentary (and Romantic) work, but he also stated, "it does me no injury for my neighbor to say there are twenty gods, or no God. It neither picks my pocket nor breaks my leg."[27] Fessenden responded, in "Democracy Unveiled," knowing that Jefferson's speculative comments played into the hands of Connecticut Congregationalists who viewed him as an atheist.

That man must have religion plenty,
Who soars from "*no* God," up to "twenty," —
No doubt, of common folks the odds,
As, "*no* God" is to "*twenty Gods.*"

Perhaps Jefferson's Romanticism, which led him to pen the Declaration of Independence, also guided him in separating church and state, his most important legacy. In this, he was far ahead of the classicists and of Ivy League graduates such as Fessenden, Dennie, and Tyler, who mocked him. New Englanders whose strong sense of God's plan led them to become outraged by social injustice found their artistic freedom constrained by Massachussetts puritanism. Tyler had to travel from Boston to New York before he could see a dramatic production that did not take place in a concealed basement. Dennie had to decamp to Philadelphia to continue his periodical for wont of New England subscribers, and the artistic and freethinking Fessenden, at least according to Hawthorne, was a rarity in parochial New England.

Ironically, Jefferson's belief in the separation of church and state helped produce an administration in which literature could thrive — even literature that was vociferously opposed to his administration. Unlike John Adams, Jefferson resisted the impulse to shut down political opponents, to censor books (as Napoleon pulped Madame de Stael's), or to exile and deport writers, though he flirted with the idea of jailing Dennie.[28] Many New Englanders who blamed Scottish and Irish writers for political dissent failed to credit Jefferson with tolerating diverse viewpoints. Fessenden, who did not miss much, perceived the irony in "Democracy Unveiled," noting that "For ere his virtues I've reported, / I shall, or ought to be — *transported!*"[29] If the success of a government can be judged by its tolerance, then Jefferson's administration looks very impressive to any reader of his clippings book.

THE OAK OF OUR FATHERS.

By R. Southey.

Alas for the Oak of our Fathers that stood
In its beauty, the glory and pride of the wood!
It grew and it flourished for many an age,
And many a tempest wreak'd on it its rage,
But when its strong branches were bent with the blast,
It struck its roots deeper and flourished more fast.
Its head tower'd high, and its branches spread round,
For its roots were struck deep, and its heart it was sound;
The bees o'er its honey-dew'd foliage play'd,
And the beasts of the forest fed under its shade,
The Oak of our Fathers to freedom was dear,
Its leaves were her crown, and its wood was her spear.
Alas for the Oak of our Fathers that stood
In its beauty, the glory and pride of the wood!
There crept up an ivy and clung round the trunk,
It struck in its mouths and its juices it drunk;
The branches grew sickly deprived of their food,
And the Oak was no longer the pride of the wood.
The foresters saw and they gather'd around,
Its roots still were fast, and its heart still was sound;
They lopt off the boughs that so beautiful spread,
But the ivy they spared on its vitals that fed.
No longer the bees o'er its honey-dews play'd,
Nor the beasts of the forest fed under its shade;
Lopt and mangled the trunk in its ruin is seen,
A monument now what its beauty has been.

The Oak has received its incurable wound
They have loosened the roots, tho' the heart may be found;
What the travellers at distance green-flourishing see,
Are the leaves of the ivy that ruined the tree.
Alas for the Oak of our fathers that stood
In its beauty, the glory and pride of the wood!

[Westbury, 1798]

1:23

Southey, who is perhaps the least read of the Romantic poets today, appealed strongly to Jefferson, who clipped six of his poems. This piece addresses the virtues of England through the metaphor of the oak tree. Did Jefferson take some delight in noting that England had entered a period of self-doubt with ivy clinging around its trunk? In some ways, the poem, written in 1798 in Westbury, could be read as a veiled allusion to the American war, or the war against France.

Federalists writing in the *Port Folio* claimed the symbol of the oak for their own party, contrasting the sturdy tree with the willow, which bends and sways with public opinion. Other Federalists viewed themselves as trees that bore fruit only to die during Jefferson's ascendancy and become nothing more than cabbage stalks, bereft of any inheritance.

Caroline.

By Thomas Campbell, Esq.

I'll bid the hyacinth to blow,
   I'll teach my grotto green to be,
And sing my true love all below
   The holly bow'r and myrtle tree.

There, all his wood scents to bring,
   The sweet south wind shall wander by,
And with the music of his wing
   Delight my rustling canopy

Come to my close and clustering bow'r,
   Thou spirit of a milder clime,
Fresh with the dews of fruit and Flow'r
   Of mountain heath and moory thyme!

With all thy rural echoes come,
   Sweet comrade of the rosy day,
Wasting the wild bee's gentle hum,
   Or cuckoo's plaintive roundelay.

Where'er thy morning breath has play'd,
   Whatever isles of ocean fann'd,
Come to my blossom woven shade,
   Thou wandering wind of Fairy Land

For sure, from some enchanted isle
   Where heav'n and love their Sabbath hold —
Where pure and happy spirits smile
   On beauty's fairest, brightest mould:

From some green Eden of the deep,
   Where pleasure's sigh alone is heav'd,
Where tears of rapture lovers weep,
   Endear'd, undoubting, undeceiv'd:

From some sweet Paradise afar
   Thy music wanders, distant, lost,

Where Nature lights her leading star,
    And love is never, never cross'd!

Oh, gentle gale of Eden bow'rs,
    If back thy rosy feet shou'd roam,
To revel with the cloudless hours
    In Nature's more propitious home.

Name to thy lov'd Elysian groves
    That o'er enchanted spirits twine
A fairer form than cherub love —
    And let the name be Caroline!

1:87/84

This engaging poem by Thomas Campbell, like
many in this section, avoids sentimentality
through inventiveness, varied poetic diction, and
concision ("Endear'd, undoubting, undeceiv'd").

A Farewell.

By Samuel Rogers, Esq.

Once more enchanting girl, adieu:
   I must be gone while yet I may;
Oft shall I weep to think of you —
   But here I will not, cannot stay!

The sweet expression of that face,
   For ever changing, yet the same:
Ah, no: I dare not turn to trace —
   It fires my soul, it melts my frame!

Yet give me, give me ere I go,
   One little look of those so blest,
That lend your cheek a warmer glow,
   And on your white neck love to rest!

Say when, to kindle soft delight,
   That hand has chanc'd with mine to meet,
How could its thrilling touch excite
   A sigh so short, and yet so sweet!

Oh, say — but no — it must not be,
   Adieu — enchanting girl, adieu!
Yet still methinks you frown on me —
   Oh! never could I fly from you!

Once more, enchanting girl, adieu!
   I must be gone while yet I may
Oft shall I weep to think of you;
   But here I will not, cannot stay!

1:91/88

Facile, like the verse of Thomas Moore, Rogers's poetry sometimes lacks force, or the quality Hazlitt called "gusto." Here he failed to particularize the person he described. Without Wordsworth's philosophical approach or Byron's incisive psychology, Rogers's verse rarely finds its way into modern anthologies, yet he was an important figure, like Leigh Hunt, who fostered the careers of his contemporaries.

Samuel Rogers published his poem *Jacqueline* with Byron's *Lara*. He introduced Caroline Lamb to the young poet, and she described him as "mad, bad, and dangerous to know." Byron thought Rogers, Campbell, and Moore the best poets of the early nineteenth century. Their reputations have been superseded by Wordsworth, Coleridge, and, to a lesser extent, Southey.

SONNET.

By Anna Seward.

Seek not, my Lesbia, the sequester'd dale,
   Or bear thou to its shades a tranquil heart;
   Since rankles most in solitude the smart
   Of injur'd charms, and talents, when they fail.
To meet their due regard: — nor e'en prevail
   Where most they wish to please: — Yet, since thy part
   Is large in life's chief blessings, why desert
   Sullen, the world? — Alas! how many wail
Dire loss of the best comforts Heaven can grant!
   While they the bitter tear in secret pour,
   Smote by the death of friends, disease, or want,
Slight wrongs if the self-valuing soul deplore,
   Thou but resemblest, in thy lonely haunt,
   Narcissus pining on the wat'ry shore.

1:91/88

Seward was a resident of Litchfield whose poem to Lesbia recalls her own struggle against bitterness and isolation (here represented as a form of narcissism). Seward struggled to care for her ailing parents at some cost to her own poetic career. Like Seward, Madame de Stael and Mary Robinson represented themselves as Sapphic figures, alienated from a society that "injur'd" their self-conception. She was a great admirer of Burger's "Leonora," which she praised to her friends in June 1796. Several politicians came to her home to hear the Gothic poem read aloud.

FROM THE *PORT FOLIO*.

The following song by M. G. Lewis, Esq. is, as we are apprized by that gentleman, derived from the *French*, though the swain who figures in it appears to be a German. The thought is pretty and the measure flowing.

A wolf, while Julia slept, had made
    Her favourite lamb his prize;
Young Caspar flew to give his aid,
    Who heard the trembler's cries.
He drove the wolf from off the green,
    But claim'd a kiss for pay.
Ah! Julia, better 'twould have been,
    Had Caspar staid away.

While grateful feelings warm'd her breast,
    She own'd she lov'd the swain;
The youth eternal love profess'd,
    And kiss'd and kiss'd again,
A fonder pair was never seen;
    They lov'd the live long day:
Ah! Julia, better 'twould have been
    Had Caspar staid away.

At length, the sun his beams withdrew,
    And night inviting sleep,
Fond Julia rose and bade adieu,
    Then homewards drove her sheep.
Alas! her thoughts were chang'd, I ween,
    For thus I heard her say:
Ah! Julia, better 'twould have been,
    Had Caspar staid away.

1:92

Casper's "aid" to Julia involves a price ("But claim'd a kiss for pay"). As with Burger's ballads, the repetition of the final line in each stanza is particularly effective because no details are given ("better 'twould have been, / Had Caspar staid away") even as words are repeated ("And kiss'd and kiss'd again"). A romance by Matthew Gregory Lewis (1775–1818), *The Monk* (1796), features Ambrosio as a confessor in Madrid who engages in scenes of erotic torture and homoeroticism. The novel's central character is at odds with himself in a contest for superiority between his real and his acquired character.[30] Magic, incest, cruelty, anti-Catholicism, and religious hypocrisy predominate as we learn about the penitents Rosario, Matilda, Agnes, Elvira, and her daughter Antonia. Lewis later became a member of Parliament and wrote a book about the plantations he owned in Jamaica; *The Castle Spectre* (1796) was very successful as well. He also wrote plays, poems, and translations featuring Gothic themes.

THE POOR NEGRO SADI.
A FRAGMENT.

OH! poor Negro, *Sadi*, what sorrow what anguish,
    Oppress the lone victim fate dooms for a slave;
What eye or what heart o'er those sorrows shall languish,
    What finger point out the lone African's grave?

First torn like a wretch from his innocent dwelling,
    And torn from *Abuka*, the wife of his soul;
Then forc'd, while his heart is indignantly swelling,
    To bow his proud neck to the despot's controul,

Think not, Europe, tho' dark his complexion,
    Dark, dark, is the hue of the African's fate,
That his *mind* is devoid of the light of reflection,
    And knows not distinctions of love or of hate.

And believe, when you see him in agony bending,
    Beneath the vile lash — if he fainting should pause,
That pure are to Heaven his sorrows ascending,
    And dear shall you pay for the torture you cause

Mark! mark! the red blood, that so eloquent streaming,
    Appeals to the Godhead thou sayest is *thine*!
Mark! mark! the sunk eye that on Heaven is beaming;
    It calls — deep revenge on oppression and crime.

                ROSA MATILDA.
                (*London paper.*)

                      1:105

Sadi is torn from Abuka, the wife of his soul. Emphasizing the human qualities of Sadi, Rosa Matilda questioned the European assumption that blacks are inferior: "Think not . . . his *mind* is devoid of the light of reflection, / And knows not distinctions of love or of hate." Jefferson wrote, "I tremble for my country when I think that God is just," in *Notes on the State of Virginia*. Rosa Matilda was also concerned with God's wrath: "dear shall you pay for the torture you cause." Like Zambo in "The Negro Boy's Tale," Sadi recognizes that if he arrives in England he will become free according to an English law of 1772.

ANACREONTIC.

[Anonymous]

Bring me wine and let me drink;
Would you have me ever think,
Always dancing after care,
Rambling on I know not where?

Wine allays my parching heat,
Bids the heart more nobly beat;
Wine dispenses mirth around,
Age more lightly treads the ground.

String me never fading bays,
Wine will yield the songs of praise,
Then I'll able join the God of Wine,
Chief of Mirth's most noble line?

1:107/015

Anacreon was known for songs that celebrated wine as a source of inspiration. "Moore and his contemporaries believed the odes he translated were the work of the sixth-century Greek poet Anacreon. The 'Anacreontic' odes are now known to be the productions of the Roman and Byzantine periods."[31] Jefferson's relationship with Thomas Moore ran the gamut from aloofness to admiration (as shown by the frequency with which poems by him appear in this volume). For his part, Moore was disgusted by the American experiment in democracy and said as much in his *Epistles, Poems, and Odes* of 1806. He wrote damaging, if accurate, lines about Jefferson's relationship with Sally Hemings, describing her as Jefferson's "sable mistress," and seems to have viewed Jefferson as a hypocrite. It seems that Jefferson followed Moore's poetic career with interest.

To My Lamp.
[Anonymous]

Fickle, flirting, wanton flame,
Life and you are just the same;
Life's inconstant, so are you,
And as idly wav'ring too.

Oft I've view'd your blazing spire,
Oft I've mark'd life's nobler fire;
Your's with sparkling brightness flies,
Life with dazzling brilliance dies.

1:107/105

Thomas Moore's libertine poems celebrated the ephemeral life of passion, which he compares, in this poem, to a "Fickle, flirting, wanton flame." Between 1808 and 1834, Moore produced ten collections of *Irish Melodies* (the first seven with tunes by Sir John Stevenson, whose songs Jefferson also collected).

Stanzas.
[Thomas Moore]

IF there exists a charm more dear
    Than Beauty's dazzling dye,
It lives in Pity's generous tear,
    And Virtue's hallowed sigh

For by that tear the soul's refin'd
    That flows at Pity's call —
The gentle sigh improves the mind
    That heaves for others thrall.

107 / 105

In addition to wine and mutability, Thomas Moore's lyrics also celebrated sensibility, the subject of several other clippings by Jefferson. "It has been too much our author's object to pander to, the artificial taste of the age; and his productions, however brilliant and agreeable, are in consequence somewhat meretricious and effeminate," Hazlitt wrote. He added that "Mr. Moore ought not to contend with serious difficulties or with entire subjects. He can write verses, not a poem. . . . He has been so long accustomed to the society of Whig Lords, and so enchanted with the smile of beauty and fashion, that he really fancies himself one of the set to which he is admitted on sufferance, and tries very unnecessarily to keep others out of it. He talks familiarly of works that are or are not read 'in our circle,' and, seated smiling and at his ease in a coronet-coach, enlivening the owner by his brisk sallies and Attic conceits, is shocked, as he passes, to see a Peer of the realm shake hands with a poet."

EPIGRAM,

Written on Mr. Kemble's Double Window in Russel Street.

[Anonymous]

Rheumatick pains make Kemble halt,
   He, fretting in amazement,
To counteract the dire assault
   Erects a double casement.

Ah! Who from fell disease can run?
   With added ills he's troubled;
For when the glazier's task is done
   He finds his *panes* are doubled.

Monthly Mirror

1:107/105

Jefferson kept an eye on the theater, clipping poems about the Young Roscius and this poem about Charles Kemble, whose brother and sister, Sarah Siddons, dominated the London stage in the late eighteenth century before being superseded by Edmund Kean and actors with more expressive, less classical, technique.

[During a period of four or five hours, in which we were indulged with the hasty perusal of a small portion of Mr. Moore's new poems, we transcribed as many pages as possible for the amusement of our readers. We will not de-lay the pleasure that our friends of sensibility and taste will derive from the following, by an expression of our own opinions or feelings. — Before a Grecian temple, we will erect no clumsy porch, but introduce at once the admiring connoisseur.]

LOVE and REASON.

'TWAS in the summer time so sweet,
    When hearts and flowers are both in season,
That — who of all this world, should meet,
    On early dawn but Love and Reason?

Love told his dream of yesternight,
    While reason talk'd about the weather;
The morn, in sooth, was fair and bright,
    And on they took their way together.

The boy in many a gambol flew,
    While Reason, like a Juno, stalk'd,
And from her portly figure threw
    A lengthen'd shadow as she walk'd.

No wonder Love, as on they past
    Should find that sunny morning chill,
For still the shadow Reason cast
    Fell on the boy, and cool'd him still.

In vain he tried his wings to warm,
    Or find a path-way not so dim,
For still the maid's gigantic form
    Would pass between the sun and him!

"This must not be," said little Love,
    "The sun was made for more than you,"
So, turning through a myrtle grove,
    He bade the portly nymph adieu.

Now gaily roves the laughing boy,
    O'er many a mead, by many a stream,

In every breeze inhaling joy,
    And drinking bliss in every beam.

From all the gardens, all the bowers,
    He cull'd the many sweets they shaded,
And ate the fruits, and smell'd the flowers,
    Till taste was gone, and odour faded!

But now the sun, in pomp of noon,
    Look'd blazing o'er the parched plains,
Alas! The boy grew languid soon,
    And fever thrill'd through all his veins!

The dew forsook his baby brow,
    No more with vivid bloom he smil'd —
Oh! where was tranquil Reason now,
    To cast her shadow o'er the child!

Beneath a green and aged palm,
    His foot at length for shelter turning,
He saw the nymph reclining calm,
    With brow as cool as Iris was burning.

Oh take me to that bosom cold,
    In murmurs at her foot he said
And Reason op'd her garment's fold,
    And flung it round his sever'd head.

He felt her bosom's key touch,
    And soon it lull'd his pulse to rest:
For ah! the chill was quite too much,
    And Love expir'd on Reason's breast!

1:108/106

This debate between "Love and Reason" recalls Jefferson's letter on the head and the heart, which he penned to Maria Cosway after jumping over a fence and spraining his wrist. His love affair with Cosway was mostly a matter of words, since she was married to Richard Cosway, a portrait painter. When Jefferson visited her again after their initial encounter in Paris, she remained aloof — some have speculated, because of the proximity and recent arrival of Sally Hemings.

In this poem, Reason is compared to a portly nymph like Juno, who throws Love's passion in the shade. He wanders away after their accidental meeting only to return to her when he finds himself exhausted. Though Love needs Reason, he expires (presumably because of her cold bosom) when he rejoins her underneath the shade of a tree. Juno was the goddess of marriage; it is perhaps fitting that a libertine poet such as Moore would represent marriage as chilling Love. The poem anticipates Keats's "Lamia" in its treatment of the tension between love and reason.

Song by the Same.
[Thomas Moore]

The wreath you wove, the wreath you wove,
    Is fair — but oh! how fair!
If Pity's hand had stolen from Love
    One leaf to mingle there.

If every rose with gold were tied,
    Did gems for dew drops fall,
One faded leaf where Love had sigh'd
    Were sweetly worth them all.

The wreath you wove, the wreath you wove,
    Our emblem well may be;
Its bloom is yours, but hopeless Love
    Must keep in tears for me.

1:108 / 106

Though these poems may seem trivial, Jefferson collected many of them. They give a good sense of what he and his contemporaries, especially the newspaper editors, valued. "Moore was not a Romantic, but an elegant poet, and elegant social climber, of the Regency," Jonathan Wordsworth ha observed. "Though not commanding his loy alty — 'Do but give Tom a good dinner, and lord . . . TOMMY *loves* a Lord' — Moore cam to be one of Byron's closest friends."

Rondeau.

By Thomas Moore, Esq.

Good night! good night! And is it so,
And must I from my ROSA go?
O! Rosa, say "good night" once more,
And I'll repeat it o'er and o'er,
Till the first glance of dawning light,
Shall find us saying still [newspaper folded] "good night!"

And still "good night!" my ROSA say —
But whisper still "a minute stay,"
And I will stay, and every minute
Shall have an age of rapture in it.
We'll kiss and kiss in quick delight,
And murmur while we kiss "good night!"

Good night! you'll murmur with a sigh,
And tell me it is time to fly;
And I will vow to kiss no more,
Yet kiss you closer than before,
Till slumber seal our weary sight,
And then, my love, my soul, "good night!"

1:108/106

This poem is one of several devoted to Rosa. It first appeared in *The Poetical Works of the Late Thomas Little*. In 1821, the London magazine predicted that "immortal he must be, as long as English ladies can *love*, or Irish gentlemen can *drink*, which, we take it, is as much immortality as any modern bard can consider himself equitably entitled to."

Moore's lascivious verse influenced Byron's *Fugitive Pieces* and other works. "I have just been turning over *Little*," Byron wrote to Moore in 1820, "which I knew by heart in 1803, being then in my fifteenth summer." At that time, Byron was in love with Mary Chaworth and was inconsolable for six weeks after she mocked him as a "lame brat." "I believe all the mischief I have ever done, or sung, has been owing to that confounded book of yours."[32] He wrote a poem in the spirit of Moore's Songs, one of which begins "So we'll go no more a-roving."

Stanzas.

By Thomas Moore,
TRANSLATOR OF ANACREON.

Come, tell me where the maid is found,
    Whose heart can love without deceit.
And I will range the world around,
    To sigh one moment at her feet.

Oh! tell me, where's her sainted home,
    What air receives her blessed sigh,
A pilgrimage of years I'll roam
    To catch one sparkle of her eye!

And if her cheeks be rosy bright,
    While truth within her bosom lies,
I'll gaze upon her morn and night,
    Till my heart leave me through my eyes!

Show me on earth a thing so rare,
    I'll own all miracles are true;
To make one maid sincere and fair,
    Oh! 'tis the utmost Heav'n can do!

1:108/106

Moore was called "Anacreon" Moore because he translated Greek poetry that treated lascivious subjects. Romantic readers allowed for sentimentality at the top of the page, as Howard Mumford Jones has noted, as long as it was balanced by erudition (in the form of footnotes) at the bottom. Moore's classicism somehow exempted him from the charge of immorality and eroticism in the United States. The speaker of Moore's poems sees no contradiction between his own libertine wandering and his desire for a maid "whose heart can love without deceit." Moore married a woman thirty years his junior.

The Exile of Erin.
[Thomas Campbell]

There came to the Beach a poor Exile of Erin,
   The dew on his thin robe was heavy and chill;
For his country he sigh'd, when at twilight repairing
   To wander alone by the wind-beaten hill: —
But the Day-star attracted his eye[']s sad devotion;
For it rose on his native Isle of the Ocean,
Where once in the flow of his youthful emotion
   He sung the bold Anthem of *"Erin, go bragh!"*,

"Oh, sad is my fate! (said the heart-broken Stranger) —
   The wild Deer and Wolf to a covert can flee;
But I have no refuge from famine and danger —
   A house and a Country remain not to me!
Ah, never again in the green sunny Bowers
Where my Forefathers lived shall I spend the sweet hour,
Or cover my Harp with the will-woven flowers —
   And strike to the numbers of *"Erin, go bragh!"*

Erin, my country, thou sad and forsaken,
   In dreams I revisit thy sea-beaten shore;
But alas! in a far foreign land I awaken,
   And sigh for the friends who can meet me no more,
Oh, cruel fate! Wilt thou never replace me
In a mansion of peace, where no person can chase me,
Ah, never again shall my brothers embrace me?
   They died to defend me, or live to deplore!

Where is my cabin-door, fast by the wild wood!
   Sitters and Sire, did ye weep for its fall?
Where is the mother that look'd on my childhood?
   And where is the bosom-friend, dearer than all?
Ah, my sad soul, long abandon'd by pleasure,
Why did it doat on a fast-fading treasure?
Tears like the rain-drop, may fall without measure —
   But rapture and beauty they cannot recall!

But yet, all its fond recollections suppressing,
    One dying wish my lone bosom shall draw: —
Erin, an Exile bequeaths thee his blessing!
    Land of my Forefather, *Erin*, go bragh!
Buried and cold, when my Heart stills her motion,
Green be thy fields, sweetest Isle of the Ocean;
And thy harp-stringing Bards sing aloud with devotion
    "*Erin*, ma vourneen — *Erin*, go bragh!"

                                                    I:113/112

Campbell was a Scottish poet who, in this
poem, takes up the theme of Ireland. *Erin go
bragh* means "long live Ireland." The third
stanza portrays Ireland as "Sad and forsaken,"
which lent itself to poetic treatment.

POEMS OF ROMANTIC LOVE

SADI THE MOOR.

[Anonymous]
TUNE — "Erin Cobrah."

The trees seem to fade as yon dear spot I'm viewing,
    My eyes fill with tears as I look on the door,
And see the lov'd cottage all sinking in ruin —
    The cottage of PEACE and Sadi the Moor,
Poor Sadi was merciful, honest and cheerly,
His friends were his life-blood, he valu'd them dearly,
And his sweet, dark ey'd Zelda, he lov'd her sincerely,
    Hard was the fate of Sadi the Moor
As Sadi was toiling — his Zelda was near him —
    His children were prattling and smiling before,
When the *Pirates* appear, from his true love they tear him,
    And drag to their vessel poor Sadi the Moor.
The forlorn one rav'd loudly, her lost husband seeking,
His children and friends at a distance were shrieking,
Poor Sadi cry'd out, while his sad heart was breaking,
    "Pitty the sorrows of Sadi the Moor!"
In spite of his 'plaint to their gally they bore him,
    His Zelda and children to mourn and deplore,
At morn from his feverish slumbers they tore him,
    And with blows hardly treated poor Sadi the Moor,
At night up a loft, while the still moon was clouding,
The thought of his babes on his wretched mind crouding,
He heav'd a last sigh, and fell dead from the shrouding,
    The sea was the grave of Sadi the Moor.

I:119

Irish music is harnessed in the cause of Sadi the Moor, who is forcibly taken from Zelda and sold to the slave trade. He dies from grief for his lost children as he falls from the "shrouding." "I wish with all my soul that the poor Negroes were all freed," Martha Jefferson wrote to her father after a boat of Algerians captured by a Virginian frigate faced the prospect of enslavement in Africa.[33]

An Elegant Morceau.

By a Caimerian Indian.

*[sung by William Walker,
collected in Southern Harmony]*

When shall we three meet again?
When shall we three meet again
Oft shall glowing hope expire,
Oft shall wearied love retire,
Oft shall death and sorrow reign
Ere we three shall meet again!

Tho' in distant lands we sigh,
Parch'd beneath a hostile sky,
Tho' the deep between us runs,
Friendship shall unite our souls;
Still in Fancy's rich domain
Oft shall we three meet again.

When around this youthful pine
Moss shall creep and ivy twine,
When our burnish'd locks are grey,
Turn'd by many a toil spent day;
May this long-lov'd bower remain,
Here may we three meet again!

When the dreams of life are fled,
When its wasted lamps are dead,
When in cold oblivion's shade,
Beauty, pow'r, and fame are laid;
Where immortal spirits reign,
Then may we three meet again!

1:123/121

In 1831, this song appeared as a hymn sung by a group of American missionaries who departed from Andover, Massachussetts, to do work in the Sandwich Islands. The missionaries included Harriet Bradford Stewart and two young, fatherless boys: Hiram Bingham and Mr. Thurston.

A Persian Gazel.
By Hindley.
The same has been translated
by Reviski *and* Sir W. Jones.

Fair maid of Shirez, would'st you take
My heart and love it for my sake,
For that dark mole my thoughts now trace
On that sweet cheek of that sweet face,
I would Bokhara, as I live,
And Samarcan too, freely give.

Empty the flagon, fill the bowl,
With wine to rapture wake the soul:
For, Eden's self, however fair,
Has nought to boast that can compare
With thy blest banks, O Rocnabad!*
In their enchanting scenery clad;
Nor ought in foliage half so gay
As are the bowers of Mosellay.†

Insidious girls with syren eye,
Whole wanton wiles the soul decoy,
By whole bewitching charms beguil'd
Our love smit town is all run wild,
My stoic heart ye steal away
As Janissaries do their prey!

But, ah! no laureat's lover's praise
The lustre of these charms can raise:
For, vain are all the tricks of art,
Which would to nature ought impart;
To tints that angelise the face,
Can borrow'd colours add new grace?
Can a fair cheek become more fair
By artificial moles form'd there?
Or, can a neck of mould divine
By perfum'd tresses heighten'd shine?

---

* The Rocnabad (Ruknabad) is a famous stream of Shiráz.
†The Mosellay (Mosalla) are celebrated gardens of Shiráz.

By wine and music, then, our theme;
Let wizards of the future dream,
Which unsolv'd riddle puzzles still
And ever did, and ever will.
By Joseph's growing beauty mov'd
Zuleikha look'd, and sigh'd, and lov'd,
Till headstrong passion shame defy'd,
And virtue's veil was thrown aside.

By then, my fair, by counsel led,
At wisdom's shrine to bow thy head;
For lovely maids more lovely shine,
Whose hearts to sage advice incline,
Who than their souls more valued prize
The hoary maxims of the wise.

But tell me, charmer, tell me why
Such cruel words my ears annoy;
Say is it pleasure to give pain?
Can sland'rous gall thy mouth profane?
Forbid it, Heav'n! it cannot be!
Nought that offends can come from thee:
For, how can scorpion venom drip
From that sweet ruby-colour'd lip,
Which, with good nature overspread,
Can nought but dulcet language shed?

Thy gazel-forming pearls are strung,
Come, sweetly, Hafiz, be they sung:
For Heav'n show'rs down upon thy lays
Thoughts, which in star-like clusters blaze.

1:132/129

Jefferson's taste in literature, like that of his
contemporary newspaper readers, was cos-
mopolitan. This poem was based on the story
of Joseph and Potiphar's wife, known in the
Koran as Zuleikha.

The following song from the pen of Sir
William Jones, has appeared in many periodical
publications but never, I believe, in the
Chronicle; the beautiful imagery, and sweetness
of numbers, which pervades the whole, and the
elegant apology for the indiscretion of
Potiphar's wife in the sixth stanza, are seldom
equalled in minor productions. Its re-publica-
tion may, perhaps, gratify many of your
readers, and none more than ROLLA.

A PERSIAN SONG.
OF HAFIZ.

SWEET maid, if thou wouldst charm my sight,
   And bid these arms my neck infold,
      That rosy cheek, that lily hand,
Would give thy poet more delight
   Than all *Rocara's* vaunted gold,
      Than all the gems of *Samaerand*.

Boy, let yon liquid ruby flow,
   And bid thy pensive heart be glad,
      What'er the frowning zealots say;
Tell them, their *Eden* cannot show
   A stream so clear as *Raenabad*,
      A bower so sweet as *Mosellay*.

O! When these fair perfidious maids,
   Whose eyes our secret haunts infest,
      Their dear destructive charms display;
Each glance my tender breast invades,
   And robs my wounded soul of rest,
      As Tartars seize their destin'd prey.

In vain with love our bosoms glow:
   Can all our tears, can all our sighs,
      New lustre to those charms impart?
Can cheeks, where living roses blow,
   Where nature spreads her richest dyes,
      Require the borrow'd gloss of art?

Speak not of fate: — Ah! change the theme,
    And talk of odours, talk of wine,
        Talk of the flowers that round us bloom:
'Tis all a cloud, 'tis all a dream;
    To love and joy thy thoughts confine,
        Nor hope to pierce the sacred gloom.

Beauty has such resistless power,
    That even the chaste Egyptian dame
        Sighed for the blooming Hebrew boy;
For her how fatal was the hour,
    When to the banks of Nisus came
        A youth so lovely and so coy!

But ah! sweet maid, my council hear,
    (Youth should attend when those advise
        Whom long experience renders sage;)
While music charms the ravish'd ear?
    While sparkling cups delight our eyes,
        Be gay, and scorn the frowns of age.

What cruel answer have I heard!
    And yet, by heaven, I love thee still;
        Can aught be cruel from thy lip?
Yet say, how fell that bitter word
    From lips which streams of sweetness fill,
        Which naught but drops of honey sip?

Go boldly forth, my simple lay,
    Whose accents flow with artless ease,
        Like orient pearls at random strung;
Thy notes are sweet, the damsels say;
    But O! far sweeter if they please
        The nymph for whom those notes are sung.

                                    1:133/130

Jefferson had much in common with Sir William Jones, who translated Arabic poetry into English. That Jefferson would compare and contrast both translations shows how he used juxtaposition in his clippings book to gain knowledge about a subject. Racine's *Phedre*, canto five of Byron's *Don Juan*, and Thomas Mann's *Joseph and His Brothers* all treat the story of Joseph.

SONG.

By Mrs. Opie.

Go, youth belov'd, in distant glades,
    New friends, new hopes, new joys to find,
Yet sometimes deign, 'midst fairest maids,
    To think on her thou leav'st behind.
Thy love, thy fate, dear youth to share,
    Must never be my happy lot,
But thou may'st grant this humble prayer,
    Forget me not, forget me not.

Yet, should the thought of my distress
    Too painful to thy feelings be,
Heed not the wish I now express,
    Nor ever deign to think on me;
But, oh! if grief thy steps attend,
    If want, if sickness, be thy lot,
And thou require a soothing friend;
    Forget me not, forget me not.

1:140/136

Amelia Opie's tender poem suggests that friendship outlasts love, though the self-abnegation of the sentimental speaker thinly veils a manipulative intent ("Heed not the wish I now express, / Nor ever deign to think on me"). Opie's novel *Fathers and Daughters* also displays the sensibility of its heroine as she struggles to please an aging father. Many of the poems Jefferson clipped, however erotic (like the Joseph poems), end with a nod toward virtue: "sometimes deign, 'midst fairest maids, / To think on her thou leav'st behind."

To Mary in Heaven.
By [Robert] Burns.

THOU ling'ring star with less'ning ray,
    That lov'st to greet the early morn,
Again thou usher'st in the day
    My Mary from my soul was torn.
O Mary! dear, departed shade!
    Where is thy place of blissful rest?
See'st thou thy lover lowly laid?
    Hear'st thou the groans that rend his breast?
That sacred hour can I forget,
    Can I forget the hallowed grove.
Where by the winding Ayr we met,
    To live one day of parting love!
Eternity will not efface
    Those records dear of transports past;
Thy image at our last embrace;
    Ah? little thought we 'twas our last!

Ayr gurgling kiss'd his pebbled shore,
    O'erhung with wilde woods, thick'ning, green;
The fragrant branch, and hawthorn hoar,
    Twin'd am'rous round the raptured scene.
The flowers sprang wanton to be prest,
    The birds sang love on ev'ry spray,
'Till too, too soon the glowing west,
    Proclaim'd the speed of winged day.

Still o'er these scenes my mem'ry wakes,
    And fondly broods with miser-care;
Time but the impression deeper makes,
    As streams their channels deeper wear.
My Mary! dear, departed shade!
    Where is thy blissful place of rest?
See'st thou thy lover lowly laid?
    Hear'st thou the groans that rend his breast?

1:141 / 137

Jefferson may have valued this piece because "Mary" was the name of his youngest child; she died, as an adult, during his second term as president. Burns's humble origins made him a favorite of American newspaper editors. One line is particularly striking: "The flowers sprang wanton to be prest."

[The following is not an European fiction (says a late English paper) but is a real *Madagascar Song*, brought from that island by the Chevalier De Porni.]

The Madagascar Mother.
[Fanny Holcroft]

"WHY shrink'st thou, weak girl! why this coward despair?
　Thy tears and thy struggles are vain;
Oppose me no more — of my curses beware!
　Thy terrors and grief I disdain."

The mother was dragging her daughter away,
　To the white man, alas! to be sold;
"O, spare me! (she cried) sure thou would'st not betray,
　The child of thy bosom for gold?

The pledge of thy love, I first taught thee to know
　A mother's affection and fears,
What crime has deserv'd thou should'st only bestow
　Dishonor and bondage, and tears!

I tenderly soothe every sorrow and care;
　To ease thee unwearied I toil
The fish of the stream by my wiles I ensnare;
　The meads of their flowers despoil.

From the bleak wint'ry blast I have shelter'd thy head;
　Oft borne thee with zeal to the shade;
Thy slumbers have watch'd on the soft leafy bed;
　The musquito oft chas'd from the glade.

Who'll cherish thy age, when from thee I am torn!
　Gold ne'er buys affection like mine!
Thou'lt bow to the earth, while despairing I mourn,
　Not my sorrows or hardships, but thine.

Then sell me not! save me from anguish & shame!
　No child thou hast, mother! but me?
Oh! I do not too rashly abjure the dear claim!
　My bosom most trembles for thee!"

In vain she implor'd, wretched maid! She was sold,
  To the ship, chain'd and frantic, convey'd;
Her parent and country ne'er more to behold,
  By a merciless mother betray'd.

1:144/140

The Madagascar mother betrays her child by
selling her into slavery. This poem is perhaps
unique in representing the mother as the
guilty party, not the slave trader.

The Old Beggar.
By Mrs. [Mary] Robinson.

DO you see the OLD BEGGAR who sits at yon gate,
    With his head silver'd over like snow?
Tho' he smiles as he meets the keen farrows Fate,
    Still his bosom is wearied with woe.

Many years has he swept the foot of the hill,
    Many days seen the summer-sun rise;
And at ev'ning the traveller passes him still,
    While the shadows steal over the skies.

In the keen blast of winter he hobbles along
    O'er the heath at the dawn of the day,
And the *dew-drops* that freeze the rude thistles among
    Are the *stars* that illumine his way!

How mild in his aspect, how modest his eye,
    How meekly his soul bears each wrong!
How much does he speak, by his eloquent sigh,
    Tho' no accent is heard, from his tongue.

Time was, when this BEGGAR, in martial trim sight,
    Was bold as the chief of his throng;
When he march'd thro' the storms of the day or night,
    And still smil'd as he journey'd along.

Then his form was athletick, his eye's vivid glance,
    Spoke the lustre of youth's glowing day!
And the village all mark'd in the combat and dance,
    The brave younker still valient as gay.

When the prize was propos'd, how his footsteps would bound,
    While the MAID *of his heart* led the throng;
While the ribbands that circled the May-pole around
    Wav'd the trophies of garland among.

But Love o'er his bosom triumphantly reign'd,
  Love taught him in fierce to pine: —
Love wasted his youth, yet he never complained
  For the *silence of Love* — is divine!

The dulcet ton'd weed, and the plaint of despair,
  Are no sign of the soul-wasting art:
'Tis the pride of Affection to cherish its core,
  And to count the quick throes of the heart.

Amidst the loud din of the battle he stood,
  Like a lion, undaunted and strong;
But the tear of compassion was mingled with blood,
  When his sword was the first in the throng.

When the bullet whizz'd by, and his arm bore away,
  Still he shrunk not, with anguish opprest;
And when Victory shouted the fate of the day,
  Not a groan check'd the joy of his breast.

To his dear native shore, the poor wanderer hied,
  But he came to complete his despair:
For the maid of his soul was that morning *a bride*,
  And a gay *lordly rival* was there!

From that hour, o'er the world has he wander'd forlorn,
  But still Love his companion would go,
And though deeply fond Memory planted its thorn,
  Still he silently cherish'd his woe!

See him now, while with age and with sorrow opprest,
  He the gate opens slowly and sighs!
See him drop the big tears on his woe-wither'd breast,
  The big tears that fall fast from his eyes.

See his habit all tatter'd, his shrivell'd cheek pale;
  See his locks waving thin in the air;
See his lip is half froze with the sharp cutting gale,
  And his head o'er the temples, all bare.

His eye-beam no longer in lustre displays
    The warm sun-shine that visit his breast;
For deep sunk is his orbit, and darken'd its rays
    And he sighs for the GRAVE'S silent rest!

And his voice is grown feeble, his accent is slow,
    And he sees not the distant hill's side;
And he hears not the breezes of morn as they blow
    Or the stream through the low valley guide.

To him all is silent, and mournful, and dim,
    E'en the seasons pass dreary and slow;
For Affliction has plac'd its cold fetter on him,
    And his soul is enamour'd of woe!

See the TEAR which, imploring, is fearful to roll,
    Though in silence he bows as you stray;
'Tis the eloquent silence which speaks to the soul,
    'Tis the *star* of his *slow-setting day!*

Perchance, ere the *May-blossoms* chearfully wave,
    Ere the *zephyr* of *summer* soft sigh,
The sun-beams shall dance on the grass o'er his GRAVE,
    And his *journey* be mark'd — TO THE SKY!

1:148/144

Jefferson's interest in Mary Robinson is striking for many reasons — and for one he may have known nothing about. Mistress of the prince regent and a well-known actress at Drury Lane, she later married the man who drove Jefferson from Monticello when he was governor of Virginia. Banastre Tarleton appears in a painting by Sir Joshua Reynolds as arrogant and self-confident as he apparently was in life. Mary Robinson became a cripple after complications resulting from her delivery of a child she conceived with Tarleton.

This poem, her account of a veteran who loses his arm and ends up poor, recalls aspects of Colonel Tarleton and Admiral Nelson's lives (only the latter was maimed in battle), though Mary Robinson found herself abandoned by the fickle Colonel Tarleton (the opposite happens in this poem). Robinson was a gifted poet whose racial tales of humble subjects recall Wordsworth's "Old Cumberland Beggar." In this poem, the soldier returns to find his heart broken and his finances in disarray. Her stress on the beggar as a walking ruin (stanza fifteen) helped inaugurate the Romantic interest in fragments and human pathos that marked the first decade of the nineteenth century.

LEONORA.
FROM THE GERMAN OF
BURGER.

Leonore fuhr um's Morgenroth
Empor aus schweren Traümen:
"Bist untreu, Wilhelm, oder todt?
Wie lange willst du saümen?"
Er war mit Konig Friedrichs Macht
Gezogen in die Prager Schlacht,
Und hatte nicht geschrieben:
Ob er gesund geblieben, etc.

1.

From visions of disastrous love
Leonora starts at dawn of day;
"How long my Wilhelm, wilt thou rove?
"Does death or falsehood cause thy stay?"
Since he with godlike Frederick's powr'rs
At Prague had foremost dar'd the foe,
No tidings cheer'd her lonely hours,
No rumour told his weal or woe.

2.

Empress and King, alike fatigued,
Now bade the storm of battle cease,
Their arms relenting friendship leagued,
And heal'd the bleeding world with peace.
They sing, they shout, their cymbals clang,
Their green wreaths wave, they come, they come;
Each war worn Hero comes to hang
With trophies his long wept for home.

3.

While from each bastion, tower, and shed,
Their country's general blessing showers,
Love twines for every laurel'd head,
His garland of domestic flowers.
How welcome husbands, sons, return'd!
What tears, what kisses greet the brave!

Alone poor Leonora mourn'd,
Nor tear, nor kiss, nor welcome gave.

4.

From rank to rank, from name to name,
The fond inquirer tremblin' flew;
But none by person or by fame,
Aught of her gallant Wilhelm knew.
When all the joyous bands were gone,
Aghast she tore her raven hair;
On the cold earth she cast her down,
Convuls'd with frenzy and despair.

5.

In haste th'affrighted mother flew,
And round her clasp'd her aged arms:
"Oh, God! her griefs with mercy view,
"Oh, calm her constant heart's alarms!"
"Oh, mother! past is past: 'tis o'er;
"Nor joy, nor world, nor hope I see;
"Thy God my anguish hears no more,
"Alas, alas! Oh, woe is me!"

6.

"Oh, hear, great God! with pity hear!
"My child, thy prayer to Heaven address;
"God does all well; tis ours tis bear;
"God gives, but God relieves distress."
"All trust in Heaven is weak and frail;
"God ill, not well, by me has done;
"I pray'd, while prayers could yet avail;
"Now prayers are vain, for Wilhelm's gone."

7.

"Oh, ever in affliction's hour,
"The Father hears his children's cry;
"His blessed sacraments shall pour
"True comfort o'er thy misery."
"Oh mother pangs like mine that burn,
"What sacrament can e'er allay.

"What sacrament can bid return
"Life's spirit to the mouldering clay!"

8.

"But if, my child, in distant lands,
"Unmindful of his plighted vows,
"Thy false one courts another's bands,
"Fresh kisses and a newer spouse,
"Why let the perjured rover go;
"No blessings shall his new love bring,
"And when death lays his body low,
"Thy wrongs his guilty soul shall sting."

9.

"My pangs no care nor comfort crave;
"Joy, hope, and life, alike I scorn;
"My hope is death, my joy the grave,
"Curs'd be the day that saw me born!
"Sink, sink, detested vital flame,
"Sink in the starless night of death:
"Not God's but Wilhelm's darling name,
"Shall faulter from my parting breath!"

10.

"Judge not, great God! this erring child,
"No guilt her bosom dwells within;
"Her thoughts are craz'd, her words are wild;
"Arm not for her the death of sin!
"Oh, child, forget thy mortal love,
"Think of God's bliss and mercies sweet;
"So shall thy soul, in realms above,
"A bright eternal Bridegroom meet."

11.

"Oh, mother! what is God's sweet bliss?
Oh! mother! mother! what is hell?
With Wilhelm there is only bliss,
And without Wilhelm only Hell!
O'er this torn heart, o'er these sad eyes,
Let the still grave's long midnight reign;

Unless my love that bliss supplies,
Nor earth nor heaven can bliss contain."

12.

Thus did the demons of despair, *the sickness unto death*
Her wildered sense to madness strain,
Thus did her impious clamours dare
Eternal wisdom to arraign.
She beat her breast, her hands she wrung,
Till westward sunk the car of light
And countless stars in air were hung
To gem the matron weeds of night.

13.

Hark! with high tread, and prancings proud,
A war horse shakes the rattling gate:
Clattering his clanking armour loud,
Alights a horseman at the grate:
And hark! the door bell gently rings,
What sounds are those we faintly hear?
The night breeze in loud murmur brings
These words to Leonora's ear.

14.

"Holla, holla! my life, my love!
"Does Leonora watch or sleep?
"Still does her heart my vows approve?
"Does Leonora smile or weep?
"O Wilhelm, thou! these eyes for thee
"Fever'd with tearful vigils burn;
"Aye, fear, and woe, have dealt with me,
"Oh! why so late thy wish'd return?"

15.

"At dead of night alone we ride,
"From Prague's far distant field I come;
"'Twas late ere I could 'gin bestride
"This coal black barb, to bear thee home."
"Oh, rest thee first my Wilhelm here!
"Bleak roars the blast through vale and grove;

"Oh come thy war-worn limbs to cheer
"On the soft couch of joy and love!"

16.

"Let the bleak blast, my child, roar on,
"Let it roar on; we dare not stay:
"My fierce steed maddens to be gone,
"My spurs are set; away, away.
"Mount by thy true love's guardian side;
"We should 'ere this full far have sped;
"Five hundred destined miles we ride
"This night, to reach our nuptial bed."

17.

"Our nuptial bed, this night so dark,
"So late, five hundred miles to roam?
"Yet sounds the bell, which struck, to mark
"That in one hour would midnight come.
"See there, see here, the moon shines clear,
"We and the dead ride fast away;
"I gage, though long our way, and drear,
"We reach our nuptial bed to-day.

18.

"Say where the bed, and bridal hall?
"What guests our blissful union greet?
"Low lies the bed, still, cold, and small;
"Six dark boards, and one milk white sheet."
"Hast room for me?" "Room, room enow:
"Come mount; strange hands our feast prepare;
"To grace the solemn rite, e'en now
"No common bridesmen wait us there."

19.

Loose was her zone, her breast unveil'd,
All wild her shadowy tresses hung;
O'er fear confiding love prevail'd,
As light on the barb she sprung.
Like wind the bounding courser flies,
Earth shakes his thundering hoofs beneath;

Dust, stones, and sparks, in whirlwind rise,
And horse and horseman pant for breath.

20.

How swift, how swift from left and right
The racing fields and hills recede;
Bourns, bridge, rocks, that cross their flight,
In thunders echo to their speed.
   "Fear'st thou, my love? the moon shines clear;
   "Hurrah! how swiftly speed the dead!
   "The dead does Leonora fear?"
   "Ah, no; but talk not of the dead."

21.

What accents slow, of wail and woe,
Have made yon shrieking raven soar?
The death bell beats! the dirge repeats,
   "This dust to parent dust restore."
Blackening the night, a funeral train
On a cold bier a coffin brings;
Their slow pace measur'd to a strain
Sad as the saddest night bird sings.

22.

   "This dust to dust restore, what time
"The midnight dews o'er grave are shed;
"Meanwhile of brides the flower and prime
"I carry to our nuptial bed.
"Sexton, thy sable minstrels bring!
"Come, priests, the eternal bonds to bless!
"All in deeps groans our spousals sing,
"Ere we the genial pillow press."

23.

The bier, the coffin, disappear'd,
The dirge in distant echoes died,
Quick sounds of viewless steps are heard
Hurrying the coal black barb beside.
Like wind the bounding courser flies
Earth shakes his thundering hoofs beneath;

Dust, stones and sparks in whirlwind rise,
And horse and horseman pant for breath.

24.

Mountains and trees, on left and right,
Swim backward from their aching view;
With speed that mock'd the labouring sight.
Towns, villages and castles flew.
    "Fear'st thou my love? the moon shines clear,
    "Hurrah! how swiftly speed the dead!
    "The dead does Leonora fear?"
    "Oh leave, oh leave in peace the dead!"

25.

See, where fresh blood-gouts mat the green,
Yon wheel its reeking points advance;
There by the moon's wan light half seen,
Green ghosts of tombless murderers dance.
    "Come, spectres of the guilty dead,
    "With us your goblin morris ply,
    "Come all in festive dance to tread,
    "Ere on the bridal couch we lie."

26.

Forward th'obedient phantoms push
Their trackless footstep rustle near,
In sounds like autumn winds that rush
Through withering oak or beech-wood sere.
With lightening's fore the courser flies,
Earth shakes his thundering hoofs beneath,
Dust, stones, and sparks, in whirlwind rise
And horse and horseman pant for breath.

27.

Swift roll the moonlight scenes away,
Hills chasing hills successive fly;
E'en stars that pave th'eternal way
Seem shooting to a backward sky.
    "Fear'st thou my love? the moon shines clear;
    "Hurrah! how swiftly speed the dead!

"The dead does Leonora fear?
"Oh God, oh leave, oh leave the dead!"

28.

"Barb! barb! methinks the cock's shrill horn
"Warns that our sun is nearly run,
"Barb! barb! I scent the gales of morn
"Haste, that our course be timely done
"Our course is done! our sun is run,
"The nuptial bed the bride attends;
"This night the dead have swiftly sped;
Here, here, our midnight travel ends!"

29.

Full at a portal's massy grate
The plunging steed impetuous dash'd:
At the dread shock, wall, bars and gate
Hurl'd down with headlong ruin crash'd.
Thin, sheeted phantoms gibbering glide
O'er paths, with bones and fresh skulls strown,
Charnels and tombs on every side
Gleam dimly to the blood red moon.

30.

Lo, while the night's dread glooms increase,
All chang'd the wond'rous horseman stood,
His crumbling flesh fell piece by piece,
Like ashes from consuming wood.
Shrunk to a skull his pale head glares,
High ridg'd his eyeless sockets stand,
All bone his length'ning form appears;
A dart gleams deadly from his hand.

31.

The fiend horse snorts, blue fiery flakes
Collected roll his nostrils round;
High rear'd, his bristling mane he shakes,
And sinks beneath the rending ground.
Demons the thundering clouds bestride,
Ghosts yell the yawning tombs beneath;

Leonora's heart, its life — blood dried,
Hangs quiv'ring on the dart of death.

32.

Throng'd in the moon's eclipsing shade,
Of fiends and shapes a spectre crowd
Dance neatly round th'expiring maid,
And howl this awful lesson loud:
   "Learn patience, though thy heart should break,
   "Nor seek God's mandates to controul!
   "Now this cold earth thy dust shall take,
   "And Heav'n relenting take thy soul!"
           K.

I:149–155 / 145–149.
[*On 149 is "Printed by Cussac, no. 33.*
rue Croix des [illegible] . . .
Price of subscription, 18 francs."]

"Leonora" was one of the most popular poems in Jefferson's day, going through seventeen editions the first year it appeared. Jefferson took special care with the poem, folding it down so it would fit on the backs of the envelopes he had pasted together. Wilhelm meets Leonora at her door for a midnight ride to his tomb, retribution for cursing God when she learned of Wilhelm's death ("God ill, not well, by me has done,"). At the end of the poem, a deus ex machina appears to join the souls of these passionate lovers. William Taylor's translation of Burger's ballad "Leonora, A Ballad from Burger" appeared in the March issue of *The Monthly Magazine* for 1796. Poet Laureate Henry James Pye, J. T. Stanley , W. R. Spencer, and Walter Scott offered other translations. Burger's three famous ballads, "Leonora," "The Lass of Fair Wone," and "The Wilde Chase," influenced Wordsworth's "The Idiot Boy," "The Thorn," and "Hart-Leap Well." William Taylor noted that the German phrases of "Leonora" match spoken language and express emotional spontaneity. "The hurrying vigour of his impetuous diction is unrivalled; yet is so natural, even in its sublimity, that his poetry is singularly fitted to become national popular song."[34]

Published in 1773, Burger's "Leonora" took England by storm twenty-three years later, when there appeared seven versions by five translators in a single year, 1796. Mr. Stanley, William Taylor of Norwich, William Spencer, Henry James Pye, and Walter Scott all took up Burger's topic, with Scott's translation, "William and Helen," becoming the most popular. Jefferson clipped Spencer's translation, which first appeared in England with illustrations by Diana Beauclerk. Jefferson also clipped other poems by William Spencer, who was himself a minor romantic poet of the period — a friend of Byron and Sheridan.

Anna Seward praised the poem for its wide appeal. "Creatures that love not verses for their beauty, like these for their horrors," Seward noted, after Lord Erskine and William Wilberforce came to her apartment "to be poetically frightened." William Spencer praised its literary quality, as well as its moral. "The story in a narrow compass unites tragic event, poetical surprise and epic regularity," he wrote, "and a moral which cannot be too frequently or too awfully enforced." M. G. Lewis, whose verse Jefferson also clipped, made his reputation with *Ambrosio, or the Monk*; he was harshly critical of Walter Scott's translation of Burger's "Leonora" for its use of half rhymes but thought enough of the poem to include Taylor's version in his *Tales of Wonder*. On the other hand, Wordsworth preferred the English to the original German.[35]

Lamb, writing to Coleridge on July 17, 1796, asked, "Have you read a ballad called 'Lenora' in the second number of the Monthly Magazine? If you have!!!! There is another fine song, from the same author (Berger), in the 3rd No. of scarce inferior merit." The other song was "The Lass of Fair Wone," which also appeared in the *Monthly Magazine* and in Jefferson's collection, translated by Rosa Matilda. Robert Southey noted that "the other ballad of Burger, in the *Monthly Magazine*, is most excellent. I know no commendation equal to its merit . . . the man who wrote that should have been ashamed of Lenora."[36]

Jefferson's interest in the supernatural is also shown in works by Fessenden ("Seduction") and Robert Merry ("The Wounded Mind"), and his poem critical of the Gothic trappings employed by Ann Radcliffe. He clipped "The Lass of Fair Wone" and collected songs by M. G. Lewis.

A BALLAD.

By Thomas Moore.

THE LAKE OF A DISMAL SWAMP.

WRITTEN AT NORFOLK IN VIRGINIA

"They tell of a young man, who lost his mind
upon the death of a girl he loved, and who suddenly disappearing from his friends, was never
afterwards heard of. As he had frequently said,
in his ravings, that the girl was not dead, but
gone to the dismal swamp, it is supposed he had
wandered into that dreary wilderness, and had
died of hunger, or been lost in some of its
dreadful morasses."   ANON.

"They made her a grave, too cold and damp
For a soul so warm and true;
And she's gone to the Lake of the Dismal-Swamp,*
Where, all night long, by a firefly lamp,
She paddles her white canoe.

And her fire-fly lamp I soon shall see,
And her paddle I soon shall hear:
Long and loving our life shall be.
And I'll hide the maid in a cypress tree,
When the footstep of death is near!"

Away to the dismal swamp he speeds —
His path was rugged and sore,
Through tangled juniper, beds of reeds,
Through many a fen, where the serpent feeds,
And man never trod before!

And, when on the earth he sunk to sleep,
If slumber his eyelids knew,
He lay, where the deadly vine doth weep
Its venomous tear, and nightly steep
The flesh with blistering dew!

And near him the she-wolf stirr'd the brake,
And the copper-snake breath'd in his ear,
Oh! when shall I see the dusky Lake,
And the white canoe of my dear?"

He saw the Lake and a meteor bright,
Quick over its surface play'd —
Welcome," he said, "my dar-one's light!
And the dim shore echoed, for many a night,
The name of the death cold maid!

Till he hollow'd a boat of the birchen bark,
Which carried him off from shore!
Far he follow'd the meteor spark,
The wind was high and the clouds were dark,
And the boat return'd no more.

But oft, from the Indian hunter's camp
This lover and maid so true,
Are seen at the hour of midnight damp,
To cross the lake by a fire-fly lamp,
And paddle their white canoe!

*The Great Dismal Swamp is ten or twelve miles
distant from Norfolk, and the lake in the middle of
it (about seven miles long) is called Drummond's
Pond.

1:156/151

Like "Leonora" (a poem that appears two pages earlier than this in Jefferson's scrapbook), Moore's "Lake of the Dismal Swamp" explores the supernatural and the boundary between love and despair. A man wanders into a dismal swamp in pursuit of his lover. Wordsworth wrote many poems that treat a landscape that becomes a *genius loci* (in Geoffrey Hartman's memorable phrase). American Indians remember a woman paddling with her canoe because she died too young to be forgotten completely.

Epitaph on a Young Lady.
By Richard Savage, Esq.

Clos'd are those eyes, that beam'd seraphic fire;
Cold is that breast, which gave the world desire;
Mute is the voice, where winning softness warm'd;
Where music melted, and where wisdom charm'd;
And lively wit, which, decently confin'd,
No prude e'er thought impure, no friend unkind.
Could modest knowledge, fair, untrifling youth,
Persuasive reason, and endearing truth;
Could honor, shown in friendships most refin'd:
And sense, that shields th'attempted, virtuous mind;
The social temper, never known to strife;
The height'ning graces that embellish life:
Could those have e'er the darts of death defy'd,
Never—ah! never had Melinda died?
Nor can she die—e'en now survives her name,
Immortaliz'd by friendship, love, and fame.

1:164/159

Though he wrote in the mid-eighteenth century, Richard Savage resembles Moore and other Regency poets. Samuel Johnson was Savage's personal friend and wrote a biography of him that, while not completely factual, has been much admired.

FROM THE POETICAL OBSERVATORY.
Poetry — A Fragment.
[Thomas Stott?]

"Lest you should think that verse shall die,
    That sounds the silver Thames along,"
Sang POPE, whose glowing numbers fly
    Above the reach of vulgar song. —

From Albion's shores how soft the sound
    Comes melting on my ravish'd ears:
Now rapt at once in thought profound —
    Now raised to mirth, now sunk in tears.

Such are th'emotions which I feel,
    Oh poetry, and such thy charms!
Permit thy votary to reveal,
    Whence swells his bosom with alarms.

Wild SHAKESPEARE, fancy's airy child,
    Shall triumph o'er the spoils of time;
Which DENHAM sung the nurses smiled
    And daring MILTON towers sublime.

With native elegance and ease,
    Forever shall my WALLER live,
And AKENSIDE shall ever please,
    And COWLEY'S lines shall morals give.

Great DRYDEN, thy immortal verse.
    Open fresh pleasures to the muse. —
Now GOLDSMITH'S numbers I rehearse;
    Now PARNELL'S melting lines I choose.

Thy church-yard strains forever, GRAY,
    Will draw from sympathy the tear;
YOUNG sings, and from the face of day,
    Night wears the sable robe of fear.

With OTWAY's fire — with softer LEE,
  The *Thespian Muse* dissolves in grief;
But now enlivening comic glee
  Returns and brings the mind relief.

When AMBROSE PHILLIPS tunes the lyre,
  Shepherds and shepherdesses dance;
Rustic swains breathe soft desire,
  And rural nymphs with smiles advance.

While Nature *"wheels the changeful year,"*
  Round THOMPSON'S brows the laurel wreath
Shall music twine — soft pity's tear
  Falls o'er the fate DODD left beneath.

Vain were the attempt at once to speak of all,
  Whose names are noted in the house of fame;
GREAT SHADES! Permit a votary, though small
  His merits are, with yours t'enrol his name.

HAFIZ.

1:189/183

This poem provides a nice overview of poets admired in Jefferson's day. Many of them are collected in Jefferson's literary commonplace book.

Thomas Parnell (1679–1718), an English poet, was born in Dublin and educated at Trinity College. Archdeacon of Clogher, he became friends with Harley, Swift, and Pope and was known for his wit. He died in Chester, while on his way to Ireland. Pope published a selection of his poems, the best known of which is "The Hermit." "The Nightpiece" and the "Hymn to Contentment" are considered better works.[37]

Abraham Cowley (1618–1667), following Westminster School attended Trinity College, Cambridge (1637), and wrote many pieces, including an epic based on King David. During the civil war he was ejected from Cambridge (1644); he studied at Oxford for another two years. In 1646, he accompanied the queen to Paris, was sent on Royalist missions, and carried on her correspondence in cipher with the king. He returned to England in 1654 and 1655, was arrested and then released on bail, and took the Oxford MD (1657). On Cromwell's death, he returned to Paris, then went back to England at the Restoration. He is the author of "Davideis," "Pindarique Odes," "Mistress," and a number of elegant essays.

Edmund Waller (1606–1687) was educated at Eton and Cambridge; he served as MP for Amersham, Ilchester, Chipping, and Amersham. In 1631, he married a London heiress who died three years later; from 1635 to 1638 he unsuccessfully courted the daughter of the earl of Leicester, Lady Dorothy Sidney, whom he referred to as "Sacharissa." In 1643, he plotted against Parliament, was arrested, and was expelled from the House. He avoided execution by confessing and paying a fine. He lived mostly in France, entertaining impoverished exiles; he returned to England in 1651. His publications include "A Panegyric to My Lord Protector" (1655) and "To the King upon His Majesty's Happy Return" (1660), addressed to Cromwell and Charles II, respectively.

Sir John Denham (1615–1669) was an English poet and the only son of an Irish judge. He wrote *The Sophy*, a tragedy, in 1641. "Cooper's Hill," in 1642, was a poetical description of the scenery around Egham; Pope's "Windsor Forest" was an imitation of Denham's poem. In 1648, Denham performed secret services for Charles I, and fled to Holland and France upon exposure. He was appointed surveyor-general of works; in 1661, he was created a Knight of the Bath. In 1665, he married a young girl who became a mistress of the duke of York.

Thomas Gray (1716–1771) attended Eton (1727) and afterward Peterhouse, Cambridge (1734). At Eton, he befriended Horace Walpole and accompanied him on the grand tour in 1739. He then traveled through France and Italy for two and a half years, departing at Reggio. Gray reached England in September 1741; in 1742, he wrote his "Ode on a Distant Prospect of Eton College." "The Elegy" was printed in February 1751. His mother died in 1753. In 1750, he began the *Pindaric Odes*. "Progress of Poesy" was finished in 1754, "The Bard" in 1757. He left Peterhouse for Pembroke Hall, Cambridge, in part because of his fear of fire. The publication of his two poems made him the leading English poet. The laureateship was offered him in 1757, but he declined it. From 1760, he devoted himself to early English poetry; he studied Icelandic and Celtic verse, producing "The Fatal Sisters" and "The Descent of Odin," precursors of Romanticism. In 1765, he visited Glamis Castle; in 1769, he visited the English Lakes; in 1768, he collected his poems in the first general edition, and accepted the professorship of history and modern languages at Cambridge.

Thomas Otway (1652–1685), an English dramatist, left Christ Church Oxford without a degree in 1672, failed as an actor, but wrote *Alcibiades* (1675). Otway fell in love with Mrs. Barry, an actress in this play. In 1676, he wrote *Don Carlos* — a good tragedy in rhyme. In 1677, Otway translated Racine's *Titus and Berenice*, as well as Molière's *Cheats of Scapin*. In 1678 and 1679 he was in Flanders; in May, he wrote *Friendship in Fashion*. In 1680, he wrote *The Orphan*, *Caius Marius*, and the important "Poet's Complaint of His Muse"; these were followed by *The Soldier's Fortune* (1681), *Venice Preserved* (1682), *The Atheist* (1684), a comedy, and "Windsor Castle" (1685), a poem addressed to James II. He died in poverty.

Ambrose Philips (1674–1749) English poet, was educated at St. John's College, Cambridge. A friend of Addison and Steele, he did hack work for Tonson, then gained a reputation by the "Winter-piece" in the *Tatler* and six pastorals in Tonson's *Miscellany* (1709). He was dubbed "Namby Pamby" by either Carey or Swift for the sentimentality of some of his poetry. "The Distrest Mother," based on Racine's "Andromaque," found favor with his contemporaries. Philips sat for Armagh, was secretary to the archbishop of Armagh, purse bearer to the Irish lord chancellor, and registrar of the Prerogative Court.

DAWN.

By Miss Owenson.

There is a soft and fragrant hour
Sweet, fresh, reviving is its power;
   'Tis when a ray
Steals from the vale of parting night
And by its mild prolusive light
   Fortells the day.

'Tis when some lingering stars scarce shed
Over the misty mountain's head
   Their fairy beam;
When one by one retiring, shrowd,
Dim glittering through a fleecy cloud,
   Their last faint gleam.

'Tis when just wak'd from transient death
(By some frail zephyrs balmy breath)
   The unfolding rose,
Sheds on the air its rich perfume,
While every bud with deeper bloom
   And beauty glows.

'Tis when fond nature (genial power)
Weeps o'er each drooping night clos'd flower,
   While softly fly
Those doubtful mists that leave to view
Each glowing scene of various hue
   That charms the eye.

'Tis when the sea girt turret's brow
Receives the East's first kindly glow,
   And the dark wave,
Swelling to meet the Orient gleam,
Reflects the warmly strength'ning beam
   It seems to have.

'Tis when the restless child of sorrow,
Watching the wish'd for rising morrow,

His couch foregoes,
And seeks midst scenes so sweet, so mild
To sooth those pangs so keen, so wild,
    Of hopeless woes.

Nor day, nor night, this hour can claim,
Nor moonlight ray, nor noontide beam
    Does it betray;
But, fresh, reviving, downy, sweet,
It hastes the glowing hour to meet,
    Of rising day.

1:200/191

A number of Romantic poems treat the
weather; this poem, by the author of *The Wild
Irish Girl*, was written by one of the best-selling
authors of the early nineteenth century.

To the Evening Star.
[Thomas Campbell]

Hail loveliest of the stars of Heaven,
    Whose soft, yet brilliant beams display,
The mildness of advancing even,
    The splendor of retiring day.

Star of delight! the rosy sky
    Sheds tears of joy for thy return!
While gentle round the breezes sigh,
    Nimphs [sic] of thy train, the planets burn.

All earth is gladdened by thy rays;
    And every flower, and shrub, and tree,
Boasts fresher bloom, and grateful pays
    A tribute of perfume to thee.

Day for thy partial smile contends;
    Night boasts, for her thy glories shine;
Before thee tranquil pleasure bends,
    And beauty whispers, "thou art mine."

Yes, thou art beauty's friend and guide;
    Conducted by thy beams so sweet,
She wanders forth at even-tide,
    The chosen of her heart to meet.

All grace she moves — with steps as light
    As rapture's bliss or fancy's dreams;
More soft her thoughts than dews of night,
    More pure than that unwaving stream.

Thy beams disclose the haunt of love,
    Conspicuous 'mid the twilight scene;
For Spring its leafy texture wove,
    And wedded roses to its green.

Fair wanderer of the sunset hour,
    Approaching to the ruddy west,

POEMS OF ROMANTIC LOVE

Where fairy forms prepare thy bow'r,
    With blooms from heavenly gardens drest.

Behold the light that fills her eye,
    The flashes o'er her cheek that move;
Can earth a sigh more sweet supply,
    Than loveliness improved by love?

"Yes, far more sweet! Methinks thee while
    I hear the accents whisper low;
'Tis beauty with her angel smile,
    Inclining o'er the couch of woe."

                         1:200/191

The evening star — which, according to Thomas Campbell, receives a tribute of perfume — becomes the occasion for a poem that celebrates nature in religious tones. More measured and restrained than Keats — less sentimental than Moore — Campbell refined his description of nature: "Can earth a sigh more sweet supply . . . ?" he asked. Yes, "'Tis beauty with her angel smile, / Inclining o'er the couch of woe." The angel smile is not meant seriously. One finishes the poem with the sense that Campbell is more pleased with himself than with the scene he describes.

LINES WRITTEN AT MIDNIGHT.
[Anonymous]

DEAR is the solemn midnight hour,
   That hour when pensive silence reigns,
Save, when low whisp'ring through the bow'r,
   The passing night-wind pours its strains:

When, stealing soft as lover's sigh,
   It breathes th'attentive ear along,
Tones sweet as fairy melody,
   Or wildest fancied spirit's song.

When the young moon, with lustre pale,
   And all the rolling planets bright,
O'er foliag'd hill, and verdant vale,
   Extend their mild, protecting light.

Dear is that hour, diffusing peace,
   A calm divine its stillness brings:
Day's little cares and sorrows cease,
   And the freed soul exalting springs:

Springs — inwards that heaven which looks so fair,
   Thro' its majestic portals flies,
And seeks with eager transports there,
   Forms that evanish'd from our eyes.

Then from bright clouds wild fancy's hand
   Shapes each lost object of our love;
Angelic visions round us stand,
   Or, warm with life and beauty, move:

And all unconscious, down the cheek,
   Steals mem'ry's pleasing, painful tear;
Nought but *that blended tear* could speak,
   The joy, the grief, that mingled there.

Dear hour! I prize thy pensive sway,
  I love thy soften'd, dubious light;
Adore who will the garish day,
  Mine be the illusive noon of night.
                              CLARA.

1:202/201

Did Jefferson place this poem next to one "From the American Citizen" to contrast British and American lyrics on a similar subject, evening? Many clippings in his book appear to be arranged with this kind of juxtaposition in mind.

LINES,

Written on the bank of a river.

[Anonymous]

HAIL, beauteous stream that smoothly glides along,
    With pleasure oft upon thy banks I've stray'd
Oft, separated from the world's gay throng,
    Reclin'd my limbs beneath thy yew trees' shade.

I love to sit beneath the foilag'd trees
    That shade thy borders from the sun's fierce beams:
O how propitious are such scenes as these
    To fancy's flights, and to poetic dreams?

When musing on my grief, I often pause
    And ponder on the follies of the great:
For ev'ry action of my life still draws
    A mournful presage of my future fate.

When spring returns to make all nature gay,
    And warblers sweet their cheerful notes employ:
When fields and flowers their various hues display,
    My soul's o'erspread with melancholy joy.

Though scenes in nature charm my woes awhile,
    And bid the anguish of my bosom rest;
Yet these are vain, they never will beguile
    The grief that constantly corrodes my breast.

Thus I must pass unfriended and unknown;
    My sorrows are so link'd they seem combin'd
Who never heard a corresponding moan,
    To sooth the troubles of his anxious mind.

So let me live whilst yet my feeling heart
    One spark of sensibility retains;
That I from nature never may depart,
    But ever sing forlorn my woe fraught strains.

A. R.

1:201/200–1:202/201

Like Campbell, who cultivated "woe" to add pathos to his description of the evening star, the author of this poem is happy to return to the melancholy — Thomas Gray called it "white melancholy" — that inspires him to sing his "woe fraught strains."

Sonnet to Night.

I love thee, mournful, sober-suited night;
    When the faint moon, yet lingering in her wane,
And veil'd in clouds, with pale uncertain light
    Hangs o'er the waters of the restless main.
In deep depression sunk, the enfeebled mind
    Will to the leaf cold elements complain,
    And tell the embosom'd grief, however vain,
To sullen surges, and the viewless wind.
Though no repose on thy dark breast I find
    I still enjoy thee, cheerless as thou art;
    For, in thy quiet gloom the exhausted heart
Is calm, though wretched; hopeless, yet resign'd:
While to th' winds and waves its sorrows giv'n
May reach (though not on earth) the ear of heaven!

Mrs. C. SMITH.

1:202/201

A third poem addressed to night, this one a sonnet by a poet who influenced Wordsworth and Coleridge, completes the thematic arrangement Jefferson intended in his clippings book. Smith is the most mournful of the three, describing the "cheerless" "quiet gloom" of "sober-suited night," which calms the "exhausted heart" into a "hopeless, yet resign'd" posture. For a man who also cultivated happiness, Jefferson did not refrain from embracing the gloom of this proto-Romantic poem.

BRYAN AND PEREENE.
A WEST-INDIAN BALLAD.
[James Grainger]
*Founded on a real fact, in the
Island of St. Christophers.*

THE north-east wind did briskly blow,
    The ship was safely moor'd,
Young Bryan thought the boat's crew slow,
    And so leap'd over board.

Pereene, the pride of Indian dames,
    His heart long held in thrall,
And whoso his impatience blames,
    I wot, ne'er lov'd at all.

A long, long year, one month and day,
    He dwelt on English land,
Nor once in thought would ever stray,
    Though Ladies sought his hand.

For Bryan was both tall and strong,
    Right blithsome roll'd his een;
Sweet was his voice, when'er he sung,
    He scarce had twenty seen.

But who the countless charms can draw,
    That grac'd his mistress true?
Such charms the old world never saw,
    Nor oft, I ween, the new.

Her raven hair plays round her neck,
    Like tendrils of the vine:
Her cheeks red dewy rose buds deck,
    Her eyes like diamonds shine.

Soon as his well-known ship she spied,
    She cast her weeds away,

And to the palmy shore she hied.
  All in her best array.

In sea-green silk so neatly clad,
  She there impatient stood;
The crew with wonder saw the lad,
  Repel the foaming flood.

Her hands a handkerchief display'd,
  Which he at parting gave;
Well pleas'd the token he survey'd,
  And manlier beat the wave.

Her fair companions, one and all,
  Rejoicing, crowd the strand,
For now her lover swam in call,
  And almost touched the land.

Then through the white surf did she haste,
  To claspe her lovely swain,
When, ah! a shark bit through his waist:
  His heart's blood dy'd the main!

He shriek'd; his half sprang from the wave,
  Streaming with purple gore,
And soon it found a living grave,
  And ah! was seen no more.

1:202/201

Jefferson's generation took pleasure in poems like Grainger's in part because of their narrative structure. A young man, Bryan, swims to meet Pereene, "the pride of Indian dames," only to be eaten by a shark before he reaches the shore. Percy's *Reliques* and *Ballads* were as popular as Blair's *Lectures on Belles Lettres* and helped popularize this genre.

ON SPRING.
[Anonymous]

WELCOME sweet cheerful spring, thy balmy breath
Infuses health, and stays the shafts of death,
With lively joy, the youthful bosom glows,
The tide of life, with rapid vigour flows

Thy presence can a ray of joy impart,
And soothe the sorrow of the aching heart.
The feeble form, new strength and firmness gains,
And circulation thrills each languid vein.

The leafless trees, their infant shoots disclose
From frost releas'd, the chrystal fountain flows,
The shining insects, sports in Pheobus' [sic] ray,
While tuneful birds, sit chirping on each spray.

All nature smiles! This variegated scene,
Fair Flora views, with countenance serene,
Her store produces, and her skill she tries
And flow'rets spring of various tints and dyes.

While youthful Fancy clad in gay attire
Attends her summons, and by her desire
O'er each unclosing bud, new grace bestows,
And gives new beauty to each op'ning rose.
                                        EMELINE.

                                                    2:55

As a gardener, Jefferson paid careful attention to the passing of the seasons. He compiled a Farm and Garden book in which he described the sequence of flowers and trees that bloomed on his estate. James Thomson's *Seasons* popularized this subject. The fourth stanza recalls Jefferson's rapturous description of nature in *Notes on the State of Virginia*. "The passage of the Potomac through the Blue ridge is, perhaps, one of the most stupendous scenes in nature. You stand on a very high point of land. On your right comes up the Shenandoah, having ranged along the foot of the mountain an hundred miles to seek a vent. On your left approaches the Potomac, in quest of a passage also. . . ."[38]

SPRING.
[Anonymous]

WHILE I with lofty lay employ,
To sing of cheerful spring's great joy,
The birds in accents nobler still,
Praise its return from every hill.
Each warbler flies from spray to spray,
Salute the Morn's returning day.
The Meads bedeck'd with vernal flow'r,
That bloom and fade in the same hour;
Declare "the Winter gone and past,
And beauteous SPRING return'd at last:"

2:76

Unlike "Remonstrance to Winter" or "Summer's Farewell," "Spring" revels in the return of a season inseparable from cheerfulness. By placing all of his poems on the seasons on a single page (including "On the Return of Spring," "Spring," "April, "On May," May," "The Rustic's May-Day," and "Summer's Farewell"[39]), Jefferson juxtaposed the moods and feelings that accompany them.

SUMMER'S FAREWELL.
AN ODE.
[Anonymous]

To Summer's sweets I bid farewell!
To the, O warbling Philomel,
To all the lovely winged tribe,
Which in thy regions now reside,
   I bid adieu! adieu ye flow'rs,
   Ye mild, ye placid, gentle flow'rs:
   Farewell ye skies of azure blue,
   Ye trails of brides, adieu! adieu.

To lovely meads, to cloud-capt hills,
To murmuring brooks, to purling rills,
To gentle streams to rural bow'rs,
To groves with their attractive pow'rs,
   I bid adieu! adieu ye vales,
   Ye fragrant, spicy, zeph'rous gales:
   Farewell ye banks of verdant hue,
   Ye woods, ye fields, adieu! adieu.

To scaly tribes, to spangled scenes,
To cool retreats to sylvan themes,
To lowing kine, to bleating flocks,
To mountains of romantic rocks,
   I bid adieu! adieu ye plains,
   Ye woodland nymphs, ye rural swains:
   Farewell ye drops of pearly dew,
   Ye pleasing shades, adieu! adieu!

To spreading tents, to humble cots,
To pebbled shores, to shelly grots,
To soothing strains, to dying lays,
To nature's mild and gentle rays,
   I bid adieu! adieu ye lawns,
   Ye tender kids, ye sportive fawns,
   Farewell ye tints which gild the view,
   Ye orient beams, adieu! adieu.

2:78

"Summer's Farewell" anticipates Wordsworth in stressing the individual's response to nature. The poem is Romantic in its protest against the fleeting character of summer. The poignancy of the poem lies in the speaker's implicit recognition that his or her enjoyment of life is as fleeting as the passing season.

A SKETCH OF THE ALPS AT DAY-BREAK.

By Samuel Rogers, Esq.

The sun-beams streak the azure skies,
    And tint with light the mountain's brow
With hounds and horns the hunters rise,
    And chase the roebuck thro' the snow.

From rock to rock, with giant bound,
    High on their iron poles they pass,
Mute, lest the air, convuls'd by sound,
    Rend from above a frozen mass.*

The goats wind slow their wonted way:
    Up craggy steeps and ridges rude,
By wild wolves destin'd for their prey
    From desert cave, or hanging wood.

And, while the torrent thunders loud,
    And, as the echoing cliffs reply,
The huts peep o'er the morning cloud,
    Perch'd, like an eagle's nest, on high.

*There are passes in the Alps where the
guides tell you to move on with speed and
say nothing, lest the agitation of the air
should loosen the snows above.

2:79

This is part of a three-poem sequence on morning, evening, and other times of the day. The Alps inspired a number of Romantic poets: Shelley and Coleridge, for example, both wrote very different poems contemplating the meaning of "Mont Blanc" (as an atheist) and as a Christian believer ("Hymn in the Vale of Chamonix"). This poem focuses on the Alps as a natural phenomenon. Neither as radical as Shelley's poem (which describes the doctrine of necessity) nor as conventional as Coleridge's (which views the Alps as an argument for religious belief), Rogers's poem retains an elegance, fluency, and charm. Like Grainger's, Rogers's lyric tries to be faithful to the scene he records. He does not seem as concerned as Shelley and Coleridge with transforming what he beholds.

The Evening Star.
By T. Campbell.

GEM of the crimson colored even,
    Companion of retiring day;
Why at the closing gates of heaven,
    Beloved Star, dost thou delay?

So fair thy pensive beauty burns,
    When soft the tear of twilight flows,
So due thy plighted step returns
    To chambers brighter than the rose

To peace, to pleasure, and to love,
    So kind a star thou seem'st to be,
Sure some enamoured orb above,
    Descends and burns to meet with thee.

Thine is the breathing blushing hour,
    When all unheavenly passions fly,
Chased by the soul subduing power,
    Of love's delicious extacy.

O sacred to the fall of day,
    Queen of propitious stars, appear,
And early rise, nor long delay
    When Caroline herself is here!

Shine her chosen green resort,
    Whose trees the sunward summit crown,
And wanton flowers, that well may court
    An angel's feet to tread them down.

Shine on her sweetly scented road,
    Thou star of evening's purple dome,
That leads the nightingale abroad,
    And guides the pilgrim to his home.

Shine where my charmer's sweeter breath
    Embalms the soft exhaling dew,

Where dying winds a sigh bequeth
    To kiss the cheek of rosy hue.

Where, winnowed by the gentle air,
    Her silken tresses darkly flow,
And fall upon her brow so fair,
    Like shadows on the mountain snow.

Thus, ever thus at day's decline,
    Is converse sweet to wander far,
O bring with thee my Caroline,
    And thou shalt be my ruling star!

                       2:80

In this poem, the speaker subordinates his
praise of the evening star to Caroline, who
rules his affections.

VERSIFICATION

[Royall Tyler]

The Northern blasts thy cloudy gates unfold,
Thy warlike form, O FINGAL, I behold;
Amid the curling gloom that wraps thee round,
Appear thy gleaming arms in fight renown'd;
Is dimly seen thy arm, so far renown'd:
Like the thin clouds the weeping stars that lave,
Thou art no more the terror of the brave.
Thy pound'rous shield, in battle once so bright,
Seems like the waning empress of the night;
A feeble vapour is the sword you bore,
Dim is the chief who walk'd in light before.
Yet still thy steps are on the distant winds,
And thy strong grasp the brewing tempest binds,
The sun thou takest in thy dreadful ire,
And quenchest in the clouds his blazing fire,
The sons of little men affrighted fly,
A thousand showers pour from out the sky;
But when thou comest forth in calmness sweet,
The gales of morning play around thy feet;
The sun shines out upon the dewy meads,
And through the vale the winding river speeds,
The bushes shake their green heads in the breeze,
The roe toward the distant desert flees.

2:91

In this "versification," Royall Tyler converts James Macpherson's poetry into heroic couplets. Jefferson admired Macpherson's poetry enough to write to Charles Macpherson, the poet's brother, to see if he could obtain the Gaelic originals. The poems turned out to be partial forgeries, but this only added luster to Macpherson's reputation as a poet, and the poems were enjoyed by Napoleon and Goethe, among many others. In Jefferson's scrapbook, Tyler's poetic rendering of Macpherson appears on the same page as "Milton," "On Health," and "Hope."

To DELLA CRUSCA.
[Robert Merry]

Blest "genius of the god of day."
  Escaped the swelling surges roar,
Receive a grateful tribute lay,
  That hails thee welcome to our shore.

In Britain's isle, subdued by love,
  Thy magic Muse in moving verse,
Confest thy pangs; whilst every grove
  Was taught "Matilda" to rehearse.

Resume once more thy "golden quill"
  A nobler theme demands thy song.
Quickly our hero's virtues tell;
  To Washington thy strains belong.

If aught can more illume his fame,
  Which soars above the Eagle's wings,
Or nations more admire his name,
  It is that Della Crusca sings.

Sing the great chief, who to his fields withdraws —
Oh, sing whilst worlds shall listen with applause!
                                        LAURA.
  Delaware State, November 6th.

2:97

Robert Merry popularized a style of poetry that was highly sentimental. While in the United States he wrote and performed several songs in praise of George Washington, as Laura urges him to do here.

SONNET.
By ANNA SEWARD

Short is the time the oldest being lives,
Nor has longevity one *hour* to waste
Life's duties are proportion'd to the haste
With which it fleets away; — each day receives
Its task; that, if neglected, surely gives
The morrow *double* toil — Ye who have pass'd
In idle sport, the days that fled so fast,
Days, that nor grief recalls, nor care relieves,
At length be wise and think, that of the party
Remaining in that vital period given,
How short the date, and at the prospect start,
Ere to the extremest verge your steps be driv'n!
Nor let a moment unimprov'd depart,
But view it as the *latest* trust of heaven!

2:103

On this page, Jefferson included "Scenes of My Youth," "To Clara," and this "Sonnet" by Anna Seward; he also placed an oak leaf here, which Robert McDonald has attributed to his close friendship with Dabney Carr.

Perhaps Carr's untimely death in 1773 made Jefferson particularly aware of the importance of seizing the moment. Seward's sonnet fits Jefferson's motto of never putting off till tomorrow what you can do today (also to be found in Lord Chesterfield's writings and Benjamin Franklin's). In a letter to Thomas Jefferson Smith, he made this adage his own.[40] Seward's concluding couplet echoes Jefferson's focus on self-improvement: "Nor let a moment unimprov'd depart, / But view it as the *latest* gust of heaven!"

The TEAR.
[Anonymous]

HOW seldom in this desert vale,
   Congenial happiness we find;
Seldom that Friendship's steady gale
   Re-animates the drooping mind.
Some passing breeze, to sorrow dear,
Dries but awhile the bitter tear!

Scarce had the wishes of the heart,
   When blighted by distrust, they die;
We feel the sun of bliss depart,
   And o'er our fairest prospects sigh!
Some passing breeze, to sorrow dear,
Dries but awhile the bitter tear.

Ah! when, to ills no more a prey,
   Shall yet the wearied soul repose?
Soon — and behold earth's toilsome day
   An everlasting sabbath close!
Fresh from the breeze of life, is near
The breeze that dries the bitter tear!

2:113

Juxtaposed with "Ode to Friendship," "The Eye," and "Memory," "The Tear" is one of three poems with this title that Jefferson clipped for his collection. Byron wrote a poem titled "The Tear" for *Hours of Idleness* (1806); Sterne's novels also feature sentimental travelers who reveal their humanity by shedding tears at the smallest provocation.

MEMORY.

[Anonymous]

AT the mild close of dewy eve,
    While the last sun-beam lingers near,
The wild and noisy throng I leave,
    To think of scenes to Memory dear.

When on the clear blue arch of heaven,
    O'er the high trees the stars appear;
I love those hours to sorrow given,
    To think of scenes to Memory dear.

Oft to the dove's sad tales I list,
    Drop to her fabled woes a tear,
And careless of the night-dew's mist,
    I think of scenes to Memory dear.

Then as the full moon signals on high,
    And brings to view the prospect drear,
Oft echo will repeat the sigh,
    That heaves for friends to Memory dear.

And when the close of life draws high,
    The thoughts of them my heart shall cheer;
And my last faultering accents sigh,
    Peace to the friends to Memory dear.

When o'er my form the green turfs swell,
    If e'er my friends should wander near,
Will they in moving accents tell,
    How died the friend to Memory dear?

2:113

Pasted directly below "The Tear," this poem considers the status of memory, an important theme treated in Wordsworth's "Tintern Abbey." As in many poems that Jefferson clipped, the mournful, simple lyric struggles to cover the whole life span, preaching a philosophy of life that will suit every occasion ("I love those hours to sorrow given").

From the Belfast News-Letter
THE UNFORTUNATE BEAUTY
OF BUTTERMERE.
A BALLAD.
[Thomas Stott]

By yonder Lake, whose crystal face
　　Reflects the scene around for e'er,
Dwells MARY, late the rural Grace,
　　The rural Boast of Buttermere.

The dew-drop on the bending blade,
　　When Summer streaks the morning sky,
A faint idea but convey'd
　　Of her bright, liquid, laughing eye.

The blushing corn-pink of the field,
　　The poppy with its silk-white vest,
In tint, to those soft colours yield,
　　That MARY's blooming cheek impress'd.

Her fame spread o'er the country wide,
　　And many a Swain, both far and near,
Sought, vainly sought, to make his Bride
　　The lovely Lass of Buttermere.

At length an artful villain came,
　　Trick'd out in Fortune's pilfer'd plumes,
And, to conceal his cursed aim,
　　An honorable Name assumes.

Deep-vers'd in all the Stygian skill
　　Of Treachery's circumventing art,
Alas! he to his wicked will
　　Soon won the simple Virgin's heart —

Gain'd her consent, in wedlock's band,
　　(O profanation!) to unite
With her's, his vile polluted hand —
　　And ev'n perform'd the hallow'd rite!

Ah! beauteous, but incautious Maid!
　　Sad victim of the Villain's guile!
Too easily wert thou betray'd
　　By SHOW's false glare, and faithless smile!

The gay illusion quickly fled —
　　The dark deceit was soon descried —
A few short suns roll'd round thy head,
　　When thou was left — a mourning Bride?

Yet, hapless Beauty of the Lake!
　　Tho' now Misfortune frowns severe,
From this reflection comfort take —
　　Thy CHARACTER, thy VIRTUE's clear.

Thy cause the Virtuous have espous'd,
　　Espous'd with more than common zeal!
Thy Wrongs have PUBLIC JUSTICE rous'd —
　　Vengeance the Traitor yet shall feel!
　　　　　　　　　　　　HAFIZ.

　　　　　　　　　　2:123

Mary of Buttermere was Mary Robinson, the Beauty of Buttermere. She was the daughter of the landlord of the Fish Inn at Buttermere, and famous in the Lake District for her charm. Her marriage in October 1802 to John Hatfield — who was already married — became the occasion for moral outrage against "artful villain[s]." Coleridge made her situation known by sending some letters on John Hatfield's bigamy to the *Morning Post*. Hatfield was hanged in September 1803.

The author of this poem, Hafiz, is most probably Thomas Stott, a poet who lived in Belfast. In book seven of *The Prelude*, Wordsworth also took up the Maid of Buttermere's cause, criticizing John Hatfield for operating "in cruel mockery; / Of love and marriage bonds."

HATFIELD, THE IMPOSTER.
(FROM A YORKSHIRE PAPER.)

We can assure the public that the following are authentic copies of Elegies, or Epitaphs, written by Hatfield whilst in the jail of Scarborough. The originals, which are now in the possession of G. Hardinge, esq. Attorney General to the Queen, were found on Sunday the 21st ult. in searching the various papers and manuscripts which Hatfield had left in a large trunk remaining in the custody of the jailer: —

Loud houl the winds around my prison house,
Dull are the days, and wearisome my nights;
Care-worn, my spirits nothing now can rouse,
Ev'n gen'rous wine itself no more delights.
Lost to the world, from ev'ry comfort torn,
Ill us'd by those who should have been my friends,
I almost curse the hour that I was born,
And sigh for that when worldly sorrow ends.
By knaves and fools I've been so long abus'd,
By sland'rous lips have been so much bely'd,
Without a cause have been so much accus'd,
And have so long in vain for justice cry'd,
That my whole soul abhors this wretched life.
One boon alone I from your town would crave,
That when I've shuffled off this mortal strife,
The Corporation may give me a grave;
On which, when some kind hand has plac'd a stone,
It may in plain but modest language tell,
And briefly to inquirers make known,
By whose vile arts the harmless stranger fell.

"Here rest the remains of John Hatfield, who died broken-hearted in the jail of this town, where he was confined by _____, at the instigation and by the advice of _____. A keen sense of the injury heaped upon him by his prosecutor, who, after confining his person, did all he could, by letters and otherwise, to vilify him, preyed too powerfully on his spirits, and he fell a victim to malicious falsehoods in his 33d year, A.D. 1792."

ANOTHER.

Lo! where the antient marbles weep,
And all the WORTHY Hatfields sleep,
Amongst them soon may I recline,
Oh! may their hallow'd tombs be mine.
When in that sacred vault I'm laid,
Heav'n grant it may with truth be said,
His heart was warm'd with faith sincere,
And soft humanity dwells there —
My children oft will mourn their father's woe,
Heart-easing tears from their sweet eyes will flow.
My — , too, relenting when I'm dead,
O'er past unkindness, tender tears will shed.

J. H. July 20, 1794 —

2:123

As if to see things from both sides, Jefferson clipped a poem by John Hatfield, who described his despair in prison after being ostracized from the community for bigamy. His incarceration seems less painful than the shame he feels. Hatfield's justification does not appear in books that treat Wordsworth's verse and is reprinted here, I believe, for the first time.

LITERARY INTELLIGENCE.
[Walter Scott]

A POEM in six cantos has just made its appearance in London, called THE LAY OF THE LAST MINSTREL. It is from the pen of Walter Scott, well known as the author of many fugitive pieces, possessing much merit, and as having favored the public with *The Minstrelsy of the Scottish Border*. The intention of the present work is thus stated in the words of the author. "The poem now offered to the public is intended to illustrate the customs and manners which anciently prevailed on the borders of England and Scotland. The inhabitants, living in a state partly pastoral and partly warlike, and combining habits of constant depredation with the influence of a rude spirit of chivalry, were often engaged in scenes highly susceptible of poetical ornament. As the description of scenery and manners was more the object of the author, than a combined and regular narrative, the plan of the ancient metrical romance was adopted, which allows greater latitude in this respect than would be consistent with the dignity of a regular poem. The machinery also, adopted from popular belief, would have seemed puerile in a poem which did not partake of the rudeness of the old ballad, or metrical romance.

"For these reasons the poem is put into the mouth of an ancient minstrel, the last of the race, who, as he is supposed to have survived the revolution, might have caught somewhat of the refinement of modern poetry, without losing the simplicity of his original model. The date of the tale is about the middle of the 16th century, when most of the personages actually flourished." The minstrel is described in the following lines, from the introduction.

[National Intelligencer.]

INTRODUCTION.

The way was lone, the wind was cold,
The Minstrel was infirm and old;
His wither'd cheek and tresses grey,
Seem'd to have known a better day;
His harp, his sole remaining joy,
Was carried by an Orphan Boy,
The last of all the bards was he,
Who sung of bolder chivalry;

For, well-a-day! their date was fled,
His tuneful brethren all were dead;
And he, neglected and oppres'd

Wish'd to be with them and at rest.
No more on prancing palfry borne,
He carroll'd, light as lark at morn;

No longer, courted and caress'd,
High plac'd in hall, a welcome guest,
He pour'd to lord and lady gay,
Th'unpremeditated lay;
Old times were chang'd, old manners gone,
A stranger fill'd the Steward's throne;
The bigots of the iron time
Had call'd his harmless art a crime.
A wandering harper, scorn'd and poor,
He begg'd his bread from door to door;
And tun'd to please a peasant's ear
The harp a king had lov'd to hear.

Amid the strings his fingers stray'd,
And an uncertain warbling made —
And oft he shook his hoary head.
But when he caught the measure wild,
The old man rais'd his face and smil'd;
And light'ned up his faded eye,
With all a poet's ecstasy!
In varying cadence, soft or strong,
He swept the sounding chords along;
The present scene, the future lot,
His toils, his wants, were all forgot;
Cold diffidence and age's frost,
In the full tide of song were lost;
Each blank in faithless mem'ry void,
The poet's glowing thought suppli'd;
And, while his harp responsive rung,
'Twas the LATEST MINSTREL sung.

2:131

The introduction to this poem explains the dilemma of poets such as Macpherson and Chatterton, who wished to emulate medieval or ancient bards but also hoped to do so in a refined way that would appeal to an urban, usually a London, audience. The "Lay of the Last Minstrel" strikes a note similar to Macpherson, who presented his poems as the last Gaelic songs of a dying and unappreciated race, but one more noble than the present.

FROM THE LAY OF
THE LAST MINSTREL,
A POEM
BY WALTER SCOTT.

BREATHES there the man with soul so dead,
Who never to himself hath said,
　　This is my own, my native land?
Whose heart hath ne'er within him burned,
As home his footsteps he hath turned,
　　From wandering on a foreign strand?
If such they breathe, go mark him well;
For him no minstrel raptures swell;
High tho' his titles, proud his name,
Boundless his wealth as wish can claim;
Despite these titles power and pelf,
The wretch, concenter'd all in self,
Living shall forfeit fair renown,
And, doubly dying shall go down
To the vile dust from whence he sprung,
Unwept, unhonor'd, and unsung.

O Caledonia! stern and wild,
Meet nurse for a poetic child!
Land of brown heath and shaggy wood,
Land of the mountain and the flood,
Land of my sires! what mortal hand,
Can e'er untie the filial band,
That knits me to thy rugged strand!
Still, as I view, each well known scene,
Think what is now, and what hath been,
Seems as, to me, of all bereft,
Sole friends, thy woods and streams were left;
And thus I love them better still,
E'en in extremity of ill.
By Yarrow's stream still let me stray,
Though none should guide my feeble way,

Still feel the breeze down Ettricke break,
Altho' it chill my wither'd cheek;
Though there, forgotten and alone,
The bard may draw his parting groan.

2:130

Scott's novels were overshadowed by his verse, but this poem's expression of nationalism — at a time when nationalism and Romanticism were inextricably combined — made both the poem and the poet extremely popular. Jefferson clipped two other extracts from the same work and pasted them underneath (this is the second of the series).

FROM THE LAY OF THE LAST MINSTREL,

A POEM

BY WALTER SCOTT

SWEET Feviot! on thy silver tide,
   The glaring bale fires blaze no more;
No longer steel-clad warriors ride
   Along thy wild and willow'd shore;
Where'er thou wind'st by dale or hill
All — all is peaceful, all is still,
   As if thy waves, since time was born,
Since first they roll'd their way to Tweed
Had only heard the shepherd's reed,
   Nor started at the bugle-horn.

Unlike the tide of human time,
   Which, tho' it change in ceaseless flow,
   Its earliest course was doom'd to know
And, darker as it downward bears,
Is stain'd with past and present tears.
   Low as that tide has ebb'd with me,
It still reflects to memory's eye
The hour my brave, my only boy,
   Fell by the side of Great Dundee.
Why, when the volleying musket play'd
Against the bloody highland blade,
Why was not I beside him laid; —
Enough — he died the death of fame;
Enough — he died with conqu'ring Graeme.

2:131

Of the three extracts from Scott's "Lay of the Last Minstrel" that Jefferson clipped, this is the third (canto 4:2). The speaker exists in a timeless state, transformed forever, by the moment his son died in the battle of Dundee. The poem's celebration of patriotic figures, inspired by the death of siblings or ancestors, recalls such poems as "Oithona" and "Fingal" in Macpherson's *Ossian*, which Jefferson and William Blake admired.

THE GRAVE.

[James Montgomery]

(A rich vein of morality runs throughout the following production)

THERE is a calm for those who weep,
A test for weary Pilgrims found;
They softly lie, and sweetly sleep,
        Low in the ground.

The storm that wrecks the winter sky,
No more disturbs their deep repose,
Their summer ev'ning's latest sigh,
        That shuts the rose.

I long to lay this painful head
And aching heart beneath the soil;
To slumber in that dreamless bed
        From all my toil.

For Misery stole me at my birth,
And cast me helpless on the wild;
I perish — O my mother Earth!
        Take home thy child.

On thy dear lap these limbs reclind,
Shall gently moulder into thee;
Nor leave one wretched trace behind,
        Resembling me.

Hark! — a strange sound affrights mine ear!
My pulse — my brain runs wild — I rave!
Ah! who art thou whose voice I hear?
        "I am the GRAVE!

"The GRAVE, that never spake before,
Hath found at length a tongue to chide:
O listen! — I will speak no more!
        Be silent, Pride!

"Art thou a WRETCH, of hope forlorn,
The victim of consuming care?
Is thy distracted conscience torn
      By fell despair?

"Do foul misdeeds of former times
Wring with remorse thy guilty breast?
And Ghosts of unforgiven crimes
      Murder by rest?

"Lash'd by the furies of the mind,
From wrath and vengeance wouldst thou flee,
Ah! think not, hope not, Fool! to find
      A friend in me.

"By all the terrors of the tomb,
Beyond the power of tongue to tell!
By the dread secrets of my womb!
      By Death and Hell!

"I charge thee LIVE! — Repent and pray;
In dust thine infamy deplore;
There yet is mercy! — go thy way,
      And sin no more.

" — Art thou a MOURNER? — Hast, thou known
The joy of innocent delights?
Endearing days forever flown
      And tranquil nights?

"O Live? — and deeply cherish still
The sweet remembrance of the past:
Rely on Heaven's unchanging will
      For peace at last.

"Art thou a WANDERER? — Hast thou e'en
O'erwhelming tempests drown thy bark?
A shipwreck'd sufferer hast thou been,
      Misfortune's mark?

"Tho' long, of winds and waves the sport,
Condemn'd the wretchedness to roam,
LIVE! — thou shalt reach a sheltering port,
  A quiet home.

"TO FRIENDSHIP didst thou trust thy fame,
And was thy Friend a deadly foe,
Who stole into thy breast to aim
  A surer blow?

"LIVE! — and repine not o'er his loss,
A loss unworthy to be told:
Thou hast mistaken sordid dross
  For Friendship's gold.

"Go, seek that treasure, seldom found,
Of power the fiercest griefs to calm,
And soothe the bosom's deepest wound
  With Heavenly balm.

" — In WOMAN hast thou plac'd thy bliss,
And did the Fair One faithless prove?
Hath she betray'd thee with a kiss,
  And sold thy love?

"LIVE! — 'twas a false bewild'ring fire;
Too often Love's insidious dart
Thrills the fond soul with sweet desire,
  But *kills the heart*.

"A nobler flame shall warm thy breast,
A brighter Maiden's virtuous charms!
Blest shalt thou be, supremely blest,
  In beauty's arms.

" — Whate'er thy lot — whoe'er thou be —
Confess thy folly, kiss the rod,
And in thy chast'ning sorrows see
  The hand of God.

"A bruised reed he will not break;
Afflictions all his children feel;
He wounds them for his mercy's sake,
    He wounds to heal.

"Humbled beneath his mighty hand;
Prostrate his Providence adore:
'Tis done! — Arise! he bids thee stand,
    To fall no more.

"Now, Traveller in the vale of tears!
To realms of everlasting light,
Through Time's dark wilderness of years,
    Pursue thy flight.

"There is a calm for those who weep,
A rest for weary Pilgrims found;
And while the mouldering ashes sleep,
    Low in the ground.

"The Soul, of origin divine,
God's glorious image, freed from clay,
In Heaven's eternal sphere shall shine,
    A star of day!

"The SUN is but a spark of fire,
A transient meteor in the sky,
The SOUL, immortal as its Sire,
    "SHALL NEVER DIE!"

2:135

James Montgomery's "The Grave" was one of his most popular poems. Like Edward Young in "Night Thoughts," the speaker of "The Grave" consoles himself for his suffering on earth by contemplating the afterlife. "The Soul, of origin divine, / God's glorious image, freed from clay, / In Heaven's eternal sphere shall shine, / A star of day!"

The poem can be read as a more extreme articulation of the retirement theme that appealed to Jefferson. With a melancholy characteristic of the graveyard poets, the speaker longs to be laid "low in the ground" in order to escape his "toil." Jefferson's letters to his daughters cast his experience in the White House in similar terms, constantly reiterating his desire to return to Monticello as a relief from strife. But the poem does not end there. With classical decorum, the speaker balances the pessimism of the first eight stanzas with a rebuke from the grave itself, to "LIVE!" The final eight stanzas of the poem link the struggle to overcome one's errors with Christian faith. "The hand of God . . . wounds to heal" and is a "chast'ning" rod.

THE BEGGAR.
[Mary Robinson]

"AH! curse me not — no crumb of bread
  "Has past these lips since yestermorn.
"No shelter for this aching head
  "Have I, abandon'd and forlorn,

"Dark is the night, and cold the blast,
  "With misery am I doom'd to roam;
"All hopeless on the wide world cast,
  "Without one friend — without a home.

"Yet, tho' by every ill opprest;
  "Tho' pining want assail my life,
"A home I had; I once was blest;
  "A mother lov'd — a happy wife.

"Think not, dear sir, it is my aim
  "A cunning, studied lie to raise,
"Like beggars bold who daily claim
  "The mite which passing pity pays.

"My husband kept a little shop;
  "And well his honesty was known;
"Of credit this the surest prop
  "His name would pass thro' all the town.

"No comforts to his wife deny'd
  "A tender husband could afford,
"Each prudent wish was gratified
  "Peace smil'd, and plenty deck'd the
board.

"Why could not this good fortune last!
  "Sure Heaven intended me for woe.
"Did I, unthinking, live too fast
  "For one so humbly placed? Ah, no!

"Indeed, dear sir, I'm not to blame,
        "The man who long had been my pride
"Grew idle, gam'd and lost to shame
        "The victim of intemperance died.

"Our few remaining goods were kept
        "For house-rent, due a year and more.
"We were turn'd out. Ah! how I wept
        "As slow I turn'd me from the door.

"Tho' now of husband, home bereft,
        "Yet I could make a living sure;
"This comfort to my heart was left,
        "I still might work, however poor.

"Buoy'd up by hope, a little hut
        "I took at twenty pounds a year.
"My daughter to a school I put;
        "'Twas not far off, nor was it dear.

"The sweet child was just turn'd of *ten*.
        "From her alone my pleasures rose;
"And she was useful too; for when
        "I wash'd, she carried home the clothes.

"Her beauty ripen'd with her years
        "A lovlier girl was never seen.
"And now, an anxious parent's fears
        "Increas'd with blooming, fresh *fifteen*.

"Those fears, alas! were too, too just
        "From a fond mother's bosom torn,
"She's now to vice and scorn reduc'd
        "Would she had died, or ne'er been born!

"A villain to seduction train'd,
        "With speech so soft, and mien so mild,
"By flattery and love well feign'd
        "Ruin'd my unsuspecting child.

POEMS OF ROMANTIC LOVE

"With me no longer would she rest,
  "I strove my spirits to sustain,
"I labour'd on, and did my best
  "A slender livelihood to gain.

"Two months past, with her paramour
  "I saw her in a *gig* quite nigh;
"Tho' finely drest, she charm'd no more,
  "Wan was her cheek and sunk her eye.

"I hurried home the blow so rude,
  "I fainted, and all thought me dead;
"A burning fever thence ensu'd
  "Which six weeks kept me to my bed.

"Confin'd by illness so severe
  "And long, my little money went,
"Doctors and nurses both were dear;
  "And I was in arrears for rent.

"When of the fever I was quit
  "I sold some clothes to buy me meat.
"Dejected, weak, for work unfit,
  "I begg'd my landlord but to wait.

"He would not. Yesterday he came;
  "With cruel taunts he bade me *"walk"*—
"Myself — I wept — but more the shame —
  "An only child — how wild I talk.

"I had one boy, and dear was he,
  "But, by a roving passion led,
"He left us all and went to sea
  "He's gone so long he must be dead.

"A sailor, by yon lamp's faint gleam
  "I see you are — alas! like you
"In garb and manner did he seem
  "When fond he breath'd his last adieu.

"With all a hapless mother's grief
    "Seven tedious years the lad I mourn.
"My darling cannot bring relief —
    "No; never shall my George return!"

"Your George!" The stranger fault'ring cried,
    "My name is George" — "George what" —
["]George Rose" —
Around her, sinking at his side
    His rugged arms he widely throws.

Loud scream'd the wretch, "O God! my boy!"
    Her woe-worn heart's sad beat was o'er.
So long unfelt the touch of joy,
    It flutter'd; burst; and heav'd no more.

2:144

Mary Robinson's poem, like Sterne's fiction, seeks to rouse the reader to a state of sensibility that will enable him or her to act on emotion. The minute particulars of Robinson's poem compel our attention and stress the difficulties faced by the indigent. One can see why, shortly after the French Revolution, such poems would achieve popularity. The absurd ending to the poem, where a mother recognizes her son George Rose, and dies of happiness, suggests that readers were not prepared to take their social criticism unembellished by sentimentality.

Jefferson endorsed sentimentality as a guide to moral action. "State a moral case to a ploughman and a professor. The former will decide it as well, and often better than the latter, because he has not been led astray by artificial rules. . . . The writings of Sterne, particularly, form the best course of morality that ever was written."[41]

The NEGRO BOY'S TALE.
By Mrs. Opie.

"Haste! hoist the sails! fair blows the wind:
Jamaica, sultry land, adieu! —
Away! and loitering Anna find!
I long dear England's shores to view."

The sailors gladly haste on board,
Soon is Trevannion's voice obeyed,
And instant, at her father's word,
His menials seek the absent maid.

But where was "loitering Anna" found? —
Mute, listening to a Negro's prayer,
Who knew that sorrow's plaintive sound
Could always gain her ready ear; —

Who knew, to sooth the slave's distress
Was gentle Anna's dearest joy,
And thence, an earnest suit to press,
To Anna flew the Negro boy.

"Missa," poor Zambo cried, "sweet land
Dey tell me dat you go to see,
Vere soon as on de shore he stand,
De help'ess Negro slave be free.

"Ah! dearest miss, you so kind!
Do take me to dat blessed shore,
Dat I mine own dear land may find,
And dose who love me see once more.

"Oh! ven no slave, a boat I buy,
For me a letel boat vould do,
And over wave again I fly
Mine own loved negro land to view.

"Oh! I should know it quick like tink,
No land so fine as dat I see,
And den perhaps upon de brink
My moder might be look for me! —

"It is long time since lass ve meet,
Ven I vas take by bad vite man,
And moder cry, and kiss his feet,
And shrieking after Zambo ran.

"O missa! long, how long me feel
Upon mine arms her lass embrace!
Vile in de dark, dark ship I dwell,
Long burn her tear upon my face.

"How glad me vas she did not see
De heavy chain my body bear;
Nor close, how close ye crowded be,
Nor feel how bad, how sick de air!

"Poor slaves! — but I had best to forget.
Dey say (but teaze me is deir joy)
Me grown so big dat ven ve meet
My moder vould not know her boy.

"Ah! sure 'tis false! But yet if no,
Ven I again my moder see,
Such joy I at her sight vou'd show
Dat she vould think it must be me.

"Den, kindest missa, be my friend;
Yet dat indeed you long become;
But now one greatest favour lend —
— O find me chance to see my home!

"And ven I'm in my moder's arms,
And tell de vonders I have know,
I'll say, Most best of all de charms
Vas she who feel for negro's woe.

"And she shall learn for you dat prayer
Dey teach to me to make me good;
Though men who sons from moders tear,
She'll tink, teach goodness never could.

"Dey say me should to oders do
Vat I vould have dem do to me; —
But, if dey preach and practise too,
A negro slave me should not be.

"Missa, dey say dat our black skin
Be ugly, ugly to de sight;
But surely if dey look widin,
Missa, de negro's heart be vite.

"Yon cocoa-nut so smooth as silk,
But rough and ugly is de rind;
Ope it, sweet meat and sweeter milk
Vidim dat ugly coat ve find.

"Ah missa! smiling in your tear,
I see you know vat I'd impart;
De cocoa husk de skin I vear,
De milk vidin be Zambo's heart.

"Dat heart love you, and dat good land
Vere every negro slave be free, —
Oh! if dat England understand
De negro wrongs, how wrath she be!

'No doubt dat ship she never send
Poor harmless negro slave to buy,
Nor vould she e'er de wretch befriend
Dat dare such cruel bargain try.

"O missa's God! dat country bless!
(Here Anna's colour went and came,
But saints might share the pure distress,
For Anna blushed at others' shame.)

"But missa, say; shall I vid you
To dat sweet England now depart,
Once more mine own good country view,
And press my moder on my heart?"

Then on his knees poor Zambo fell,
While Anna tried to speak in vain:
The expecting boy she could not tell*
He'd ne'er his mother see again.

But, while she stood in mournful thought,
Nearer and nearer voices came;
The servants 'loitering Anna' sought,
The echoes rang with Anna's name,

Ah! then, o'ercome with boding fear,
Poor Zambo seized her trembling hand,
"Mine only friend," he cried, "me fear
You go, and me not see my land."

Anna returned the artless grasp:
I cannot grant thy suit," she cries;
"But I my father's knees will clasp,
Nor will I, till he hear me, rise.

"For, should thine anxious wish prove vain,
And thou no more thy country see,
Still, pity's hand might break thy chain,
And lighter bid thy labours be.

"Here wanton stripes, alas! are thine,
And tasks, far, far beyond thy powers;
But I'll my father's heart incline
To bear thee to more friendly shores.

---

* "I could not tell the imp he had no mother." — Vida Series of Plays on the Passions, by Miss Baillie, —
Count Basil, page III.

"Come! to the beach! for me they wait!"
Then, grasping Zambo's sable hand,
Swift as the wind, with hope elate,
The lovely suppliant reached the sand.

But woe betides an ill-timed suit:
His temper soured by her delay,
Trevannion bade his child be mute,
Nor dare such fruitless hopes betray.

"I know," she cried, "I cannot free
The numerous slaves that round me pine;
But one poor negro's friend to be,
Might, (blessed chance!) might now be mine".

But vainly Anna wept and prayed,
And Zambo knelt upon the shore;
Without reply, the pitying maid
Trevannion to the vessel bore.

Mean while, poor Zambo's cries to still,
And his indignant grief to tame,
Eager to act his brutal will,
The negro's scourge-armed ruler came.

The whip is raised — the lash descends —
And Anna hears the sufferer's groan;
But while the air with shrieks she rends,
The signal's given — the ship sails on.

That instant, by despair made bold,
Zambo one last great effort tried:
He burst from his tormentor's hold, —
He plunged within the foaming tide.

The desperate deed Trevannion views,
And all his weak resentment flies:
"See, see! the vessel he pursues!
Help him, for mercy's sake!" he cries:

"Out with the boat! quick! throw a rope!
Wretches, how tardy is your aid!"
While, pale with dread, or flushed with hope,
Anna the awful scene surveyed.

The boat is out, — the rope is cast,
And Zambo struggles with the wave; —
"Ha! he the boat approaches fast!
O father, we his life shall save!"

"But low, my child and lower yet
His head appears; — but sure he sees
The succour given — and seems to meet
The opposing waves with greater ease: —

"See, see! the boat, the rope, the rope he nears!
I see him now his arm extend! —
My Anna, dry those precious tears;
My child shall be *one negro's friend!"*

Ah! Fate was near, that hope to foil: —
To reach the rope poor Zambo tries; —
But, ere he grasps it, faint with toil,
The struggling victim sinks, and dies.

Anna, I mourn thy virtuous woe;
I mourn thy father's keen remorse;
But from my eyes no tears would flow
At sight of Zambo's silent corse: —

The orphan from his mother torn,
And pining for his native shore, —
Poor tortured slave — poor wretch forlorn —
Can I his early death deplore? —

I pity those who live, and groan:
Columbia countless Zambos sees;
For swelled with many a wretch's moan
Is Western India's sultry breeze.

Come, Justice, come! in glory drest,
O come! the woe-worn negro's friend, —
The fiend-delighting trade arrest,
The negro's chains asunder rend!

2:148

Many poems in this section owe their existence to a strain of "sorrow" that permeates romantic verse. For Sterne, as for Jefferson, reflection leads to moral improvement. Amelia Opie's affecting tale of the Negro boy graphically depicts the brutality of separating people from their native land, a theme picked up by Walter Scott in "Breathes there the man. . . ."[42] Opie moved in the radical circles of William Godwin and Joseph Johnson in the 1790s and converted to Quakerism after her husband's death. Though crude, her use of the vernacular foreshadows works by Mark Twain and, later, Ralph Ellison. Anna becomes a heroine because she can feel for Negroes' woe.

Taken from his home in Africa, Zambo is a slave in Jamaica. He tries to persuade "loitering" Anna to allow him to board their ship bound for England, knowing that once he arrives there he will be free. (By law, a slave from the West Indies became free once he or she landed in England.) Zambo's plea falls on deaf ears, but when he is whipped and struggles, by swimming, to board the departing ship, Anna's father, Trevannion, relents ("thy father's keen remorse"). It is too late, however, and Zambo drowns in the attempt to reach the boat. Abolition of the transatlantic slave trade (the "fiend-delighting trade") finally occurred in 1807.

OSMAM and ZORIDA

(*Altered from* FLORIAN)

[adapted and attributed, by an
American newspaper, to Thomas Chatterton.]

YOUNG OSMAN the valiant, by fortune betray'd
The MOSLEMS by baseness a captive had made;
A fair Moorish princess Zorida by name,
Soon father enthrall'd him than did slavery's chain,
As oft'times the tale of his miserys he drew,
Her pity was chang'd into LOVES tender hue.
Bright *love* does high honors and riches despise,
But when heart beats to heart gives delight to his eyes.
A long time in silence they cherish'd the flame,
While *eyes* spoke those feelings their *tongues* dare not name;
The captives they glow'd with the ardour of love,
While her's did declare, that his love she approv'd.
One evening, ah! fatal to the Lovers so true,
They rov'd near a mountain the landscape to view,
At the foot of the mountain a river did flow,
Whose waves sped with rage to the ocean below.
In scenes so well suited for tales of fond *Love*.
They plighted their faith by the PROPHET above;
For constant to be till they breath'd their last breath
And they below did sleep in the iron arms of death.
But woe to the lovers! the monarch Marmoud,
ZORIDA'S own father their steps had pursu'd.
His soldiers with fury he urg'd through the wood,
Towards the dark cliff where the lovers they stood;
The lovers fled swift their pursuit to evade,
Around the brown mountain and thro' its dark shade,
At length gain'd the height they resolv'd for to throw
Themselves from the steep in the river below;
"O stay" cry'd Zorida "O stay thy swift steed
While I for my *Love* now your mercy will plead.
O stay! cruel fire, or we plunge from this steep,
And escape from thy rage in the realms of the deep."
Great MARMOUD was mov'd, and his speed he suspended,
But while in his bosom his passions contended;
A swift-footed soldier straight forward now sprung,

To where the fond maid to her OSMAN fast clung;
They saw and they sprung both a down from the height,
Embrac'd and embracing they plung'd in dark night.
The dark waves receiv'd them, ah! how hapless their state,
They sunk ne'er to rise, 'twas the mandate of fate.

CHATTERTON.

2:150

As Marmoud, the father of Moorish princess Zorida, contemplates whether to attack his future son-in-law and risk the death of his daughter, Zorida and Osman themselves plunge to their deaths. Chatterton's poem makes use of the conventions of Orientalism. This poem is conventional in its stereotype of Easterners as controlled by "the mandate of fate," as with Byron's "Eastern Tales" and Moore's *Lallah Rookh*. Jefferson clipped two additional poems by Chatterton, which he placed side by side: "Resignation" and a poem inspired by Chatterton's untimely death.

THE LASS OF FAIR WONE*

**Extract from the admirable Poem under the above
title, from Rosa Matilda's "Hours of Solitude."**

[G. Burger, translated by Rosa Matilda]

Up the harsh rock so steep and slim'd,
    The mourner had to roam;
And faint, on tott'ring feet she clim'd,
    To see her lover's home.

Alas! my blood-stain'd bosom see,
    The drooping-sufferer cried!
A *Mother* hast thou made of me,
    Before thou mad'st a *Bride*.

This is thy ruthless deed, behold,
    And sinking on the floor,
Ah! let thy love with honor hold,
    My injur'd name restore.

Poor Maid, I grieve to see thy woe,
    My folly now lament,
Go not while harsh the tempest blow,
    Thy Father shall repent.

I cannot stay, she shuddering cried,
    While dubious hangs my fame;
Alas! forswear thy cruel pride,
    And leave me not to shame.

Make me thy wife, I'll love the true,
    High Heav'n approves the deed;
Alas! for me some pity shew,
    E'en while for thee I bleed!

What honor bids, I'll do for thee,
    My *huntsman* shall be thine,
While still our loves voluptuous free,
    No *shackles* shall confine.

Damn'd be thy soul! and sad thy life,
    May pangs in Hell await,
Wretch! if too humble for thy *wife*,
    Oh, why not for thy *mate*.

May God attend my bitter pray'r,
   Some *high* born spouse be thine,
Whose wanton arts shall mock thy care,
   And *spurious* be thy line.

Then traitor feel how wretched those
   In hopeless *shame* immerst,
Strike thy hard breast with vengeful blow,
   While curses from it burst.

Roll thy dry eyes, for mercy call,
   Unfoot thy grinning woe,
Through thy pale temples fire the ball,
   And sink to fiends below!"

They starting up, she wildly flew,
   Nor felt her bleeding feet,
Nor knew how keen the tempest blew,
   Nor heard the hissing fleet.

2:151

  * From the German of Burger.

Burger's poem treats a woman who murders herself and then her infant, the victim of a "Bacchanalian lord" who seduces her. Dacre suppressed both the hanging of the heroine and the description of her running a pin through the heart of her young child.

Jefferson may have been intrigued by the class conflict between this professed libertine and the young woman whom he impregnates. Rejected by her father after her pregnancy becomes visible, the young woman pleads for the young man to marry her, asking a question with Jeffersonian overtones: "if too humble for thy wife, / Oh, why not for thy mate?" Her curse on her former lover betrays sharp insight into what the lord might gain from marrying a woman of his own class: "Some *high* born spouse be thine, / Whose wanton arts shall mock thy care, / and *spurious* be thy line." In England, "women of fashion in London are accountable to nobody after they are married," Lady Teazdale observed in Sheridan's *School for Scandal*;[43] in fact, aristocratic women were only responsible for the paternity of their first

son, obeying the laws of primogeniture. Jefferson enjoyed contrasting sexual mores in Europe with those in America, a factor that may have influenced his clipping of this poem. "Conjugal love having no existence among them, domestic happiness, of which that is the basis, is utterly unknown."[44] In 1786, he informed Lucy Ludwell Paradise that family life in America was "infinitely more replete with happiness than . . . in Europe."

Published in *Hours of Solitude* (1805), this translation from Burger, as Dacre has noted, came as a result of reading Burger's poem in 1800 ("four or five years ago"). Her comments are condescending for a youth of twenty-three: "conceiving it extremely interesting, but yet susceptible of some improvement, I ventured to make in it such alterations as I flattered myself without deducting from the sense or substance of the original, might render it, in some measure, more acceptable to the English reader; for the Germans, in an overstrain'd attempt at nature, often pourtray her in her worst and plainest garb."[45]

NATIVE POETRY

[With pride and pleasure, we cull the following effusion, to bedeck our Wreath — with pride, because the author is a young American — with pleasure, because we wish to show how much we admire a man, *as a poet*, whom we are compelled to consider, *politically*, as our enemy. *Editor of the Balance*].

EXTRACT

FROM AN UNFINISHED
DRAMATICK MANUSCRIPT.

By Sellick Osborn.

I MET, as near the Forest's skirts I stray'd,
A remnant of a man; wooing the gloom
Of twilight shade, congenial to his soul.
He threw askance a look of wild reproach,
That seem'd to say, "avaunt! unkind intruder,
These haunts are consecrated to DESPAIR!"
Then turning, sought the bosom of the wood,
I follow'd him, aloof; and oft observ'd
His comely, though emaciated form,
Alternate, gilding 'neath the hemlock boughs,
Or slowly climbing o'er the craggy steep.
At length, beneath a huge and shelving rock
He sat him down; its high projecting brow
A hemlock met, whose thick entangled limbs
Flung o'er the ground beneath a sombrous shade —
And near the root, in subterraneous course,
A grumbling streamlet flow'd, whose hollow round
Rose through the crannies of the broken earth —
"Fit temple of despair!" he said, and then
With eyes that gleam'd a sullen satisfaction,
He view'd the gloomy scene. "Here haggard fiend
Thou sitt'st enthron'd in ghastly majesty —
Here will I raise an altar, and thereon
Lay these week limbs, a wretched sacrifice!"
Then from his bosom he a phial drew,
And view'd it with a grim hysterick smile —
"Oh! precious draught!" he said — "thou art, to me,
Like a cool fountain to a thirsty Pilgrim —
Thy Cordial pow'r shall lull the racking pain

That rings my tortur'd heart?" then to his lips
He raised, with eager hand, the deadly potion.
"Hold! wretched man!" I cry'd — and rushing forth,
Seiz'd his rash hand — while with a ghastly state,
He ey'd me, as an evil genius, sent
To cross the fondest purpose of his soul.
His cheeks were lean and haggard, and he seem'd
A wreck of man, a monument of woe!
(I saw him once in happier days, when joy
Beam'd in each feature, and the admiring world
Deny'd him not the early wreath of fame —
But, in a sanguine moment of his youth,
Fell dissipation led his steps astray —
Then did his friend, with mild solicitude,
Reach out a gentle hand, to stay his course,
Or to restore him to the path of virtue —
Then, lorn and destitute, he keenly felt
The scorn of an uncharitable world —
Whose cool reproach, & frown contemptuous weigh'd
His spirit down, and drove him to despair!)
I press'd his hand, and with a tender smile
Proffer'd my service — and while yet I spoke,
I saw a tear roll down his faded cheek,
Which was a stranger there — for scorching grief
Had dry'd, long since, the moisture of his eyes.
And then me thought I saw a gleam of hope,
Born in a languid smile, illume his face —
A gradual increasing smile, which seem'd
Like the returning of the vernal sun,
Which comes to chase the win'try cloud away,
And bid reviving nature bloom again!

    . . .

And now, with health and happiness elate,
He lives, to virtue and to friendship true —
Oft with the grateful musick of his thanks,
He serenades my ear — and blesses oft
The guardian pow'r that led my curious steps
To the intended scene of self destruction.
Now do I feel more pride, in having thus
Restor'd a youth, from misery and vice

To virtue's path — his sorrows sooth'd, and pour'd
The balm of friendship on his wounded heart —
Pluck'd from his breast the canker of despair,
And planted hope's delightful promise there,
Than I should feel to rule the state alone,
Or wade, through bleeding millions, to a throne!

2:158

Selleck Osborn served as editor of the *Litchfield Witness* and other papers. As the introduction by the editor of the *Balance* suggests, Osborn was a firm supporter of Jefferson's democratic politics and served a prison term for one year because of a libel against a Federalist lawyer. This work, "Extract . . .," does not appear in Osborn's collected poems.

Osborn's extract resembles the plot of Goethe's *Faust* (1801), which was translated by Madame de Stael (1813) and influenced Byron; it is not unlikely that Osborn also read Goethe's play. In the beginning of Goethe's drama, the scholar Faust contemplates drinking a vial of poison, but is interrupted by the bells that announce Easter. Like Faust and Manfred, the observed figure is a "monument of woe." By telling the story of this "remnant of a man" from the third-person point of view, however, Osborn provides some distance and perspective on his suffering. The ending of this manuscript is thoroughly conventional: "Now, with health and happiness elate, / He lives, to virtue and to friendship true — ." A mild political criticism (perhaps of Napoleon) seems intended, for the speaker makes a point of preferring the saving of souls to the ruling of states: "Now do I feel more pride, in having thus . . . Pluck'd from his breast the canker of despair, / And painted hope's delightful promise there, / Than I should feel to rule the state alone, / Or wade, through bleeding millions, to a throne!" In 1826, Osborn published an effective satire of Napoleon titled "Elba."

FROM ST[R]ANGFORD'S CAMOENS.
CANZON.

"Se as penas com que Amor tao mal me trata
Permiterem que en tanto viva dellas," &c.

Should I but live a little more,
    Nor die beneath thy cold disdain,
These eves shall see thy triumphs o'er,
    Shall see the close of Beauty's reign.

For Time's transmuting hand shall turn
    Thy locks of gold to "silver wires;"
Those starry lamps shall cease to burn,
    As now with more than heav'nly fires:

The ripened cheek no longer wear
    The ruddy blooms of rising dawn!
And every tiny dimple there
    In wrinkled lines be roughly drawn!

And, oh! what show'rs of fruitless woe
    Shall fall upon that fatal day —
How wilt thou weep the frequent "No,"
    How mourn occasion past away!

Those vain regrets, and useless sighs,
    Shall in my heart no pity move —
I'll deem them but a sacrifice
    Due to the shade of buried Love!

2:152

Jefferson clipped this poem on the ravages of time, a theme Selleck Osborne explored in "On Time." On an earlier page (2:151), he juxtaposed "The Lass of Fair Wone" with some "Lines written in a blank leaf of Strangford's Translations from Camoens."

THE WOUNDED SOLDIER.

[Robert Merry]

The sun was just retir'd, the dews of eve
    Their glow-worm lustre scatter'd o'er the vale:
The lonely Nightingale began to grieve,
    Telling, with many a pause, her tend'rest tale.

No clamours rude disturb'd the pensive hour.
    And the young moon, yet fearful of the night,
Rear'd her pale crescent o'er the burnish'd tow'r,
    That caught the parting orb's still ling'ring light.

'Twas then, where peasant footsteps mark'd the way,
    A wounded Soldier feebly mov'd along,
Nor aught regarded he the soft'ning ray,
    Nor the melodious bird's expressive song.

On crutches borne his mangled limbs he drew,
    Unsightly remnants of the battle's rage;
While Pity, in his youthful form, might view
    The helpless prematurity of age.

Then, as with strange contortions, lab'ring slow,
    He gain'd the summit of his native hill,
And saw the well-known prospect spread below,
    The farm, the cot, the hamlet, and the mill.

In spight of fortitude, one struggling sigh
    Shook the firm texture of his tortur'd heart,
And from his hollow and dejected eye
    One trembling tear hung ready to depart.

"How chang'd," he cried, "is the fair scene to me
    "Since last across this narrow path I went!
"The soaring lark felt not superior glee,
    "Nor any human breast more true content.

"When the fresh hay was o'er the meadow thrown,
    "Amidst the busy throng I still appear'd;

"My prowess too at harvest time was shown,
  "While Lucy's carol ev'ry labour cheer'd.

"The burning rays I scarcely seem'd to feel,
  "If the dear maiden near me chanc'd to rove;
"Or if she deign's to share my frugal meal,
  "It was a rich repast — a feast of love.

"And when at ev'ning, with a rustic's pride.
  "I dar'd the sturdiest wrestlers on the green;
"What joy was mine! to hear her at my side
  "Extol my vigour, and my manly mien.

"Ah! now no more the sprightly lass shall run
  "To bid me welcome from the sultry plain;
"But her averted eye my sight shall shun,
  "And all our cherish'd fondest hopes be vain.

"Alas! my parents, must ye too endure
  "That I should gloom for e'er your homely mirth,
"Exist upon the pittance ye procure,
  "And make ye curse the hour that gave me birth?

"O hapless day! when at a neighb'ring wake,
  "The gaudy Serjeant caught my wond'ring eye;
"And as his tongue of war and honour spake,
  "I felt a wish to conquer or to die.

"Then while he bound the ribbons on my brow,
  "He talk'd of Captains kind and Gen'rals good;
"Said a whole nation would my fame avow,
  "And *bounty* call'd the purchase of my blood.

"Yet I refus'd that *bounty*, I disdain'd
  "To *sell* my service in a *righteous cause*;
"And such to my dull fence it was explain'd
  "The cause of monarchs, justice, and the laws:

"The rattling drums beat loud, the fifes began,
  "My king and country seem'd to ask my aid;

"Thro' ev'ry vein the thrilling ardour ran;
   "I left my humble cot — my village maid.

"O hapless day! torn from my Lucy's charms,
   "I thence was hurried to a scene of strife;
"To painful marches, and the din of arms,
   "The wreck of reason, and the waste of life.

"In loathsome vessels now with crowds confin'd,
   "Now led with hosts to slaughter in the field;
"Now backward driv'n, like leaves before the wind,
   "Too weak to stand, and yet asham'd to yield.

"Till oft repeated victories inspir'd
   "With ten-fold fury the indignant foe,
"Who ruthless still advanc'd as we retir'd,
   "And laid our boasted, proudest honours low.

"Thro' frozen desarts then compell'd to fly,
   "Our bravest legions moulder'd fast away,
"Thousands of wounds and sickness left to die,
   "While hov'ring ravens mark'd them for their prey.

"Ah! sure remorse *their* savage hearts must rend,
   "Whose festive, des'prate phrenzy could decree,
"That in one mascot murder MAN should blend,
   "Who sent the *Slave* to fight against the *Free*.

"Unequal contest — at fair Freedom's call,
   "The lowliest Hind glows with celestial fire;
"SHE rules, directs, pervades, and conquers all,
   "And ARMIES at her sacred glance expire.

"Then be this warfare of the world accurs'd
   "The Son now weeps not on the Father's bier;
"But grey-hair'd Age, for Nature is revers'd,
   "Drops o'er his children's grave an icy tear."

Thus having spoke — by varying passions tost,
   He reached the threshold of his Parent's shed,

Who knew not of his fate, yet mourn'd him lost
AMIDST THE NUMBER OF THE UNNAM'D DEAD

Soon as they heard his well-remember'd voice,
    A ray of rapture chas'd habitual care;
"Our Henry lives! we may again rejoice!"
    And Lucy sweetly blush'd, for she was there.

But when HE ENTER'D in such HORRID GUISE,
    His Mother shriek'd and dropp'd upon the floor;
His Father look'd to Heav'n with streaming eyes,
    And Lucy sunk, alas! to rise no more!

O may this Tale, which Agony must close,
    Give deep contrition to the *self-call'd great*;
And shew the POOR how hard the Lot of those
    Who shed their blood for MINISTERS of STATE!
                DELLA CRUSCA.

                        2:162

Many of the poets Jefferson admired exhibit the sentimental style popularized by British poet Robert Merry. Merry took the pen name of Della Crusca and wrote sentimental, often highly artificial, poems to Hannah Cowley, whom he addressed as Anna Matilda.

Merry's reference to "the melodious bird's expressive song" echoes the many other poems in this section that refer to birds. According to his Account Book, Jefferson kept mockingbirds at Monticello and compared them favorably with nightingales. In 1793, he encouraged Martha to "venerate it as a supe- rior being in the form of a bird." At the president's house, Margaret Bayard Smith noted that "whenever [Jefferson] was alone he opened the cage and let the bird fly about the room. . . . Often when retired to his chamber it would hop up the stairs after him and while he took his siesta, would sit on the couch and pour forth its melodious strains. How he loved this bird! How he loved his flowers! He could not live without something to love, and in the absence of his darling grandchildren, his bird and his flowers became objects of tender care."[46]

FROM THE PALLADIUM.

SEDUCTION,

OR,

THE BEAUTIFUL MANIAC.

AN ELEGY.

By Thomas Green Fessenden, A. N.

Now night's sullen noon spread her mantle around,
    And menacing thunders roll solemn in air,
AMANDA's sad accents the woodland resound,
    Dark mountains re-echo the plaints of despair!

See now the gloom deepens, the rude tempest roars,
    And loud the rough north winds howl thro' the expanse,
Old Ocean, hoarse murmuring, lashes the shores,
    And phantoms of night o'er the wild desert dance!

The prominent cliff, that impends o'er the flood,
    Responds to the ominous scream of the owl,
Grim wolves rave infuriate through the dark wood,
    Their orgies, nocturnal, discordantly howl!

Here, pensively straying, I'll climb the tall steep,
    While night's leaden sceptre bids nature repose
From the brow of the precipice plunge in the deep
    And thus put an end to my numberless woes.

In the gay morn of life, surely none was more blessed,
    To the blithe song of pleasure, I danced o'er the green,
Of innocence, beauty, and fortune possess'd,
    While sportive festivity hail'd me her queen.

To solace my parents, my pleasing employ,
    Their life's rugged passage with flow'rets to strew,
AMANDA their hope, and AMANDA their joy,
    Her happiness, all that they wish'd for below.

Thus fifteen fair summers roll'd swiftly away,
    Ere man, base deceiver, to ruin me strove,

Ere CLEON, false hearted, but witty and gay,
   First melted my heart to the raptures of love.

Spring, sweetly luxuriant, deck'd the gay lawn,
   The dew-drop, nectarious, bespangled the grove
When CLEON first met me, one beautiful morn,
   With trembling solicitude whisper'd of love!

His person was graceful, his manners refin'd,
   A pupil of Chesterfield, easy and free,
But night's darkest gloom, not so dark as his mind
   Not half so deceitful yon treacherous sea!

"With eyes beaming rapture he swore to be true,"
   Can cruelty dwell with a cherub so fair,
Will you make me unhappy, who live but for you,
   Ah, why will you drive a fond youth to despair?

"With fatal success were his stratagems pli'd,
   To ruin a blooming and innocent maid,
Full often he promised to make me his bride,
   But basely deserted the nymph he betray'd.

The news to my parents convey'd sad surprise,
   Oppress'd with keen anguish they tore their grey hair,
Till pitying death clos'd their sorrowing eyes,
   But left me a prey to the pangs of despair!

Impell'd by rude frenzy I wandered from home,
   That house, once delightful, where once I was bless'd,
Now indigent, hopeless, distracted I roam,
   Till death's cold embrace lull my sorrow to rest.

But hah! the wild horrors of madness return,
   To rive every nerve in my tremelous frame,
Forbear my pain'd head any longer to burn,
   Cease, anguishing heart, to enkindle the flame!

Roar louder, ye winds! spread destruction around!
   Let thunders, loud bellowing, shake the firm pole,

Let earthquakes impel, o'er the shuddering ground
   To mimic the passions which torture my soul!

Ah! Cleon, thou false, thou perfidious swain,
   My spectre shall haunt thee in night's solemn gloom!"
She spoke, and precipitan [sic] plung'd in the main,
   And a requiem sought in the cold wat'ry tomb.

2:163

"Seduction" appeared as "The Beautiful Maniack" in Green's collection of poems. In "The Beautiful Maniack," Fessenden alluded to Chesterfield's *Letters to His Son*. Samuel Johnson thought Chesterfield's complete manual of education for a young man (addressed to his son Philip and dating from 1737, but not intended for publication) taught the "morals of a whore and the manners of a dancing-master." Jefferson also clipped Fessenden's "Ode (for the Anniversary of the Massachusetts Charitable Fire Society),"[47] a patriotic and anti-French poem.

"Seduction," by Fessenden, also uses Gothic trappings ("ominous scream of the owl"), which Radcliffe and Lewis employed; poets such as Royall Tyler and Samuel Taylor Coleridge ("Christabel") satirized such conventions as sentimental and predictable hyperbole. Ruskin charged Romantic poets with "pathetic fallacy," or attributing human emotions to inanimate objects: "sullen noon," "menacing thunders," "dark mountains re-echo the plaints of despair!" In this poem, the speaker describes a landscape that echoes back human emotions, creating, however temporarily, the sense of a world sympathetic to unrequited love: "Let thunders, loud bellowing, shake the firm pole, / Let earthquakes impel, o'er the shuddering ground / To mimic the passions which torture my soul!" The poem ends, however, with the heroine destroying herself.

Jefferson collected a number of poems about sexual betrayal, including Bellamy's poems about his abandonment of the Maid of Buttermere. This poem is unique for describing an American love affair, cast in the neoclassical manner, with Amanda and Cleon as the representative figures. Fessenden locates libertinism as a British strategy by linking Cleon's behavior to his reading of Lord Chesterfield: "His person was graceful, his manners refin'd, / A pupil of Chesterfield, easy and free."

Fessenden's poem represents moods of despair and hope as products of night ("Now night's sullen noon spread her mantle around") and morning ("gay morn of life"). Edward Young's *Night Thoughts*, which Jefferson showed interest in as a student at William and Mary, makes use of the same strategy.

TO VIRTUE.
[Anonymous]

WHAT tho' beneath a humble roof,
I live, and die, unknown to fame!
From courts and cities far aloof,
And Great ones ne'er pronounce my name.

Though soon, beside some lonely heath,
I'm lodg'd, mid undistinguish'd dead,
With not a friend to weep my death,
Nor place a marble at my head; —

Yet, VIRTUE! thou shalt make me blest,
Thy hand shalt lead, thy arm sustain;
And *life*, with thee shall lack no rest,
And *death*, with thee shall give no pain!

2:163

This poem appears directly under "Seduction," providing yet another example of Jefferson's interest in complementarity. For the classical republican, virtue was inextricably tied to modesty and self-sacrifice. Jefferson did not live "unknown to fame," but his posture of indifference to it helped him, paradoxically, achieve public recognition. The contrast with the blatantly ambitious Alexander Hamilton and Aaron Burr is striking.

REMONSTRANCE to WINTER.

By J. Montgomery.

AH! why, unfeeling *Winter!* why,
　　Still flags thy torpid wing?
Fly, melancholy Season, fly,
　　And yield the year to *Spring*.

Spring — the young cherubim of love,
　　An exile in disgrace,
Flits o'er the scene, like Noah's dove,
　　Nor finds a resting place,

When on the mountain's azure peak,
　　Alights her fairy form,
Cold blow the winds — and dark and bleak,
　　Around her rolls the storm.

If to the valley she repair
　　For shelter and defence,
Thy wrath pursues the mourner there,
　　And drives her weeping thence.

She seeks the brook — the faithless brook,
　　Of her unmindful grown,
Feeds the chill magic of thy look,
　　And lingers into stone.

She wooes her embryo flowers in vain,
　　To rear their infant heads; —
Deaf to her voice her flowers remain
　　Enchanted in their beds.

In vain she bids the trees expand
　　Their green luxuriant charms; —
Bare in the wilderness they stand,
　　And stretch their withering arms.

Her favourite birds, in feeble notes,
　　Lament thy long delay;

And strain their stammering throats,
  To charm thy blasts away.

Ah! *Winter*, calm thy cruel rage,
  Release the struggling year;
Thy power is past, decrepid [sic] Sage!
  Arise and disappear.

The stars that graced thy splendid night
  Are lost in warmer rays;
The Sun, rejoicing in his might
  Unrolls celestial days.

Then why, usurping *Winter*, why
  Still flags thy frozen wing?
Fly unrelenting tyrant, fly —
  And yield the year to *Spring*.

2:166

Montgomery displays a proto-Romantic passion in "remonstrating" with his subject — quarreling with nature rather than simply observing it. The subtitle of Edward Young's "Night Thoughts" ("The Complaint") fits the tone of this poem.

SONNET TO THE WHITE BIRD
OF THE TROPIC.
By Helen Maria Williams.

BIRD of the TROPIC, thou who lov'st to stray
   Where thy long pinions sweep the sultry line,
   Or mark'st the bounds which torrid beams confine
By thy averted course, that shuns the ray
Oblique, enamour'd of sublimer Day;
   Oft on yon cliff thy folded plumes recline,
   And drop those snowy feathers Indians twine
To crown the Warrior's brow with Honours gay.
Oe'r trackless Oceans what impels thy wing?
   Does no soft instinct in thy soul prevail?
No sweet affection to thy bosom cling,
   And bid thee oft thy absent nest bewail? —
Yet thou again to that dear spot can spring:
   But I my long-lost home no more shall hail!

2:167

Invited to Paris in 1790, Helen Maria Williams supported the Revolution and published *Letters Written from France* (1790). She returned to Paris in 1791 and became a supporter of the Girondins. In October 1793, Williams was under house arrest in Paris and her papers, as well as several poems, were confiscated. "White Bird of the Tropics" was published in 1795.

CAMPBELL'S HOHEN LINDEN.
[Thomas Campbell]

On Linden when the sun was low,
All bloodless lay the untrodden snow,
And dark as winter was the flow
    Of Iser rolling rapidly.

But Linden show'd another sight,
When the drum beat, at dead of night,
Commanding fires of death to light,
    The darkness of the scenery

By torch and trumpet fast array'd,
Each horseman drew his battle blade,
And loudly every charger neigh'd,
    To join the dreadful revelry.

Then shook the hills by thunder riven!
Then flew the steed to battle driven;
And louder than the bolts of Heaven,
    Far flash'd the red artillery.

But redder still the light shall glow,
On Linden's tops of stained snow,
And bloodier far the torrents flow,
    Of Iser rolling rapidly.

The combat thickens — on ye brave!
Who rush to Glory, or the Grave;
Wave, Munich, all thy banners wave,
    And charge with all thy chivalry!

It is morn! and scarce yon level sun,
Can pierce the war clouds' rolling dun,
Where furious Frank and fiery Hun
    Shout in the sulph'rous canopy.

Few, few shall part where many meet,
The snow shall be their winding-sheet,
And every turf beneath their feet,
    Shall be a Soldier's Sepulchre!

2:172

"Hohen Linden" is one of three poems (with "Ye Mariners of England" and "The Battle of the Baltic") that Campbell wrote after observing an Austrian cavalry charge in the village of Hohenlinden in December 1800; Campbell viewed the battle from a nunnery in Ratisbon. Napoleon's General Moreau, commanding a French and Bavarian force, defeated an Austrian contingent in this battle. The emperor of Austria had to submit to Napoleon's peace terms in order to save his capital, Vienna. During his return home, Campbell witnessed a battle between the Danish batteries and the British fleet, part of the battle of Copenhagen. Campbell received a government pension in 1805 in recognition of his patriotic verse. Campbell's "Hohen Linden" inspired an imitation in the *Morning Chronicle*:[48] "Low gasping on the battle plain, / No friend shall sooth their dying pain, / No sculptur'd stone, no mourning train, / Grace the dead hero's memory." Exhibiting the sense of complementarity he showed throughout his scrapbook, Jefferson pasted an extract from Anne Bannerman's pacifist "War" next to Campbell's patriotic poem.

WAR.

By MISS BANNERMAN.

O! could some spirit from the fields of day,
To this fair planet wing his vent'rous way,
Inhale the freshness of the vernal breeze,
And mark the sun reflected in the seas;
View where, abundant, on a thousand shores,
The waving harvests yield their golden stores
Gay beauty smiling in the sweets of morn
Th op'ning violet, and the flow'ring thorn,
Th'expanding fields of every varied hue,
And the clear conclave of unclouded blue!
Then let him stand where hostile armies join —
By the red waters of the rushing Rhine,
Amid thick darkness, hear the trumpets blow,
And the last shriek of nature quiver low,
Mark the full tide of de[s]olation spread,
And count at eve the dying and the dead:
How would he pause! — how seek in vain to find
Some trace in Man of an immortal mind;
Man, who can glory in a scene like this,
Yet look to brighter world for endless bliss!

2:172

This is an excerpt from Anne Bannerman's "War" (stanza thirty of a thirty-four-stanza poem), the subtitle for which is "Verses on an Illumination." During the Napoleonic Wars, the city of London was often "illuminated" after a victory over Napoleon. "Is this a time for triumph and applause," Bannerman asks in the poem's second stanza, "when shrinking Nature mourns her broken laws?" The poem describes a mother's separation from her son "The frantic mother's cries of Heaven implore / Some youthful warrior — she shall meet no more"), though it does so in general terms. Bannerman's poem reflects the politics of her mentor, Robert Anderson, especially when she questions how a Christian can believe in the afterlife if he glories in "the red waters of the rushing Rhine." Though dark, the final note struck is uplifting: "Time's feeble barrier bounds the painful course, / But joy shall reign, eternal as its source." Jefferson shared Bannerman's pacifism, avoiding war with Great Britain by means of an embargo.

Bannerman's "War" is juxtaposed with "The Soldier's Dream" and Campbell's "Hohen Linden."

HYMN to CONTENT.
By Mrs. Barbauld.

O thou, the Nymph with placid eye!
O seldom found, yet ever nigh!
    Receive my temp'rate vow:
Not all the storms that shake the pole
Can e'er disturb thy halcyon soul,
    And smooth unalter'd brow.

O come in simple vest array'd,
With all thy sober cheer display'd,
    To bless my longing sight;
Thy mien compos'd thy even pace,
Thy meek regard, thy matron grace,
    And chaste subdued delight.

No more by varying passions beat,
O gently guide my pilgrim feet
    To find thy merit's cell;
Where in some pure and equal sky
Beneath thy soft indulgent eye
    The modest virtues dwell.

Simplicity in Attic vest,
And Innocence with candid breast,
    And clear undaunted eye;
And Hope, who points to distant years,
Fair op'ning thro' this vale of tears
    A vista to the sky.

There Health, thro' whose calm bosom glide
The temp'rate joys in even tide,
    That rarely ebb or flow;
And Patience there, thy sister meek,
Presents her mild unvarying cheek
    To meet the offer'd blow.

Her influence taught the Phrygian sage
A tyrant master's wanton rage
   With settled smiles to meet;
Inur'd to toil and bitter bread,
He bow'd his meek submitted head,
   And kiss'd thy sainted feet.

But thou, oh Nymph retir'd and coy!
In what brown hamlet dost thou joy
   To tell thy tender tale?
The lowliest children of the ground,
Moss-rose and violet blossom round,
   And lily of the vale.

O say what soft propitious hour
I best may choose to hail thy pow'r,
   And court thy gentle sway?
When Autumn, friendly to the Muse,
Shall thy own modest tints diffuse,
   And shed thy milder day:

When Eve, her dewy star beneath,
Thy balmy spirit loves to breathe,
   And every storm is laid
If such an hour, was e'er thy choice,
Oft let me hear thy soothing voice
   Low whisp'ring thro' the shade.

2:190

Anna Barbauld was the favorite poet of Martha Jefferson, who used Barbauld's *Lessons for Children* to teach her daughters to read.

Barbauld makes use of a number of personifications ("Patience," "Simplicity," and "Health") to teach female resignation.

AN ODE FROM HAFIZ.
TRANSLATED.

With pleasure I talk of my pain,
   To the world I my secret confide;
For the slave of Love's powerful chain,
   Is released from all trouble beside.

But alas! who shall give me the pow'r,
   E'en the half of my woes to declare?
I'm the bird of a sanctified bow'r,
   Say how did I fall in the snare?

I once was an angel of light,
   Yes, Eden has been my abode:
Nor should I, had Eve stept aright,
   Have e'er trod this disastrous road.

You ask me, how can I forget
   Fair Tooba's heart-ravishing tree
And the Hoories with eye balls of jet;
   I forget them, my charmer — for thee.

"Tis true — in the page of my heart,
   Thy name I can only explore:
For Love, when he taught me this art,
   Tho' with chastisement, taught me no more.

As yet no diviner has told,
   What complexion my fortune has got,
Be it thine then, my fair, to unfold,
   What stars have determin'd my lot.

Thee, Love, since I first understood,
   New pains were my portion each hour:
My heart has run currents of blood,
   Since first I experienc'd thy power.

My cheeks are with weeping defil'd,
   Give thy tresses to wipe it away;
Or Hafiz's roundelay wild,
   In silence forever 'twill lay.

2:190

This poem, by Hafiz, should be distinguished from the works of British and American poets who used *Hafiz* as a nom de plume. Here the voice of Hafiz sounds like a libertine ("I forget them, my charmer — for thee"). The poem appears on the same page as Barbauld's "Hymn to Content."

The following lines were occasioned by observing in a late publication an account of the insanity of Mrs. Radcliffe, author of the Italian Mysteries of Udolpho, Romances of the Forest, &c &c.

THE WRECK OF REASON.

Would your imagination stray;
To scenes of horror make its way;
Would it from sorrow take its flight;
From scenes of pleasure, to affright;
Would it, reluctant, slowly creep,
And o'er the WRECK OF REASON weep;
— Hither come, ye blithe and gay;
Come, and throw your mirth away.
Weeping beauty, hither hie,
And o'er the ruin breathe a sigh:
Come and see, ye giddy vain,
A sadder sight than "CRAZY JANE."

The tender heart, the lib'ral mind;
The soul by sentiment refined,
The modest mien, the graceful air,
Are gone, and all is ruin there:
The matchless whole, divine grac'd,
Is chang'd into chaotic waste;
The timid mind, with terror fated,
Starts at the phantoms it created.

— See the MANIAC's ghastly stare!
See her loose, dishevell'd hair!
See her wildly rolling eyes,
Distorted form, and piercing cries!
See she trembles, writhes and groans,
And fills the air with piteous moans!
— O Radcliffe! this at last thy fate,
To sink to such a dreadful state! —
See she shudders, starts and raves
Of grinning ghosts and gaping graves,
Of antique arms, and haunted halls,

Of tot'ring turrets, mouldering walls,
The fulgent cross, the monkish cowl,
The raven's flap, the boding owl,
The warning knell, the mystic roll,
With horror strike her frenzied soul.
The murky vault's terrific gloom,
The echoes from the dismal tomb,
The quiv'ring pail, the crimson'd knife,
All gory with the blood of life,
The secret self, the glimmering light,
The putrid corse, the flitting sprite,
The pendant charm, the magic chest,
With terror fills her frantic breast.

No more she'll pen the fairy dream,
The awful, yet the pleasing theme;
No more portray with matchless art,
To frighten, yet delight the heart;
Genius in her, has left the throng,
And madness now usurps alone,
Let frozen souls precise and nice,
Call her the native child of vice
Let torpid spirits and care
Affect to startle and beware
A potent reason all may bring,
They in her *moral* find a *sting* —
E'en savage minds to feeling dead,
And icy hearts by *virtue led*,
When pitying death relieves her woe,
And lays the hapless victim low,
Might come, and on the maniac's bier
Shed pensive pity's softest tear.

2:192

This poem, which has proven very difficult to trace and is therefore included in an incomplete form, criticizes the Gothic novel, implicitly, by linking Ann Radcliffe's insanity to the exercise of her imagination. Jefferson thought novels unhealthy reading for his daughters because they left the imagination "bloated."

ON TIME.

By SELLECK OSBORNE.

Mov'd by a strange, mysterious pow'r,
Who hastes along the rapid hour,
   I touch the deep-ton'd string;
Ev'n now, I see his wither'd face,
Beneath yon tower's mould'ring base,
   Where mossy vestments cling.

Dark roll'd his cheerless eye around,
Severe his grisly visage frown'd,
   No locks his head array'd;
He grasp'd a hero's antique bust,
The marble crumbled into dust,
   And sunk amidst the shade!

Malignant triumph fill'd his eyes;
"See, hapless mortals, see," he cries,
   "How vain your idle schemes:
"Beneath my grasp the fairest form
"Dissolves and mingles with the worm;
   "Thus vanish mortal dreams.

"The works of God and man I spoil;
"The noblest proofs of human toil
   "I treat as childish toys:
"I crush the noble and the brave;
"Beauty I mar; and in the grave
   "I bury human joys."

Hold ruthless phantom — hold, I cried,
If thou canst mock the dreams of pride
   And meaner hopes devour,
Virtue, beyond thy reach, shall bloom,
When other charms sink to the tomb,
   She scorns thy envious power.

On frosty wings the demon fled;
Howling, as o'er the walls he sped,
  "Another year has gone!"
The ruin'd spire, the crumbling tower,
Nodding, obey'd his awful power,
  As Time flew swiftly on.

Since beauty, then, to *Time* must bow,
And age deform the fairest brow,
  Let brighter charms be yours;
The female mind, embalm'd in truth,
Shall bloom in everlasting youth,
  While *Time*, himself, endures.

2:193

This melodramatic poem appears to be addressed to a woman, who is advised to develop her mind rather than her appearance: "The female mind, embalm'd in truth, / Shall bloom in everlasting youth." Though this poem shows the influence of the Gothic novel in its depiction of a morbid melancholy, Osborn later repudiated this literary style. In his preface to his poems of 1823, he claimed to admire Homer, Milton, Young, and Goldsmith, and lamented the "extravagant ravings of a Maturin, the cynical moroseness of a Byron, and the intoxicating witcheries" of the numerous novelists who made the "gruel and barley water of every-day verse."[49] He was a strong supporter of Jefferson and went to jail for his beliefs as editor of the *Litchfield Witness* in 1806. His imprisonment became a national issue. Though this is the last poem in volume two of Jefferson's scrapbooks, he chose to insert a speech by Curran as the final entry in his book of poetry ("A Speech Delivered Before the Lord Chief Justice," 1802; the speech is treated in Golden and Golden's volume *Jefferson and the Rhetoric of Virtue*).

APPENDIX ONE
A NOTE ON THE TEXT

Textual description: The page is 8.75 by 5.75 inches; the book, bound in brown boards, is 9.25 by 6.25 inches; it is 1.75 inches thick; on the frontispiece appears "His Excellency FREE / L'Louis July 21st / Thomas Jefferson, President / of the United States / Washington City / By Mail" (in brown pen); A .J. Laird's letter from Staunton, Virginia, of April 8, 1851, follows; a discolored sheet with "5948-a" in the top corner follows.

Thomas Jefferson's Scrapbooks are based on two of the four volumes housed at the Alderman Library that consist primarily of poems. The other two volumes focus on prose extracts clipped from the newspapers.

Where possible, I have traced attribution for a number of these poems by consulting indices of poets who wrote at this time. Some poems must necessarily remain anonymous. As Thomas Tanselle notes in his study of Royall Tyler, "Contributions to newspapers and magazines at this time were generally anonymous or pseudonymous, and, in the absence of a record kept by the author himself or by the editor, it is now virtually impossible to establish the complete canon of any particular writer's periodical work."[1] Books on pseudonymous authors and the *PMLA* article on attributions from the Hall file (for Joseph Dennie's *Port Folio*), while initially promising, have proved of limited use. My hope is that scholars of American literature will be able to further advance knowledge in this area, but attribution of all poems (or the precise newspaper in which they appeared) is not the primary purpose of the present edition. I have not altered punctuation, choosing, instead, to transcribe the poem as it appeared in the newspaper Jefferson clipped. More modern editions of these poems can be found in anthologies of Romanticism. I have been interested in preserving the poem or translation that Jefferson actually read.

I have counted leaves in both volumes, which are not numbered consistently, and assigned them as they appear at the end of each poem. The attribution 1:1 refers to volume one of the clippings book; 2:1 refers to volume two. Each section of *Thomas Jefferson's Scrapbooks* proceeds in more or less chronological order throughout both volumes. Several leaves in the original volumes have shifted over time; the microfilm copy reflects a pagination that no longer exists. For this reason, I have constructed a new numbering system from both volumes as they appeared in 2003–2004. Readers who consult the original volume will find a poem within one or two pages of the number assigned in this text.

Numbers after a slash mark (1:2/1) refer to penciled annotations at the bottom of the page, presumably Jefferson's original numbering system for the volumes, which is no longer recoverable and is inconsistent.

Volume one, which contains most of the political poems, is located in the visitor center at Monticello and was obtained by special permission through Carrie Taylor, curator of the Jefferson Library. My thanks to her and to Bryan Craig for arranging my visits to Monticello in 2003.

N.B.: Some of these poems are pasted on envelopes; most on gray papers. "To My Infant Asleep," for instance, is on an envelope, yet "The Mansion of Rest" is on recycled paper that has been previously printed. Pages 189–204 are printed on paper that is French; pages 1–2 are fairly thick; pages 3–6 appear with architectural drawings; 7–38 on gray paper; 39–74 on thicker envelopes; 75–82 on thin gray paper again; 83–88 on thick paper; 89–92 on thin gray; 93–100 on recycled printed paper; 101–112 on gray paper; 113–128 on recycled printed paper; 129–146 on gray paper; 147–152 on thick paper; 153–154 on thin gray; 155–204 on thick printed paper. The volume ends with three thin gray sheets.

Volume two, which includes the epigrams on marriage and domestic subjects, is housed at the Alderman Library, University of Virginia. The first four pages, from "The Patriot . . ." to "From the Norristown Herald, August 13, 1804," are loose sheets and may not have been the first few pages of the book; the first page bound in this book is titled "Alarming!" (p. 7). I have confined my comments on the physical description of the text to volume one, which is identical in size to volume two. There is a leaf pressed in page 103 of this volume. Earlier microfilming of this volume suggests that the leaf has been on this page for at least the last fifty years.

TABLE OF CONTENTS FOR
JEFFERSON'S NEWSPAPER CLIPPINGS

Note: There are four volumes of newspaper clippings: two poetry volumes, and two prose volumes. Below is a complete list of poems included in the poetry volumes. The pages listed correspond with my own numbering of the manuscript pages for the volumes of poetry, which will take the reader within one or two pages of the numbering systems inconsistently employed on the books themselves.

Volume One (407 poems total)

APPENDIX TWO

Volume Two (477 poems)

FAVORITE EPIGRAMS OF JEFFERSON

These poems open volume two of Jefferson's newspaper clippings book. They are retained as a sequence because of the insight they give into Jefferson's juxtapositions. He moves from commemorating a man fallen in the Revolutionary War to considering the absurdities of Bonaparte, before he turns to the poem on Thomas Paine that is included under Poems of Nation.

The first four pages, from "The Patriot . . ." to "From the Norristown Herald," are loose sheets and may not have been the first few pages of this notebook; the first page bound in this book is titled "Alarming!"

[Anonymous]
The Patriot, the Soldier and the Christian who visit
these mansions of the dead, view this Monument with
Respect. Beneath it are deposited the remains of
JOHN BARRY.
He was born in the country of *Wexford*, in *Ireland*,
but *America* was the object of his patriotism, and the
theatre of his usefulness and honour. In the revolutionary
war, which established *The Independence of the United
States*, he bore the commission of a Captain
in their infant Navy afterwards became its
COMMANDER IN CHIEF.
He fought often, and once bled, in the cause of
Freedom — His habits of war, did not lessen in him,
the peaceful virtues which adorn private life: he was
gentle, kind and just, and not less Beloved by his
family and friends, than by his grateful country.
In a full belief of the doctrines of the Gospel,
he calmly resigned his soul into the arms of his
REDEEMER,
ON THE 13th OF SEPTEMBER 1803.
IN THE 59th YEAR OF HIS AGE.
His affectionate WIDOW has caused this
MARBLE TO BE ERECTED,
To perpetuate his name, after the hearts of
his fellow-citizens had ceased to be the living records of his
PUBLIC AND PRIVATE VIRTUES.

2:1

An EPITAPH.

[Anonymous]

FAREWELL vain world I've had enough of thee,
And now am careless what thou sayest of me;
Thy miles I court not, nor thy frowns I fear,
My days are past, my head lies quiet here;
What faults in me you've seen, take care to shun,
And look at h[eaven], enough there's to be done.

2:1

EPITAPH for a POET.

[Anonymous]

"Mirabile dictu!"

THESE lines record what many will *forget*.
A POET now has paid great Nature's debt,
Let satire cease, and peaceful rest the grave;
Tis the *first debt* the POET ever paid.

2:1

[Anonymous]

The author of the elegant and spirited work entitled an Examination of the Pursuits of Literature,
to which we have adverted twice or thrice in the
course of the week, gives the following French
epigram as a specimen of *Reignier's* [sic], no old
French poet's manner — it was an epitaph written
for himself, a translation is subjoined — *Aurora*.

FROM REGNIER.

J'ai vécu sans pensement.
Me laissant aller doucement,
   A la bonne loi naturelle;
Et je m'étonne fort purquai,
Lamort osa songer a moi,
   Qui ne songeai jamais a elle!
TRANSLATION.
A life devoid of care and thought,
I led, as nature's maxims caught,

A life of frolic whim:
Then how astonish'd must be
That death should dare to think of me
Who never thought of him.

2:1

REGNIER EPITAPH,
WRITTEN BY HIMSELF.
Often called the bill of life,
Nor e'er the cloud of care or strife,
The smiling prospects dim
As thus I journey'd, careless, free,
'Tis strange that death should think of one
Who never thought of him!

2:1

EPIGRAM.
On the Marriage of Mr. Smart to Miss Pain.
[Anonymous]
TWO lovers, pierc'd by Cupid's dart;
Long sigh'd for Hymen's chain,
She kindly wish'd to have his SMART,
And he to have her PAIN.

A priest they call'd nor call'd in vain,
His blessings to impart;
He soon gave longing Collin PAIN,
And made fond LUCY SMART.

2:2

THE IMPORTANCE OF FIVE MINUTES.
[Anonymous]
At the edict of king Francis, the first, we are told;
To crack jokes on a lord, his buffoon had made bold,
Who swore by his wife (let us hope by a good one)
He'd cut [off t]he head of king Francis' Jack Pudding
The buffoon told his king what his lordship had said,
As he firmly believ'd he would cut off his head;

'Aye, aye,' said the king, between anger and laughter,
'If he does, Jack, I'll hang him up five minutes after;'
'You'd oblige me great sire,' said the jester, 'much more,
'If you'd hang up his lordship *five minutes before.'*

2:2

From a late **LONDON PAPER.**
IMPROMPTU,

On the late Marriage of the Hon, and Rev.
Mr. *Howard*, to Miss *Idle*, Niece of Sir
Philip Musgrave, Bart.

[Anonymous]

MOST men, left to their choice, I know,
  Would lead an idle life,
But few there will be found, I trow,
  Would choose an *Idle* wife.

RESPONSE.

Thy wit is futile on my life,
  So learn thy tongue to bridle,
Tis clear the mind, become a wife;
  Is now no longer *Idle*.

2:2

EPIGRAM.

On the Report of an intended MARRIAGE *between
the* Emperor *of Germany and the* Empress *of*
Russia.

[Anonymous]

SOME say the Imperial Monarch has try'd
  To gain a fair mate to his bosom,
To make the Czarina of Moscow his bride,
  Nor did she incline to oppose him.
But faith there's still this insurmountable bar,
  The bargain old *Kate* will ne'er close, if
She finds him as *tardy* in Love as in War,
  For she swears that in both he's — A JOSEPH.

2:2

IMPROMPTU.

On an expected Marriage of Mr.
Frederick Lamb to Miss Monk.

[Anonymous]

In times remote when Heathens sway'd,
A sacrifice was often made,
    Their Deities to quiet;
And by the Priest the Lamb was led,
Unto the altar, where he bled,
    Without the smallest riot,

Mark how revers'd the blissful scene,
No Heathen rites now intervene,
    To bid the timid faulter;
For, lo! The MONK! — how strange to say,
Is by the LAMB now led away,
    Quite willing, to the altar!

[Eng. Pap.]

2:2

THE FAIR EQUIVOQUE.

From a pleasant little work called the Journey of Life,
is taken the following neat epigram.

[Anonymous]

As blooming HARRIET moved along,
The fairest of the beautious throng,
The beaux gazed on with admiration,
Avow'd by many an exclamation —
What form! what naivete! what grace!
What roses deck that Grecian face!
"Nay," Dashwood cries, "that bloom's not Harriet's;
'Twas bought at Reynold's, Moore's, or Harriot's.
And though you vow her face untainted,
I swear, by God, your beauty's painted."
A wager instantly was laid,
And Ranger sought the lovely maid;
The pending bet he soon reveal'd,
Nor e'en the impious oath conceal'd.

Confused — her cheek bore witness true,
By turns the roses came and flew.
"Your bet," she said, "is rudely odd —
But I am painted Sir — by God."

2:2

THE MUSEUM.
ADDRESSED TO A LADY,
WITH A BEAUTIFUL HAND AND ARM.
[Anonymous]

WHEN at the Bar of Love you stand,
For pilfering hearts in idle sport,
The moment you hold up that hand,
'Twill prove your guilt to all the COURT!

2:2

Answer to the question, What is Happiness?
[Joseph Brown Ladd]

'TIS an empty fleeting shade,
By imagination made;
'Tis a bubble, straw, or worse;
'Tis a baby's hobby horse;
'Tis a little living clear;
'Tis ten thousand pounds a year!
'Tis a title, 'tis a name;
'Tis a puff of empty fame,
Fickle as the breezes blow:
'Tis a lady's YES or NO!
And, when the description's crown'd,
'Tis just *no where* to be found.

2:3

THE MISTAKE.
[Anonymous]

A cannon ball, one bloody day,
Took a poor sailor's leg away;
And, as on his comrade's back he made off,
A second fairly took his head off.
The fellow, on this odd emergence,
Carries him pick-back to the surgeons.

Z——ds! cries the doctor, are you drunk,
To bring me here a headless trunk?
A lying dog! cries Jack — he said
His leg was off, and not his head.

2:3

EPIGRAM.
[Anonymous]
TWO lawyers, when a knotty case was o'er;
Shook hands, and were as good friends as before:
"Zounds!" says the losing client, "how came you
"To be such friends, who were such foes just now?["]
"Thou fool," says one, "we lawyers, tho' so keen;
"Like sheers, ne'er cut *ourselves, but what's between.*"

2:3

BONAPARTE IN STILTS;
Or, "FORTUNE'S FROLIC" illustrated.
[Anonymous]
WHEN *"Robin Rough-head,"* from the plough,
Became a *Lord* — the Lord knows how —
The farce he acted had less fun,
Than *that* at Paris going on;
For *little Bonny* made a King,
O'ertops in *mock'ry* every thing,
That ever was, or e'er will be,
Ridiculous in *mimicry.*
Made a *Great Emp'ror* by the *Gulls,*
Whom, by the bye, he's made *great fools,*
The laughing world he's all surprised,
And *"Fortune's Frolic"* realized.

2:3

THE MISER.
[Anonymous]
Iron is his chest — Iron is his door —
Iron is his hand, and his heart more.

2:3

I. Jefferson and the Newspapers

Jefferson's attitude toward newspapers changed over the course of his thirty-five-year career in government. During the Revolutionary War, Jefferson complained about the misrepresentations of American life he witnessed in British papers. British newspapers were "those infamous fountains of falsehood," with reporters remaining in their garrets instead of doing research;[1] they were marked by a "deep rooted hatred, and fear of emigration."[2]

After the war was over, Jefferson established his reputation "as the foremost exponent in history of the necessity of a free speech."[3] In 1787, he wrote that "were it left to me to decide whether we should have a government without newspapers or newspapers without a government, I should not hesitate a moment to prefer the latter."[4] As secretary of state under George Washington, he encouraged Philip Freneau to found the *National Gazette* as a Republican response to John Fenno's popular *Federalist Gazette*, even finding funds to support its cause.[5] He hired James Callendar to help advance Republican ideas and combat what he thought of as Hamilton's pernicious influence. He helped pen the Kentucky Resolutions as a protest to the Alien and Sedition Acts passed by Congress in 1798, and supported, financially, Republican papers charged with sedition. When he became president, he freed those who "were under the persecution of our enemies, without instituting any prosecutions in retaliation."[6] His two inaugural addresses stress the importance of free speech.

By the sixth year of his presidency, however, Jefferson began to chafe under the rhetorical attacks conducted by Federalists. He flirted with the idea of prosecuting Joseph Dennie for libel. By the time a young Kentucky journalist asked, in 1807, how a newspaper should be conducted (during the trial of Aaron Burr), Jefferson could not restrain his cynicism, noting that a paper that limited itself to facts would not find many subscribers. "Nothing can now be believed which is seen in a newspaper," he wrote. "Truth itself becomes suspicious by being put into that polluted vessel."[7] Papers reflected a coarsening of American culture, which Federalist critics had also noted. "An editor would have to set his face against the demoralizing practice of feeding the public mind habitually on slander, and the depravity of taste which this nauseous ailment induces. Defamation is becoming a necessary of life; insomuch that a dish of tea in the morning or evening cannot be digested without this stimulant . . . it is not he who prints, but he who pays for printing a slander, who is its real author."[8] Having paid Callendar for such slanders, however, Jefferson was not exempt from the practices he bemoaned.

Jefferson, then, was a product of his time. But he also shaped that time. Jefferson's two favorite newspapers were practically organs of his administration — the *National Intelligencer* (1800) and *Richmond Enquirer* (1804). He praised the editors he helped place in their positions, Samuel Harrison Smith and Thomas Ritchie, for they "cull what is good from every paper, as the bee from every flower."[9] After he retired, he claimed that he read only the *Richmond Enquirer*.[10] At the same time, he kept a great many newspapers, from states as far-flung as Kentucky, Maryland, and Massachusetts. Perhaps most significantly, he read the literary journal of his most vociferous rival, the Federalist journal *Port Folio*, edited by Joseph Dennie.

II. Jefferson and His Literary Critics:
Dennie, Moore, Fessenden

Joseph Dennie was a Harvard-trained lawyer from New England who edited the first and most influential literary journal in the United States. Nathaniel Hawthorne described him as "once esteemed one of the finest writers in America."[11] If Dennie did not feel that Federalists had a monopoly on good writing, he came close to suggesting this. "The republican faction not only think erroneously," he noted, "but write incorrectly." Dennie further noted that "the effusions of every republican rascal and scribbler are *always* incorrect in expression."[12] Dennie took particular relish in evaluating Jefferson's language in the Declaration of Independence. In the literary journal issue for April 25, 1801, he urged an author who signed himself "Common Sense" to scrutinize its style, promising that he would "cheerfully and promptly print, whatever will acutely detect the lurking gallicisms, *false* politics, *false* logic, and *false* metaphysics of a rambling declaration, whose language, like that of a huffing bully, supplies by hardihood, and audacity of assertion the place of good manners, reason, and truth." Recent books on the Declaration (Becker, Maier, Wills) do not even quote Federalist criticisms of the document (Dennie, Fessenden, and Tyler), which provide interesting insight into how it was read by Jefferson's contemporaries.[13]

What prompted Dennie's hostility? To begin with, Jefferson's election lost him a position as private secretary to Timothy Pickering, secretary of state under John Adams. Ideologically, however, he was a supporter of Adams and a dyed-in-the-wool New Englander. Dennie thought Jefferson a demagogue who helped coarsen American culture by endorsing unmixed democracy and mob rule.[14] "A democracy is scarcely tolerable at any period of national history," Dennie wrote. "Its omens are always sinister. . . . It was weak and wicked in Athens. It was bad in Sparta, and worse in Rome. It has been tried in France, and has terminated in despotism. It was tried in England, and rejected with the utmost loathing and abhorrence. It is on its trial here, and the issue will be civil war, desolation, and anarchy."[15]

Brought up on charges of libel for these speculative remarks, Dennie toned down his attacks. Yet he continued to ridicule celebrations of the Fourth of July, which play such a prominent role in Jefferson's poems of nation. "Unsatisfied with *Acting* like fools," Dennie wrote of the July 4, 1801, celebrations, "Men begin to enlarge their schemes, and talk and write from the vocabulary of folly."[16] But Dennie was not alone. In *Democracy Unveiled*, Thomas Fessenden lampooned Jeffersonians who celebrated Independence Day by impaling an ox's head on a stake.[17] Such a vulgar exhibit proved that mobs could not be trusted, even when celebrating their own liberty.

Federalists like Dennie battled with Jeffersonians for the contested mantle of classical republicanism, as Joyce Appleby has explained. "For federalists like Dennie and Ames, . . . there remains constant in every human society that principle of irrationality, of pure egoistic self-gratification, that in ancient political theory was always embodied in the uncontrolled *demos* or *vulgus*, the people viewed under the aspect of mob or crowd response."[18] A writer for the *Port Folio* noted that, while he is the last person in the world "to desire to strip the people of all power, for then slavery would ensue," nonetheless "their uncontrolled power is despotism, in its least hopeful form."[19] Hence the *Port Folio*'s complaints about "turbulent demagogues, and beer house politicians."[20] For these writers, Jefferson's America was hopelessly squalid.

Both Dennie and Jefferson were interested in shaping American tastes in literature and, by extension, American politics. One question was whether classical principles would prevail. Where the Federalists urged the continuation of a curriculum of Latin and Greek in college, for example, Jefferson came down firmly on the side of eliminating these languages from his own alma mater, William and Mary, as a requirement for admission and, ultimately, from the required curriculum; the University of Virginia also eliminated Greek and Latin as a requirement,[21] though translating Latin was still required for graduation with a BA.[22] For the Federalists, a knowledge of Greek and Latin writers produced selfless, patriotic citizens. Jefferson, like Benjamin Rush, hoped to diffuse learning more broadly. "While Greek and Latin are the only avenues to science (i.e. knowledge), education will always be confined to a few people," Rush wrote. "It is only by rendering knowledge universal, that a republican form of government can be preserved in our country."[23] Dennie worried about such educational trends; he preferred the dictionary of Samuel Johnson to Noah Webster's and deliberately adopted English spellings in preference to American innovations by Caleb Alexander (*Columbian Dictionary*), which Dennie ridiculed as "a record of our imbecility."[24] Jefferson, by contrast, endorsed Noah Webster's dictionary and approved of Webster's observation that colleges had become "nurseries of Inequalities, the enemies of liberty."[25]

In his collection of newspaper verse, Jefferson became a kind of editor himself. Like Dennie, he juxtaposed poems, arranging them according to topic (seasons, elegies, epigrams, political verse). For all their differences, Dennie and Jefferson admired similar writers, such as Thomas Moore. Jefferson even clipped several poems from Dennie's *Port Folio*, which he obviously read with interest, and both Dennie and Jefferson admired the writings of women. "The editor is anxious . . . to give the most liberal encouragement to the genius, talents, and virtue of the ladies," Dennie wrote, adding that "the influence of women over the fate and fortune of this paper is much greater than that of statesmen."[26] Jefferson featured works by Anne Bannerman, Fanny Holcroft, Amelia Opie, Helen Maria Williams, and even girls in their early teens, such as Helen and Maria Falconar. Nor did Jefferson neglect American writers: Verses by William Cullen Bryant (a youth of thirteen), Philip Freneau, Joel Barlow, Selleck Osborn, Thomas Green Fessenden, and William Ray appear, sometimes juxtaposed, favorably, with British treatments of the same subject (George III, "Evening").

At first, Dennie embraced the poetry of Wordsworth and Coleridge, printing "She Dwelt Among Untrodden Ways" and admiring "Rime of the Ancient Mariner,"[27] though politics soon won out. Dennie ultimately rejected the verse of Wordsworth and Coleridge as too democratic. "Wordsworth stands among the foremost of those English bards, who have mistaken silliness for simplicity,"[28] Dennie wrote. "It appears that Southey and a Mr. Coleridge, another *democratic poet*, were educated together and mutually inflamed with French liberty," he continued. "The poems of Southey and his companions are recited with *patriotic* emphasis, by the whole tribe of dissenters, innovators, wishers for parliamentary reform, and haters of church and king."[29] It is tempting to speculate that Jefferson would have admired Wordsworth for the very reasons that Dennie objected to him.

Joseph Dennie cultivated several poets who were hostile to Jefferson's administration. Thomas Moore's attitude toward Jefferson was no doubt soured by his companion Thomas Merry, the British ambassador, whose wife (and Merry himself) took umbrage at the "pell-mell" style of seating Jefferson employed, and by the third American president's predilection for wearing courduroys and slippers to greet heads of state.[30] Moore was only twenty-four at the time, and he admitted that he found Dennie's society more congenial than the American president he had come to visit. "In the society of Mr. Dennie and his friends, at Philadelphia, I passed the only agreeable moments which my tour through the States afforded me," Moore remarked.[31] Thomas Moore paid homage to Dennie's friendship, but also criticized the Federalists for their intemperate attacks. In fact, one of Moore's chief complaints about America was the uncivil tone in which political life was conducted — something to which he contributed, of course, with his lines alluding to Sally Hemings.

Moore's patrons were English, and it appears that *Odes, Epistles, and other Poems*, dedicated, as it was, to the military hero Lord Rawdon, was also written to please them. His "Epistle VII: To Thomas Hume, M.D., Esq. From the City of Washington" sees Washington, DC, from the vantage point of a British patriot, as a place where English liberty does not flourish:

> 'Tis evening now; the heats and cares of day
> In twilight dews are calmly wept away.
> The lover now, beneath the western star,
> Sighs through the medium of his sweet segar,
> And fills the ears of some consenting she
> With puffs and vows, with smoke and constancy!
> The weary statesman for repose hath fled
> From halls of council to his negro's shed,
> Where blest he woos some black Aspasia's grace,
> And dreams of freedom in his slave's embrace![32]

At twenty-four, Thomas Moore still had a fortune to make, which was no doubt in his mind when he closed his poem to Lord Hume.

> So here I pause — and now, my HUME! we part;
> But oh! full often, in magic dreams of heart,
> Thus let us meet, and mingle converse dear
> By Thames at home, or by Potowmac here!
> O'er lake and marsh, through fevers and through fogs,
> Midst bears and yankees, democrats and frogs,
> Thy foot shall follow me, thy heart and eyes
> With me shall wonder, and with me despise![33]

Anti-democratic with one stroke of the pen ("democrats and frogs"), Moore could be sycophantic in another ("and now, my HUME, we part"). "Tommy loves a Lord," Byron wrote sarcastically of his future biographer, providing (as usual) sharp psychological insight into the social-climbing propensity of one of his closest friends.[34] Even Wordsworth, however, "could do no better, when he stood in the face of American democracy than 'keep the secret of a poignant scorn.'"[35]

In alluding to Sally Hemings, Moore simply versified claims that Joseph Dennie had been making in his *Port Folio*.[36] Moore's own comments on Negroes in Virginia are hardly flattering,[37] for Moore seems to have been a parlor dandy and a social snob. Thirty years later, the bitter nature of Moore's attack on Jefferson was linked, by *Harper's Magazine*, not to politics but to personal pique: "the President had a habit of casting a cold first look at a stranger; and on this occasion, standing erect, six feet two inches and a half, he gazed for a moment silently down upon the perfumed five-foot poet."[38] Though he did not retract the lines, Moore wrote that "there are few of my errors I regret more sincerely than the rashness I was guilty of in publishing those crude and boyish tirades against the Americans. My sentiments both with respect to their National and individual character are much changed since then, and I should blush as a lover of Liberty, if I allowed the hasty prejudices of my youth to blind me to the bright promise which America affords of a better and happier order of things than the World has perhaps ever yet witnessed."[39] Two years later, he noted that "the little information I took the trouble of seeking came to me through twisted and tainted channels — and in short I was a rash boy and made a fool of myself."[40] All was apparently forgiven, though Moore never retracted a line when he had the poems reprinted in 1847. Well before that time, when Moore's *Irish Melodies* came out during Jefferson's second term, Jefferson's granddaughter gave him a copy. Jefferson, when he saw Moore's name, said, "Why this is the little man who satirized me so!" In the letter he wrote to his daughter when he was dying, Jefferson quoted several lines from Moore.[41]

Another writer who took up the cudgels against Jefferson was Thomas Green Fessenden. Fessenden excelled at satirizing American manners, but is represented by two rather tame works in Poems of Nation: "Soldier's Return" and "Epigram."

> When cannons roar, when bullets fly,
> And shouts and groans affright the sky,
> Amid the battle's dire alarms,
> I'll think, my Mary, on thy charms,

APPENDIX FOUR

The crimson field, fresh proof shall yield,
Of thy fond soldier's love;
And thy dear form, in battle's storm,
His guardian angel prove.[42]

This poem, "Soldier's Return," appears as "Song Written for July 4, 1805" in Fessenden's *Poems* (1806). Fessenden apparently first called the poem "Soldier's Return" with a newspaper audience in mind. It is surprisingly sentimental, given Fessenden's reputation for satire (his pen name was Christopher Caustic). The second poem in Jefferson's collection, "Epigram," is more political.

Some wicked people in the nation,
Find fault with our administration;
But if the whole truth were unfurl'd,
They're not the worst men in the world:
They lack but two things, I suspect,
Viz. *honesty* and *intellect*.[43]

Fessenden might have smiled to see his criticisms of Jefferson's administration reduced to a somewhat innocuous epigram. After all, Fessenden excoriated Jefferson's politics in *Democracy Unveiled* in cantos with titles like "Mobocracy" and "The Jeffersoniad." Nevertheless, Fessenden would have been proud to note that the president took account of his work as poet, even if they differed in politics.

Despite these two brief poems in the collection, Fessenden is worth special attention. This is so because he represents a group of Dartmouth, Harvard, and Yale graduates — many of them lawyers — who found themselves frustrated by Jefferson's political style. He had spent three years in England, becoming one of the best-selling authors abroad, before returning to the United States in 1806 and taking on Jefferson's policies. "Devoid of influence or fear, I trace Democracy's career," Fessenden wrote in the preface to *Democracy Unveiled*.

And paint the vices of the times,
While bad men tremble at my rhymes

And I'll unmask the Democrat,
Your sometimes this thing, sometimes that,
Whose life is one dishonest shuffle,
Lest he perchance the *mob* should ruffle.

For Fessenden, politics was a moral crusade ("bad men tremble at my rhymes"). He saw himself as a scourge who would cleanse the commonwealth of the "wicked men" who corrupted it. While Robert Merry could write a poem praising the French National Assembly, a sentimental poem Jefferson would no doubt have admired, Fessenden felt it incumbent upon him to explain that the leaders of a mob "are, generally speaking, haughty and imperious demagogues."[44] Lest Jefferson miss his target, Fessenden went farther, alluding to "the genuine-republican-slave-driving nabobs of Virginia, who would fain conceal their designs of domination beneath the mask of liberty, and a *pretended* zeal for the rights of the people."[45] When Thomas Moore objected to the uncivil political discourse he witnessed in America, he might have had these lines in mind, though they were published after his visit.

In *Democracy Unveiled*, Fessenden saw "the spirit of the rebellion of 1786 [Shay's Rebellion] is represented as *preparing the way* for French revolutionary principles." He explained that "Ridicule seems to be the only weapon which has not fallen blunted from the buckler of Democracy, like the dart of Priam from the bosses of Pyrrus."[46] He blamed Randolph, Nicholson, and Duane for the low state of political debate in the United States. "It is time that the community were well and truly informed for the characters of the principal performers on our political theatre; . . . If our *political* rights are undefined and insecure, our *civil rights* among which is the right of property, will not long be respected."[47] Fessenden wrote like the attorney he had trained to be. "I consider myself as having brought a set of culprits to trial before the tribunal of *public opinion*."[48] Published under the innocuous title of *Original Poems*, Fessenden's satire did not result in the fines, imprisonment, or exile he sometimes professed to fear.

While Thomas Jefferson and Joel Barlow admired French institutions, Fessenden insisted that America's proper ally was England. In fact, most of the trouble that the United States faced, in the views of Federalists such as Dennie and Fessenden, came from immigrants like Albert Gallatin and Irish newspaper editors.

> When braggart Swiss, and Irish paddies,
> With pride and nonsense, overweening,
> Absurdly blunder round their meaning; —
> . . . Fellows, who sped away, betimes
> To seek a refuge from their crimes
> Who, if transported back to Europe,
> Each hangman there would lack a new rope.[49]

Fessenden was not inaccurate: Callendar was a fugitive from Scotland; Thomas Paine had a dubious reputation in England; and William Duane, like many American newspaper editors, hailed from Ireland. The tone of Fessenden's satire, however, lost him readers, except among those who could appreciate his clever wordplay. Soon his politics would be relegated to the ash heap of history, however, only to be resurrected by a new species of Republicans, such as Patrick Buchanan. But Fessenden was no crank. Nathaniel Hawthorne, who knew him well, wrote a moving essay honoring him as a man of "genius." "The severe simplicity of our republic recognizes no Poet Laureate," Hawthorne wrote, "but the poets of America might place a laurel crown upon his honoured head, and acknowledge him the leader of their choir."[50]

Fessenden's satire of Jefferson's embargo, *Pills, Poetical, Political, and Philosophical* (1809), came out too late to sell well.[51] Yet William Cullen Bryant was a fellow traveler, writing "The Embargo, or Sketches of Our Times" when he was only thirteen.[52] At his father's suggestion, Bryant enlarged the 244-line poem to 420 lines after passage of the Embargo Act of January 9, 1809, inflamed public opinion. Bryant's poem is marked by the kind of scurrilous abuse that characterized political debate during Jefferson's administration: "Go, wretch, resign the presidential chair, / Disclose thy secret measures foul or fair, / Go, search, with curious eye, for horned frogs, / 'Mongst the wild wastes of Louisianian bogs." Dumas Malone has written that Jefferson "is not known ever to have seen it,"[53] but Jefferson certainly did, for he pasted the poem in his clippings book; nevertheless, eighteen of the most ad hominem lines (included those quoted above) do not appear in the newspaper version Jefferson clipped. As the seven poems dedicated to the topic of the embargo reveal, poets treated every aspect of the policy, including the burden on American women forced to wear coarse homespun cloth in lieu of imports. In some ways, Jefferson averted war with Great Britain, which would occur under James Madison's administration, by pursuing a policy of neutrality during England and France's battles for supremacy of the seas. Henry Mellen, Spunky Jonathan, and others all weighed in. While the Louisiana Purchase was almost beyond reproach, the embargo, and the war with the Barbary nations, reveal the difficulties Jefferson faced in leading a country without a sufficient navy to protect its commerce and trade.

III. Jefferson and Women's Education

Jefferson's attitudes toward women's education emerges indirectly in these clippings. On the one hand, he cultivated a relationship with his granddaughters and clipped verse for them. On the other, he considered child rearing their most important function. In a letter to Anne Randolph Bankhead, for example, he compared women, however playfully, to flowers, whose "more interesting office" is reproduction.[54] In choosing novels for his daughters, he kept the values of domesticity constantly in mind (he did not share his love of Laurence Sterne with them!). In the same letter to Anne quoted above, for example, he noted the dangers of Maria Edgeworth's *Modern Griselda*, which was making the rounds of the Jefferson family. "I have just received a copy of the Modern Griselda which Ellen tells me will not be unacceptable to you. I therefore enclose it. The heroine certainly presents herself as a perfect model of ingenious perverseness, and of the art of making herself and others unhappy. If it can be made of use in inculcating the virtues and felicities of life, it must be by the rules of contraries."[55]

If men and women were to enjoy happiness rather than simply pursue it, a plan of education was clearly required. Jefferson set forth his most extended remarks on the subject of female education in a letter to Nathaniel Burwell:

> A plan of female education has never been a subject of systematic contemplation with me. It has occupied my attention so far only as the education of my own daughters occasionally required. Considering that they would be placed in a country situation, where little aid could be obtained from abroad, I thought it essential to give them a solid education, which might enable them, when become mothers, to educate their own daughters, and even to direct the course for sons, should their fathers be lost, or incapable, or inattentive.[56]

Jefferson went on to describe his view of women's education in terms not far different from Mary Wollstonecraft's.

> A great obstacle to good education is the inordinate passion prevalent for novels, and the time lost in that reading which should be instructively employed. When this poison infects the mind, it destroys its tone and revolts it against wholesome reading. Reason and fact, plain and unadorned, are rejected. Nothing can engage attention unless dressed in all the figments of fancy, and nothing so bedecked comes amiss. The result is a bloated imagination, sickly judgment, and disgust towards all the real businesses of life. This mass of trash, however, is not without some distinction; some few modelling their narratives, although fictitious, on the incidents of real life, have been able to make them interesting and useful vehicles of a sound morality. Such, I think, are Marmontel's new Moral Tales, but not his old ones, which are

really immoral. Such are the writings of Miss Edgeworth, and some of those of Madame Genlis. For a like reason, too, much poetry should not be indulged. Some is useful for forming style and taste. Pope, Dryden, Thomson, Shakespeare, and of the French Molière, Racine, the Corneilles, may be read with pleasure and improvement.[57]

Like the barber and the priest in *Don Quixote* ("Inquisition in the Library"), Jefferson could barely stand to part with the novels and poetry he condemned ("Some is useful for forming style and taste," he said of poetry). Yet Ellen Coolidge seems to have agreed with her grandfather that "much poetry should not be indulged." Poetry encouraged "quick feelings, & a lively imagination," qualities that did not help the owners of large Virginian plantations that were becoming increasingly expensive to maintain. When Jefferson's granddaughters faced the prospect of poverty, "they chafed at the fact that they could not work," Joyce Appleby has noted. "Cornelia Randolph wrote with some bitterness that not until they sank entirely would it 'do for the granddaughters of Thomas Jefferson to take in work or keep a school,' to which Ellen Coolidge penned an echoing note: 'My sisters are losing heart. . . . My sisters wish to work for their own support, but [they are] the granddaughters of Thomas Jefferson.'"[58]

IV. Jefferson and His Granddaughters

Jefferson was disappointed in the amount of time he could spend with his daughters while vice president; as president, he seemed determined to rectify this by bridging the distance between Washington and Monticello. He began by sending a story for Anne for her scrapbook on January 16, 1801: "I inclose for Anne a story, too long to be got by heart, but worth reading. Kiss them all for me: and keep them in mind of me. Tell Ellen I am afraid she has forgotten me."[59] Compared with Martha, who had learned French and accompanied her father to Paris, Anne and Ellen were educated at home. He sent "a little story of Anne . . . as I have sometimes done before," on June 25, 1801. He already had Ellen in his sights. "Tell Ellen as soon as she can read them, I will select some beautiful ones for her."[60] Apparently, Jefferson sent the stories on colored paper. "They shall be black, red, yellow, green and of all sorts of colours."[61]

Jefferson took an interest in his granddaughters' writing skills. To Ellen he sent two books, encouraging her to write herself. "When I left Monticello you could not read," he wrote on November 27, 1801, "and now I find you can not only read, but write also. I inclose you two little books as a mark of my satisfaction, and if you continue to learn as fast, you will become a learned lady and publish books yourself."[62] Martha was pleased by the encouragement. "I really think we are indebted to your letter expressing your surprise at her having in so short a time learned to read and write."[63] Only with restraint could Ellen be kept from learning to write and read at the same time. "I *feel* that I never can sit down quietly under the idea of their being blockheads," Martha wrote. Anne seemed more reluctant. "I inclose poetry for Anne's book. I must pray her to become my correspondent," Jefferson wrote to Martha. "It will be useful to her, and very satisfactory to me."[64] In her letter of February 14, 1804, Anne apparently obeyed her mother's command. "I am much obliged to you for it and the poetry also. I will very gladly undertake to write to you every post," she wrote.[65] Once Anne's scrapbook was large enough, he turned his attention to Ellen. "As I expect Anne's volume is now large enough, I will begin to furnish you with materials for one. I know you have been collecting some yourself; but as I expect there is some tag, rag, and bobtail verse among it you must begin a new volume for my materials."[66] Anne's letter to her father shows that she could also have high expectations. "This is the fourth letter I have written to My Dear Grand Papa without receiving an answer. I suppose you have not received them or else your business prevented your answering them." Working on Ellen's book now, he wrote, "I send you some pieces for your volume of poetry, some of which have merit."[67] Jefferson also sent Mrs. Barbauld's first lessons for Cornelia. On July 20, 1805, Ellen wrote, "I am very obliged for the poetry you sent me. Little John and the Ode to Modesty."[68] Jefferson wrote to Martha, "I look over the two ensuing years as the most tedious of my life." On November 30, 1806, he wrote, "I send you enclosed much newspaper poetry"; on March 1, 1807, "I send for little Cornelia a poem, the Grasshopper's ball to begin her collection. The Yankee story is for yourself." Martha wrote back: "Cornelia is very much pleasd with the piece of poetry you sent her."[69] Physical discomfort did not prevent Jefferson from communicating with his granddaughters. "Even with headache I send Ellen a little piece of poetry." Since he sent poetry to Ellen and Anne, Martha's children, it seems clear that the poetry he kept for himself reflected, at least in part, his own tastes. On June 1, 1807, he sent "a piece of poetry for Ellen. Tell her she is to consider this as a substitute for a letter and I debit her account accordingly."[70] On June 9, 1807, he wrote, "I send you some poetical gleanings; our newspapers have been barren in that ware for some time past."[71] He was careful to add, "A good housewife is worth more than the whole family of the muses." He then sent poetry by Peter Pindar and "some poetry but I am not sure whether I may not have sent you the same pieces before."[72] His letter was acknowledged.[73] In a letter to Jefferson on March 11, 1808, she wrote, "I am sorry there is so little poetry in the newspapers as my book is not full. If I can fill it sister Ann and I will have together an excellent collection. We each have books in which we copy such poetry as we cannot get in the newspapers."[74] Later Jefferson recommended Madame de Seveigne's letters to Ellen.

On March 29, 1808, the dearth of poetry in the newspapers continued. "Our newspapers are so barren that I have been obliged to go to Paris for a piece of poetry for you, or at least to a Paris paper."[75] Jefferson included a poem he had known as a child. Ellen wrote to tell him that "Cornelia was very much delighted with your letter, she easily found out the verse as she had seen many before of the same kind."[76] The source was J. Harvey Dalton, *Children's Books in England*. On December 26, 1808, Jefferson congratulated Cornelia on acquiring the "art of writing," and inclosed a copy of "The Terrapiniad."

Bear and Betts have noted that the grandchildren's scrapbooks were lost, but Jefferson's survived: "TJ's own volume 'The Jefferson Scrapbook' is in the Alderman Library at the University of Virginia," they wrote. "This contains a great variety of material, including several poetical works sent to his grandchildren for their scrapbooks."[77] In their work, only one volume is referenced as "The Jefferson Scrapbook." In fact, there are four surviving books, two of which are poetry; the other two are short stories and prose works. The second volume of poetry, not alluded to by Bear and Betts, was housed at the visitor center in Monticello for a number of years. Depending on how one interprets the phrase "in the press," the binding of these scrapbooks may have begun as early as November 10, 1801: "Make hast to come home to see us and all our books in the press," Ellen Wayles Randoolph wrote that month.[78]

V. Jefferson's Witty Epigrams

Jefferson's sense of humor and wide-ranging interests play havoc with the three categories I have sometimes imposed upon this collection. I include an appendix, therefore, that allows a reader to experience the diverse interests of the "whirligig" Jefferson and to see them in all the glory of their juxtapositions. Jefferson included a number of epigrams on marriage.

> Most men, left to their choice, I know,
> Would lead an idle life,
> but few there will be found, I trow,
> Would choose an *Idle* wife.[79]

Jefferson particularly enjoyed poems in which a person's flaws come back to haunt him or her. One poem describes marriage as an exchange of goods.

TWO lovers, pierc'd by Cupid's dart,
Long sigh'd for Hymen's chain,
She kindly wish'd to have his SMART,
And he to have her PAIN.

A priest they call'd nor call'd in vain,
His blessings to impart;
He soon gave longing Collin Pain,
And made fond LUCY SMART.[80]

This poem mocks the meddling priest who makes things worse than before; his thwarted effort to guide his flock toward contentment prepares us for the next poem in the collection, "Answer to the Question, What Is Happiness?"

'TIS an empty fleeting shade,
By imagination made;
'Tis a bubble, straw or worse;
'Tis a baby's hobby horse;
'Tis a little living clear;
'Tis ten thousand pounds a year!
'Tis a title, 'tis a name;
'Tis a puff of empty fame,
Fickle as the breezes blow:
'Tis a lady's YES or NO!
And, where the description's crown'd,
'Tis just *no where* to be found.[81]

This poem appears anonymously in the collection, but is by the South Carolina bard Joseph Brown Ladd, whose wry sense of humor captures the flavor of many of the epigrams Jefferson clipped.[82] If he could be sentimental about the right to "pursue happiness" at thirty-three (when he wrote the Declaration), he became facetious about achieving it at fifty-seven.

The poem that follows this shows how happiness must compete with the exigencies, even the tragedies, of everyday life. Armed with wit, a person has a better chance at happiness, for he or she will not be surprised by life's misfortunes, as "The Mistake," makes clear:

A cannon ball, one bloody day,
Took a poor sailor's leg away;
And, as on his comrade's back he made off,

A second fairly took his head off.
The fellow, on this odd emergence,
Carries him pick-back to the surgeons.
Z — ds! cries the doctor, are you drunk,
To bring me here a headless trunk?
A lying dog! cries Jack — he said
His leg was off, and not his head.[83]

In this case, wit forestalls a sentimental response.

One page of Jefferson's epigrams describes a poet who cannot pay his debts. The page closes with Regnier's depiction of a thoughtless man's death: "That death should dare to think of me, / Who never thought of him."[84] These witty, if somewhat morbid, reflections precede a page announcing several marriages: Mr. Smart and Miss Pain, Mr. Howard and Miss Idle, and an actual betrothal of Mr. Frederick Lamb (plenipotentiary to Vienna), son of Lady Melbourne, and Miss Monk. In each case, the divergent natures of the married couple are resolved through wit; beauty, which leads to marriage, is shown to be illusory, as in the Swiftian squib "The Fair Equivoque."[85] Sometimes an apparently face-tious poem includes cutting political commentary. A poem announcing the marriage between the emperor of Germany and the empress of Russia, for example, impugns the German emperor's courage by depicting him as "*tardy* in Love as in War."[86]

Though Jefferson negotiated with Bonaparte for the purchase of the Louisiana territories, the following poem gives new insight into what America's third president thought of the newly crowned emperor.

BONAPARTE IN STILTS;
Or, "FORTUNE'S FROLIC" illustrated.

WHEN "Robin Rough-head," from the plough,
Became a Lord — the Lord knows how —
The farce he acted had less fun,
Than that at Paris going on;
For little Bonny made a King,
O'ertops in mock'ry every thing,
That ever was, or e'er will be,
Ridiculous in mimicry.
Made a Great Emp'ror by the Gulls,
Whom, by the bye he's made great fools,

The laughing world he's all surprised,
And "Fortune's Frolic" realized.[87]

Jefferson was perceptive enough to recognize that Bonaparte, for all his rhetoric about liberty, was more bent on becoming a king ("little Bonny made a King") than on establishing a democracy. His keen eye for political fraud, whether in Alexander Hamilton, Aaron Burr, George Washington, John Adams, Thomas Paine, or Napoleon Bonaparte, made Jefferson a formidable advocate for democratic principles.

The facetious poem on Bonaparte follows a poem mocking lawyers (Jefferson's own profession) and the radical rhetoric of Thomas Paine, to which Jefferson was so susceptible. Jefferson's efforts to husband his resources — the very recycled nature of the commonplace book, the nail factory at Monticello,[88] his concern with profit and loss at his estate — ultimately gave way to reckless spending on wine and books. If he became something of a spendthrift, endangering his family's resources, Jefferson could comfort himself that he had avoided the fate of the miser, to which he probably considered himself susceptible.

Iron is his chest — Iron is his door —
Iron is his hand, and his heart more.[88]

Jefferson's daughter seems to have described him well when she noted that "He enjoyed jests, provided it were to give pain to noone, and we were always glad to have any pleasant little anecdote for him — when he would laugh as cheerily as we'd do ourselves."[89]

VI. The Literary Value of the Selected Poems

Connoisseur as he was of wine, architecture, and fine arts, Jefferson does not seem to have been a revolutionary in his literary preferences. He valued the sentiment as much as the substance of the poems he collected on domestic affections. For Jefferson, as for Royall Tyler and T. G. Fessenden, literature was a pleasant diversion from the rigors of law, the field in which they were all trained. This led Jefferson to interesting inconsistencies. On the one hand, he could clip, with apparent approval, a sentimental poem by Mr. Upton that exposed the health dangers posed to chimney sweepers (not included in this collection); on the other, he dismissed Phyllis Wheatley's equally didactic poetry as "beneath the dignity of criticism" in Notes on the State of Virginia.

Despite his remarks on Phyllis Wheatley's verse, Jefferson clipped poems that reflect the democratic ideology he hoped to instill through his own conduct in the White House. For Jefferson saw himself as setting an example for others even in minute particulars, such as walking to his own inaugural (rather than arriving in a pompous horse and carriage) or greeting guests at the White House with red slippers and worn slacks, or seating foreign dignitaries pell-mell, without regard to their rank. The case was no different with his clippings book. In this sense, the book itself conveys a message.

Jefferson's preference for clipping poetry from the newspaper to buying bound volumes of the stuff reminds one today of someone recording music off the radio rather than purchasing the CD. Jefferson was certainly a frugal man. But this may not go all the way toward explaining why he constructed a newspaper clippings book rather than purchase the miscellanies in which many of these poems appeared. Jefferson seems to have been chiefly interested in verse that circulated publically, for this allowed him to keep his finger on the pulse of the times. An academic might compare this "pulse" with what Jürgen Habermas called the "public sphere," for Jefferson regarded newspaper verse as a mediating force between the people and the government that represented them. Jefferson rejected the idea that poetry was something for elite and sophisticated palates.[90] For a committed republican, poetry could serve the function of an opinion poll. Poetry, especially verse published in the newspapers, formed what Benedict Anderson has called an imagined community. The modernism of Ezra Pound and T. S. Eliot clouds our sense of the public function poetry once had, as late as the Victorian era. Jefferson seemed bent on enjoying homely verse, doggerel, and commonplace subjects in such poems as "To My Segar."[91] The feeling was, in some ways, more important than its expression. Without pushing the point too far, one finds a love of conviviality in this collection — of fellowship — that might be expected in a Masonic meeting, the subject of several poems in this collection.[92]

Though Jefferson admired poetry, he was not afraid to ridicule versifiers, or to clip the verse of well-known friends (such as Benjamin Franklin) who did: this, too, was part of his balance, his love of complementarity. Like other Americans, he could be suspicious of his own intellectuality. He collected Benjamin Franklin's witty dismissal of poets in a brilliant sketch titled "Paper," which compares a number of different men to different types of paper, concluding with this devastating stanza:

> What are our poets, take them as they fall,
> Good, bad, rich, poor, much read, not read at all.
> Them and their works in the same class you'll find;
> They are the mere *waste-paper* of mankind.[93]

Jefferson's modest collection of verse reverses Benjamin Franklin's prediction, for he preserved poetry by pasting over old correspondence. Jefferson's scrapbook is thus a palimpsest that becomes one with the ephemeral material upon which it appears. If the medium is the message, as Marshall McCluhan observed of an electronic age, Jefferson's scrapbook cannot be understood apart from the recycled materials it comprises. Jefferson's charming regard for the scarcity of resources such as paper, as well as his choice of verse by women and unknown Americans, makes his work as resonant in our time as it was in his own.

BIOGRAPHIES

Pseudonyms and Pen Names

Hafiz ("A Persian Song," "Unfortunate Beauty of Buttermere"). This pen name was used by both Thomas Stott and John Haddon Hindley; see their separate entries.

Peter Pindar is the pseudonym used by John Wolcot.

Rosa Matilda is the pseudonym used by Charlotte Dacre (née Byrne).

Rusticus ("Embargo — A New Song") was also the author of "Liberty: A Poem by Rusticus" (1768); *The Plain Truth, by Rusticus* (1776), a response to James Chalmers; and *The Good of the Community impartially considered, in a letter to a merchant in July 15* (1754). Rusticus's "Liberty: A Poem" was republished with Alexander Martin's (1740–1807) "America: A Poem" (1769).

S. C. ("A Song, for the New-Hampshire Election, 1805") was the pen name of William Butler (1759–1821), a supporter of the embargo.

S. K. ("An Ode, Most Respectfully Inscribed to His Excellency General Washington"), possibly John Armstrong (1717–1795).

Authors

Anderson, Robert, MD (1750–1830) ("The Slave"), studied divinity at Lanark and medicine at St. Andrews (1778). When his wife died (1784), he was left with three infant daughters. An annuity allowed him to end his medical practice. Anderson edited the *Edinburgh Magazine* (1784–1803) before it was incorporated into *Scots Magazine*. He also edited *The Works of John Moore, M.D., with Memoirs of His Life and Writings* (1820), and the poems of Robert Blair (1826). In 1793, he began preparing his edition of the *British Poets*, which was published in thirteen volumes (1795–1807). Anderson helped promote the career of Anne Bannerman by supporting her financially after the death of her mother in 1802. He introduced Thomas Campbell to his literary circle in Edinburgh in 1797, assisting him with the publication of "The Pleasures of Hope," which Campbell dedicated to Anderson. Anderson wrote biographies of Smollett and Dr. Johnson. His abolitionist poem "The Slave" would have appealed to Jefferson's idealistic views, though Jefferson himself was caught in the dilemma of a man whose inherited wealth was inextricably bound up with the slave economy.

Bannerman, Anne (1765–1829) ("War"). Jefferson adopted strategies such as the embargo in order to avoid military conflict. He would have approved of Bannerman's poem, which is critical of Britain's aggressive foreign policy.

Born in Edinburgh, Bannerman was the daughter of William Bannerman and his wife, Isobel Dick. She formed part of Edinburgh's literary circle, which included John Leyden, Thomas Campbell, and Dr. Robert Anderson. Through the efforts of Anderson and Thomas Park, Bannerman found her work read by James Currie (Burns's first biographer), Bishop Percy (editor of *Reliques of Ancient English Poetry*), and Joseph Cooper Walker (Irish writer on Italian tragedy and lifelong friend of Charlotte Smith). Bannerman was an old friend of John Leyden (Scott's co-editor of *The Minstrelsy of the Scottish Border*, 1802–1803), whose best-known ballad, "The Mermaid," appeared two years after Bannerman's own ode "The Mermaid" appeared in *Poems* (1800).

The Monthly Magazine, the *Poetical Register*, and the *Edinburgh Magazine* published Bannerman's work under the pseudonyms "Augusta" and "B," and under her own name. Bannerman's *Poems* (1800) included two sonnet sequences that also drew inspiration from Joanna Baillie's theory of dramatic composition. Her second volume, *Tales of Superstition and Chivalry* (1802), published anonymously, included ten Gothic ballads and four engravings, the fourth of which, "The Prophecy of Merlin," scandalously included a nude female figure. In 1802, she translated several verse passages for Joseph Cooper Walker's *An Historical and Critical Essay on the Drama in Italy* (1805). After her mother died in 1803, Anderson and Park helped her publish *Poems: A New Edition* (1807), by subscription, which included most of the poems in the 1800 and 1802 volumes, along with some new works, including "To Miss Baillie." Park obtained twenty pounds from the Royal Literary Fund for her in 1805, but she could not obtain a pension. With Anderson's help, Bannerman accepted the position of governess for Lady Frances Beresford's daughter in Exeter. She visited Hampstead and by the early 1810s was back in Scotland, existing partially through gifts from the Beresford family, and visiting writer Anne Grant in 1824. In 1829, she died an invalid and in debt in Portobello, near Edinburgh, with two of her poems appearing in *The Laurel* (1830) and *The Casket* (1829). Lady Frances Beresford destroyed all of Bannerman's letters. Scott praised her *Tales of Superstition and Chivalry* (1802); Bannerman was the only female poet Scott included in this essay on Scottish ballads, and she remains significant for her Gothic ballads, as well as for her innovative sonnet series and her bold original odes.

Barbauld, Anna (née Aikin) (1743–1825) ("Hymn to Content"). Jefferson's daughter Martha asked him to purchase a copy of Barbauld's *Lessons* in 1801 for her own child. "Will you be so good as to bring Cornelia *Mrs. Barbauld's first* *lessons.* She is so young at reading that the print of the books common to children of her age puzzles her extremely whereas Mrs. Barbauld is allways printed in large type in 4 small volumes."[1] Martha Jefferson Randolph left Barbauld's "Pure spirit! O where art thou now!" in Jefferson's commonplace book as a "valedictory of her father."[2] Three years after Jefferson stepped down as president, Barbauld published "England in 1811," which condemned English imperialism but criticized American provincialism. There is no evidence that Jefferson read "England in 1811" or John Wilson Croker's savage review.

The daughter of a tutor in languages, literature, and divinity at Warrington Academy, Anna Letitia Barbauld made lifelong friends with Joseph Priestley (1733–1804), his wife Mary (1742–1796), and William Enfield (1741–1797). She shared literary and scientific tastes with her brother John Aikin (1747–1822). In the mid-1760s, she began to write poetry. *Poems* (1773) was a success, reaching five editions by 1777 (with another in 1792). This was followed by *Miscellaneous Pieces in Prose* (1773), a collection of essays. She opened Palgrave School, with her husband, attracting William Taylor (1765–1836) and Thomas Denman (1779–1854), drafter of the Reform Act of 1832. The book resulted in publication of Barbauld's *Lessons for Children* (four volumes, 1778–1779), written to teach Charles to read, and *Hymns in Prose for Children* (1781) a primer in religion: both became important pedagogical tools.

In 1785, the Barbaulds resigned from Palgrave School and traveled in France. Her brother edited *Monthly Magazine* (1796–1802), to which she contributed. She also wrote for the *Annual Review* (1803–1809), edited by nephew Arthur Aikin (1773–1854), and wrote prefaces to editions of Mark Akenside (1794), William Collins (1797), and Addison and Steele (1804). She edited Samuel Richardson's correspondence in six volumes (1804) and wrote prefaces for a fifty-volume collection, *The British Novelists* (1810). In 1809, she began to write for the *Monthly Review*, contributing approximately 340 reviews during six years. She also brought out a literary anthology titled *The Female Speaker* (1811), which was designed for young women. Her last separate publication and most ambitious work was *Eighteen Hundred and Eleven* (1812), which was negatively reviewed by Tory John Croker for its prophecy of England's economic decline and protracted war against France.

In 1802, Barbauld's associates included her publisher Joseph Johnson (1738–1809) and such literary figures as Joanna Baillie, George Dyer, Maria Edgeworth, William Godwin, and Henry Crabb Robinson. Barbauld's support of a young Samuel Taylor Coleridge resulted in his turning against her, which injured her posthumous reputation; Charles Lamb also criticized her work in children's literature. Her husband committed suicide in 1808, and she died of asthma in 1825. Lucy Aikin (1781–1864), her niece, edited her *Works* (1825), adding fifty-two poems to the fifty-five Barbauld had published, and a volume of teaching pieces and essays called *A Legacy for Young Ladies* (1826).

Barlow, Joel (1754–1812) (*The Columbiad*). Barlow became friendly with Thomas Jefferson, who invited him to Monticello in 1806 after his return from France. Jefferson urged Barlow to write a history of the United States and provided him with boxes of private papers to do so, though the project never came to fruition. Barlow attended Dartmouth, transferred to Yale, and became a schoolmaster, but then returned to Yale to pursue an MA in theology. He joined the Third Massachussetts Brigade in 1780, married Ruth Baldwin in 1781, joined Elisha Babcock, published the *American Mercury* (1784), and opened a bookstore in 1785. In 1786, he began his law practice, which led to positions in business and government. He began "The Vision of Columbus" in April 1779 but did not complete it until 1787. Barlow's *The Columbiad* (1807) was a revised version of "The Vision of Columbus," composed after spending seventeen years in France. Completed with the financial assistance of Robert Fulton (the inventor of the steamboat), *The Columbiad* included eleven lavish engravings, and was one of the most expensively produced volumes in America. "As a poem of the Epic character it can never rank high," he wrote in his complimentary copy to Jefferson. "As a patriotic legacy to my country, I hope it may prove acceptable."[3] Federalists criticized the epic, and Noah Webster faulted its atheism. Of Barlow's works, "The Vision of Columbus" and "Advice to a Raven" — a criticism of Napoleon — are highly regarded by recent critics; "The Hasty-Pudding" is widely anthologized. His poems include "The Prospect of Peace" (1778), "Poem, Spoken at the Public Commencement at Yale College" (1781), "The Conspiracy of Kings" (1792), "The Hasty-Pudding" (1793), "Advice to a Raven in Russia" (1812, published in 1838), "The Vision of Columbus" (1787), and *The Columbiad*; his "Advice to the Privileged Orders in the Several States of Europe, Resuming from the Necessity and Propriety of a General Revolution in the Principle of Government" (1792) is an essay.

Braham, John (177?–1856) ("Domum! Sweet Home! Composed and sung by Mr. Braham"), was most likely educated at the Great Synagogue in Duke's Place, Aldgate, London. At nineteen, he made his reputation in *Mahmoud*, which received its premiere (after the composer's death) on April 30, 1796, at Drury Lane. On November 26, he appeared at the King's Theatre in Gretry's *Zemire et Azor* and performed in operas by Sacchini and Martin y Soler. He was one of the few British tenors to sing, to favorable reviews, at La Scala in Milan. He toured with Nancy Storace (1797–1801), singing for Napoleon and Josephine, and meeting Napoleon's brother, Jerome; they performed in operas by Moneta and Basili. Braham impressed Giacomo Davide, the leading Italian tenor. From December 1798 to March 1799 he sang at La Scala in Nasolini's *Il Triono di Clelia*, alongside British soprano Elizabeth Billington. In August 1799, Braham and Storace moved to Livorno, where they met Horatio Nelson, Emma Hamilton, and the queen of Naples. In 1831, Braham invested disastrously in the Colosseum in the Regents Park, losing forty thousand pounds; in 1836, he built St. James' Theatre at a significant loss. In 1838, he sang the part of William Tell at Drury Lane, and in 1839 the part of Don Giovanni. His last public appearance was at a concert in March 1852. He is the author of several songs, the most notable being "The Death of Nelson" (1811).

Bryant, William Cullen (1794–1878). Bryant wrote his poem on "The Embargo" at the urging of his Federalist father, a distinguished physician in Massachussetts, though he did not include this poem in his later collections; the poem came out in two editions, the second inspired by an intensifying of the embargo legislation. Like Jefferson, Bryant was a close observer of nature, influenced by the English Romantic poets. He served as a lawyer and later as editor of the *New York Evening Post* for fifty years. His blank verse "Thanatopsis" appeared in the *North American Review* and is, perhaps, his best-known work. His collection *Poems* (1821) included "To a Waterfowl," "The Yellow Violet," and "Green River." He translated the *Iliad* (1870) and *Odyssey* (1872) into blank verse and published one of the earliest examples of American literary theory applied to poetry, *Lectures on Poetry* (1825).

Burger, Gottfried August (1747–1794) ("Leonora," "The Lass of Fair Wone"). J. T. Stanley, William Taylor, H. J. Pye, W. R. Spencer, and Walter Scott all translated Burger's ballad "Lenore" (1773) for an English audience; Jefferson clipped Spencer's translation. Charlotte Dacre translated Burger's "The Lass of Fair Wone," which Jefferson also clipped. Though Jefferson criticized the excessive use of imagination, he remained interested enough in Gothic sensationalism to collect these poems. Burger's work is the longest poem Jefferson included; the top of the clipping is carefully folded down into the book itself, exceeding the page size imposed by the scrapbook.

Burger was born at Molmerswende, near Halberstadt, son of a Lutheran pastor. In 1764, he studied theology; in 1768, he migrated to Göttingen and studied jurisprudence. He formed a friendship with Voss, the two Stolbergs, and others. He was influenced by Shakespeare and Percy. Burger married unhappily, three times, once to his wife's sister; he was a favorite poet of the German nation who nevertheless died poor.

Burns, Robert (1759–1796) ("To Mary in Heaven"). Jefferson's poems about young girls, particularly this one by Burns, reflect his interest in Mary's emotional life (Burns wrote to a woman of the same name). At the same time, Burns, like Macpherson, celebrated Scottish values. "Jefferson lauded the poetry of Robert Burns as an illustration of how the Scottish dialect he used enriched the beauty of the message he sought to convey."[4] His songs, like Thomas Moore's *Irish Melodies*, would also have appealed to Jefferson. Where Moore translated Anacreon, earning a reputation as a classicist, Burns turned to rural subjects. Poems such as "Tam O'Shanter," written in a single day, express democratic sentiments that Jefferson would have admired. Burns's ballads had an especial appeal for Jefferson, who seemed to have admired the form. Jefferson's interest in Scottish heroes is also apparent in his clipping of "The Death of Wallace."

Burns was educated at Alloway Mill and by John Murdoch. He was influenced by popular tales and the ballads and songs of Betty Davidson, an older woman who lived with the family. He read Alan Ramsay and became acquainted with sailors and smugglers. When his father died in 1784, Burns tried to farm, though he had little money to invest. His association with Jean Armour began this same year. In 1785, he produced "Epistle to Davie," "Death and Dr. Hornbook," "The Twa Herds," "The Jolly Beggars," "Halloween," "The Cotter's Saturday Night," "Holy Willie's Prayer," "The Holy Fair," and "The Address to a Mouse." In 1786, he wrote a number of satires, including "The Twa Dogs," "The Lament," and "Despondency," which recalls Regnier. Burns's affair with Highland Mary (Mary Campbell), and her subsequent death, led him to plan to leave the country. In order to emigrate to Jamaica, Burns published the Kilmarnock edition of his poems (1786). Burns was about to sail but was persuaded to stay in Scotland because of the popularity of this edition. In winter, he went to Edinburgh, where he was lionized. He returned to Jean Armour and then, after a Highland tour, went back to Edinburgh and began epistolary flirtations with "Clarinda." Burns's democratic sentiments and his close ties to the land would have had obvious appeal. He came from humble origins, identified with the Scottish folk tradition, and, like Macpherson, helped establish its literary merit.

Byrne, Charlotte (née King) (1782–1825) (pseudonyms Charlotte Dacre and Rosa Matilda; "The Poor Negro Sadi," partial translation of "Lass of Fair Wone"). Byrne was the daughter of Jonathan King, whose real name was Jacob Rey (1753–1824). Rey was a moneylender and radical writer who divorced her mother, Deborah (1785), to marry the dowager countess of Lanesborough. In 1798, Charlotte King published *Trifles of Helicon*, a volume of Gothic verse, with her sister Sophia Fortnum (1781–1805). The reappearance of poems from this volume in *Hours of Solitude* (1805) was published under the pseudonym Charlotte Dacre. She also wrote verses for the *Morning Post* and *Morning Herald* under the name Rosa Matilda, inspired perhaps by the demonic lover in Matthew Lewis's *The Monk* (1796). Dacre had three children by the editor of the *Morning Post*. *Hours of Solitude*, which included a fashionable self-portrait, influenced Byron's *Hours of Idleness* (1807). She published *The Confessions of the Nun of St. Omer* (1805); *Zofloya, or, the Moor* (1806), which influenced Shelley's Gothic novels; *Zastrozzi*; and *St. Irvyne*. In 1807, Dacre wrote *The Libertine*. The *Morning Post* defended the novel's "liberality of sentiment" and "utmost purity of morals" against those who thought it "prurient trash." Her last novel, *The Passions* (1811), exposed the danger of "swerving, even in *thought* from the sacred line of virtue." Her newspaper verse of the next decade shows her reactionary politics, and in 1822, she published a royalist poem, "George the Fourth."

Campbell, Thomas (1774–1844) ("To the Evening Star," "To Caroline," "Hohen Linden," "Exile of Erin"), was an important Scottish poet educated in Glasgow. Thomas Campbell's father's fortunes were ruined during the American Revolution. In 1797, he moved to Edinburgh to study law. *The Pleasures of Hope*, which treats the partition of Poland, appeared in 1799, going through four editions; Campbell was a lifelong supporter of the Polish people. During a tour of the Continent (1800–1801), Campbell visited Hohenlinden, in the forests of Upper Bavaria, and witnessed the battle between General Moreau's French and Bavarian forces and Austria, which resulted in a French victory. Campbell's patriotic verse earned him a government pension in 1805. Two years before that, he had married and settled in London, contributing articles to the *Edinburgh Encyclopedia* and compiling *The Annals of Great Britain from George II to the peace of Amiens*. In 1809, he published *Gertrude of Wyoming*, one of the first Romantic poems set entirely in the United States; in 1818, *Specimens of the British Poets* appeared. In 1820, he delivered a course of lectures at the Surrey Institution; from 1820 to 1830, he edited the new *Monthly Magazine*, contributing "The Last Man" and other poems. He served as lord rector of the University of Glasgow in 1827–1829 and helped found the University of London. "Hohen Linden," "Ye Mariners of England," and "The Battle of the Baltic" are his best-known poems.

Carolan, Turlough (1630–1738) ("Shelah na Gira," "The Clare Rambler," "Humours of Glen," "Gramachree," "My Lodging Is on the Cold Ground," "Boyne Water," "Erin go Brah"). Carolan was a blind Irish bard who became well known for his musical accompaniment to a number of poems included in this collection. His works appeared frequently in American newspapers. Jefferson collected Irish and Scottish verse with enthusiasm, having himself written "Thoughts on Prosody."

Chatterton, Thomas (1752–1770) ("Osmam and Zoraida," "Sympathy"). Jefferson clipped several poems by Florian, translated by Chatterton, but not listed, in Chatterton's complete works. Chatterton's "editing" of the Rowley manuscripts exhibits the kind of exhibitionist antiquarianism that Jefferson admired in Macpherson. Charges of forgery and plagiarism, some of which were revealed in Jefferson's lifetime, did not change Jefferson's view. Chatterton was born at Bristol; his father died shortly after his birth. His mother was a schoolmistress. Chatterton grew up near St. Mary Redcliffe, a church where his ancestors had been sextons or masons since the time of Queen Elizabeth. Chatterton forged a number of pseudo-antiquities, including "Elinour and Juga," which he claimed he found in Canynge's Coffer, in the muniment room of St. Mary's. In 1769, he sent Horace Walpole a "transcript" of "The Ryse of Peyncteyne yn Englande, wroten by T. Rowleie 1469, for Mastre Canynge." Walpole was duped at first, but showed the work to Mason and Gray, who judged the poems forgeries. In London, he wrote satires, squibs, stories, political essays, burlettas, epistles in Junius's style (for "Wilkes" and "liberty"), and the "Balade of Charitie." On August 24, 1770, after refusing his landlady's meal, he locked himself into his garret, tore up his papers, and was found the next morning dead of poison. They buried him in the paupers' pit of the Shoe Lane Workhouse. Scholars took sides evaluating the Rowley manuscripts, with Jacob Bryant (1781), Dean Milles (1782), and Dr. S. R. Maitland (1857) supporting their authenticity and Tyrwhitt (1777–1782) and Warton (1778–1782) denying it. Samuel Johnson was ambivalent but took the trouble to inspect the chest where the Rowley manuscripts were "discovered."

Chaucer, Geoffrey (1345–1400) ("Good Consaile"). Like many other writers in this collection, Chaucer does not appear in Jefferson's literary commonplace book, so his presence in the newspaper clippings book is of some interest. "I learn . . . with great pleasure," Jefferson wrote in 1825, "that a taste is reviving in England for the recovery of the Anglo-Saxon dialect of our language; for a mere dialect it is, as much as those of Piers Plowman, Gower, Douglas, Chaucer, Spenser, Shakespeare, Milton, for even much of Milton is already antiquated."[5]

Chaucer may have attended Oxford or Cambridge. In 1357, he was page to Lionel, duke of Clarence. In 1359, he served in the French campaign; his wife appears to have been Philippa Chaucer (a member of the queen's bed-chamber), who had two sons and a daughter. In 1369, he published *Book of the Duchess* on the death of John of Gaunt's wife. Between 1369 and 1387, he published *The Parliament of Fowls*, *The House of Fame*, *Troilus and Cressida*, and *The Legend of Good Women*, as well as the Clerk's, Man of Law's, Prioress's, Second Nun's, and Knight's Tales in the *Canterbury Tales*. He translated part of the *Roman de la Rose*, which shows his interest in French literature, though Italian writers such as Boccaccio exerted greater influence on Chaucer's imagination.

Cottle, Joseph (1770–1853) ("The Affectionate Heart"). Jefferson enjoyed this poem enough to paste two copies of it in this clippings book. Cottle was an important bookseller who encouraged Wordsworth and Coleridge at early stages in their careers; he published Coleridge's *The Watchman* (1796), enlisted subscribers, and lent Coleridge money. In 1798, Cottle formed a partnership with printer Nathaniel Biggs, with whom he printed Coleridge's *Poems* (1797), *The Lyrical Ballads* (1798), Southey's *Poems* (1799), and *Thalaba the Destroyer* (1801). Cottle's tastes as a bookseller and editor closely resemble Jefferson's own, though Wordsworth and Coleridge do not seem to have been popular enough to be published in American newspapers except, anonymously, in the *National Intelligencer*.

Between 1791 and 1800, Cottle had sold, printed, or published 114 works, mainly religious writings, medical tracts, and topical pamphlets. He published *Poems* (1795) and *Malvern Hills* (1798) with Joseph Johnson, Benjamin Flower, and H .D. Symonds; *Alfred* (1800) and *The Fall of Cambria* (1808), the latter of which Byron mocked in *English Bards and Scotch Reviewers* (1809). His grandniece remembered him as deeply religious, with long hair, a skullcap, and weak blue eyes.

Cowper, William (1731–1800) (poetry from "The Task"). Jefferson included several poems by Cowper, whose political liberalism, concern for the poor, and delicate sensibility match other works in Jefferson's newspaper clippings collection. Educated at Westminster, Cowper was destined for a legal career but failed to appear for a position as clerk in the House of Lords (1763). Morley and Mary Unwin nursed him through a subsequent mental crisis. Mrs. Unwin inspired his moral satires (1782); Lady Austen encouraged him to pen *The Task* (1785). He translated Homer (1791), along with Milton's Latin poems and French and Italian works. Cowper's "Yardley Oak" (1791) prefigures Wordsworth as a poet of nature. He also anticipated the Clapham sect and nineteenth-century evangelical movements for reform. "The Task" depicts the English park (the Throgmortons' estate) as it existed in the eighteenth century.

Dacre, Charlotte, see Byrne, Charlotte.

Dennie, Joseph (1768–1812) (numerous prose introductions to works by Thomas Moore). After graduating from Harvard, Dennie studied for law with Benjamin West of Charlestown, New Hampshire. In 1792, he began writing essays called "The Farrago," which first appeared in *Morning Ray; or, Impartial Oracle*, a newspaper from Windsor, Vermont. In 1793, he wrote for the *Eagle; or, Dartmouth Centinel*, which was located in Hanover, New Hampshire. In 1794, Dennie met Royall Tyler, who practiced law in Guilford, Vermont. Both were Federalists who collaborated on prose and poetry contributions, using the title "From the Shop of Colon and Spondee." Dennie wrote theatrical criticism for a Boston paper, the *Federal Orrery*, in early 1795. Dennie started his own magazine in Boston, the *Tablet*, in May 1795. The journal lasted for thirteen numbers, subsiding in August. Dennie then changed residence from Charlestown to Walpole, New Hampshire, where he wrote for the *New Hampshire Journal; or, Farmer's Weekly Museum*. Dennie was a lay reader for two churches in 1792, which inspired a new essay series titled "The Lay Preacher," which he began in October 1795, using a Bible passage to begin each essay. He began to oppose champions of democracy such as Thomas Paine. Dennie also served as paid editor for *Museum* from 1796 to 1799. His models were Joseph Addison and Oliver Goldsmith, earning him the sobriquet "the American Addison." In addition to Tyler, his collaborators included Roger Vose and Thomas G. Fessenden. He began a literary club that met at Crafts Tavern in Walpole.

Dennie ran for Congress unsuccessfully in 1798; a bachelor, he moved to Philadelphia in 1799 and served as private secretary to Timothy Pickering, the secretary of state, but lost his position when Pickering left the cabinet in May 1800. He then wrote for *Gazette of the United States*, a Federalist paper in Philadelphia. Dennie opposed Thomas Jefferson's election, which he connected with French revolutionary principles. In January 1801, he began the first issue of *Port Folio*, which made his reputation and was considered the leading literary journal in the United States. Writing under the name of Oliver Oldschool, Dennie praised the "simplicity" of writers such as Goldsmith and criticized the language of common people. In 1803, he was prosecuted for sedition when he predicted civil war, though he was acquitted. Dennie supported writers such as Joel Barlow, Charles Brockden Brown, Philip Freneau, and Washington Irving, who also tried, more successfully than Dennie, to be an "English man of letters in America."[6] Contributers to the *Port Folio* included John Quincy Adams, Nicholas Biddle, and Thomas Moore.

Dyer, G. ("A Glee"). *The Cabinet of Poetry, containing the best entire pieces to be found in the works of the British Poets* (1808), by Samuel Pratt, contains the following poems by Dyer: "Grongar Hill," "The Country Walk," "To Mr. Savage," and "An Epistle to a Friend in Town."

Ferguson, Elizabeth Graeme (1737–1801) ("To Della Crusca" [Robert Merry]), is the author of *Poems on Several Occasions* (1772).

Fessenden, Thomas Green (1771–1837) ("Epigram," "Seduction"), was a writer, inventor, and lawyer, born in Walpole, New Hampshire. He attended Dartmouth (1792–1796), paying for his expenses by teaching in a village school and giving evening lessons in the writing of psalms. Fessenden also studied with Nathaniel Chipman at Rutland, Vermont (1796). Between 1795 and 1800, Fessenden published poetry in serials, broadsides, and pamphlets. "Jonathan's Courtship" (1795) earned the praise of Hawthorne, who enjoyed the depiction of American rustic manners and colloquial diction. "The Rutland Ode" was a popular, early political poem of Fessenden's. This anti-French work was set to music and performed at Rutland's Fourth of July celebration in 1798. In 1801, Fessenden traveled to England to apply for a patent on a hydraulic pump constructed by Barnabas Langdon of Vermont. Without funds in England and with few prospects, Fessenden turned to literature and wrote *Terrible Tractoration!!* (1803), in which he satirized the sanguine hopes of science at the time. "He defended Dr. Elisha Perkins' 'Metallic Tractors' — a pair of nail-like metal pieces supposed to relieve pain by galvanic action when applied to an inflamed spot — by having the unsympathetic persona of Dr. Christopher Caustic attack the medical device."[7] Fessenden became known as "The American Butler" for his successful use of the verse form that English poet Samuel Butler (d. 1680) popularized in "Hudibras." Fessenden published *Original Poems* (1804), which included a preface critical of Jefferson's administration. These pieces included poems published separately in newspapers before he had traveled to England. In 1804, Fessenden returned from England to Boston, publishing *Democracy Unveiled* (1805) the following year, in which he used the persona of Christopher Caustic to satirize Jeffersonian democracy, including cantos titled "Mobocracy" and "The Jeffersoniad." Fessenden also attempted to establish a Federalist paper in New York, the *Weekly Inspector* (1806–1807). *The Inspector* failed because Fessenden's high-Federalist opinions were unpopular in democratic New York, and because he was competing with the periodical *Salmagundi* (1807–1808). In 1808, with *Register of Arts* (1808), he shifted his attention from politics to scientific discoveries once again. Between 1809 and 1822, Fessenden lived in Brattleboro and Bellows Falls, Vermont. He published *Essay on the Law of Patents for New Inventions* (1810). At forty-two, he married twenty-eight-year-old Lydia Tuttle of Littleton, Massachusetts. He edited two weekly papers, the *Brattleboro Reporter* (1815–1816) and the *Vermont Intelligencer* (1817–1822). He produced *The American Clerk's Companion* (1815), a collection of legal forms, and *The Husbandman and Housewife* (1820), which contained directions for agriculture. Fessenden defended farming in the *New England Farmer*, which became a model of its kind, promoting scientific agricultural methods. Fessenden also helped promote silk manufacturing in the Massachusetts Silk Company in 1836. In 1830, he produced a patent for "Portable Steam and Hot Water Stove." He was elected to the Massachusetts legislature in 1835. Hawthorne lodged in the Fessenden house for a few months in 1836 and commented on the hot-water stove that Fessenden kept in his kitchen, along with writing a sympathetic sketch of his career in 1838. Jefferson also clipped "Ode," "Morning," and "Ode" (Massachussetts Charitable Fire Society).[8]

Florian, Jean P. Claris de (1755–1794) ("Osmam and Zorida"). French novelist and poet.

Fox, Charles James (1749–1806) ("On the Death of Lord Nelson"), was an English liberal statesman, the third son of first Lord Holland. Born in London and educated at Eton and Hertford College, Oxford, he became MP for Midhurst at nineteen and supported Lord North, under whose leadership he became a lord of the admiralty. In 1772, he resigned, but the next year was made a commissioner of the treasury before being dismissed by North in 1775. After North's departure (1782), he was one of the secretaries of state and formed a coalition with North in 1783, resuming his former office. Pitt came into power in 1784. The regency, the trial of Warren Hastings, and the French Revolution led to protracted conflict with Pitt. He opposed the American war and the war with France, advocating nonintervention. After Pitt's death in January 1806, Fox began negotiations with France, but he died that same year. His last bill proposed the abolition of the slave trade. He was buried near Pitt, in Westminster Abbey.

Freneau, Philip (1752–1832) ("The Jug of Rum"). Editor of the *National Gazette* (1791–1793), Freneau was a friend of James Madison and Jefferson. Jefferson claimed that Freneau's newspaper prevented the United States from "galloping fast into monarchy." Hamilton later accused Jefferson of setting up Freneau's paper, which Freneau denied under oath. In 1768, Freneau enrolled in the College of New Jersey, later named Princeton University, where he was a precocious and respected student. At college, Freneau's friends included

James Madison, Hugh Henry Brackenridge, and William Bradford. In 1775, he published patriotic poems such as "American Liberty" and "General Gage's Soliloquy," which earned him the sobriquet "Poet of the Revolution." He worked as secretary to a prominent planter in Santa Cruz, and wrote verse on the cruelty of slavery. "Jamaica Funeral" was written during this time. In May 1780, he served on the *Aurora*, which was captured by the British; his 1781 work "The British Prison-Ship" was inspired by this event. Freneau published two volumes of poetry before his death in a snowstorm.

Grainger, Dr. James (1721?–1767) ("Bryan and Pereene. A West-Indian Ballad, Founded on a real fact, in the Island of St. Christophers"). Grainger was a physician and poet, born in Dunse, Scotland, whose liberal beliefs echoed Jefferson's own. He served as a surgeon during the rebellion in Scotland and published a treatise in Latin on diseases related to army life (1753). While residing in London, Dr. Grainger became acquainted with Shenstone, Dr. Percy, Glover, Dr. Johnson, and Sir Joshua Reynolds. After publishing "Ode on Solitude," which gained positive notice, he helped Miller complete the second volume of Maitland's *History of Scotland*. In 1758, he published a translation of the "Elegies of Tibullus." He became embroiled in a controversy with Smollett shortly after this, though the origins of the quarrel are not known.

Soon after publishing "Elegies," Dr Grainger visited St. Christophers Island as a physician and planter. Returning to England, he published "Sugar Cane,"a summary of his West India experience. In the same year (1764), he also produced "An Essay on the more common West India diseases, and the remedies which that country itself produces; to which are added, some hints on the management of Negroes." Besides these works, Dr. Grainger's "Bryan and Pereene" was a very popular ballad collected in a number of miscellanies in the 1790s. After a short residence in England, he returned to St. Christophers, where he died on December 24, 1767.

Gurney, G. H. or Hudson (1775–1864), was the translator of "Cupid and Psyche: A Mythological Tale" from *The Golden Ass of Apuleius* and other works.

Hayley, William ("Charm for Ennui: A Matrimonial Ballad"). Jefferson seems to have admired Hayley's conventional sentiments on marriage. Hayley could recognize genius and sometimes maddened the artists he patronized by setting them to tasks they could not perform, as Blake once observed. A poet and biographer who was a close friend of William Blake and William Cowper, Hayley moved in a circle of painters and artists for whom he provided patronage. George Romney painted him in a gathering at Hayley's Sussex estate, Eartham, in summer 1792 with Cowper and Charlotte Smith. He helped Charlotte Smith publish her first volume of poems by accepting her dedication; Smith had Dodsley print the poems at her expense. Hayley came in touch with Cowper when both were preparing editions of Milton for the press and invited him to Sussex. This was the first time Cowper had left home in twenty-five years. According to the *Dictionary of National Biography*, Hayley secured a royal pension of three hundred pounds for Cowper in 1794; he also wrote a memorial inscription on Cowper's tomb in 1800, along with the poet's biography (1803), which revealed the charm of Cowper's letters. Benjamin Franklin received a copy of *Poems* in 1780. Published in 1785, "The Task" condemned slavery and advocated the humane treatment of animals.

Hindley, John Haddon (1765–1827) (pseudonym Hafiz), was born in Manchester, the son of Charles Hindley, a cloth merchant. He enrolled in Brasenose College on April 21, 1784, graduating with a BA (1788) and MA (1790). He became chaplain of Manchester Collegiate Church and librarian of Chetham's Library. The valuable Oriental manuscripts at Chetham's Library led Hindley to study Persian. He translated several books from Persian, including works by Hafiz, Attar, and Jami. His versions from Hafiz are in both prose and verse. Several other poets used this pen name, which means "observer," including Thomas Stott, an Irish poet. Hindley seems the most likely author of the Joseph translations that Jefferson collected and contrasted with translations by William Jones, another Orientalist.

Holcroft, Fanny (1780–1844) ("The Madagascar Mother"). Fanny was the daughter of Holcroft's third wife, Dinah, and was baptized on June 11, 1785, at St. Andrew's, Holborn, London. She was devoted to her father, from whom she received a broad education in modern languages and the arts; she shared her father's liberal political opinions and assisted his literary work. In 1802, William Godwin recommended her as governess for Lady Mountcashel, a position once held by Mary Wollstonecraft, but Holcroft lost the job when *The Times* accused her of being a French spy. Fanny Holcroft provided the incidental music for her father's successful melodrama, *The Lady of the Rock* (1805). She also wrote translations of politically liberal plays by Alfieri, Weisse, Lessing, Calderon, and Moratin for her father's periodical *The Theatrical Recorder* (1805–1806). She published *Memoirs of the Life of the Great Conde* (1807), a translation of a biography of the French prince and military leader during the seventeenth-century French civil wars. After her father's death, Fanny Holcroft published two novels, *The Wife and the Lover: A Novel* (three volumes, 1813) and *Fortitude and Frailty: A Novel* (four volumes, 1817), dedicated to her father's memory.

Hopkins, Lemuel (1750–1801) (Jack Ratline, "A Tickler for Timothy"). One of the Connecticut Wits and a Yale graduate, Hopkins collaborated with several others in writing popular political satires. He was one of the most distinguished physicians of his time, founding the Medical Society of Connecticut. "A Tickler for Timothy" has been traced to him in the *Dictionary of American Biography*, for he was satirizing democratic senators who opposed Jay's treaty. The Connecticut Wits were at first devoted to modernizing the Yale curriculum and declaring the independence of American letters. They jointly wrote a number of works including *The Anarchiad* (in the *New Haven Gazette*, 1786–1787), *The Political Greenhouse* (in the *Connecticut Courant*, 1799), and *The Echo* (in the *American Mercury*, 1791–1805). Members of the group included Timothy Dwight, David Humphreys, John Trumbull, Lemuel Hopkins, Richard Alsop, and Theodore Dwight. Joel Barlow, once a member, changed his views during the French Revolution and supported Jefferson's policies, visiting him at Monticello after his seventeen-year absence in Europe.

Jones, Sir William (1746–1794) ("Persian Gazel"), was a British Orientalist who helped trace Indo-European languages to a common root. Educated at Harrow and University College, Oxford (1765), he became tutor to the son of Earl Spencer; in 1774 he was called to the bar; and in 1776 became commissioner of bankrupts, publishing *Persian Grammar* (1772), *Latin Commentaries on Asiatic Poetry* (1774), and translations of seven ancient Arabic poems (1780). He became a judge in the Supreme Court of Judicature in Bengal, and was knighted in 1783. He studied Sanskrit and was the first to point out its resemblance to Latin and Greek (1787). He established the Asiatic Society of Bengal (1784), serving as the first president. He completed translations of *Sakuntala*, the *Hitopadesa*, parts of the Vedas, and the Manu, before his death.

Kelly, Hugh (1739–1777) ("The Bottle"). Hugh Kelly was a London journalist and playwright who had the type of itinerant career one notes in Joel Barlow and Philip Freneau on the American side of the Atlantic. Jefferson enjoyed a number of poems on the subject of drinking, including Freneau's "Jug of Rum" and the anonymous "Drunkenness Cured." In 1766, Kelly published "Thespis," a couplet poem examining the performance of Drury Lane actors, which won David Garrick's favorable notice. The poem is in the tradition of Charles Churchill's "The Rosciad." Under the pseudonym Numa, Kelly published a series of letters in the *Public Advertiser* supporting Britain's colonial policies. In 1767, he published his only novel, *Memoirs of a Magdalen, or, The History of Louisa Mildmay* (two volumes), which was influenced by Samuel Richardson. Kelly's first play, *False Delicacy*, opened in January 1768 and ran for twenty nights. Garrick's preference for Kelly's play over Goldsmith's *The Good Natur'd Man* sowed enmity between Kelly and Goldsmith, which Goldsmith described in his poem "The Retaliation." Kelly's *False Delicacy* makes use of courtship plots to make comic points, while Goldsmith, R. B. Sheridan and Samuel Foote were still using class and wealth as their comic resources for scenes of duplicity and deception."[9] Kelly wrote *A Word to the Wise* and *The School for Wives* (1774), the most successful drama in Drury Lane's 1773–1774 season. The play ran for twenty-four nights; it was printed in five editions and seen in 1805 in Bath. In 1773, Kelly worked for the *General Evening Post*; his next drama was *The Romance of the Hour* (1774); his final production was *The Man of Reason* (1776), which was unsuccessful. He was financially successful, earning between two and three hundred pounds a year. *The Works of Hugh Kelly*, to which is prefixed *The Life of the Author*, was published in 1778 for the benefit of his widow, a year after his death in 1777.

La Fontaine, Jean de (1621–1695) ("The Spirit of Contradiction"). Born in Champagne, La Fontaine produced a verse translation of Terence's *The Eunuch*; Fouquet became his patron. His *Contes et nouvelles en vers* appeared in 1665, his *Fables choises mises en vers* in 1668, and his *Amours de Psyche et de Cupidon* in 1669. Frivolous and dissipated, this poem parodies the trait of querulousness that Jefferson and Franklin went out of their way, as diplomats in Paris, to avoid.

Macdonald, Andrew (1757–1790) ("A Matrimonial Thought"), was a poet and playwright who wrote under the name Matthew Bramble; the pseudonym may well come from Smollett's *Humphrey Clinker*. Educated at Leith and at Edinburgh University, under the sponsorship of Bishop Forbes of Ross and Caithness, who shared his father's Stuart sympathies, Macdonald became a deacon in the Scottish Episcopal church in 1775. In 1782, he published *Velina, a Poetical Fragment*, and the following year, *The Independent*, a novel. His tragedy, *Vimonda*, was performed in Edinburgh. As Matthew Bramble, he wrote poetic burlesques modeled on John Wolcot (Peter Pindar), which brought him popularity but little money. He died on August 22, 1790, leaving a widow and infant daughter. His sermons were published (1790), as well as his *Miscellaneous Works* (1791).

Macpherson, James (1736–1796). Jefferson admired Macpherson's "translations" of a third-century Celtic bard. Recent scholars have shown that Macpherson did considerable archival and anthropological work for this project, visiting the homes of Scottish peasants familiar with oral traditions. Nevertheless, Macpherson's poems owe more to his own imagination and to classical and biblical precedent than they do to the third century. Some scholars have expressed annoyance that Macpherson appropriated Irish poetry for Scottish purposes and Scottish nationalism. In his day, Macpherson's *Fragments of Ancient Poetry Collected in the Highlands of Scotland and Translated from Gaelic or Erse Language* (1760) received favorable notice. In the interests of Scottish pride, the rhetorician Hugh Blair, another writer Jefferson admired, took up Macpherson's cause and encouraged Macpherson to produce *Fingal, An Ancient Epic Poem* (1762), which included a number of shorter poems. Samuel Johnson doubted the work's authenticity, as he would later doubt Chatterton's, but Macpherson was admired by Thomas Gray, Goethe, and Napoleon, who appreciated his nationalist themes regardless of the poem's origins.

Jefferson's literary commonplace book shows fourteen entries from Macpherson, and Jefferson even wrote to Macpherson's brother, Charles, to obtain information about their veracity. "I am not ashamed to own that I think this rude bard of the North the greatest Poet that has ever existed. Merely for the pleasure of reading his works I am become desirous of learning the language in which he sung and of possessing his songs in their original form." When the marquis de Chastellux visited Jefferson at Monticello in 1782, they spoke positively of the poetry of Ossian. "It was a spark of electricity which passed rapidly from one to the other," Jefferson remembered. "We recalled the passages of those sublime poems which had particularly struck us, and we recited them for the benefit of my traveling companions. . . ." Jefferson placed Macpherson at the level of Milton, Pope, and Swift, recommending that Peter Carr, his nephew, examine the work for its style. After the poems were proved fraudulent, Jefferson did not retract his opinion. Of Frances Wright's *A Few Days in Athens*, he wrote that "like Ossian, if not ancient, it is equal to the best morsels of antiquity." Macpherson later became a member of Parliament.[10]

Matilda, Rosa ("The Lass of Fair Wone," "The Poor Negro Sadi"). See Byrne, Charlotte.

Mellen, Henry (1757–1809) ("The Embargo"). Henry Mellen's poem ridiculed Jefferson's policy on the embargo and produced Simon Pepperpot's satiric response. He is the author of "Sketches of Masonic History," an oration delivered July 25, 1798, at St. John's Chapel, Portsmouth, before the Grand Lodge of New Hampshire.

Montgomery, James (1771–1854) ("Remonstrance to Winter," "The Fowler," "The Grave," "The Wanderer of Switzerland"), a hymn writer and poet, was born in Irvine, Ayrshire, the second of four children by John Montgomery (1734–1791) and his wife Mary, née Blackley (d. 1790). Montgomery's parents, who did not see their son after 1783, served as missionaries in Barbados, where they died when he was twenty. By the age of fifteen, Montgomery composed three volumes of poems. He served as an apprentice to a baker in 1787; he played oboe and composed verses. In April 1792, he secured work with the *Sheffield Register*, edited by the radical reformer Joseph Gales, who fled to America to escape prosecution for alleged sedition. Montgomery edited a reconstituted version, called the *Sheffield Iris*. Benjamin Naylor, a Unitarian minister, helped finance the paper for a year. In January 1795, he was prosecuted for publishing a supposedly seditious poem that hailed the fall of the Bastille. In January 1796, he reported the militia's use of arms against a Sheffield crowd and served six months in York. The government's prosecution of dissidents included the use of spies, however, and Montgomery earned the respect even of the man he libeled, Colonel Athorpe, commander of the militia. In *Prison Amusements* (1797), he wrote about his incarceration; he also published *The Whisperer* (1798), a volume of essays. He founded the Sheffield Literary and Philosophical Society and worked for the abolition of the slave trade. Deeply religious, he was ecumenical, moving among Methodist, Baptist, and Anglican chapels. He was readmitted as a member of the Moravian Church in 1814.

The Ocean was published in 1805. *The Wanderer of Switzerland and other Poems* (1806) made him a national figure. By 1850, it ran to thirteen editions. Southey and Scott praised it; Byron wrote that *The Wanderer* "was worth more than a thousand Lyrical Ballads."[11] The poems addressed Britain's concern for liberty, recently threatened by Napoleon's subjugation of Switzerland. Montgomery wrote "The West Indies" (1809) to support the abolition of the slave trade. A religious epic, "The World Before the Flood," appeared in 1812; *Greenland* (1819), in heroic couplets, treats the accomplishments of Moravian missionaries in Greenland. "The Pelican Island" (1827) explores the topic of evolution in blank verse. "The Grave" (1806) and "The Peak Mountains" (1812) were popular shorter pieces. The fact that Jefferson included "The Grave" in his collection shows that he followed the development of poetry while president. Like Byron, Jefferson admired "The Wanderer of Switzerland"; he also clipped "The Fowler." Montgomery contributed reviews to *The Eclectic Review* (1833) and composed articles on Dante, Ariosto, and Tasso for Lardner's *Cabinet Cyclopedia*. As a hymnist, he is valued alongside Wesley and Watts. *The Christian Psalmist* (1825) includes such works as "Angels from the Realm of Glory." Montgomery received a pension of 150 pounds from Robert Peel.

Prone to melancholy and hypochondria, he nevertheless succeeded as a small businessman. "He was, perhaps, too sociable, too fond of local position, to be a really good poet," his most recent biographer concluded.[12]

Moore, Thomas (1779–1852) ("Song," "Rondeau," "Stanzas," "A Ballad," "Love and Reason," "The Lake of the Dismal Swamp"). Jefferson collected Moore's "translations" from Anacreon and his Irish melodies. With the exception of Peter Pindar (who has seventeen entries), Moore is the poet most often represented in Jefferson's volume, with more than ten poems. The two met in Washington, DC, when Moore was staying with the British ambassador, Anthony Merry, who had felt slighted by the republican president when he failed to greet him with the diplomatic courtesy he expected. Anthony Merry and his wife prepared Thomas Moore to dislike Jefferson, and the Irish poet promptly took offense at Jefferson's apparent aloofness. The feeling was not reciprocated, for Jefferson admired Moore's anacreontic verses, his *Two-Penny Post-Bag* (1812) for its mockery of English royalty, and *Irish Melodies* (1807–1834), which survive in Monticello scrapbooks and music books. As the mother of five in Boston in 1831, Ellen Coolidge, Jefferson's granddaughter, gathered the words of two "wilde Moore-ish" songs, admitting that "Ill as I thought of Moore the man, I greatly admired his poetry."[13] Jefferson's daughter Martha regretted the reception of Moore as late as 1807, when a new British diplomat, Augustus Foster, recorded her reaction: "She told me she had much regretted Mr. Moore's reception had not been more flattering to him, but that from his low stature and youthful appearance her father had taken him for a boy, and as he had always professed to be of the liberal party in England he felt rather surprised at this bitter censure of a person so devoted to the cause of liberty as was the President." Moore noted: "My single interview with this remarkable person was of very short duration; but to have seen and spoken to the man who drew up the Declaration of Independence was an event not to be forgotten."[14]

The son of a Dublin grocer, Moore attended Trinity College, Cambridge, and a statue of him can be seen just outside the entrance. His translation of *Anacreon* (1800) made his reputation, though these poems are now known to be written by Roman and Byzantine poets rather than by the sixth-century Greek poet Anacreon. Moore was appointed registrar of the admiralty court at Bermuda; he arranged for a deputy and toured the United States and Canada, mocking Jefferson and embracing Jefferson's Federalist critic Joseph Dennie and his circle in Philadelphia. Moore wrote damaging stanzas on Jefferson's relations with Sally Hemings and was harshly critical of the poor roads and lack of culture among American inhabitants he met. He later regretted his remarks against America, especially since he came to admire aspects of the American democratic experiment. In 1811, he married actress Bessy Dyke, who was thirty years younger than him, and settled in Wiltshire. In 1817, *Lalla Rookh* appeared, for which Longmans had paid three hundred guineas; *Irish Melodies* was also commercially successful, bringing a yearly income. But Moore's Bermuda deputy embezzled a large sum of money, and in 1819, to avoid arrest, he visited Italy and Paris, where he met Byron, with whom he had become friendly as early as 1807 after nearly fighting a duel with him (due to Byron's mockery of Moore's duel with Francis Jeffrey). He returned in 1822 to Wiltshire, where he spent his last thirty years. He wrote lives of Sheridan, Byron, and other works. In 1835, he received a pension of three hundred pounds. His two sons died shortly before his own death. Moore was as popular as Byron in his day. His poetry has been characterized as "light, airy, graceful, but soulless," though American newspapers praise his gifts.[15]

Osborn, Selleck (1783–1826) ("On Time," "Seduction"). Born in Trumbull, Connecticut, Osborn was educated in England and worked in a printing office in Danbury, Connecticut, at the age of twelve. His name is misspelled "Sellick Osborn[e]" in newspapers; his 1823 publication is the source for the spelling here. From June 19, 1802, to January 3, 1803, he edited the *Suffolk County Herald* in Sag Harbor, New York. In 1805, he joined Timothy Ashley in editing the *Litchfield Witness*. Litchfield included a number of outspoken Federalists who were openly critical of Thomas Jefferson. Democrats helped found the *Witness* to expose Federalist bias. One victim of his anti-Federalist satire was Julius "Crowbar Justice" Deming, who sued the editors for libel. Ashley paid the fine, but Osborn continued to edit the journal from prison and soon became a martyr to the Democratic party. John C. Calhoun, then studying law at Litchfield, compared him to John Wilkes. A committee visited his jail, and weekly bulletins circulated describing his mistreatment. On August 6, 1806, public indignation led to his release; he resumed control of the *Witness*, which folded in the summer of 1807.

Osborn served as a lieutenant in the U.S. Army (1808) and was promoted in February 1811. In 1810, he married Mary, daughter of Barnabas Hammond, by whom he had two children. He served in the War of 1812 in Canada, but left the service in 1814 and returned to journalism, editing a paper in Bennington, Vermont. For three years (1817–1820), he served as owner and editor of the *American Watchman* in Wilmington, Delaware. In 1823–1824, he used his journalistic gifts to support his friend John C. Calhoun, editing and printing the *New York Patriot*.

Osborn wrote verses as a young man and included his verse in the poet's corner portion of the newspapers he edited. His most popular poem was "The

Ruins." He published *Poems, Moral, Sentimental, and Satirical* in Boston in 1823. In the preface to that work, he indicated his preference for the poetry of Milton, Young, and Goldsmith over Byron, Monk Lewis, and Gothic novelists. Osborn published many poems, the fair copies of which he lost; he was content, he claimed, to see them in print and afterward indifferent as to their fate: "Such as I have reclaimed have been collected with much labor and considerable expense."[16] In several of his poems, which range in quality, Osborn celebrated the Sabbath morning before the arrival of vice-ridden man; he mocked officious neighbors who, ignorant of their status, saw tales of intrigue in the embrace of husband and wife; and praised the army and navy. In "Peace," he took a Jeffersonian perspective on war with England, declaring his pleasure at learning that war was not necessary. His verse is sunnier than Fessenden's or Tyler's, recalling George Crabbe and Leigh Hunt; Jefferson also clipped Osborn's "The Sailor," which was written in prison.[17]

Opie, Amelia (1769–1853) ("The Negro Boy's Tale," "Song"). Jefferson did not comment directly on Amelia Opie, but she belonged to an intellectual circle that would have appealed to him. In 1798, she married John Opie, a protégé of John Wolcot (Peter Pindar), and associated with the Godwin circle, which included Thomas Holcroft, Elizabeth Inchbald, and Mary Wollstonecraft. They met Charles James Fox, Benjamin West, the Polish patriot Kosciuszko, the painter David, the actor Talma, and Helen Maria Williams in Paris in 1802. That year, she published "An Elegy to the Memory of the Late Duke of Bedford," which celebrates a man who was also championed by Lady Melbourne (Bedford's lover). *The Father and Daughter* was highly successful, and turned into a play titled *Smiles and Tears* (1815) by Maria Kemble; W. T. Moncrieff adapted a "domestic drama" titled *The Lear of Private Life*, which was based on it. *Adeline Mowbray* is a work inspired, in part, by the marriage of William Godwin and Mary Wollstonecraft. Other works include *Simple Tales* (four volumes, 1806), *Tales of Real Life* (1813), *New Tales* (1818), and *Tales of the Heart* (1820). Her three-volume novels included *Temper, or, Domestic Scenes: a Tale* (1812), *Valentine's Eve* (1816), and *Madeline: a Tale* (1822). An anonymously published novel titled *Self-Delusion* (1823) was attributed to her by the *Ladies' Monthly Museum* (1823). Her story "The Ruffian Boy" was turned into a chapbook by Sarah Wilkinson and dramatized by Thomas Dibdin and Edward Fitzball (1820).

After the period during which Jefferson collected her verse (1800–1808), Opie became friendly with Richard Brinsley Sheridan, Germaine de Staël, Lord Byron, and Walter Scott. She published *The Warrior's Return, and other Poems*

(1808) during the last year of Jefferson's presidency. This collection includes poems that treat pacificism ("The Warrior's Return," "Lines on the Opening of a Spring Campaign"), slavery ("The Lucayan's Song"), political violence ("Lines on the Place de La Concorde at Paris"), and courtly decadence ("To Lothario" and other songs). She composed several verse letters supposedly written by Mary, queen of Scots, for *The European Magazine* (1823). She supported religious toleration, as Jefferson did, and Catholic emancipation. "The Negro Boy's Tale" became popular as a children's poem when published by Harvey and Darton. She composed another anti-slavery poem titled "The Black Man's Lament, or, How to Make Sugar" (1826). "Illustrations of Lying in All Its Branches" (1825) is an interesting satire exposing social hypocrisy. *Lays for the Dead* (1834) was her last collection of poems. According to the *New Dictionary of National Biography*, her tales and novels made Opie the most respected woman fiction writer of the early nineteenth century after Maria Edgeworth.

Owenson, Sydney, Lady Morgan (1777–1859) ("Dawn"). Sydney Owenson produced more than seventy volumes of fiction, poetry, nonfiction prose, and opera. She was the first woman to be granted a pension for her services to literature, in 1837. Her *Poems* appeared in 1801. She collected Irish tunes, composed lyrics, and published them; her example was copied by Thomas Moore. Her first novel was *St. Clair, or the Heiress of Desmond* (1803), an imitation of the *Sorrows of Werther*. Her novel *The Novice of St. Dominick* was very successful and enjoyed by William Pitt; Richard Phillips, her publisher, offered her three hundred pounds for *The Wild Irish Girl* (1806); Charles Maturin imitated her work, with a novel called *The Wild Irish Boy* (1808). Her opera, *The First Attempt*, appeared at the Theatre Royal, Dublin, March 4, 1807. She then published *The Lay of an Irish Harp; or Metrical Fragments*, her most important collection of poems. *The Poetical Register* assessed her poetry as follows: "In most of these little poems there is great elegance, fancy, command of language, and melody of versification. Their chief fault is an occasional glitter and gaudiness, which, in her future compositions, Miss Owenson will do well to avoid. Let her beware of ridicule, by enlisting in the band of Della Cruscan rhymes. She has talents to entitle her to hold a respectable rank among female authors."[18] *The Monthly Review*, with an eye on the political dimension of her verse (her nationalism), wrote that her fault was "the language of feeling carried to excess."[19] Percy Shelley enjoyed *The Missionary* (1811), an Indian novel. "Since I have read this book I have read no other — but I have thought strangely," he wrote to Hogg in June 1811. She was a friend of Mary Tighe, Lady Caroline Lamb, and Madame de Stael.

Paine, Robert Treat (1731–1840) ("Song in Celebration of July 4th"). Educated at Boston Latin School, Robert Treat Paine graduated from Harvard at eighteen and taught theology. He enrolled as a merchant marine to strengthen his constitution, visiting the southern colonies, Spain, the Azores, and England. He became a lawyer in Massachusetts in 1757, working in Portland, Maine, and Taunton, Massachusetts. He served as a prosecuting attorney in the trial of the British soldiers involved in the Boston Massacre. He attended the first Continental Congress, writing the final appeal to the king, known as the Olive Branch Petition, in 1775. Paine was reelected to represent Massachusetts at the Continental Congress of 1776. He participated in the debates leading to the resolution for independence, and his signature appears on the Declaration of Independence. According to comments made by Benjamin Rush, Paine was known in Congress as the "Objection Maker," because of his habit of frequent objections to the proposals of others. In 1777, he was elected attorney general of the state of Massachusetts. He was then serving on the legislative committee to draft the first constitution of the state under the new federation. In 1780, he moved back to Boston, where he helped found the American Academy of Arts and Sciences. Governor Hancock offered him an appointment to the bench of the Supreme Court in 1783. He turned this offer down but accepted it, when renewed, in 1796. After fourteen years in the job, he retired due to failing health, dying at age eighty-three.

Paine, Thomas (1737–1809) ("Land of Love and Liberty"). Born in Thetford, Norfolk, Thomas Paine was the son of a Quaker. In England, he met Benjamin Franklin, who encouraged him to emigrate. Paine was an officer of the excise before he took up political pamphleteering, shortly after his arrival in Philadelphia in 1774. His first pamphlet was *African Slavery in America*, which criticized slavery as an institution as unjust and inhumane. He became co-editor of the *Pennsylvania Magazine*. On January 10, 1776, he published *Common Sense*, which influenced the Declaration of Independence. Paine joined the Continental army and published his sixteen *American Crisis* papers between 1776 and 1783. In 1777, he served as secretary of the Committee of Foreign Affairs in Congress, before being dismissed from that post in 1779 because he disclosed secret information.

In 1787, Paine left for England to raise funds for the construction of a bridge he had designed. Between March 1791 and February 1792, he published numerous editions of his *Rights of Man*, in which he defended the French Revolution against the attacks by Edmund Burke, in Burke's *Reflections on the Revolution in France*. Paine's work was banned in England because it opposed monarchy. Elected to the National Convention in Paris, Paine opposed the execution of Louis XVI, for which Robespierre imprisoned him in 1793. During his incarceration, he wrote *The Age of Reason*, which earned him the title of atheist. Jefferson met Paine when the former served as ambassador to France. Paine embarrassed Jefferson, however, by including Jefferson's private letter praising *Rights of Man* in a preface to Paine's new edition. In 1802, Jefferson invited Paine to return to the United States, where he continued his critical writings against the Federalists and on religious superstition. After his death in New York City on June 8, 1809, he was regarded as someone who did "some good and much harm." Jefferson valued Paine as an inventor and a writer, though relations between the two seem to have cooled in the early 1800s.

Pindar, Peter (John Wolcot) (1738–1819) ("The Owl and the Parrot," "Conscience," "Tooth-Ache," "A Cure for Bad Razors," "Alexander's Feast"). Jefferson clipped seventeen poems by Peter Pindar, more than any other poet in his collection. Like the American editors who published his work, Jefferson seems to have admired Peter Pindar's shrewd insights into human nature. Both Jefferson and Pindar admired General Kosciuzko, who visited Pindar in London. The liberal tone of Pindar's satire sustained Kosciuzko during his imprisonment in Russia. Peter Pindar was the pen name for John Wolcot, an English satirist, born at Dodbrooke, Devon, who studied medicine for seven years and took his MD at Aberdeen (1767). He traveled to Jamaica, where he became physician-general of the island. He returned to England to take orders, but began medical practice at Truro. He discovered John Opie (Amelia's future husband) and moved to London with him in 1780, where he began writing squibs and satires in verse. His sixty or seventy poetical pamphlets (1778–1818) include *The Lousiad*, *The Apple-Dumplings and a King*, *Whitbread's Brewery visited by their majesties*, *Bozzy and Piozzi*, and *Lyrical Odes on the Royal Academy Exhibitions*. Witty, he was nevertheless considered "coarse" and "ephemeral" by *Chambers Biographical Dictionary*.

Pratt, Samuel Jackson (1749–1814). Pratt was a poet, essayist, biographer, playwright, and novelist. He contributed to the *Morning Post* (where Robinson was poetry editor) and wrote Robinson's epitaph.

Pye, H. J. (1745–1813). Born in London, Pye studied at Magdalen College, Oxford. He is the author of *Alfred: An Epic* (1801) as well as numerous birthday and New Year's odes.

Ratline, Jack ("A Tickler for Timothy"). See Hopkins, Lemuel.

Ray, William (1771–1827) ("Cash," "Patriotic Song, by William Ray," "War, or a prospect of it"). Ray was the author of *Poems on Various Subjects* (1826). He supported Jefferson's policies. His experiences as a prisoner in Tripoli would have brought home to him the importance of Jefferson's embargo and of fighting the impressment of American sailors. Ray was strongly in the Jeffersonian camp: "More free than the Mohawk that glides thro' our plains, / Republicans! Meet round this joyous libation," he wrote. "While Jefferson o'er us sublimely sits head, / No treason the league-union's states can dissever; / Of freedom the guardian — of tyrants the dread — / His name will grow dearer and dearer forever."[20] When war with Great Britain threatened in 1808, Ray published "War, or a Prospect of it." The last lines were "Unite, and side by side / Meet vict'ry or your graves; / That moment we in War divide, / That moment we are slaves."

Robinson, Mary (1758–1800) ("The Old Beggar"), attended a school in Bristol run by Hannah More's sisters. Her first volume, *Poems* (1775), was supported, in part, by Georgiana, duchess of Devonshire; she then published *Captivity: A Poem* (1777). Through Garrick and Sheridan, Mary Robinson worked as an actress at Drury Lane, attracting the attention of the prince regent when she played the part of Perdita in 1779. She obtained five thousand pounds from the royal family after the Prince Regent abandoned her; subsequent lovers include Charles James Fox and Colonel Bastre Tarleton, a war hero who led an advance guard assigned the task of driving Jefferson from his home at Monticello. At twenty-four, Robinson suffered a miscarriage from Tarleton's child that left her paralyzed from the waist down. She spent several years on the Continent with Tarleton before returning to England in 1788. Between 1775 and 1800, she produced six volumes of poetry, eight novels, and two plays. Her novel *Vancenza, or The Dangers of Credulity* (1792) sold out in a day. Her *Poems* (1791) brought together her Della Cruscan poetry and sold very well; she composed *Sappho and Phaon* (1796) when she was already altering her style. Journalists wrote about her as follows: "Mrs. R was one of the chief disciples of what was called the Della Cruscan School, a sect of harmonious drivellers, who bewitched the idle multitude for a time with a sweet sound which passed for fine poetry, and an extravagant and affected cant which was mistaken for the language of exquisite feeling."[21] Despite such misplaced condescension, she earned the respect of fellow poets. Coleridge sent her a manuscript copy of "Kubla Khan." Her *Lyrical Tales* (1800) almost inspired Wordsworth to change the title of the second edition of *Lyrical Ballads*.[22] Coleridge described her as "a woman of undoubted genius," in January 1800.[23]

Robinson was friends with Samuel Jackson Pratt, to whom she wrote in 1800, mentioning a list of her acquaintances: William Godwin (whom she knew through Robert Merry); Jane Porter, the author of *Thaddeus of Warsaw* (1803); and Anna Maria Porter, a novelist. She was also friendly with "Mrs. Parsons," probably Elizabeth Parsons (author of *The Castle of Wolfenbach*), Eliza Fenwick (a close friend of Mary Hays, educator, and author of *Secresy*), and "Mrs. Bennet," probably Agnes Maria Bennet (a novelist, the author of *Agnes de Courci*).

Rogers, Samuel (1763–1855) ("A Sketch of the Alps at Day-Break," "Farewell"). Born at Newington Green, London, Rogers gave up his desire to enter the Presbyterian ministry in order to join his father's banking business in Cornhill. Poor health led him to study literature, particularly the work of Johnson, Gray, and Goldsmith, who influenced his contributions to *Gentleman's Magazine* and his first volume of poetry (1786). He met Adam Smith, Henry Mackenzie, the Piozzis, and others in 1788. In 1791, he was in Paris, and enjoyed the art collection of Philippe Egalite at the Palais Royal, which he later acquired. *The Pleasures of Memory* (1792) reflects the poetic diction of the eighteenth century. Rogers, like Campbell, elevated and refined familiar themes by abstract treatment and lofty imagery. Campbell's *Pleasures of Memory* was written in imitation of Rogers's work.

"An Epistle to a Friend (Richard Sharp)," published in 1798, describes Rogers's ideal of a happy life. "The Voyage of Columbus" (1810) followed, and then "Jacqueline" (1814), a narrative poem using the four-accent measure that had become popular, published in the same volume with Byron's "Lara." "Human Life" (1819), which he worked on for twelve years, was written in his earlier manner. His collection of verse tales, *Italy* (1828), was successful when re-released with illustrations from J. M. Turner, Thomas Stothard, and Samuel Pratt, which Rogers commissioned. Fanny Kemble remembered his kind heart and sharp tongue. He helped the poet Robert Bloomfield, reconciled Moore with Jeffrey and with Byron, and relieved Sheridan's economic difficulties in the last days of his life.

Roscoe, William (1753–1831) ("The Butterfly's Ball, and the Grasshopper's Feast"), was an author, historian, and, by 1774, member of the English bar. He became a member of Parliament, opposing the slave trade (1806). His *Life of Lorenzo de' Medici* (1795) did well, but his four-volume *Life of Leo X* (1805) did not. In 1806, he submitted to *Gentleman's Magazine* "The Buttlerfly's Ball, and the Grasshopper's Feast"; it was highly successful, being one of the first non-didactic poems written for children during this period. William Mulready (1786–1863), an Irish genre painter, provided the illustrations.

Savage, Richard (1697?–1743) ("Epitaph on a Young Lady"), claimed to be the illegitimate son of Richard Savage, fourth and last Earl Rivers, and the countess of Macclesfield. In 1724, he published in *The Plain Dealer*. In 1727, he killed a gentleman in a tavern brawl. He wrote "The Bastard" (1728) and "The Wanderer" (1729). On Queen Caroline's death (1737), Pope tried to help him, but after about a year he went to Bristol, where he was incarcerated for debt and died. Samuel Johnson knew him when they both were suffering through hard times in London, a factor that led Johnson to write a moving biography of him — portions of which have proven to be inaccurate.[24]

Scott, Sir Walter (1771–1832) ("From The Lay of the Last Minstrel, a Poem"). Scott was a Scottish novelist and poet, influenced by Fielding and Smollett, Walpole's *Castle of Otranto*, Spenser and Ariosto, and Percy's *Reliques and German Ballad poetry*. In 1792, he became a lawyer after apprenticing in his father's law office as a clerk. At his grandfather's farm at Sandy-Knowe, he became familiar with the Border country, which he used often as a fictional setting. His first publication was an adaptation of Burger (1796), whose work appears twice in Jefferson's clippings books. Scott was a volunteer in the yeomanry, where he met Mademoiselle Charpentier, daughter of a French émigré, whom he married in 1797. He wrote "Glenfinals" and "The Eve of St. John" before translating Goethe's *Goetz von Berlichingen*. His first major work was *The Border Minstrelsy* (volumes 1 and 2 in 1802; volume 3 in 1803). "The Lay of the Last Minstrel" (1805) made him the most popular author of the day. He also wrote "Marmion" (1808) and "The Lady of the Lake" (1810), as well as "Rokeby "(1811) and "Lord of the Isles" (1815) before turning his attention to the novel. His brother John joined James Ballantyne as his publishers in the Canongate; he went bankrupt in 1826. He wrote *Guy Mannering* (in six weeks), *Heart of Midlothian*, *Old Mortality*, and *Bride of Lammermoor*, the latter of which is influenced by the ballad. He treated medieval subjects in *Ivanhoe*; the Reformation in *The Monastery* and *The Abbot*; and made use of the ballad motif in *Woodstock* (1826) and *The Fair Maid of Perth* (1828). He is also the author of *The Antiquary* and *Redgauntlet*. He wrote three letters under the pen name of Malachi Malagrowther (1826), revealing his interest in Scottish subjects, though E. M. Forster charged him with a "lack of ideas." His epitaph reminds people of the high esteem in which he was held: "Scott is greater than anything he wrote." Lockhart's life (1837–1838) of Scott is highly regarded.[25]

Seward, Anna (1747–1809) (two versions of "Sonnet"), was an English poet. Jefferson's clipping of Anna Seward's verse inspires interest since she touched upon the lives of those, like George Washington and Samuel Johnson, who knew Jefferson well. Dubbed the "Swan of Lichfield," Seward had a contentious relationship with a number of important writers, including Samuel Johnson and Erasmus Darwin. William Hayley paid her court in Litchfield, and Josiah Wedgwood encouraged her to write abolitionist verse, though she felt Thomas Day and Hannah More were more successful than she would be. Her letters, signed as "Benvolio" in the *Gentleman's Magazine* (1786–1787), reveal her annoyance at the "servile adulation granted to Johnson, especially by Boswell." She wrote "Elegy on Captain Cook" (1780), a poem that celebrated Cook's achievement, which attracted Hayley's attention. She memorialized John Andre in "Monody on Major Andre" (1781), a poem protesting Andre's court-martial and hanging at Tappan by the Americans who condemned him as a British spy. Andre's capture proved crucial in exposing Benedict Arnold's treachery. In her poetry, Seward denounced George Washington for his part in ordering Andre's execution (Seward's friend was Andre's fiancée); Washington sent an emissary to Seward with evidence demonstrating his limited role.

In 1784, she published *Louisa: a Poetical Novel, in Four Epistles*, an experimental form she considered her best work. The poem went through four editions, and a fifth in 1785. Her *Original Sonnets on Various Subjects* and *Odes Paraphrased from Horace* (1799) collected poems from the 1770s to 1799, some of which had been published in periodicals. She defended the sonnet, despite Johnson's dismissal. In 1804, she published her *Memoirs of The Life of Dr. Darwin*, a biography of Darwin's early life in Litchfield (1756–1781). The title poem of *Llangollen Vale with other Poems* (1796) honors the home and garden of Butler and Ponsonby that attracted so many celebrities to the site. In 1768, she fractured her kneecap, causing an incurable limp that worsened as she aged. Walter Scott noted her "great command of the literary anecdote" and her delightful company.[26]

Smith, Charlotte (1749–1806) ("Sonnet to Night," "The Mimosa"). Jefferson collected several sonnets by Smith, whose work was much admired by Wordsworth and Coleridge, among other poets. Patronized by Georgiana, duchess of Devonshire, during the 1790s, Smith nevertheless led a difficult life due to a protracted lawsuit that kept her husband's wealth inaccessible to her. Her husband, Benjamin, was sent to the king's bench for debt in December 1783. She served part of the seven-month sentence with him. Smith sent her poems to her Sussex neighbor, the poet and biographer William Hayley. Hayley was friendly with John Flaxman, George Romney, William Cowper, and William Blake. *Elegiac Sonnets, and other Essays by Charlotte Smith of Bignor Park, Sussex* (1784) went into more than nine editions by 1800. Jefferson enjoyed Smith's melancholy poetry, which was a precursor of Romanticism and reflects verse he copied in his literary commonplace book, but she wrote equally gloomy novels, beginning with *Emmeline, the Orphan of the Castle* (1788), which went into three editions. Nine others followed, most of them written to sustain herself financially, though *The Old Manor House* and *Desmond* are highly regarded: *Ethelinde, or, the Recluse of the Lake* (1789), *Celestina* (1791), *Desmond* (1792), *The Old Manor House* (1793), *The Wanderings of Warwick* (1794), *The Banished Man* (1794), *Montalbert* (1795), *Marchmont* (1796), and *The Young Philosopher* (1798) represent her prodigious output.[27] She also published *The Letters of a Solitary Wanderer*, in five volumes (1801–1802), and a comedy, *What Is She?* (1799), anonymously. Like Barbauld, Smith published works for children, including *Rural Walks* (1795), *Rambles Farther* (1796), *Minor Morals* (1798), and *Conversations Introducing Poetry* (1804). *Beachy Head, Fables, and other poems* (1807) includes an uncompleted but highly regarded poem. Smith died at fifty-seven.

Southey, Robert (1774–1843) ("Oak of Our Fathers," "Hymn to Content," "The Death of W. Wallace," "The Old Man's Comforts," "The Widow" [Southey wrote more than one poem titled "The Widow"; this version may have been misattributed by an American newspaper]). Born at Bristol, Robert Southey was a close friend of Samuel Taylor Coleridge and William Wordsworth, and became an important influence on the second generation of Romantic poets, including Lord Byron, who satirized his role as poet laureate in the mock dedication to *Don Juan*. Educated at Balliol in 1793, Southey became influenced by Coleridge's idea of a "pantisocracy," a plan that involved relocating to the banks of the Susquehanna River. The plan was only partially completed when Southey married Edith Fricker (with Coleridge marrying her older sister), and further utopian ideas were abandoned. Southey visited Lisbon in 1795; in 1800, he moved to Great Hall, Keswick, where Coleridge and his wife lived. He received a pension of 160 pounds a year from his school friend Wynn, which was transformed into an annuity (1835). Peel raised this to three hundred pounds in 1835; he served as poet laureate from 1813. He enjoyed a happy domestic life, one reason why Jefferson may well have enjoyed his verse; in 1837, however, his wife died insane. His ballads, particularly "Holy Tree," "Battle of Blenheim" (clipped by Jefferson), and "Old Woman of Berkeley," had an important influence. He wrote many epics, using rhymeless meter rather than blank verse, such as *Joan of Arc* (1795), *The Curse of Kehama* (1810), and *Roderick* (1814). He wrote biographies of Nelson (1813), Wesley (1820) and Bunyan (1830). He also wrote "A Vision of Judgment" (1821), "Book of the Church" (1824), "Colloquies on Society" (1829), "Naval History" (1833–1840), and "The Doctor" (1833–1947), which includes "The Three Little Bears." Jefferson seems to have been attracted to his reverence for the past, his love of national themes, and his sense, like Macpherson, that heroic action springs from developing one's moral imagination.

Stott, Thomas (d. 1829), wrote poetry for his own amusement, under the pseudonym *Hafiz* (Arabic for "observer"). "They are the recreations of solitary hours snatched from the hurry of business," he said of his poems, "furnishing innocent amusement and a proof that literary recreation is not altogether incompatible with the pursuits of commerce." Stott contributed regularly to numerous journals and newspapers, including the *Belfast Newsletter* and *London Morning Post*. Byron satirized him in *English Bards*. He was the son of a prosperous Hillsbourgh linen merchant, and he also went into the linen business. In 1777, he married Mary Ann Gardiner.[28]

Tyler, Royall (1757–1826) ("Versification of a Passage from Ossian"), associated with Federalists and entertained opinions that Jefferson would have found objectionable, although they shared an admiration for the poetry of James Macpherson. Tyler graduated from Harvard (1776) and received his degree from Yale that same year; he served in the colonial army during the American Revolution and later in the suppression of Shay's Rebellion (which Jefferson supported). Tyler practiced law in Portland, Maine, then Quincy, Massachusetts. He left Quincy after his engagement to Abby Adams, daughter of John and Abigail Adams, came to an end. In Vermont, where he settled in 1790, he served as chief justice of the Supreme Court (1807–1813) and professor of jurisprudence (1811–1814) at the University of Vermont. *The Contrast* (1787) was the first American comedy produced professionally. He also wrote other plays and a novel, *Algerine Captive* (1797). With Joseph Dennie, he wrote witty Federalist verse and essays for the *New Hampshire Journal*; he also contributed to *The Polyanthos*, the *Port Folio*, and *The Analectic Magazine*. In 1794, he married Mary Palmer, with whom he had eleven children.

Walker, William ("Indian Song"). Walker seems to have been the author of the hymn "Indian Song," an extract of which Jefferson included in his newspaper clippings book. Walker's poem inspired several missionaries to the Sandwich Islands, though Jefferson seems to have admired the poem's sentimental invocation of loss.

Williams, Helen Maria (1761–1827). Born in London, Helen Maria Williams was a successful poet whose friends included Fanny Burney, William Hayley, Samuel Johnson, Elizabeth Montagu, Anna Seward, and the Wartons. Williams published her first poem, "Edwin and Eltruda, A Legendary Tale"

(1782), with the assistance of Andrew Kippis. Kippis, a well-known dissenter, was one of Godwin's tutors at Hoxton. He introduced her to Johnson, Montagu, and Seward, as well as notable dissenting radicals such as Priestley, Price, and Godwin. In 1783, she published "An Ode on the Peace" and "Peru, A Poem" (1784), which she dedicated to Elizabeth Montagu. Her *Poems* (1786) met with fifteen hundred subscribers. Wordsworth addressed a sonnet to her in March 1787, and his "Vale of Esthwaite" was influenced by "Part of an Irregular Fragment, found in a Dark Passage of the Tower," which the *European Magazine* considered her finest work.

Williams's political radicalism was expressed in "Poem on the Bill Lately Passed for Regulating the Slave-Trade" (1788). She wrote *Julia, A Novel; Interspersed with Some Poetical Pieces* (1790), which responds to Rousseau's *Nouvelle Heloïse*. In one poem in this collection, "Bastille, A Vision," she criticized the French ancien régime. She became one of the strongest supporters of the French Revolution, describing her visit to the Bastille in *Letters Written in France in the Summer of 1790*. In "A Farewell, for Two Years, to England. A Poem" (1791), she described her opposition to the slave trade, connecting it to the quest for liberty in revolutionary France. Wordsworth visited her in Paris in 1791, with a letter of introduction from Charlotte Smith, and was inspired to write a pamphlet praising regicide, which, prudently enough, was never published. In Paris, she was friendly with Thomas Paine and Mary Wollstonecraft. Anna Seward wrote an open letter to her that appeared in the *Gentleman's Magazine* (February 1793) shortly before the beheadings of Marie Antoinette and Louis XVI. "Fly, dear Helen, that land of carnage!" Seward wrote.

Confined during the revolution, Williams translated St. Pierre's *Paul and Virginia* (1796) and recorded her response to revolutionary France in *Letters Containing a Sketch of the Politics of France* (1795). She emphasized the heroic role French women played, but the poem earned her rebukes from the *British Critic* for its lack of patriotism. A letter she wrote to Joseph Priestley in America was published in the *Anti-Jacobin Review* as evidence of her treachery. In 1794, her *Tour of Switzerland* was also published. She died in Paris, having become a naturalized French citizen in 1817. She published her collected poems in 1823. Jefferson's sympathy for the French Revolution may well have made her a figure of interest to him.

Wolcot, John. See Peter Pindar.

NOTES

Introduction

1. In the late eighteenth century, there were no "envelopes." Letters were written on paper that would then be closed with sealing wax. In England, parliamentary figures could mail letters for free (*franking* was the term used).

2. Randolph, *Domestic Life*, 347.

3. Golden and Golden, *Rhetoric of Virtue*, 473.

4. Burstein, *Jefferson's Secrets*, 102.

5. Bear and Betts, *Family Letters*, 203.

6. Writers who have treated Jefferson's literary interests have studiously avoided this collection. John Wayland was the first scholar to take the collection seriously, yet his important article in the *Sewanee Review* (1911) has been ignored. Julian Boyd went so far as to say that he "does not find Jefferson's literary tastes to be important" (Golden and Golden, *Rhetoric of Virtue*, 134). James and Alan Golden's *Jefferson and the Rhetoric of Virtue* treated the collection in an appendix.

7. Church, *Jefferson Bible*, 18.

8. Jefferson began editing the volume for two nights in February 1804; he returned to the task fifteen years later, finishing it in 1820 (Church, *Jefferson Bible*, 18; Burstein, *Jefferson's Secrets*, 252).

9. Church, *Jefferson Bible*, 18.

10. Jefferson, *Correspondence*, 1801 Ford edition, 8:65. This letter has been cited as the final word on his mature interests in literature: "Imaginative literature became something of a lapsed interest in his later years," Wilson has noted (*Literary Commonplace Book*, 5). The rhetorical context for his letter to Burk, however — presumably the source for this judgment — has too often been ignored.

11. Wilson, *Literary Commonplace Book*, 8.

12. Golden and Golden, *Rhetoric of Virtue*, 127.

13. Burstein, *Jefferson's Secrets*, 129.

14. Karl Lehmann has emphasized the classical reading of Jefferson. Though he acknowledged that Jefferson kept a clippings book, he concluded that poetry was not the vehicle by which Jefferson sought to understand history; Jefferson was "not at all influenced by poetical references to historical personalities" (*American Humanist*, 91). Lehmann argued that John Wayland seriously misunderstood the significance of the book he had unearthed (94, 232). Frank Shuffleton also raised questions in his *Thomas Jefferson: A Comprehensive, Annotated Bibliography of Writings About Him, 1826–1997* (2001), #3401, which dismissed Wayland's *Sewanee Review* findings: "Discusses a scrapbook of newspaper verse supposedly collected by TJ; highly unlikely." I concur with Dan Jordan, James Horn, and Robert McDonald, who view the work as Jefferson's, noting Jefferson's penciled emendations in the collection. No major biography of Thomas Jefferson, except Fawn Brodie's, treats this important archival discovery.

15. Joseph Priestley, January 27, 1800; William Peden, in Jefferson, *Life and Selected Writings*, 1944 Koch and Peden edition, 507.

16. Wilson, *Jefferson's Literary Commonplace Book*, 172.

17. Jefferson, *Life and Selected Writings*, 1944 Koch and Peden edition, 398.

18. April 16, 1802; Bear and Betts, *Family Letters*, 223.

19. "To Cornelia Jefferson Randolph," April, 3, 1808; Bear and Betts, *Family Letters*, 339.

20. The books were attributed to Jefferson by Robert McDonald. Articles in the local press covered the story in 1999 (www.virginia.edu/insideunva/1999/33/scrapbook.html, *Inside UVA Online*, 1999).

21. *Life*, "Over the Hills and Far Away," 32.

22. Ibid., 32–33. My thanks to Eleanor Sparagana for sending me a copy of this article. New York architect William Adams Delano built Kenwood between 1939 and 1941 for Major General and Mrs. Edwin M. Watson; Watson's wife, Frances Nash Watson, was a noted concert pianist (www.monticello.org/jefferson/dayinlife/sanctum/moern.html, July 2, 2005).

23. McLaughlin, *Jefferson and Monticello*, 327.

24. Burstein, *Jefferson's Secrets*.

25. Randolph, *Domestic Life*, 369.

26. Dershowitz, *Sexual McCarthyism*.

27. Burstein, *Jefferson's Secrets*, 110.

28. "To Ellen." Digital Archives, Miscellaneous. The poem appears next to a few clipped pages from Oliver Goldsmith's *Vicar of Wakefield*. I have consulted the original in 2001 at the Library of Congress, but a digitized version can be seen at http://memory.loc.gov/cgi-bin/query/P?mtj:1:/temp/~ammem_ZdJx:, image 318 of 357.

29. "I think this is the most extraordinary collection of talent and of human knowledge that has ever been gathered together at the White House — with the possible exception of when Thomas Jefferson dined alone." John F. Kennedy's April 29, 1962, dinner honoring forty-nine Nobel laureates (*Simpson's Contemporary Quotations*, 1988, from *Public Papers of the Presidents of the United States: John F. Kennedy, 1962*, 347).

30. Ellis, *American Sphinx*, 220.

Part One: Poems of Nation

1. Ellis, *American Sphinx*, 310.

2. April 7, 1775; Boswell, *Life of Johnson*. With Jefferson's declaration in mind, Johnson memorably asked, "How is it that we hear the loudest *yelps* for liberty among the drivers of negroes?" (*Taxation no Tyranny*). Jefferson thought Samuel Johnson's *Dictionary* as pernicious as David Hume's *History of England*. Both promoted a Tory version of political history that Jefferson thought exceedingly damaging for young, impressionable readers.

3. Adams, *History of the United States*, 115, 107.

4. Jefferson, *Life and Selected Writings*, 1944 Koch and Peden edition, 300.

5. Peterson, in Weymouth, *Thomas Jefferson*, 30.

6. 1:152.

7. 1:112.

8. Jefferson viewed Hamilton as "not only a monarchist, but for a monarchy bottomed on corruption": the West Indian immigrant was insufficiently grateful "to a nurturing country whose republican spirit was responsible for his promotion in its society" (Burstein, *Inner Jefferson*, 215). In Hamilton's defense, one might note that Hamilton's wartime service as aide to General Washington helped create a nation and prevent it from civil unrest.

9. Ibid., 220.

10. Burstein, *Jefferson's Secrets*, 228.

11. Chernow, *Alexander Hamilton*, 80, 163.

12. Ibid., 172.

13. 2:16.

14. 1:31.

15. Burstein, *Jefferson's Secrets*, 224.

16. Maier, *American Scripture*, 35.

17. Ibid., 217–224.

18. Malone, *Jefferson and His Time*, 3:274.

19. Dennie, *Letters*, 178.

20. To Thomas Jefferson Randolph, November 24, 1808; to Waterhouse, 1822; Jefferson, *Correspondence*, 1801 Ford edition, 10:220.

21. Ibid.

22. Ellis, *American Sphinx*, 346.

23. Ibid., 30; Bear and Betts, *Family Letters*, 13, 18, 72.

24. Fliegelman, *Declaring Independence*, 14.

25. 1:65/63.

26. Weymouth, *Thomas Jefferson*, 33.

27. Ellis, *American Sphinx*, 284.

28. Jones, *The Harp*, 80.

29. My thanks to Andrew Burstein for this information, letter of January 17, 2006. See also Irwin, *Daniel A. Tompkins*, 52-53.

30. Woodress, Luddington, and Arpad, *Essays Mostly on Periodical Publishing*, 252.

31. Onuf, *Jeffersonian Legacies*, 116.

32. Jefferson, First Inaugural Address, March 4, 1801; *Correspondence*, Ford edition, 8:1.

33. Malone, *Jefferson and His Time*, 5:605.

34. Ibid., 5:606.

35. Ibid.

36. Bear and Betts, *Family Letters*, 329.

37. Bryant, *Facsimile Reproductions*, 1955 Mabbott edition, 11.

38. Ibid., 23.

39. Jones, *The Harp*, 80.

40. Jefferson, First Inaugural Address, March 4, 1801; *Correspondence*, Ford edition, 8:1.

41. Blake, *Blake's Poetry and Designs*, 1979 Johnson and Grant edition, plate 14, line 4.

42. Ellis, *American Sphinx*.

43. Malone 3:377–8.

44. To William Duane, June 1807; Jefferson, *Correspondence*, Ford edition, 9:120.

45. Sowerby, *Catalogue of the Library of Thomas Jefferson*.

46. To William Short, 1819; Jefferson, *Correspondence*, Ford edition, 10:146.

47. Jefferson, *Writings*, 1854 Washington edition, 7:40.

48. Sowerby, *Catalogue of the Library of Thomas Jefferson*.

49. Jefferson, *Correspondence*, Ford edition, 7:204.

50. Chernow, *Alexander Hamilton*, 199.

51. Shakespeare, *As You Like It*, act two, scene seven.

52. Onuf, *Jeffersonian Legacies*, 123.

53. Stanton, "Looking for Liberty," 660–663.

54. Wills, *Negro President*, 1–13.

Part Two: Poems of Family

1. Bear and Betts, *Family Letters*, 11.
2. Cappon; in Wills, *Inventing America*, 274.
3. To Charles Bellini, 1785; Jefferson, *Papers*, 1950 Boyd and Butterfield edition, 8:569; Scheick, "Chaos and Imaginative Order," 224.
4. Jefferson, *Papers*, 1950 Boyd and Butterfield edition, 9:592; Scheick, "Chaos and Imaginative Order," 224.
5. McLaughlin, *Jefferson and Monticello*, 153.
6. To Chastellux, November 26, 1782; Jefferson, *Life and Selected Writings*, 1944 Koch and Peden edition, 340.
7. Bear and Betts, *Family Letters*, 7.
8. To Barbe-Marbois, December 5, 1783; Bear and Betts, *Family Letters*, 8.
9. Ellis, *American Sphinx*, 161.
10. January 7, 1798; Bear and Betts, *Family Letters*, 151.
11. Ibid.
12. Bear and Betts, *Family Letters*, 10.
13. Bear and Betts, *Family Letters*, 284, note 1.
14. Weymouth, *Thomas Jefferson*, 17.
15. Lewis, *Pursuit of Happiness*, 115.
16. March 11, 1808; Bear and Betts, *Family Letters*, 333.
17. Randolph, *Domestic Life*, 347.
18. Ibid., 401.
19. Wordsworth, *Prelude*, book 14, lines 446–447.
20. Bear and Betts, *Family Letters*, 320.
21. I have checked the *National Intelligencer*, *Richmond Enquirer*, and *Gentleman's Magazine* for 1807–1808. I'd be grateful if future researchers who might discover this poem contact the author at jgross@depaul.edu.
22. 2:132.
23. Lewis, "Domestic Society," 136.
24. 1:145/141.
25. Recent studies, such as Nancy Cott's *Bonds of Womanhood* and Jan Lewis's *Pursuit of Happiness*, give insight into what such balance, in fact, meant for women's lives.
26. 1:145/141.
27. 2:22.
28. 1:127.
29. November 24, 1808; Jefferson, *Life and Selected Writings*, 1944 Koch and Peden edition, 543.
30. 2:15.
31. Halliday, *Understanding Thomas Jefferson*, 102.
32. Wills, *Inventing America*, 273.
33. Sowerby, *Catalogue of the Library of Thomas Jefferson*, 4:446; Burstein, *Inner Jefferson*, 200.
34. 1:102/100.
35. March 27, 1801; Lewis, quoted in Onuf, *Jeffersonian Legacies*, 139.
36. "The Affectionate Friend"; 1:102/100.
37. 1:100/98.
38. Ibid.
39. Ibid.

40. "Jug of Rum"; 2:53.

41. "Address to My Segar," 2:42.

42. 1:132.

43. 1:136.

44. Ibid.

45. Nathaniel Hawthorne copied several stanzas of this poem in his notebook, though he is not the author of it, as the 1994 Woodson, Simpson, and Smith edition of his works assumes (23:3).

46. 1:169.

47. Ibid.

48. McLaughlin, *Jefferson and Monticello*, 379.

49. "Letter to Charles James Fox" (January 14, 1801), in Merchant, editor, *Wordsworth: Poetry and Prose*, 839.

50. Lewis, "Domestic Society," 101.

51. Randolph, *Domestic Life*, 429.

52. *Brewer's Concise Dictionary*, 258.

53. Ellis, *American Sphinx*, 258.

54. Sowerby, *Catalogue of the Library of Thomas Jefferson*.

55. Ovid, *Metamorphoses*, translated by Dryden; book one: the transformation of Daphne into a laurel.

56. Wordsworth, "Tables Turned," line 16.

57. Randolph, *Domestic Life*, 341.

58. Jones, *The Harp*.

59. Randolph, *Domestic Life*, 284.

60. To Bishop James Madison; Jefferson, *Correspondence*, Ford edition, 7:419.

61. Jefferson, *Correspondence*, Ford edition, 4:387.

62. Hawthorne, *Centenary Edition of Complete Works*, 23:3.

63. Reissued by Woodstock Books (Oxford), 1990.

64. Wilson, *Jefferson's Literary Commonplace Book*, 70, 73, 76, 174.

65. Aeschylus, *Oresteia*, 70.

66. January 7, 1798; Bear and Betts, *Family Letters*, 15.

67. To James Madison, December 16, 1786; Jefferson, *Life and Selected Writings*, 1944 Koch and Peden edition, 378.

68. Paris, 1787; Jefferson, *Correspondence*, Ford edition, 4:432.

69. *Brewer's Concise Dictionary*, 193.

70. Jefferson Looney, letter of January 30, 2006; contra Ellis, *American Sphinx*, 277.

71. Jefferson, *Correspondence*, Ford edition, 9:329.

72. *Brewer's Concise Dictionary*, 136.

73. Byron, *Don Juan*, 2:169.

74. Kerber, *Women of the Republic*, 120.

75. Ibid.

76. Bear and Betts, *Family Letters*, 278.

77. Ibid.

78. Ibid., 22.

79. Jefferson, *Life and Selected Writings*, 1944 Koch and Peden edition, 259.

80. Halliday, *Understanding Thomas Jefferson*, 189.

81. January 31, 1801; Bear and Betts, *Family Letters*, 192; quoted in Onuf, *Jeffersonian Legacies*, 137.

82. February 5, 1801; Bear and Betts, *Family Letters*, 195, quoted in Onuf, *Jeffersonian Legacies*, 137.

83. 1800?; Jefferson, *Correspondence*, Ford edition, 7:477.

84. Swift, "Voyage to Brobdingnag," *Gulliver's Travels*, 2:102.

85. Randall, *Thomas Jefferson: A Life*, 469.

86. 2:56.

87. Byron, *Sardanapalus*, act 1, line 191.

88. Pope, *Moral Essays*, 2:1:207.

89. Austen, *Sense and Sensibility*, 82.

90. September 1782; Onuf, *Jeffersonian Legacies*, 101.

91. Herold, *Mistress to an Age*, 419; quoted in Melbourne, *Byron's "Corbeau Blanc,"* 48.

92. Byron, *Don Juan*, 12:96:524.

93. September 18, 1812; Byron, *Byron's Letters*, 2:199.

94. Halliday, *Understanding Thomas Jefferson*, 102.

95. Sterne, *Tristram Shandy*, 104.

96. Jefferson, *Life and Selected Writings*, 1944 Koch and Peden edition, 197.

97. December 11, 1783; Bear and Betts, *Family Letters*, 21.

98. Burstein, *Jefferson's Secrets*, 32.

99. November 24, 1808; Randolph, *Domestic Life*, 318.

100. Leary, *Soundings*.

101. Jefferson, *Correspondence*, Ford edition, 10:125.

102. 2:54 and 2:118.

103. To Thomas Jefferson Randolph, November 24, 1808; Jefferson, *Writings*, 1854 Washington edition, 541.

104. February 7, 1799; Bear and Betts, *Family Letters*, 173.

105. Bear and Betts, *Family Letters*, 134.

106. McLaughlin, *Jefferson and Monticello*, 323.

107. March 3, 1802; Onuf, *Jeffersonian Legacies*, 137.

108. Byron, *Don Juan*, 1:994.

109. Ellis, *American Sphinx*, 31.

110. Ibid., 52.

111. Bear and Betts, *Family Letters*, 71.

Part Three: Poems of Romantic Love

1. Burstein, *Inner Jefferson*, 56.

2. Wilson, *Jefferson's Literary Commonplace Book*, 132n.

3. Burstein, *Inner Jefferson*, 62; Randolph, *Domestic Life*, 64; Lehmann, *Thomas Jefferson*, 54.

4. Randolph, *Domestic Life*, 340–341. Ellen Coolidge's description of her grandfather's interests was no doubt partly accurate, but smacked of hagiography and seemed to have been written with posterity in mind. It is strange, for example, that she made no mention of the poems he shared with her during his White House years — relegating this, perhaps, to his private rather than his public life as a scholar and intellectual. "Books were at all times his chosen companions, and his acquaintance with many languages gave him great power of selection. He read Homer, Virgil, Dante, Corneille, Cervantes, as he read Shakespeare and Milton. In his youth he had loved poetry, but by the time I was old enough to

observe, he had lost his taste for it, except for Homer and the great Athenian tragics, which he continued to the last to enjoy." Burstein's *Jefferson's Secrets* noted how Coolidge helped to shape historians' perceptions of her grandfather through letters she wrote, going so far as to refute allegations about Sally Hemings.

5. Halliday, *Understanding Thomas Jefferson*, 55, 189, 103.

6. Byron, *Letters and Journals*, 3:227.

7. "Declaration," Jefferson, *Life and Selected Writings*, 1944 Koch and Peden edition, 26.

8. Byron, "The Vision of Judgment," lines 352–356.

9. This was the Southey whom Byron recalled later when Southey attacked Byron as a member of "the Satanic school of poetry." Jefferson had also been accused of atheism but he never answered his accusers in the newspapers, as Byron did in the literary journal he edited with Leigh Hunt, *The Liberal*, where "The Vision of Judgment" first appeared (1821). Jefferson preferred dreaming of domestic tranquility at Monticello (without a wife) to tasting the sardonic humor of the discontented narrator of *Childe Harold's Pilgrimage* or the cynical urbanity of *Don Juan*, which John Quincy Adams enjoyed. By 1824, when Byron died fighting for a cause Jefferson might have championed, the Greek War of Independence, Jefferson was busy building the University of Virginia. He died two years after Byron, in 1826.

10. Blake, *Blake's Poetry and Designs*, 1979 Johnson and Grant edition, plate 14, line 16.

11. Not surprisingly, Jefferson appeared in the curated exhibit, Wordsworth and the Age of Romanticism, that toured North America and England in the late 1980s.

12. To John Waldo, 1813; Jefferson, *Writings*, 1854 Washington edition, 6:184. Jefferson's allusion to the "beautiful poetry" of Burns is worth noting, for nine Burns poems appear in this collection—yet few other records give evidence for the particular poems by Burns that Jefferson admired.

13. Fliegelman, *Declaring Independence*, 10.

14. Ibid., 12–14.

15. Tanselle, *Royall Tyler*, 114.

16. Kroeber, *Romantic Narrative Art*, 35.

17. Jones, *The Harp*, 110.

18. 1:108.

19. McLaughlin, *Jefferson and Monticello*, 5.

20. Burstein, *Jefferson's Secrets*, 66–67.

21. Isaac Jefferson, a slave on Jefferson's plantation, noted that "Monticello was pulled down in part and built up again some six or seven times. One time it was struck by lightning. . . . They was forty years at work upon that house before Mr. Jefferson stopped building," (Burstein, *Jefferson's Secrets*, 67).

22. Kelsall, *Iconography of Romanticism*, 59, 86.

23. Royall Tyler, for example, mocked women led astray by the sentimentalism of Sterne, Richardson, and Mackenzie. In Tyler's *The Contrast*, Charlotte failed to value Sir Manley's virtue because he did not display the manners she had come to expect from rakes in English novels (thanks in part to Lord Chesterfield's letters to his son). Tyler was more critical of England than Dennie, who looked to the mother country for literary and social models, especially after Jefferson's election.

24. January 30, 1808; Dennie and Dickens, *Port Folio*, 66–67.

25. Though Merry bemoaned political injustice, the sexual politics of his verse reinforced it, as several poems titled "To Della Crusca" reveal. In one of these, not in Jefferson's collec-

tion, the point is especially obvious. Anna Matilda (Hannah Cowley), the poet, longs for the poetic skill of Merry:

> Ambiguous Nature form'd the *female heart*
> So proud, capricious, cold and warm,
> That much she fear'd her FIRST COMMAND
> *Inert* would prove, throughout the land;
> So gave the counteracting charm—
> ON *favour'd Man* bestow'd sagacious ART.
>
> (To Della Crusca, 1789; Anna Matilda, *British Album*, 73)

That women used their "charm" rather than their reason was something that Mary Wollstonecraft bemoaned and Anna Matilda celebrates.

26. Jefferson, *Life and Selected Writings*, 1944 Koch and Peden edition, 258.
27. Ibid., 254.
28. Malone, *Jefferson and His Time*, 4:228.
29. Fessenden, "Democracy Unveiled," 101.
30. Lewis, *Monk*, 239.
31. Stanton, "Looking for Liberty," 673.
32. Moore, preface, *Thomas Little*, 3.
33. May 3, 1787; Boykin, *Girls and Boys*, 34.
34. *Romanticicsm on the Net*, http://www.ron.umontreal.ca/, May 1996, 15.
35. "Burger's 'Lenore,'" *Western Reserve Studies*, 32.
36. Ibid., 33.
37. Thorne and Collocott, *Chambers Biographical Dictionary*, 1021.
38. Jefferson, *Life and Selected Writings*, 182.
39. 2:76–78.
40. Jefferson, *Correspondence*, Ford edition, 10:341.
41. August 10, 1787; Jefferson, *Life and Selected Writings*, 1944 Koch and Peden edition, 398.
42. Wu, *Romantic Women Poets*, 348.
43. 2:134, Melbourne, *Byron's "Corbeau Blanc,"* 22.
44. To Charles Bellini, September 30, 1785; Jefferson, *Papers*, 1950 Boyd and Butterfield edition, 8:569; Scheick, "Chaos and Imaginative Order," 224.
45. Dacre, *Hours of Solitude*, 2:40.
46. Burstein, *Inner Jefferson*, 40.
47. 1:187.
48. *Morning Chronicle*, January 16, 1815.
49. Osborn, *Poems*, ix.

Appendix 1

1. Tanselle, *Royall Tyler*, 109.

Appendix 4

1. Golden and Golden, *Rhetoric of Virtue*, 148.
2. Ibid.
3. Ibid., 147.

4. Ibid., 146.

5. Ibid., 149.

6. Ibid., 147.

7. Malone, *Jefferson and His Time*, 5:384.

8. Ibid., 5:385. Yet reading was also a necessity of life, to borrow the title of William J. Gilmore-Lehne's interesting study of the rising tide of literacy in Vermont, *Reading Becomes a Necessity of Life: Material and Cultural Life in Rural New England, 1780–1835*.

9. Golden and Golden, *Rhetoric of Virtue*, 152.

10. Ibid.

11. January 1838; Hawthorne, *Miscellaneous*, 1994 Woodson, Simpson, and Smith edition, 23:96.

12. Randall, "Joseph Dennie's Literary Attitudes," 64.

13. Joseph Dennie and Thomas Fessenden were critics of Jefferson's administration whose comments do not appear in Ellis, Halliday, Onuf, Randall, Wills, or Malone (Dennie receives a brief paragraph about his libel against Jefferson in Malone, *Jefferson and His Time*, 4:228; and Cunningham, *In Pursuit of Reason*, 270). The result is that the Sally Hemings story and other controversies appear to be the sole work of calumniators or scandalmongers such as James Callendar, though Dennie, Fessenden, Moore, and others circulated them in mock-epics like *Democracy Unveiled* and respected journals. Linda Kerber has treated the topic thoroughly in *Federalists in Dissent*, as has William Dowling, in *Literary Federalism in the Age of Jefferson*. I am indebted to these fine studies for the account that appears here.

14. Dowling, *Literary Federalism*, 2.

15. Dennie and Dickens, *Port Folio*, 3:135; Dowling, *Literary Federalism*, 1.

16. Randall, "Joseph Dennie's Literary Attitudes," 64.

17. Fessenden, *Democracy Unveiled*, 3:67.

18. Dowling, *Literary Federalism*, 4.

19. Dennie and Dickens, *Port Folio*, 3:137.

20. Ibid., 1:38.

21. Dowling, *Literary Federalism*, 34.

22. Lehmann, *Thomas Jefferson*.

23. Rush, *Essays*, 26–27.

24. Dennie, *Port Folio*, June 5, 1802, 176; quoted in Randall, "Joseph Dennie's Literary Attitudes," 64.

25. Dowling, *Literary Federalism*, 47.

26. Dennie and Dickens, *Port Folio*, 1:35.

27. Randall, "Joseph Dennie's Literary Attitudes," 77.

28. March 1, 1809; *Port Folio*, 1:286.

29. August 29, 1801; Dennie and Dickens, *Port Folio*, 1:274; Randall, "Joseph Dennie's Literary Attitudes," 79.

30. He greeted him "in an old brown coat, red waistcoat, old corduroy small-clothes (much soiled), woolen hose, and slippers without heels," (White, *Tom Moore*, 46).

31. Moore, *Epistles, Odes, and Other Poems*, 268.

32. Moore, *Epistles, Odes, and Other Poems*, "Epistle VII" 214, lines 1–10.

33. Moore, *Epistles, Odes, and Other Poems*, "Epistle VII" 215, lines 87–103.

34. Moore, *Epistles, Odes, and Other Poems*, 3.

35. Wordsworth, "The Excursion," 3:890–909, quoted in Henry Adams, *History of the United States*, 123.

36. Dennie and Dickens, *Port Folio*, 3:6, 22, 52, 92, 122.

37. Moore, *Poetical Works of the Late Thomas Little*, 5.

38. White, *Tom Moore*, 47.

39. June 1816; ibid., 50; Stanton, "Looking for Liberty," 654.

40. Letter to John Hall, July 12, 1818; Moore, *Letters*, 1:458.

41. White, *Tom Moore*, 47.

42. 1:122.

43. 2:6.

44. Fessenden, *Democracy Unveiled*, xvi.

45. Ibid., xv.

46. Ibid., xviii.

47. Ibid., xvi.

48. Fessenden, *Original Poems*, preface.

49. Fessenden, *Democracy Unveiled*, prologue.

50. Hawthorne, *Centenary Edition*, 12:231.

51. Ibid.

52. Malone, *Jefferson and His Time*, 5:606.

53. Ibid.

54. May 26, 1811; Bear and Betts, *Family Letters*, 400.

55. Ibid.

56. March 14, 1818; Jefferson, *Life and Selected Writings*, 1944 Koch and Peden edition, 628.

57. Ibid., 628–629.

58. Lewis, *Pursuit of Happiness*, 148–149, quoted in Appleby, *Inheriting America*, 98.

59. Bear and Betts, *Family Letters*, 191.

60. Ibid., 207.

61. Ibid.

62. Ibid., 214.

63. April 16, 1802; ibid., 223.

64. January 27, 1803; ibid., 242.

65. Ibid., 257.

66. March 4, 1805; ibid., 269.

67. June 28, 1805; ibid., 274.

68. Ibid., 278.

69. Ibid., 298.

70. Ibid., 306.

71. Ibid., 309.

72. January 12, 1808; ibid., 320, 321.

73. January 15, 1808; ibid., 321.

74. Ibid., 332.

75. March 29, 1808; ibid., 338.

76. April 14, 1808; ibid., 341.

77. Ibid., 203.

78. November 10, 1801; ibid., 212.

79. 2:2.

80. Ibid.

81. 2:3.

82. Leary, *Soundings*, 110.

83. 2:3.

84. 2:1.

85. 2:2.

86. Ibid.

87. 2:3.

88. Ellis, *American Sphinx*, 167.

89. Burstein, *Inner Jefferson*, 97.

90. The "public sphere" is a realm "in which opinions are exchanged between private persons unconstrained (ideally) by external pressures. Theoretically open to all citizens and founded in the family, it is the place where something approaching public opinion is formed. It should be distinguished both from the state, which represents official power, and from the economic structures of civil society as a whole. . . . it is the arena in which the public organizes itself, formulates public opinion, and expresses its desires vis-à-vis the government." This is a summary of ideas expressed in Habermas's *The Structural Transformation of the Public Sphere* (1962); see *Johns Hopkins Guide*, 1994.

91. 1:97/94 and 2:36.

92. 1:19, 1:96, and 1:108.

93. 1:181. Jefferson added a new wrinkle to Byron's claim that poetry would be used to line the pans of pastry chefs or portmanteaus:

> Young men should travel, if but to amuse
> Themselves; and the next time their servants tie on
> Behind their carriages their new portmanteau,
> Perhaps it may be lined with this my canto.
>
> (DJ 2:127)

In the eleventh canto of *Don Juan*, Byron mocked the bluestockings for wearing bonnets lined with poetry. Wastepaper (often poetry) was used for such purposes, and in *The Blues*, Byron noted that he would read Wordsworth's latest poem in the bonnet of a lady's cap: "I shall think of him oft when I buy a new hat: / There his works will appear," (*The Blues*, 2:60–61).

Appendix 5

1. Bear and Betts, *Family Letters*, 278.

2. Wilson, *Jefferson's Literary Commonplace Book*, 225.

3. Leary, *Soundings*, 249.

4. Golden and Golden, *Rhetoric of Virtue*, 94.

5. Wilson, *Jefferson's Literary Commonplace Book*, 175.

6. *Dictionary of American Biography*.

7. Ibid., 860.

8. Charles Zarobila, in ibid., 859–860.

9. Thorne and Collocott, *Chambers Biographical Dictionary*.

10. Wilson, *Jefferson's Literary Commonplace Book*, 172–173.

11. Byron, "English Bards and Scotch Reviewers," note to line 425 in Byron, *Complete Poetical Works*.

12. Tolley, in *New Dictionary of National Biography*.

13. Stanton, "Looking for Liberty," 655.

14. Ibid., 668.
15. Thorne and Collocott, *Chambers Biographical Dictionary*, 950.
16. Osborn, *Poems*, vii.
17. *Dictionary of American Biography*, 70.
18. Wu, *Romantic Women Poets*, 465.
19. Ibid.
20. 2:34.
21. Wu, *Romantic Women Poets*, 181.
22. Ibid., 180.
23. Ibid., 177.
24. Makower, Richard. *Savage: A Mystery in Biography*, 1909.
25. Thorne and Collocott, *Chambers Biographical Dictionary*.
26. Scott, in DNB.
27. *New Dictionary of National Biography*.
28. Gamble, "Thomas Stott."

BIBLIOGRAPHY

Archives and Newspapers

Alderman Library, University of Virginia
Jefferson's Newspaper Clippings Book, Alderman Library at the University of Virginia.
Volume Two, mss. 5948, 5948-a; Volume B-3.

American Antiquarian Society, Massachusetts
National Intelligencer
Richmond Enquirer

Library of Congress, Washington, DC
"To Ellen." Digital Archives, Miscellaneous. Thomas Jefferson Papers Series I. General
Correspondence. 1651–1827 (http://memory.loc.gov/cgi-
in/query/P?mtj:1:/temp/~ammem_ZdJx:, image 318 of 357).

Visitor center, Charlottesville, Virginia
Jefferson's Newspaper Clippings Book. Visitor center, Thomas Jefferson Memorial Library (on
display at visitor center, but a copy exists as Volume One, mss. 5948, 5948-a, donated by A.
T. Laird in 1851, Robert H. Smith International Center for Jefferson Studies library).

Internet Sources on Jefferson's scrapbooks
"A Day in the Life of Thomas Jefferson: The Robert H. Smith International Center for Jefferson
Studies," July 19, 2005. www.monticello.org/jefferson/dayinlife/sanctum/modern.html.
All Things Considered, September 30, 1999, NPR online.
"Scrapbooks show Jefferson was a voracious and sentimental clipper of newspapers." *Inside
UVA Online*, October 15–21, 1999.
http://www.virginia.edu/insideunva/1999/33/scrapbook.html.

Primary Sources

Ashfield, Andrew, ed. *Romantic Women Poets, 1770–1838*. Manchester: Manchester University
Press, 1995.
Bannerman, Anne. *Poems by Anne Bannerman*. Edinburgh: Mundell Son, Longman & Rees, and
J. Wright, 1800.
———. *Tales of Superstition and Chivalry*. London: Vernor and Hood, J. Swan, 1802.
Bear, James, ed. *Jefferson at Monticello*. Charlottesville: University Press of Virginia, 1967.
Bear, James A., and Edwin Morris Betts. *Family Letters of Thomas Jefferson*. Charlottesville:
University Press of Virginia, 1966.
Bernard, John. *Retrospections of America, 1797–1811*, edited from the manuscript by Mrs. Bayle
Bernard, with an introduction, notes, and index by Laurence Hutton and Brander
Matthews. New York: Harper & Brothers, 1887.
Blake, William. "America." In *Blake's Poetry and Designs*, edited by Mary Lynn Johnson and
John E. Grant. New York: Norton, 1979.
Boswell, James. *Life of Samuel Johnson*. Oxford: Oxford University Press, 1980.
Boykin, Edward, ed. *To the Girls and Boys, being the delightful, little-known letters of Thomas*

Jefferson to and from his children and grandchildren. New York: Funk & Wagnalls Company, 1964.

Bryant, William Cullen. "The Embargo by William Cullen Bryant: Facsimile reproductions of the editions of 1808 and 1809, with an introduction and notes by Thomas O. Mabbott." Gainesville, Florida: Scholars' Facsimiles and Reprints, 1955.

Byron, Gordon George Lord. *Lord Byron: The Complete Poetical Works*. edited by Jerome McGann. 7 volumes. Oxford: Clarendon Press, 1980–93.

Byron, George Gordon Lord. *Don Juan*, edited by Truman Guy Steffan and Willis W. Pratt. New York: Penguin, 1988.

———. *Letters and Journals*, edited by Leslie Marchand. 12 volumes. Cambridge: Harvard University Press, 1973–1982.

Campbell, Thomas. *The Poetical Works of Thomas Campbell*. Philadelphia: J. Criss and J. Grigg, 1827.

Chinard, Albert, ed. *The Commonplace book of Thomas Jefferson, a repertory of his ideas on government, with an introduction and notes by Gilbert Chinard*. Baltimore: Johns Hopkins Press, 1926.

Church, Forrest, ed. *The Jefferson Bible: The Life and Morals of Jesus of Nazareth*. Boston: Beacon Press, 1989.

Clinton, William Jefferson, and Al Gore. *Putting People First*. New York: Random House, 1992.

———. *Between Hope and History: Meeting America's Challenges for the 21st Century*. New York: Random House, 1996.

Cottle, Joseph. *Poems*. Bristol: G. G. and J. Robinson, 1796.

Dacre, Charlotte. *Hours of Solitude: A Collection of Original Poems*, 2 volumes, 1801. Reprinted New York: AMS Press, 1974.

Dennie, Joseph. *The Letters of Joseph Dennie, 1768–1812*, edited by Laura G. Pedder. Orono, Maine: University of Maine Press, 1936.

Dennie, Joseph, and Asbury Dickins. *Port Folio*, by Oliver Oldschool, Esq. Philadelphia: The Editor and Asbury Dickens, printed by H. Maxwell, 1801–1808.

Fessenden, Thomas Green. *Democracy Unveiled, or, Tyranny stripped of the garb of patriotism. By Christopher Caustic* [pseud.], 3rd ed. New York: Printed for I. Riley & Co. 1806.

———. *Original Poems*. Philadelphia: Branson, 1806.

Hawthorne, Nathaniel. *Centenary Edition of the Complete Works of Nathaniel Hawthorne*, edited by Thomas Woodson, Claude M. Simpson, and L. Neal Smith, 23 volumes. Columbus: Ohio State University Press, 1994.

———. *Complete Works of Nathaniel Hawthorne*, 13 volumes, edited by George Lathrop and Julian Hawthorne. New York: Sully and Kleinteich, 1932.

Hazlitt, William. *Complete Works of William Hazlitt, edited by P. P. Howe after the edition of A. R. Waller and Arnold Glover*. London: J. M. Dent and Sons, 1930–1934.

Jefferson, Thomas. *Jefferson's Literary Commonplace Book*, edited by Douglas Wilson. Princeton, New Jersey: Princeton University Press, 1989.

———. *The Life and Selected Writings of Thomas Jefferson*, edited and with an introduction by Adrienne Koch and William Peden. New York: Modern Library, 1944.

———. *The Papers of Thomas Jefferson*, edited by Julian P. Boyd, Lyman H. Butterfield, et al., 31 volumes, 1760–1800. Princeton, New Jersey: Princeton University Press, 1950– .

———. *The Writings of Thomas Jefferson*, edited by H. A. Washington. Washington, DC: Library of Congress, 1854.

———. *Thomas Jefferson correspondence, printed from the originals in the collections of William K. Bixby with notes by Worthington Chauncey Ford*, 10 volumes. Boston: 1916.

Kames, Henry Home, Lord. *Elements of Criticism*, 3rd edition. Edinburgh: A. Millar, 1765.

Melbourne, Elizabeth. *Byron's "Corbeau Blanc": The Life and Letters of Lady Melbourne*, edited by Jonathan David Gross. Houston: Rice University Press, 1997.

Moore, Thomas. *Complete Poems of Thomas Moore*. Boston: Phillips, Samson, and Company, 1851.

———. *Epistles, Odes, and Other Poems*. London: James Carpenter, 1806.

———. *The Letters of Thomas Moore*, edited by Wilfred S. Dowden, 2 volumes. Oxford: Oxford University Press, 1964.

Osborn, Selleck. *Poems, Moral, Sentimental, and Satirical*. Boston: J. P. Orcutt, 1823.

Pope, Alexander. *The Twickenham Edition of the Poems of Alexander Pope*, edited by John Butt, et al., 11 volumes in 12. London: Methuen; New Haven, Connecticut: Yale University Press, 1939–1969.

Randolph, Sarah N., ed. *The Domestic Life of Thomas Jefferson*. 1871. Reprinted Charlottesville: University Press of Virginia, 1978.

Rush, Benjamin. *Essays, literary, moral and philosophical*. Philadelphia: Thomas and William Bradford, 1798.

Shelley, Percy Bysshe. "Defense of Poetry." In *Shelley's Poetry and Prose: Authoritative Texts, Criticism*, edited by Donald H. Reiman and Neil Fraistat. New York: Norton, 2002.

Staël-Holstein, Madame de. *De L'Allemagne, with notes and Appendices*. Translated by O. W. Wight, A.M., 2 volumes. New York: Hurd and Houghton, 1864.

Tyler, Royall. *The Contrast; a comedy in five acts*. Boston: Houghton Mifflin, 1920.

Whitman, Walt. *Leaves of Grass*. New York: Oxford University Press, 2005.

Wordsworth, William. "Letter to Charles James Fox" (January 14, 1801), in *Wordsworth: Poetry and Prose*, edited by W. M. Merchant. 1839. Reprinted London: Rupert Hart-Davis, 1955.

———. "Preface to Lyrical Ballads"; "Prelude" (1850). *Complete Poetical Works of William Wordsworth*. London: Macmillan, 1924.

———. *The Early Letters of William and Dorothy Wordsworth (1787–1805)*, edited by Ernest de Selincourt. London: Oxford University Press, 1935.

Wu, Duncan, ed. *Romantic Women Poets*. London: Blackwell, 1998.

Secondary Sources

Adams, Henry. *The History of the United States of America During the Administrations of Jefferson and Madison*, edited and abridged by Ernest Samuels. Chicago: University of Chicago Press, 1943.

Anderson, Benedict. *Imagined Communities: Reflections on the Origin and Spread of Nationalism*. London: Verso, 1983.

Appleby, Joyce Oldham. *Inheriting America: The First Generation of Americans*. Cambridge: Belknap Press of Harvard University, 2000.

Brewer's Concise Dictionary of Phrase and Fable, edited by Betty Kirkpatrick. New York: Helicon, 1992.

Brodie, Fawn. *Thomas Jefferson: An Intimate History*. New York: W.W. Norton and Company, 1998.

Burstein, Andrew. *America's Jubilee*. New York: Knopf, 2001.

———. *Jefferson's Secrets: Death and Desire at Monticello*. New York: Basic Books, 2005.

———. *The Inner Jefferson: Portrait of a Grieving Optimist*. Charlottesville: University Press of Virginia, 1995.

Chernow, Ron. *Alexander Hamilton*. New York: Penguin, 2004.

Cott, Nancy F. *Bonds of Womanhood: "Woman's Sphere" in New England, 1780–1835.* New Haven: Yale University Press, 1997.

Cox, Stephen. "The Literary Aesthetic of Thomas Jefferson." In *Essays in Early Virginia Literature Honoring Richard Beale Davis,* edited by J. A. Leo LeMay. New York: Burt Franklin, 1977, 235–256.

Cunningham, Noble, Jr. *In Pursuit of Reason: The Life of Thomas Jefferson.* New York: Ballantine Books, 1987.

Dershowitz, Alan. *Sexual McCarthyism: Clinton, Starr, and the Emerging Constitutional Crisis.* New York: Basic Books, 1998.

Dictionary of National Biography, edited by Sir Leslie Stephen and Sir Sidney Lee. 24 vols. Oxford: Oxford University Press, 1949–50.

Dowling, William C. *Literary Federalism in the Age of Jefferson: Joseph Dennie and the Port Folio, 1801–1812.* Columbia: University of South Carolina Press, 1999.

Ellis, Joseph. *American Sphinx: The Character of Thomas Jefferson.* New York: Knopf, 1997.

Emerson, O. F. "The Earliest English Translations of Burger's 'Lenore.'" Cleveland, Ohio: *Case Western Reserve Studies,* (1911):1–108.

Fliegelman, Jay. *Declaring Independence: Jefferson, Natural Language, and the Culture of Performance.* Stanford, California: Stanford University Press, 1993.

Foreman, Amanda. *Georgiana, Duchess of Devonshire.* New York: HarperCollins, 1998.

Gamble, Roy. "Thomas Stott — Dromore's Forgotten Poet." *Dromore and District Local Historical Group Journal* 1 (1991).

Gates, Henry Louis. *Trials of Phyllis Wheatley.* New York: Basic Civitas Books, 2003.

Gellner, Ernest. *Nationalism.* New York: New York University Press, 1997.

Gilmore-Lehne, William J. *Reading Becomes a Necessity of Life: Material and Cultural Life in Rural New England, 1780–1835.* Knoxville: University of Tennessee Press, 1989.

Golden, James L., and Alan L. Golden. *Thomas Jefferson and the Rhetoric of Virtue.* Lanham, Maryland: Rowman & Littlefield, 2002.

Halliday, Ernest Milton. *Understanding Thomas Jefferson.* New York: HarperCollins, 2001.

Herold, Christopher J. *Mistress to an Age: A Life of Madame de Stael.* New York: Harmony Books, 1958.

Howard, Leon. *The Connecticut Wits.* Chicago: University of Chicago Press, 1943.

Irwin, Ray W. *Daniel D. Tompkins: Governor of New York and Vice President of the United States.* New York: New York Historical Society, 1968.

Isaac, Rhys. "The First Monticello." In *Jeffersonian Legacies,* edited by Peter S. Onuf, with a foreword by Daniel P. Jordan and afterword by Merrill D. Peterson. Charlottesville: University Press of Virginia, 1993.

"It's Over the Hills and Far Away: PA Watson's Little White Guest House Lodges a Distinguished Weekend Visitor." *Life Magazine* 10:26 (May 19, 1941), 32–33.

Johns Hopkins Guide to Literary Theory and Criticism, edited by Michael Groden and Martin Kreiswirth. Baltimore: Johns Hopkins University Press, 1994.

Jones, Howard Mumford. *The Harp That Once — : A Chronicle of the Life of Thomas Moore.* New York: H. Holt and Company, 1937.

Kelsall, Malcolm. *Jefferson and the Iconography of Romanticism: Folk, Land, Culture and the Romantic Nation.* New York: Macmillan Press, 1999.

Kerber, Linda K. *Federalists in Dissent: Imagery and Ideology in Jeffersonian America.* Ithaca, New York: Cornell University Press, 1970.

———. *Women of the Republic: Intellect and Ideology in Revolutionary America.* New York: Norton, 1986.

Kroeber, Karl. *Romantic Narrative Art*. Madison: University of Wisconsin Press, 1960.

Leary, Lewis. *Soundings: Some Early American Writers*. Athens: University of Georgia Press, 1975.

Lehmann, Karl. *Thomas Jefferson: American Humanist*. Charlottesville: University Press of Virginia, 1985.

Lewis, Jan. "'The Blessings of Domestic Society': Thomas Jefferson's Family and the Transformation of American Politics." In *Jeffersonian Legacies*, edited by Peter S. Onuf, with a foreword by Daniel P. Jordan and afterword by Merrill D. Peterson. Charlottesville: University Press of Virginia, 1993.

———. *The Pursuit of Happiness: Family and Values in Jefferson's Virginia*. New York: Cambridge University Press, 1993.

Maier, Pauline. *American Scripture: Making the Declaration of Independence*. New York: Knopf, 1997.

Malone, Dumas. *Jefferson and His Time*. 6 volumes. Boston: Little, Brown, 1948–1981.

McGann, Jerome. *Fiery Dust: Byron's Poetic Development*. Chicago: University of Chicago Press, 1968.

———. *The Poetics of Sensibility*. Oxford: Clarendon Press, 1996.

McLaughlin, Jack. *Jefferson and Monticello: The Biography of a Builder*. New York: Henry Holt, 1988.

McLuhan, Marshall. *Understanding Media: The Extensions of Man*. Cambridge, Massachusetts: MIT Press, 1994.

Moore, Thomas. "Preface." In *The Poetical Works of the Late Thomas Little*, edited by Jonathan Wordsworth, 1801. Reprinted Oxford: Woodstock, 1990.

Onuf, Peter S., ed., with a foreword by Daniel P. Jordan and afterword by Merrill D. Peterson. *Jeffersonian Legacies*. Charlottesville: University Press of Virginia, 1993.

Randall, Randolph C. "Authors of the *Port Folio* Revealed by the Hall Files." *American Literature* 11 (1940): 379–416.

———. "Joseph Dennie's Literary Attitudes in the Port Folio, 1801–1812." In James Woodress, Townsend Ludington, and Joseph Arpad, *Essays Mostly on Periodical Publishing in America: A Collection in Honor of Clarence Gohdes*. Durham, North Carolina: Duke University Press, 1973, 57–91.

Randall, Willard Sterne. *Thomas Jefferson: A Life*. New York: HarperPerennial, 1993.

Safire, William. *Scandalmonger*. New York: Simon & Schuster, 2000.

Scheick, William J. "Chaos and Imaginative Order in Thomas Jefferson's *Notes on the State of Virginia*." In *Essays in Early Virginia Literature Honoring Richard Beale Davis*, edited by J. A. Leo LeMay. New York: Burt Franklin, 1977, 221–234.

Sears, Louis Martin. *Jefferson and the Embargo*. Durham, North Carolina: Duke University Press, 1927.

Smith, Lee. "Scrapbooks Believed to Be Work of Jefferson." *Washington Post* (September 30, 1999).

Sowerby, E. Millicent, compiler. *Catalogue of the Library of Thomas Jefferson*, 5 volumes. Washington, DC: The Library of Congress, 1952–1959.

Stanton, Lucia. "Looking for Liberty: Thomas Jefferson and the British Lions." *Eighteenth-Century Studies* 26 (1993): 649–668.

Tanselle, G. Thomas. *Royall Tyler*. Cambridge, Massachusetts: Harvard University Press, 1967.

Thorne, J. O., and T. C. Collocott. *Chambers Biographical Dictionary*. Edinburgh: W. & R. Chambers, 1985.

Wayland, John W. "The Poetical Tastes of Thomas Jefferson." *Sewanee Review* 18 (1911): 283–299.

Weymouth, Lally, ed. *Thomas Jefferson: The Man . . . His World . . . His Influence.* New York: G. P. Putnam's Sons, 1973.

White, Terence De Vere. *Tom Moore: The Poet.* London: Hamish Hamilton, 1977.

Wills, Garry. *Inventing America: Jefferson's Declaration of Independence.* New York: Houghton Mifflin, 1978.

———. *Negro President: Jefferson and the Slave Power.* Boston: Houghton Mifflin Company, 2003.

Wilson, Douglas. "Jefferson and the Republic of Letters." In *Jeffersonian Legacies*, edited by Peter S. Onuf; with a foreword by Daniel P. Jordan and afterword by Merrill D. Peterson. Charlottesville: University Press of Virginia, 1993.

———. "Jefferson and Literacy." In *Thomas Jefferson and the Education of a Citizen*, edited by James Gilreath. Washington, DC: Library of Congress, 1999.

———. *Jefferson's Books.* Charlotte: University of North Carolina Press, 1996.

———. "The American *Agricola*: Jefferson's Agrarianism and the Classical Tradition." *South Atlantic Quarterly* 80:3 (summer 1981): 339–354.

Wood, Gordon S. *The Americanization of Benjamin Franklin.* New York: Penguin, 2004.

Wordsworth and the Age of English Romanticism, edited by Jonathan Wordsworth, Michael C. Jaye, and Robert Woof. Newark, New Jersey: Rutgers University Press, 1987.

Wordsworth, Jonathan. "Introduction," in *The Poetical Works of the Late Thomas Little*, edited by Jonathan Wordsworth, 1801. Reprinted Oxford: Woodstock, 1990.

INDEX

NOTE: The initials TJ refer to Thomas Jefferson. Page numbers in italics type are for the photography section.

nourished by scrapbook, 9
on novels, 461
oak leaf placed, 3, 3, 407
on open disagreement, 280
and Orientalism, 334, 337
pacifism, 18, 455
and Paine, Thomas, 504, 529
personal attacks on, 8–9
philosophical distillation, 230
and poetry, xv, 5, 330, 331, 505, 549n93
on Poland, 168
political with domestic comparison, 183, 214, 437
on politics, 214, 504
presidency, 117, 181, 244
and press/newspapers, 12, 15, 144, 489–90
privacy need, 308
progeny, 175–76
as proto-feminist, 180
public sacrifices, 184
pursuit of happiness, 231, 263, 502
to Randolph, Ellen Wayles (TJ granddaughter), 93
and rationality, 95, 218, 329
and reflection, 433
remarriage, foresaking, 176, 214, 262
on republican creed, 12
on Republican virtues, 120
and retirement, 6, 7, 7, 176, 177, 183, 184, 185, 225, 330, 422
on revolution, 11–12
romanticism/neoclassicism, 332
romanticism of, 330, 338
and rural life, 197
as scrapbooker, 2
as secretary of state, 13, 489
on seizing the moment, 407
self as exemplar, 504–5
self-description, xv
on self-improvement, 407
self-promotion, 15
and self-sacrifice, 449
and sentimentality, 181, 239, 301, 330, 337, 338, 426, 445, 504, 536
sexual betrayal interest, 448
to Short, William, 164
as slave owner, 171
and slavery, 338, 347, 540n2
and sorrow, 409
as spendthrift, 504
spirit of '76, 117, 129
states' rights, 12, 15
on Sterne, Laurence, 426
stoicism of, 221
and sweetness, 315, 316
and theater, 351

"Thoughts on Prosody," 332, 513
tombstone, 244
and travel, 231, 271 (*See also* in France *in this section*)
and underdogs, 16
and vernacular, 332
views changing, 334
as Virginian, 231, 244
and virtue, 120, 164, 205, 365
on *The Vision of Columbus* (Barlow), 4–5
on Washington, George, 46
on Webster, Noah, 492
and wife, 180–81, 214 (*See also* Jefferson, Martha Wayles Skelton)
wife's final illness, 185, 262
William and Mary College student, 5, 331
and women, 180–81, 182–83, 228, 243, 296, 492;
on education of females/granddaughters, 497–501
women/men comparison, 214
Jefferson, Thomas, and daughters, 461. *See also* Eppes, Mary (Maria/Polly) Jefferson (TJ daughter); Randolph, Martha (Patsy) Jefferson (TJ daughter)
on appearance, personal, 285
biographical information, 177
as charitable, 214
confides unhappiness in White House to, 422
on deathbed, 185
as doting single parent, 327
education of, 304
and grandchildren, 243
as happiness, 303
Maria's death, 337
on mockingbirds, 445
on novels, 461
respecting intellect of, 180
selection of reading material for, 498
Jefferson, Thomas, and grandchildren. *See also* Bankhead, Anne Randolph/Randolph, Anne Cary (TJ granddaughter); Randolph, Anne Cary/Bankhead, Anne Randolph (TJ granddaughter); Randolph, Cornelia Jefferson (TJ granddaughter); Randolph, Ellen Wayles (TJ grandaughter); Randolph, Thomas Jefferson (TJ grandson); Trist, Virginia J.
absence of, 445
appreciate poems sent by TJ, 243
cherishing company, 218
on disagreement, 280
on domesticity, 178
and emotional life, 304
on granddaughters' education, 499–501
poetry appreciation, 243
poetry gift to TJ, 494
relationship cultivation, 497–98

"Lines Written on the Bank of a River" (Anon.),
332
Literary Commonplace Book (TJ), 180, 329–30, 386–87
Literary Federalism in the Age of Jefferson (Dowling),
547n13
"The Litigiousicals" (Anon.), 282
Little, Thomas, 355. *See also* Moore, Thomas
Logan, George (Dr.), 142
"On a Long Nose" (Sterne), 181
Looney, Jefferson, 2
Louisiana Purchase, 18, 325, 497
"Love and Reason" (Moore), 211, 335
love/despair (Moore), 383
Lowell, James Russell, 144
Lyrical Ballads (Wordsworth and Coleridge), 17, 332,
515

Macdonald, Andrew, 522
Mackenzie, Henry, 337, 545n23
Macpherson, James, 329
    ancient bard emulation, 415
    ballad tradition, 332
    biographical sketch, 522–23
    "Fingal," 418, 523
    nationalism/lost causes, 236
    "Oithona," 418
    Ossian, 130, 161, 303, 333, 335, 418, 523
    Scottish values, 512
    and TJ, 5–6, 122, 233, 244, 405, 523
"The Madagascar Mother" (Holcroft), 331, 334, 367,
520
Madison, James, 13, 497
"The Maid of Buttermere" (Wordsworth), 236
Maier, Pauline, 15
Malone, Dumas, 83, 327, 497, 547n13
Mann, Thomas, 364
Man of Feeling (Mackenzie), 337
"The Mansion of Rest" (Anon.), 184, 225, 466
The Many-Headed Hydra (Linebaugh and Rediker),
136
Marvell, Andrew, 310
"To Mary in Heaven" (Burns), 337, 512
Matilda, Hannah (Cowley, Anna), 445, 545–46n25
Matilda, Rosa (Charlotte Dacre), 6, 381. *See also*
Byrne, Charlotte (née King)
    biographical sketch, 512–13
    and nature, 333
    self-editing, 437
    on slavery, 337, 347
    as translator, 437, 511
"A Matrimonial Ballad" (Hayley), 333, 519
"On May," 399
McCarthyism, sexual, 8–9
McDonald, Robert, 2, 3, 407, 539n14
melancholy, 394, 422
Mellen, Henry, 83, 497, 523

Melville, Herman, 274
"Memory" (Anon.), 408
"To the Memory of Gen. Hamilton" (Anon.), 13
men
    advice as husbands, 256
    husbands/wives, 256, 258
    and marriage, 256, 258, 264, 297
    perfect husbands, 241
Merry, Anthony, 145
Merry, Robert (Della Crusca), 333, 336, 337, 381, 406,
496, 545n25
Merry, Thomas, 492–93
Mill, John Stuart, 302
"Milton" (Anon.) , 405
Milton, John, 5, 161, 228, 329, 544n4
Mirror for Magistrates, 3–4, 16, 183, 244, 245
missionaries to Sandwich Islands (Hawaii), 360, 536
"The Mistake," 502–3
"Mistress" (Cowley), 386
Modern Griselda (Edgeworth), 498
The Monk (Lewis), 346
Monroe, James, 216
"Mont Blanc" (Shelley), 402
Montesquieu, 163
Montgomery, James, 422, 523–24
Monticello, 6, 156, 171, 218, 330
    classic/romantic dichotomy, 335–36
    compared to scrapbook, 4
    debts incurred, 193
    entrance statuary, 14
    farm and garden book by TJ, 398, 504
    hospitality, 237, 252, 308
    as idealized retreat, 214, 545n9
    Jefferson Memorial Library, 1
    missed by TJ, 252
    mockingbirds at, 445
    nail factory, 504
    Poplar Forest, 308
    rebuilding of, 545n21
    as retirement idealization, 184, 422
    and Roosevelt, Franklin D., 1, 7
    Roosevelt cottage, 1, 7, 8
    sold, 184, 193
    as theme, 6, 184
    TJ routed from, 145, 371
    vineyard, 227
Moore, Thomas, 111, 207, 344, 492
    in America, 525
    "Anacreon," 337, 525
    and Anacreon, 348, 356, 525
    "Anacreontic Verses," 330, 334
    biographical sketch, 525–26
    and Byron's memoirs, 3
    dueling, 212, 526
    elegance of, 354
    Epistles, Odes, and Poems, 171, 212, 348, 493–94